B____Y
PEOPLE
UP FOR
A LIVING
DON'T YOU
MUMMY?'

Inside the World of the Dominatrix
Compiled and edited by Roy Turner

Absolute Elsewhere

First published in Great Britain in 2001 by
Absolute Elsewhere, PO Box 2, Brighton,
East Sussex, BN1 4LQ, United Kingdom.

www.absolute-elsewhere.co.uk

You Beat People Up For A Living, Don't You, Mummy?
Compiled and edited by Roy Turner.
Absolute Elsewhere © 2001

British Library Cataloguing in Publication Data. A CIP record of
this book is available on request from the British Library.

ISBN 0 9540777 0 9

10 9 8 7 6 5 4 3 2 1

For Doreen, my Mother and Father,
and lastly Freya Viking Goddess,
Patron Saint of the Dominatrix!

Born in South London in 1952, Roy Turner graduated from Middlesex University and Saint Martin's School of Art. He has studied sociology and anthropology and written several historical biographies and novels inspired by his extensive travels and adventures around the world.

Today, Roy Turner is perhaps best known as the founder and editor of the fetish magazine Domina. Earlier career re-incarnations included teaching, acting, painting and decorating, both window-dressing and window cleaning, a spell working on a rodeo in Arizona and a shot at being a bullfighter in Spain! These days he divides his time between Britain and Spain.

GLOSSARY OF TERMS AND ABBREVIATIONS

AC/DC: Bi sexual
CP: Corporal punishment
Fem Dom: Female domination
SM: Sado masochism
TS: Transsexual
TV: Transvestite
Water-sports: Sex games involving urine
Hard-sports: Games involving excretion.
Safe Words: Agreed word or phrase used by the submissive to pause or stop the action.
Sub/Dom: Submission and Domination
Vanilla Sex: Conventional sexual activity

CONTENTS

INTRODUCTION

This book was not consciously embarked upon at all, but rather evolved with a life force all its own. Throughout its existence, interviews and 'real life' contributions by both professional and lifestyle dominatrixes have been the mainstay and 'life blood' of our publications. As editor, it was always my aim to bring to readers the reality of the Fem-Dom scene. This book came about as a natural progression from that. I also thought it was about time someone brought a glimmer of 'truth' about the fetish 'scene' into the public arena.

Throughout I have sought to eliminate the interviewers 'voice' completely. In so doing, I have presented the words of each mistress undiluted and unblemished by any intrusions on my part. Each interview, therefore, stands as an extended essay on each woman's point of view. No censorship, no comments and no judgments.

The emergence of Aids brought new concerns about sexual lifestyles in the closing years of the last century and a growing interest in sado-masochism and fetishism. As people realised they could no longer 'swing' quite so freely as they did in the 1970's, they looked for more imaginative forms of sexual expression within a monogamous relationship. Within this context, SM was seen as the ultimate form of safe sex, and the dominatrix its high priestess!

As such, the genuine practitioner of Fem-Dom will take supreme pride in her skills and in her professionalism, and will disparage 'working girls' who add the euphemism of 'personal services' to their menus (or the 'whip and wank brigade' as one interviewee succinctly put it) as being interlopers into her area of expertise and for giving her chosen vocation a bad name. A genuine, professional dominatrix or mistress will never offer her client sexual favours. This 'no sex clause' is referred to again and again in these interviews as the yard stick by which to appraise the genuineness of a particular mistress.

Unlike a prostitute, who may be forced by circumstances to 'sell' sex, the dominatrix sees herself as offering a legitimate service through her role-playing and fantasy skills, that is very much on par with a therapist or counsellor. Indeed, the reader will note how similar the language of the dominatrix is to that of these other professionals. Interestingly, many come from the field of nursing, psychiatric or other caring services; including some who actually are trained therapists. Others have been high flying achievers in the world of business, commerce or teaching. Many will apprentice themselves initially to other, more experienced, mistresses at the outset of their careers in order to learn their dungeon craft. Almost without exception, in my experience, the dominatrix will be well educated, intelligent and a highly skilled communicator.

During my years of involvement in the Fem-Dom subculture, I've encountered a spectrum of attitudes and approaches to the art of Female Domination that proved to be as diverse and individualistic as the dominatrixes themselves. These ranged from the light-hearted to the deeply committed, and from the politically militant to the spiritually esoteric. Many dominatrixes have a deep interest in tarot and astrology, for example. While others, particularly in America, see themselves as the vanguard of a new world order. Indeed, a strong theme of pagan-based Goddess spirituality recurred again and again. Yet, in my opinion, all these diverse aspects form an equally important and valid part of a fascinating whole.

The world of the dominatrix encompasses all facets of human desire and imagination. It is a world where eroticism coexists with horror, humour and downright weirdness; while fantasy merges with madness. I encountered many outrageously funny incidents in the life of the dominatrix. From the slave who wanted to be mummified in newspaper to the submissive who wanted his artificial leg put into bondage! The kidnap that went hysterically wrong to the client who wanted to be ironed and then baked in the oven!

Then there were tales that left me gasping in amazement at the sheer strangeness of some client's fantasies; such as slaves who want teeth knocked out, foreskins nailed to tables or testicles blown up to the size of footballs! And even a totally unique theory of alien abduction! Then there are the harsh realities of the job: the stalkings by obsessive slaves, the dangers of dealing with a violent client, the mind games and manipulations of the 'pretend' submissive, police harassment, exploitative landlords, the immoral tactics of tabloid newspapers, the suburban 'witch hunts' by neighbours, and even a slave who drugged and enslaved his own mistress!

Over the past decade, I have met literally hundreds of dominatrixes and have been privileged to gain, through their friendship and trust, an insight into their unique world. The ideas and philosophies

I have encountered over the years, and the unique perceptions on life and sexuality have been, well, little short of mind-blowing! Freud and Jung would have been left open mouthed by the insights into human behaviour and psychology these women have reached! I can only hope this book will have the same effect on you.

Roy Turner,
Brighton, England

MISTRESS ASH

*As a lifestyle (as opposed to a professional) dominatrix, Mistress Ash spe-
cialises in the initiation of novice, younger male slaves who are interested
in older women. At present, she keeps her SM side as a hobby, combining
it with a highly successful business career and an active interest in wiccan
paganism.* Interviewed March 2001

I first discovered I was dominant in my mid-teens, but it was a long
time before I found any 'scene' to support those early fantasies. It
may sound a bit weird, but my domination side has always been
linked to lunar cycles. This, in turn, seemed to tie in with my own
monthly cycles. Basically, when my periods started, I used to get
these 'feelings'. Every three or four weeks I was having very strange
fantasies! At the time, I didn't have any good words to describe it. It
was a sexuality that was tied in with gothic and vampire imagery,
because that was the only 'dark side' stuff I knew at the time. It was
a very velvet and leather and lace kind of thing. I used to manage to
slip out of my carefully controlled life and go 'slumming around', for
want of a better phrase, in a sort of underworld of sleazy bars in parts
of London that were quite different from the kind of life that I lived
the rest of the month, in order to try and get this predatory yearning
out of my system. For about ten days a month I would turn into this
other creature, and I had no idea what it was, really. I thought I was
crazy for a long time.

I must have lived with that for nearly ten years before I discovered the right words for my kind of sexuality – like sado-masochism
or sub-dom. Back then there wasn't really any politically correct way
of describing it; sadism and masochism were always seen as very negative, and there wasn't any information around to help people like me
to come to terms with what we were feeling. It was very hard to find
out about this stuff and, when you did, it was always about very
heavy-duty extreme stuff that would be enough to put most beginners into shock! There certainly wasn't any SM safe sex information
around. When I started to find the words, it took me even longer
before I found a community. This was partly, as I say, because there
wasn't the information on where to find it, but I was also scared wit-

less as the only information I did manage to dig up was so frightening! I was about twenty five or so before I found out what SM was, and probably about thirty before I went out and found a community. I found it eventually because I was lucky enough to pick up an experienced submissive who took me into the scene, otherwise I may never have blossomed as a mistress at all!

I was actually out looking for 'prey', for want of a better phrase, when I met this sub. I knew it was a part of me that I wanted to get around to exercising. I was about four months out of a really heavy duty relationship at that time, and I felt it was either now or never to let this SM side of me out to play! I still didn't know what the scene was about, but I'd got a vocabulary by this time and had read enough to be able to do things safely; plus I had my fantasies to guide me, so I was looking for someone to play with, and he came along at the right time. I was so lucky to find a 'sub' who knew exactly what he wanted and felt a lot better about himself in his liking for this kind of thing than I did at the time, so he was a very positive role model for me.

I believe we dominants can learn a lot from our submissives, if we manage to keep our egos out of the way! I've got enormous respect for a *true* sub; maybe that's because I seem incapable of playing that role myself. Thinking it might make me a better dominant if I knew what it was like to be on the other side of things, I have tried playing the submissive role, but it completely freaks me out and I just can't deal with it. However, my sub experience has made me very respectful of people who can play that role. I'm one of those strange creatures who isn't really a 'switch'. I'm about 95% dominant, I think.

When I first got my submissive and I started acting out the kind of fantasies that I'd had, it became a very intense part of my life for a while. I found out that not only did I have a sexuality I wanted to explore, but I had a whole emerging personality in there that wanted to dress in a different way (*she* had a quite unexpected taste for corsets and Victoriana, for example!) and do things that I hadn't done. It was absolutely fascinating, but also quite problematic. I found the easiest way of dealing with it was to split her off as a separate person. That's how the character of Mistress Ash came into being.

It sounds a bit schizophrenic, doesn't it? But, really, *she* wanted to do things with my credit cards that absolutely alarmed the 'normal' me! *She* wanted to buy toys and clothes and subscriptions to fetish clubs and magazines. It really was a problem! In fact, at one point, I had to order my sub to keep my credit cards away from me, or rather her! I also started writing about her, which is something I haven't done before or since. Writing seemed a way of processing this huge upsurge of creative energy that came about from me finally being able to liberate this part of myself. That was when I accepted that I really was a dominant and that it was a part of who I am. As time went by, Mistress Ash and I became closer and closer, until eventually *she* integrated altogether and we're one person now. These days I can make fairly rational decisions about whether I can actually afford that pair of boots or not!

In playing out scenes, what really interests me is the relationship between the dominant and the submissive. How I can earn the trust of that person, and how I can lead them to figure out exactly what it is that they want and to tell me about it. The partners I enjoy most are the newcomers to the scene, who are often pretty nervous. I guess I like working in this area because I remember what it was like to be out there with no information about this side of yourself. I always want to make sure their first SM experience is a wonderful and positive one, and I'll often go to a lot of effort to make sure that happens. With slaves I've met on-line, I've often become a sort of informal one woman information service, if you like. So, yes, I enjoy teaching beginners, and I enjoy playing with them, obviously. It's about how their minds work and making them feel good about what they are. I like helping them find out exactly what it is that turns them on, and making them feel good about themselves.

Often, when I first meet them, they're a jumble of imagery – a bit like I was! Maybe they've seen a couple of images on the Internet that turned them on. Maybe it was an advert for a fetish event that they thought looked interesting, but didn't have the nerve to go along. They've picked up bits and pieces and got some idea, but have never gone inside themselves and found out what their personal 'turning point' is that truly excites them. It's trying to find out what that is that I find very challenging, because it often comes down to a really tiny thing. It could be a particular word said in a particular tone of voice in a particular set of circumstances and that's it! Press that point and you've made someone's dreams come true! It's about finding the key that unlocks the door and, usually, people don't know what that is. Once you've found that, it's wonderful. You can just keep pushing that 'button' and you all get very happy! You'll then have a very happy submissive on your hands, and nothing makes me happier than seeing a slave who's simply pleasured out of their brains! That's why I do this, really.

It's also a big 'power rush' for the dominant. When you give someone *the* sexual event of their life, an experience that they'll never forget and that nothing will ever measure up to, it's really quite a rush! As I said, I go to quite a lot of trouble to make sure that happens! My pet hate is the kind of submissive who gives me no feed-back at all. Though they might be tied up behind their gags and can hardly move a muscle, there are *still* numerous ways of expressing that they're having a good time! They only have to find the ways! Selfish slaves who simply lie there are just dreadful. If I wanted that I might as well beat up the cushions! No feed-back equals no excitement on my part. This, in turn, means I get bored; which means things end rather quickly!

I don't tend to have short SM affairs, because I do try to be responsible about my playing around. For instance, I'll never play a one night stand with someone new and then leave them without my phone number, because some people tend to freak out somewhere between a week and a month after their first scene and will need some support. They often go through the whole: "Oh God, did I really do that?" or "Did I really *want* to do that?", "What's wrong with me? What's wrong with *her*?" thing, and they'll need to talk it through and, hopefully, do it again! So, they don't tend to be short-lived things, by any means. With new slaves I always try and get them to make friends with another slave of the same gender, so they don't just get my point of view. Boy-slaves especially seem to need to talk to another bloke (and, no, *not* a master!) while they adjust their heads to what it feels like to give their power away in a scene.

I do have a variety of media that I use in my search for slaves. While I'm playing with people in real life, I'll also have a number of people I'm talking to on the Internet. I'll probably never meet them but, hopefully, I'm helping them to get to the right place. Initially, I always like to talk on the phone at least with a prospective new slave before we meet to make sure we're looking for the same thing. Also, I must admit that I find inarticulate slaves who can't express what they want, and certain accents, a real turn-off, so a phone call gets that out of the way. Then I'll arrange to meet them somewhere safe during the day. I *always* tell friends where I'm going, and wouldn't be at all offended if they did the same! After all, there are some very 'twisted' (and I don't mean in a *nice* way) people out there! Play tends to take place at my house which, though I have quite a range of kit and dress-up clothes, doesn't incorporate a dungeon. In my place, I'm afraid it was a choice between a dungeon and a study. And, as I work from home a lot, the study won! I also enjoy playing in clubs with someone if they're into it, and once we've got to know each other well.

When I meet people online or for real, I always recommend my favourite books on the subject. The number of recommendations that I put out, I ought to get commission! I also tell people to get along to the London Fetish Fair so they can see there's a whole positive community out there and that they're not on their own My number one book to recommend for beginners is *Sensuous Magic* by Pat Califia. She's not my role model, but I have complete respect for that woman. I think she's a goddess! Plus she's a pagan, as well as a dominant. And she loves cats, so that's something else we've got in common! In fact, that's one main reason I'd like to find a live-in submissive, so I could have someone to look after my cats when I'm away on business. Because I get rushed off to wherever at short notice, I can't have cats at the moment, so my slave could look after the cats when they're not looking after me!

Although I play with a whole variety of slaves, I do tend to attract, and enjoy, 'toy-boys'. Because I'm playing with people who are new to the scene, they're usually under thirty and often under twenty five. I try to make sure they're over twenty one – but they lie, so what can you do? However, my playmates tend to be separate from people that I have actual relationships with. To try and have a relationship with someone that's also got an SM component is, I've found, a very interesting challenge. In fact, it's a huge and extremely difficult question that I'm still trying to work out. I tried having a relationship with the slave who first introduced me to the scene and we tried all sorts of combinations to try and get it to work, but it's hard to deal with that 'balance of power' thing. When you go from your role-playing to being complete equals (as you have to for a real-world relationship to work, I believe) it's a tricky head game to play. On the other hand, if you have your SM life separate from your main relationship, then you need to have a very understanding partner or you lie! Unfortunately, that seems to be what the majority of people resort to. This happens, especially, when they're married and find out about this aspect of their sexuality *after* they've made the commitment.

In fact, I have been credited with the breakup of one marriage on the Internet, which is something I'm not very proud of. I'm sure there were other problems in the relationship before I came along though. Basically, I got chatting to a chap in Canada who, at the age of thirty four and having been married since he was eighteen, had come to realise that he was very submissive. He'd tried talking to his wife about this, but wasn't getting anywhere. She wasn't interested in discussing it or taking him seriously on the topic, so he went on the Internet in order to try and understand himself a bit better and to try and find a sympathetic ear, as he was going through that whole 'what's wrong with me' kind of voyage of discovery. We formed a very close friendship and talked a lot and exchanged e-mails, though we never actually met. Unfortunately, his wife found one of these e-mails and threw him out, and that was it. It wasn't an obscene e-mail at all. I think it was just the fact that he had felt so strongly about his SM side that he would seek out someone else he could to talk about it with that caused the final rift in their relationship.

I do sympathise with partners who suddenly find that their beloved is submissive, particularly wives. It's great if a submissive has a wife who can be dominant but, as far as I can figure out, not everyone has got what it takes, no matter how willing they are! I don't know what you'd call it: the 'manner' or the 'gift'? I know men who've confessed they're submissive, and their wives have been quite willing to try and dominate them, but they've just never made a very convincing dominant. There's nothing sillier than someone trying to do it when they really can't. Having said that, I certainly wouldn't want to discourage anyone who had the nerve to want to give it a whack, as it were! There are some great books around now for novice 'tops' of all genders, which are supportive and full of good ideas. But you certainly need a very supportive and encouraging sub partner and, of course, to be reasonably assertive yourself anyway in order to carry it off.

I think part of the reason for a shortage of dominant women is that, considering the way society is set up, women who want to be dominant are moving much further away from their accepted social roles than men are by being submissive. Men are used to going out into the world and *thrusting* and making stuff happen, and they often have the responsibility for providing for a family on their shoulders. So, when they come home, they just want to lay their burdens aside for a little while by being submissive. That's okay, because in the 'real' world they can pick up their power again after the session. Whereas for women, to step from what's generally regarded as a less powerful position into being dominant is a bloody great psychological leap and quite difficult to do! For a woman to become dominant, she's taking on an *extra* set of responsibilities (which she needs to learn about and master) rather than *relinquishing* responsibilities, as the man does when he becomes submissive. What's more, she's taking on a stack of things that are completely against the way she's been socialised. For men, it's taking two small steps to gear down in order to be submissive. Whereas, the woman needs to 'gear up' ten steps to somewhere she's never been before! It's a difficult thing to do and, I think, that's why there aren't that many of us doing it!

Looking back, I'm sure that one of the reasons I chose to have a career rather than just a job is that it gave me an outlet for the kind of strength of character you need to be a dominant female. I also chose a career, quite unconsciously, that challenged me to raise my self confidence and self reliance, and my ability to deal with people and to manage situations. If you're lifestyle domina, it goes right through you like a stick of rock. It doesn't just stay in the bedroom. You're constantly challenging the way that women are meant to be behaving out there, and where our boundaries are exactly meant to be, and what we're meant to be capable of.

For me, consent is the *absolute* central point about sexy SM play– as they say: "if it ain't sensual, and it ain't mutual, it ain't SM!" So I don't play with anyone or anything unable to give their full consent. This includes children, animals, and adults who are too drunk or stoned to engage their judgment fully. I also steer clear of play that is likely to transfer 'interesting' bugs! I'm talking about things like shit-related stuff. Obviously, safe sex is a must for scenes that involve penetration of any kind, and requests for unsafe sex are the ones that I most often have to turn down. As a community, I believe we can choose to 'eroticise' safe sex through the porn we read and the images we choose to use in our play and our publications; and I believe that is the responsible thing to do, especially with AIDS diagnosis exploding at such an alarming rate this year! After all, many of us say we find rubber sexy, so let's do something really constructive with our fetishes and lead the erotic world in safe sex!

Though I respect people on the scene who want to reclaim the word 'perv' or 'pervert', I would never describe myself like that. I think it's an unfortunate word because it's very broad in it's meaning, so it doesn't just apply to SM or sub-dom. It applies to child molesters, as well! Plus a whole range of other illegal and unpleasant activities that our community is trying to disassociate itself from. So I see it as pretty risky to associate ourselves with the word 'perv'. I mean, we've got enough PR troubles as it is, right?

I would call myself a Domme or a Domina. I find I quite often get a friendly reaction to that because there are so many submissive males out there. However, even though there are quite a few, it's still difficult for a single dominant female to find slaves. I mean, where are you going to go to find these people? You could look for them on the Internet, but that takes an awful long time. It's also quite a dangerous way to go about it because you don't know who you're talking to, plus you can waste an awful lot of typing on someone you just don't fancy! The most obvious thing to do is to go along to clubs, but doing that as a single female is also tricky. Although you'd imagine the average dominant female is probably fairly assertive and isn't going to be shy about walking into a club on her own, we're also not stupid! You become a bit of a moving target in some establishments, and being a lone female in a sex-oriented establishment is always a risk, even if you are carrying a big whip! It's kind of a *Catch-22* situation. You want to get to know some people on the scene, but you haven't got anybody to go to the scene with unless you already know some people! Plus the music is often so loud that, once you get there, you can't even hear your potential new friends talk, let alone hear a 'safe word' from someone you want to play with!

At the moment, for instance, I'm single and would love to meet some more submissive men, but I would be hesitant about dressing up in a corset and going off to a fetish event on my own to find them. I really think they should add an event to the fetish scene that's aimed at single people into this kind of stuff where it's absolutely okay to go on your own; possibly even ban couples! Maybe things need to be a bit organised when you get there, with people put into groups for discussions and then circulated or something, so you don't have the chance to be a wallflower. I think I'm beginning to sound like an old-fashioned society hostess, I'm afraid! I don't know quite how it would work, but we do need an SM social. I think the Fetish Fair is the nearest we've got to that, because it's fairly informal and relaxed with friendly people and no dress code.

My own experience 'on the scene' is pretty limited. I've never spoken to women who do this for money (though I'd like to!) or guys who pay for it. I don't even know how many women there are like me who do this without any thought of earning a living at it. Maybe one of the reasons I enjoy playing with beginners is that they haven't had much exposure to the scene either, so their reactions and their fantasies are very fresh, very original and very heartfelt. They haven't picked up a whole load of stereotypes from magazines or the Internet, and they haven't had a chance to alter themselves to fit in with what people might think.

As I haven't had any contacts with other dominants, I'm completely self taught. I've read books and found that for me a lot of it is instinctual. I really don't know if I'm what 95% of men who are looking for a dominant would call a 'domina'. Maybe I wouldn't suit most people. Maybe I've just been lucky enough to attract people that suit my style. But there lots of different styles, aren't there? If someone was looking for the kind of mistress who was going to march around and pose and shout at them and play the complete and utter *prima donna,* then they're not for me. It just wouldn't be the kind of thing I'd enjoy doing. I like to think I'm a lot more subtle about it. That doesn't mean that I don't get extremely intense sometimes, but I'm not a 'caricature' or standard kind of dominant – if there is such a beast?

I find other people's sexual fantasies intensely horny, which is one of the reasons I'm hanging out with them in the first place! I remember I had what I thought was a straight, submissive who wanted me to arrange a scene where he was buggered by another guy. It was, shall we say, interesting and unexpected! Especially from someone who defines themselves as 'straight'! Yet they had their SM persona, same as I have, and their SM persona turned out to be bi-sexual. That one really came out of left-field. But this kind of sexual adventure can be such an amazing way to learn about yourself, can't it?

Someone else wanted me to take him to a club and sort of hang him near the entrance with a sign in lipstick around his neck saying 'Has been a very bad slave. Please help yourself', so everyone could do what they wanted to him. It was complete *slutism*! I found those two fantasies rather exciting but, for some reason, people who want to play around with water-sports invariably make me giggle. I just find that very funny. All those kind of scenarios are not that unusual, though. In fact, they're probably quite common. Again, it's the psychology of it. To me, playing with someone who discovers more of their SM possibilities during the months that you're playing together and then, without any prompting from books or community or anything else, comes to realise that, in a purely SM way, they're attracted to the same sex is quite a miraculous thing. It's just incredible!

Another area of fantasy that interests me is 'sissy maids'. There seems to be a large community of guys who are attracted to that particular transvestite imagery. And it's very specific imagery, isn't it? It makes you wonder how so many people can manage to find that out for themselves, and *about* themselves, and all arrive at such a similar image. It's like the fashion shows each season. They're all supposed to be top secret yet, when they put on the catwalk shows, you find they've all got the same things in common. It's the same with sissy maids, in my experience.

Usually, my 'sissy maid' scenes involve 'forcible' cross-dressing of the guy (including make-up, lingerie, hair ornaments and maids outfit), followed by a few hours of servitude. I particularly enjoy getting my tea made, my supper cooked and my toenails painted. However, all scenes are discussed with the 'maid' beforehand, so I understand what is really exciting for them in a scenario and try to build it in. I knew one guy who only wanted to scrub floors! Nothing else. But he looked so pretty doing it, and was *obviously* so excited about it, that I came to enjoy my sessions with him immensely.

As a pagan myself, I'm also particularly interested in the spiritual aspects of SM. There's a definite similarity between pagan ritual and SM ritual, as both of them are capable of taking people to transcendent places. Regular beating often causes someone to trance out, and that has been used by shamanism and other pagan practices for many centuries. It's a form of physical self hypnosis that can be used to bring about an altered state of consciousness. This is something you have to be aware of, and responsible about, when you're playing with a submissive as sometimes they will go into a different head-space (sometimes called 'going away' or 'space out') where they can become non-verbal or too tranced to be able to use safe words. This state can be used, by prior mutual consent, for virtual self development or shamanic journeying. In fact, in the back of one my Pat Califia books is a reference to someone called a *Ka-See-Ka* who is defined as an experienced 'top' who knows how to create a certain transcendental or spiritual experience for the bottom. I thought that was really interesting, because I had no idea there was that kind of role when I first started noticing the similarities between the two worlds. There's definitely quite a bit of cross-over there.

Also, some people would say that, by acting out the part of the dominant, you're enacting one of the feminine goddess archetypes. I'm thinking more of the Dark Lady archetypes or the destructive Goddess aspects, which is a very powerful one, and something people need to encounter in their own psyche just as much as they need to look to what people see as the more 'positive' Mother Goddess image. The Dark Lady is something that men, in particular, need to encounter; but probably won't find unless they deliberately go seeking Her, I think. And that seems to come out quite strongly in the way the scenes develop. So, as a pagan *and* a dominant, I hope I'm well placed to try and work consciously with that kind of energy when it comes up in a scene.

Mind you, just because I'm a dominant, doesn't mean I'm one *all* the time. No one is twenty four hours a day, apart from in fantasy. We have our off-duty times when we need a good cuddle like the rest of the world, and a good Domme won't be too concerned with keeping up her image not to admit that! Hopefully, a good and caring slave will be able to spot when it's appropriate to offer a hug, as well as when to offer other services!

In a few years time, I can imagine living near a beach somewhere with big picture windows looking out onto the surf and being attended to by my perfect slave, who would look after my house and do chores for me during the day *and* be my equal partner and love of my life in the evenings! Is that too much to ask? I've met some wonderful playmates along the way, but I'm still hoping to find that elusive slave-lover of my life!

11

MISTRESS MAI-LING

A Chinese psychiatric nurse from Singapore, turned professional dominatrix, Mai-Ling retired from the scene a year after this interview took place and is now running her own highly successful property development company in the midlands. Interviewed May 1995

I first got into the scene by accident, really. I used to work in the field of psychiatric medicine. I had a friend of a friend who owned a studio. I was very dissatisfied with my job in the medical profession. I knew I wasn't going to get anywhere. I was looking for a way out when this fellow suggested I get into the S&M scene. I said: "What's that? What are you talking about?"

He offered to bring round a few magazines to show me. He also asked me if I wanted to go to a party that Saturday. Remember, I didn't know anything at this point. I didn't even have any clothes. I had to borrow some from the Mistress of the House where the party was being held. I decided not to think about anything. I thought I'd just leave my mind a blank and go with a completely open mind about things.

I was introduced to the people there as a 'Mistress in the Making', and I'd reply that I was thinking about it. I spoke to a transsexual mistress called Sadie and she was really nice. She told me to stick by her throughout the evening and I'd learn a thing or two. She showed me how to use the whip and all of that. Though, to be honest, watching all these people walking around half naked, I was secretly thinking: "Oh, no. This isn't my scene at all!"

At one point, as I was sitting down, someone said to me: "Mistress, can I be your footstool?" So, I said, rather casually: "Okay, yeah." He lifts my feet up and lays them across his naked back. I had really high heels on and I didn't want to hurt him. I didn't even realise at this point that that was what he wanted more than anything in the world. But he said: "It's alright, Mistress, dig them in a little deeper." Well, if that's what he wants, I thought, okay. But I was also bursting to go to the toilet and I was wondering: "What do I do now?" The drink was beginning to go to my head, so I just kicked him and said: "Out of my way, I'm going for a pee". And he said: "Oh, Mistress, may

I accompany you to the toilet?" I didn't have a clue to what to say to that, so I simply shouted: "How dare you!"

Later, the man who took me to the party asked me how I was getting on, so I told him about the fellow and what had happened. And he just fell about laughing and said: "Why didn't you just piss on him and make him drink it?" I said: "What! Why should I?" Well, according to him that's what you should do. I didn't know! Anyway, that party was my introduction to the world of Fem-Dom. I soon got the hang of it, though. In fact, the very next day, the same guy phoned me up and asked me to go round to his house the next weekend and try my hand as a mistress. I said: "I don't think so, it's too much for me. I can't whip people like that."

Look at it from my point of view. I was very straight. I'd never dressed up, never done anything like that. I didn't know anything at all. But he was very insistent that I should go and see this other mistress and watch how she worked. So I went along when she had one of her regular slaves with her. Remember, this is the time I'd ever walked into a dungeon. I said: "What's this, for heavens sake?" He replied, very matter-of-factly: "This is a dungeon and this is a slave. And these are the weights you put on his balls."

He went on like this, talking about all the things they use. Then the mistress took over and told me to watch her whip the slave's backside, saying that I could take over later. When I took over, I hit him a few times and the slave started complaining, saying: "Mistress, I don't think she's doing it hard enough." The mistress told me I had to really give it to him. So, I thought to myself: "Okay, I will!" I really started whacking him harder after that! But still not too hard because the blood put me right off, you know.

Afterwards, I asked the mistress if that was it? Was there anything else I needed to know? She said: "A lot. You've got to learn everything about this business. The best thing to do is to come and work with me now and again to get the hang of things". I didn't want to disappoint her, so I said alright. Later, I thought to myself: "Oh God, I've committed myself to something here! I don't know what I'm letting myself in for". Now and again I went down to see her and that's how I started to learn. But all the while, I was thinking: "I really can't do this. It's too harsh for me". Then my friend said: "I think you're looking at it from the wrong angle. There are other aspects to it. It's a big field that ranges from whipping to water sports". It was at the next party that I really started getting into domination. But it still took me another two years to build up enough courage to become a full-time mistress.

It was when I was on holiday in Italy that I thought to myself: "I think I'm going to go into that". When I came home I literally threw myself into it. I didn't think about anything else. I immediately made inquiries about taking a dungeon. By that time I'd seen a lot of videos and read a lot of books on the subject and felt ready. I gave a months notice at work and left. I knew this was something I wanted to do.

I still remember my very first client. He wanted a really good beating. I thought: "What shall I do? I'll just clear my mind and give it to him". And, amazingly enough, he came back for more! In fact, he ended up being one of my long term regular clients. It just started from nothing. That was six years ago now. Obviously, I've progressed a lot since then and got better and better. Each mistress develops her own style and individual techniques as time goes on.

Above all, to be a good mistress, you have to be confident. As soon as a slave walks through the door you have to take over. What happens is that when they arrive, after making an appointment first, of course, my maid lets them in and shows them around the dungeon. They never see me at this point. When I come in I am dressed in ordinary clothes and I'll tell you why. We'll spend about ten minutes discussing exactly what they want out of the session. Some might just want to be a naughty boy and stand in the corner. Others might want to be a real slave. We'll both sit down, but I always make sure I'm sitting higher than they are. I've got a list of about a dozen rules written down which they must read so they'll know exactly how to behave in my presence. They are also given a choice of what they want me to wear. Remember, the session is their fantasy, not mine. So I try to make it real for them. I ask them what they like. Leather, rubber, PVC? High heels, thigh boots? Whatever they like, I try and get it for them. By the time they see me again in the dungeon, I am dressed for their fantasy. Now the session starts.

First of all, I will humiliate them. Not in a big way, but in a small way. However, I make sure they know who is the mistress and who is the slave. I look down on them, see? It doesn't matter if it's only a couple of inches, but they always have to raise their eyes to look up at me. Once I'm dressed and the session starts, I don't stop for anything. That's the whole idea of sitting them down at the beginning, so that later I can just run smoothly with them. They understand that once I walk in dressed in full uniform it doesn't stop until the time is up. They're already acquainted with my rules, so they know what to expect of me. If they forget, then I have to forcibly remind them.

But it is more than just the physical side. Take humiliation as an example. The real humiliation comes from the mouth. It's in what I say and the way I say it. Although I'm doing what they want, I'm making them do it my way. For instance, if they want to worship my body, I tell them where to worship and for how long. If they want to lick my boots, I make sure they do a really good job and lick all the dirt off. They must only touch me where we have agreed beforehand they can touch. Absolutely nowhere else. If I tell them they may kiss my bottom and they start holding me there with their hands, I let them know that it is wrong! And I make sure they won't do it again, believe me!

The kind of punishments I meter out varies from one slave to another. Not everyone likes heavy punishment, but the point is to find out what they like and what they don't like first. My kind of punishment is to give them a little of what they don't like! They won't do it again! The kind of situation where I would give out what I call 'real' punishment would be, for example, when they are not supposed to touch me unless I tell them to. Even if they just brush against me without permission they will be punished. If they tell me they don't like to be marked, then I will mark them! But only for a short period, though. By the time they leave the marks will be gone, but it will be enough to make my point. It's the fright you put into them that counts. Not all of my slaves can afford to go home with marks on them for their wives to see. Another slave may have told me he doesn't like his nipples played with, so what do I do if they're naughty? I'll tie them up and yank their nipples a little bit. Of course, you gag them first so they don't scream. And, again, you don't do it too long. Just long enough to let them know that they should never disobey. If they do, they'll know what they'll get! And the next time it will be harder. Above all, never let them know when the punishment is coming. Most of the time they will learn to like it.

I never work on the basis that I know what a slave wants, because

I don't. They have to tell me and then I carry it out. For instance, some slaves like to take Amyl Nitrate. Personally, I don't like the stuff. But, if that's what they want, then they have it. Also, although they tell you what they want, they expect you to fill in the gaps between. It's difficult to explain what that means, really. For example, they might give me a piece of paper. Maybe three or four sheets. I can scan through it, but there's usually no way I can carry all this stuff out in an hour or an hour and a half. The theory that's in their heads doesn't translate into reality, so I say to them: "Well, we'll do most of the things you want and I'll fill in the gaps". Others don't actually know what they want, so again I have to fill in the gaps and make it last. Just because I'm a mistress the slave thinks I know everything, but I don't.

Even when trained slaves come to me, who may have served another mistress for years, I still say to them: "You must forget your old mistress completely and go my way". And that's how we do it. I tell them I'm going to break them body and soul. I tell them: "You're new to me and I'm new to you. I don't even want to know what you've been through before". I don't mess around with them. It's the only way to do it, really.

There are some so-called mistresses who haven't a clue what they're doing and that's the truth. I have rules and regulations that all my slaves understand so they know how to treat me Once I'm dressed up and in the working room I will break them into my rules, but within the constraints of what they want. At the end of the day, you have to remember it's the man who's coming to you and you're the one who's got to please him. You can see I'm being very frank with you. I'm not cutting out anything.

When I come to the end of the session and want to end it, I give them permission to dress and see them to the door. At that point we're back to normal. If they're new ones I will ask them if they are happy or if they have any complaints. So far I haven't had any complaints. Sometimes with the new ones, if I have the time, I will sit down with them and explain why I did this or that during the session. If they're the sort who have come with unrealistic scenarios, I'll tell them to go away and think about what they really want and to read some books on the subject. That way we can progress in the next session.

As a mistress you have to be a good actress. You've also got to be

17

able to read people's minds which, fortunately, I can due to my training as a psychiatric nurse. Above all, you've got to be in command throughout the whole session. Never relax. Never let them know if you don't know or are unsure. You, as a mistress, must surround them, in a sense. They're watching you all the time, so you've got to be on top from the first minute to the last. If they talk without permission, tell them to shut up. And when you punish them, smile at them. And they will smile back at you and say: "Thank you".

I always use hand contact between whippings to relax them and bring them to attention. Any mistress or master will tell you that. You can't just hit someone anywhere and anyhow. That's not domination. That's just beating someone black and blue. Domination is an art and the person doing it is an artist. What I do is very classy. I combine hard and soft techniques. I have lots of little brushes and other equipment as well as my fingers to relax them. So you've got to be an artist, you've got to be able to read their minds and you've got to be dominant without being forceful. But, most of all, you've got to be natural.

I never swear at them. Well, I don't know how to swear to be honest with you. I'll call them names, but I don't like ugly words. I'll call them 'cabbage-brains' or something like that. The beauty of it is that they respect me and I respect them and we have a relationship. They phone up and say: "Hello, Mai-Ling. How are you?" I don't like to be called 'mistress' when I'm not actually working. I don't think it's on. I keep the dungeon separate from normal life. It's beautiful. I love my work.

In the course of a day, I may cover all sorts of things. Torture scenes and interrogations. I have to treat them as terrorists or prisoners or whatever. For this I'll put them in the cage or tie them up and blindfold them. Then I treat them rough. I mean very, very rough because they love it. I do a lot of threatening and I put a lot of panic and fear into them. It's like acting in a film. You have to treat them like dirt. Grab their hair and all sorts. Whatever it takes. It's hard sometimes because some of them hold on for an hour or more before I can get information out of them. A favourite one for them is to pretend they're in Changie prison in Singapore. Other times I am a customs officer. But I always give some leeway. That is, I give with one hand and take back with the other. The trick is never to let them know when you are going to give it to them and when you are going to take away.

I also have a room set aside for TV's and Adult Babies, too. When I do something I like to do it properly. In there they've got the wigs, the dresses, the shoes, everything. Sometimes at parties I will dominate other women, but it doesn't really do anything for me. I can do any male–young, old or in between. Most of the men I see are between twenty and sixty five. Not younger or older. But they've got to be strong physically and not ailing. I won't see anyone who is ailing at all, because there is the risk that they might drop down dead! And I'm not joking! The other thing is that I won't put people at unnecessary risk. Nothing has happened so far, but I won't put people's lives in danger. It's a game and I keep it as a *safe* game. I don't do degradation or shitting on people. Definitely not, under any circumstances. If anyone phones me for that, I'll say no. If they call again, I'll just put the phone down. There are lots of other mistresses who will do it, but I've got limits to what I'll do. The clients I see are more than happy with me and I am happy with them. Once they know what I do and don't do, that's okay.

I'm not looking for people who don't respect themselves. And I don't want someone who is just coming here for one day to get a kick out of it. I want someone who has a genuine interest. Someone who says: "Mistress, I'm in your hands. Do what you want with me". Within reason, obviously. Someone who wants me to teach them how to be a proper slave and who sincerely wants to learn how to worship a mistress. Once they tell you that you know they will keep coming back. These are the sort of clients I want.

I like to tie people up and tease them silly in lots of different positions. These people are not into the heavy S&M thing. That's what they want and that's what they get. No marks, no nothing. I never go over the top with anyone. If they say that's all they can take I respect their limits. Unless they're doing something they shouldn't. That's a different matter. Then, obviously, I do what I want with them because I'm the mistress and they have to take it whether they like it or not!

They never know what I'm going to do next. I'm very unpredictable, and everytime they come it's a different thing altogether. Never do the same thing over and over again. It's boring and I lose interest very quickly. So I tell them that next time they come we'll do what they've set out, but then they're going to learn. I'll introduce new things for them, but I'll always give them what they want first. A bit of body worship, whatever. And then introduce something else. There's so much you can do with them. It can go on and on and on. But never give to them all in one go – prolong it!

Of course, I have been occasionally asked to be submissive, but I can't do it because I'm naturally dominant. Sometimes I'll get a call from someone asking me to be submissive for them. This is very, very rare. When it happens I'll ask them where they got that information? They will read out my ad over the phone and I say: "Where does it say about being submissive? It doesn't. You'd better find someone else". If I'm in a bad mood, I'll just slam the phone down. I give and they take. That's the whole idea of them being here and there's no in-between. But the genuine people don't waste my time because they're wasting their own time, too. If you're genuinely dominant, then you can't be submissive. These people are worms, they can't read. All they see is a phone number. If they're here in the room and they ask for that then I really give it to them hard because they're stupid.

What I plan for the future is to take in overnight stays and week-end visits on a one to one basis. They will have to write me a formal letter of introduction for this service as I am only interested in very genuine scene players. I'm having a booklet printed which will be sent to each applicant, so they will know what they're letting themselves in for. At the same time they must explain exactly what they want. I don't know anyone else who is providing this service, but I think there is a call for it. I'm really looking forward to starting.

I'm often asked about the funniest or weirdest requests I've ever had, but it would be impossible to list them all because there have been so many! When I first started I was very shocked by some of the requests I got, but I never showed it. I pretended I knew what I was talking about, even though I didn't! But I'm doing this five days a week for six years now, so I think I've heard it all! I don't let anything shock me now. Why should I? There's nothing to be shocked about. Sometimes I might wonder where he gets his ideas from? I look at the client and the paper he has written. I look back at him again and tell him that I don't think I can carry this out, not to this extent. I mean some of the ideas clients have are just too fantastical, there's nothing you can do with them.

Yet it's like you're in a glass house. You're being watched all the time. You've got to be competent, confident and in total control. If you take on something you can't do, you've lost it. They're not coming back to you, so it's best to be honest with them. I don't cheat clients with their time or their money. That's why I always sit and discuss everything with them before hand and, if I can't do what they want, I tell them straight I can't do it. It's just not applicable – but we can do this and this.

You can see by now that being a true dominatrix is very hard work. I've got so many role-plays and so many screen-plays. Sometimes they will come to me and want us to pretend we're at a party. Do to me what you'd do at an S&M party, they'll say. He's *never* been to an S&M party in his life, never even been to a fetish club, yet he's asking me to take him there in my workroom in fantasy! Now what do I do with him? Do you see how hard it is? He doesn't have the chance to go in real life, but he'd love to go. His fantasy is that he's on stage at a party. It's so hard to put on that sort of thing. But whatever they want, I can't smile or laugh. I have to be serious. Obviously, if it's something funny we'll have a good laugh about it afterward, but I can't laugh in the workroom.

I had one slave in particular I must tell you about. He had a wife he loved, but she didn't love him. The arrangement between them was that he was her slave, but she could take any man she fancied. So, she brought this new man home and introduced her husband as her 'slave', and told him he had to serve both of them. This new man was very dominant and started taking over. Pretty soon his wife is dressing him up in a maids uniform and sending him over to me for further training, because she couldn't even be bothered to train him herself anymore – not now that she had her 'dream lover', as she called her boyfriend.

Meanwhile, the poor chap is having to call the boyfriend 'Master'. He used to force my slave to come into the bedroom and watch him make love to his wife. This went on for four months. Then the boyfriend decides to move some of his stuff into the house and stay over most nights. At this point, I said to the slave: "Do you think you can handle this?" He says: "Sure. No problem".

He had to do things like clean the boyfriend's car every Sunday.

Outside in the road, this is. All dressed up in pink knickers and everything. But it did start to get a little bit out of hand when some of the boyfriend's mates were brought back and he had to serve them drinks and wait on them and curtsey like a maid and everything, while they all got drunk and took turns having sex with his wife.

He started getting really unnerved about that. He wasn't getting anything, you see. No sex, nothing. Meanwhile, she's going out dressed really teasingly with short, tight skirts. When she comes back she would take off her knickers and let him smell them and then she'd tell him about all the men who had spunked over them that night. This was the nearest he was allowed to get to sex with his own wife now. He wasn't even allowed to touch her. Then the boyfriend banned him from even sniffing his own wife's knickers. Instead, they got him a blow-up doll and he was allowed to sleep with that for a couple of nights a week.

Things became really heavy for him when his wife's lover (who was a builder) decided to take him away on a six week contract. He was made to work all day for nothing. But worse than that, the boyfriend had another mate on the building site. He told everything to this chap about what went on. How he has sex with the man's wife and everything. So this mate started taking the mickey out of him, saying things like: "You've got a really nice wife. We're all going to come round and fuck her for you". Things like that. On top of this, he became the dogsbody to everyone on the building site. If they wanted anything from the shops, he would have to get it. For the whole six weeks they treated him really rough, making him work from seven in the morning till seven at night.

Back home he was forced to live in the box room of his own house. No furniture, nothing. Now and again the boyfriend might allow him to watch them having sex and then punish him if he got an erection. Then the boyfriend announced that he was going to leave his own wife and move in permanently. At this point the fellow phoned me and he was not too happy. He visited me to talk about it, yet even then he still thought he could cope with it.

Shortly afterward, the boyfriend went away on another contract and the wife started pining for him, saying how much she missed his cock. Her husband offered to fuck her in his absence and she got really angry. She said: "How dare you" and slapped his face and then proceeded to beat him very hard. Anyway, during this period she started letting another boyfriend come round to satisfy her. The two boyfriends didn't know about each other, you understand, only the husband knew. But he still insisted he could cope with it because he loved her so much.

Finally, and I don't know exactly what happened to trigger it, but the boyfriend was making the husband call him 'Master', as usual, and forcing him to get on the floor to lick his wife's boots, as he did everyday, when he must have said something to make the husband snap. He went completely over the edge and grabbed a baseball bat and chased both the boyfriend and his wife down the street, hitting him all the time with the bat while the neighbours watched. This is while he's wearing stockings and his maids uniform, remember! So, in the end it was too much for him and he couldn't cope with it. Now he's decided he doesn't want to do the slave thing anymore. He wants to try straight forward S&M for a change.

Now you understand that I always have to keep my mind a blank in this business, because I never wonder who's coming. It could be someone I've seen ten thousand times, but I still ask them what they want to be, what they want me to do with them today. He might have changed his mind from the last time. How do I know? He might have read some books and got some new ideas. Every day is a new day and every time they come I treat them like a new client. That's why they love coming to me. I don't just ask them what they want and get on with it, because they'd get fed up and so would I. Then I'd get lax in my work and start getting angry, and when they come next time, I'd say: "Oh no, not you again!" See what I mean? It's got to be new all the time. They come to me to be relaxed in their own specific way and I give them exactly what they want. It's as simple as that!

To any woman who wants to become a mistress, I would say this: don't try to be mistress all the time. You need time away from it to develop new ideas and different ways of dealing with your slaves. Ensure that each session is new and exciting for both you and your slave. Always make the slave wonder what he can expect, what will be done to him today. Make it work for him and don't forget to enjoy yourself, too. Above all, give your all to each session. Give it your heart.

MADAM KARRA

Boy meets girl. Boy and girl fall in love and get married. Pretty usual stuff so far, isn't it? After all, that's what people do. However, what happens when boy also wants girl to be his mistress? In other words, what do you do when one partner is in the "scene", while the other thinks it's just all plain weird? Well, that's exactly the situation that faced slave-husband Richard and his lady love, the divine Madam Karra. Interviewed March 1996.

Several years ago, my husband Richard got bitten by the bug that breeds submissiveness towards the Superior Female. I'm afraid I was, in the early days, a very reluctant mistress who just didn't realise her potential. My poor husband would meticulously detail a sub-dom session on reams of paper in the hope that his 'mistress' would follow it word-for-word. Sadly, he was mistaken and had to settle for a rushed version of his masterpiece. Admittedly, for someone like myself, who didn't really understand the reasoning behind a male wishing to be bossed about and disciplined by a female, his written compositions were quite off-putting.

In those days, a typical 'session' would begin with his preparing an outfit for me to wear, and changing into something effeminate himself. He would arrange all the instruments in a neat row, then inform me that my outfit was prepared. Then he'd wait patiently in the corner, probably going over the 'agenda' in his head. Eventually, I would appear in something *completely* different to what he'd so lovingly prepared! The outfits he had selected were designed to give a female a sense of 'power-dressing'. Inevitably, my version would be more like 'half-throttle' dressing! Not to be deterred though, he accepted my choice and looked forward to the meaty stuff. Topics for his sessions varied from schoolgirl to housemaid, to effeminate slave. Basically, anything which allowed him to wear women's clothes, especially lingerie. Every session involved housework, inspections of chores, discipline and lots of standing in corners!

Due to my lack of understanding, there was never any genuine anger in my commands, I'm afraid. Punishments would be rushed and meaningless – punished for no reason, so to speak. Inspections were also rushed and he was praised for good work a lot of the time. This avoided me having to punish him, so that I could carry on watching television. In short, I'd try and get the whole business over with as quickly as possible, hoping it was just a phase he was going through.

These sessions progressed for some years and up to six months apart. Frustration was an understatement for my poor slave! Over the years he managed to tone down his desire to wear women's clothes and adopted simple thongs instead. This helped a bit, as I felt more at ease with him as a 'male' slave, and things improved slightly. Then one day, after reading a story in a Fem Dom publication, he hit upon an idea or rather, an ultimatum! He decided he would risk his whole fantasy life in one last attempt to make or break the woman who was his wife! There would be no reams of paper and no dressing-up – just seven whole days of continuous 'make-it-up-as-you-go-along' mistress/slave scenarios! His only conditions were that he would do *anything* for me and would be punished at least once a day. Well, seven days turned into twenty one days and, by the end of it, he was begging for no punishments at all! Don't ask why or how it happened! But I am now his 'Mistress' as well as his 'Governess': Madam Karra, a Superior Female with a *total* commitment to dominance of the inferior male. She who must be addressed as 'Ma'am'!

The way it came about was that I had, by this stage, become so extremely irritated with my husband's demands for a 'Domination Session', that I decided to call his bluff and, hopefully, put a stop to his perversions once and for all! It was time to take him up on his ultimatum, and a week-long session-to-end-all-sessions might be just what was needed!. I was tired of getting home from work only to find him 'demanding' to be dominated! He'd spend an absolute fortune on gear to satisfy his *own* fantasies, and hope to get me to wear the stuff for him! Occasionally, I would agree to carry out a session and have to work through his long and detailed transcripts of 'how it must be done'. Needless to say, I skipped the parts I didn't like and invariably rushed through the rest. Now my conditions were that I must control the entire session for the whole seven days, and there was to be no silly 'pieces of paper' with endless scripts. One hint of interference would terminate the session and disrupt any future sessions. I felt pretty confident that he wouldn't be bugging me anymore once I'd finished with him! I reckoned three or four days would be all that it would take.

I began the first day by giving him a huge list of chores to complete. This kept him occupied for most of the evening, and I soon detected that he hated doing them! I deliberately ignored him the whole evening and simply instructed him to complete every chore before reporting to me. This really annoyed him as well, because it meant he wouldn't receive any punishments at all until right at the end. As the evening went on, I sensed a weird kind of 'evilness' inside me. I knew what I was doing was totally against his own desires, as my denial was more of a 'punishment' to him than actually giving him what he wanted!

When the moment of completion finally came, I was simply going to pass every chore and praise him for being such a good boy. However, during the inspection of his first task, I suddenly decided to look *very* closely at his efforts. I can't really describe exactly what came over me, but I just became very 'nit-picking'. His face dropped as I began to ask for his excuses for such sloppy work. Of course, he couldn't come up with anything except: "I have failed you, Mistress. I beg your forgiveness, Mistress". Oh, how boring this pathetic phrase had become by now! I went to town on all his other tasks and really let him have it! I insisted that to be a slave of mine would require a lot more effort than what he'd put in so far!

By the time the full inspection was over, I wasn't very pleased at all! To make things worse, when I informed him that he'd have to be punished severely for his lax efforts, his little face positively lit up! Now this made me genuinely angry! In fact, my rage actually frightened him as he'd never experienced any real anger on my part during a session. I decided to tie him to the bed to receive his punishment (which was another unusual move that worried him) and informed him that he would be caned *and* whipped! The first salvo involved a thin, bamboo cane which snapped after several extremely hard strokes. My next selection was a riding crop which also came to pieces after an enthusiastic beating. My slave was writhing about in agony by this time, and close to tears. Another mean-streak came over me and made me ignore his welfare and really make him cry! I fetched a stranded whip that, ironically, he'd made himself and began to lash his body with it. He gritted his teeth, made muffled screams into the pillow and jerked as much as his bonds would allow. It was all to no avail though, because I'd already detected an anger in him that he was using to counteract his tears!

Because I'd succeeded in making him angry, I felt that I had defeated him; which, in turn, gave me a huge thrill! I'd never felt so good before now at seeing someone in true pain! I was convinced that this would put him off sooner than I had thought but, at the same time, I secretly hoped I'd have the opportunity to repeat the treatment! I decided it was best to leave him tied for twenty minutes, so he could cool off. I admit I was a bit worried that he may have taken it badly and retaliated. This had been one of my main concerns in the past. Before we went to bed that night I asked how he was feeling, as I was still wondering if I had gone too far. His response was not the one I wanted to hear! He said: "That's how I've always wanted it done, Mistress". I immediately tasked him for the morning chores *and* made him write out a list of jobs that were to be completed once he had returned from work!

The next couple of days went much the same as the first. In fact, it was soon turning into something of a routine. Around the middle of that week I realised I was beginning to enjoy the situation. I was getting home from work to discover that everything was done and a meal would be ready for me! Simple little things that a woman could normally not expect. Usually, of course, it's the wife who has to cook, clean and run about after her man. I was very quick to realise that I could live a life of luxury as far as housekeeping was concerned!

Interest soon got the better of me and I decided to experiment further. A short list of rules were drawn up to test *exactly* what power I had. Things such as having him massage my feet as soon as I had come home, warming up the toilet seat before I sat on it, cleaning me after I had been to the toilet, having him make me a coffee at one snap of my fingers and generally running around fetching things for me. All these were factors that slowly drew me into the world of Female Domination. Each day passed with surprising ease and I could sense that I was becoming more and more dependent upon the services of my 'slave'. He showed no signs of giving in to the harsh chastisements I was inflicting on him each day. In fact, I noticed him adopting an even more obedient attitude as he grew tired of the beatings.

Near the end of the seven-day period, I increased his workload substantially. By this stage, he was doing absolutely everything about the house *and* running about for all my personal needs. This was becoming sheer bliss for me, as you can imagine. My stress-levels were falling and I found myself becoming happier, both at work and at home. Being pampered and waited on was an experience I wanted to last forever. Not only was I enjoying the experience of having a personal servant, I was also beginning to enjoy inflicting pain. For some reason, which I can't explain to this day, I started to feel great delight in chastising his vulnerable flesh! If I ever felt some tension, or had been annoyed by something during the day, I'd instantly make it an excuse to punish my husband. He provided the punch-bag upon which all my tension could be taken out! He never once complained, retaliated or walked away. It was my own power of dominance that kept him there, and I could see that he accepted it totally and without question.

My thoughts soon turned to prolonging this situation indefinitely! I still wasn't happy with the fact that most of the week had been conforming, in the main, with *his* ideas of Female Dominance, rather than mine! Sure, I had introduced some of my own ideas and he'd been quite happy to carry them out, but I still needed to condition him to my way of thinking and my way of doing things. During his last evening of slavery, I drafted out some of my own ideas and methods. While doing this, I realised that I was actually composing a list of ideas that would demand absolute perfection in order to be achieved! Well, if perfection requires a strict set of rules which must be intricately detailed, then so it shall be! Before that evening was over I had dictated a huge list of rules and regulations to my slave. I instructed him to learn these off by heart, and to abide by them from now on. He dared to raise the question that a set of such detailed rules was a bit late to enforce at this stage of the session. My response provoked a mixed reaction from him. I simply informed him: "I may wish to extend the session!"

One of the first major changes was my title and form of address. I'd become so engrossed with the situation that I decided to adopt the Female Dominant title of Madam Karra. I'd once read a book which characterised a female executive called Karra. She was ruthless and insisted on perfection from her male underlings. The form of address had to change as well because, personally, I don't like to be referred to as a 'Mistress'. Seeing as I was a Madam, I thought that 'Ma'am' sounded more appropriate, and instructed Richard accordingly. The ground work had now been laid for my *total* control over his life.

Surpassing the seven-day deal saw a change in me that made me realise that dominating the male of the species is what I should have done years ago. It's the only thing I've experienced that has made me content and confident as a woman. My life was very routine and average before, but now I feel I have a real vocation in life. As each day progressed, I became aware of new ideas that would groom my husband into an obedient and well-disciplined personal servant. I had to change his way of thinking, of course, so that all his actions would conform to my ideals. His workload increased, too, as I became even more demanding, but he soon began to carry out tasks as if it were second nature. I must stress at this point that I had introduced a severe punishment policy. Any mistake, sign of disobedience or lax discipline, no matter how trivial, was met with harsh chastisement. I felt that the only way to prevent him from deliberately making mistakes was to punish him very severely in the first place. A second offense would merit automatic doubling of a previous punishment. A third offense would triple it, and so on. By this stage he was working as I wanted him to. He'd learned his lessons the hard way and was aware of the consequences in the future. I had converted my husband into an obedient, well-disciplined personal servant who worked hard in order to avoid the wrath of my punishments. I became increasingly aware of my endless power over him and was determined to take him to the utmost limits of obedience!

One day, while we were out shopping, I got the urge to make him display his subservience then and there. Knowing that such displays in public are limited, I got the idea of having him kneel at my feet, but in a way that would *seem* quite normal. Instructing him to re-tie the laces on my boots provoked a surprised look from him. So I gave him one of my angry stares, snapped my fingers, then pointed to the ground and said: "Boots! Laces! Now!" No further prompting was needed as he dropped onto both knees and re-tied my laces to perfection. I actually enjoyed the feeling of power as other men passed by and stared. The moment they realised that I was watching them they averted their eyes and scurried away. It felt wonderful to watch the so-called 'macho' sex squirming with embarrassment. As soon as we'd got back home, I gave him such a severe caning that he has never again refused or questioned one of my commands in public!

I felt that I'd now created a new lifestyle for us both. He's now actually *doing* what he'd merely fantasised about before, except for the fact that he has to do it my way and not his! And I'm beginning to enjoy the advantages of having my own personal servant. You could say that he treats me like royalty: serving, obeying and protecting me. Another thing I drastically changed was his time off. With both of us working in full-time employment, we find it hard to get compatible days off. Before, I'd have to get up and go to work while he still lay around in bed. This had to stop, of course! I decided to enforce a routine where he would have to get up early and prepare my breakfast. On his days off, he'd also attend to my morning shower and prepare everything I would normally do myself. When it came to my days off, and he was working, I would waive the breakfast chore. Compatible days off were best of all. I would instruct him to get up early as usual and give him a list of chores to complete. This ensured that he maintained his routine and left me to enjoy a longer sleep. Because a lot of his chores would have been completed early in the day, it also left more time for me to have some fun with him!

These periods of fun now occur on a regular basis and involve physical exercise/endurance, obedience re-training and humiliation. His exercises consist of either static repetitions or a run. Obedience re-training involves his abilities to control himself and, as far as humiliation is concerned, I usually 'transform' him. Physical exercises which can be conducted in-house are usually press-ups, sit-ups, squat-thrusts, 'burpees', and the like. I'll make him sweat for at least an hour. Running is a completely different ball-game. I will designate a particular place he must run to and return in a specific time. Failure means a repeat of the run and embarrassment for him. Why embarrassment? Simply because the designated point is a particular shop which I know stocks its own brand of goods or has pre-printed price labels and receipts. This ensures that no cheating is possible. Returning to the shop for the second or third time for one item will baffle the staff and cause him some embarrassment as he tries to explain away his reasons.

One thing that I capitalise on whenever he is carrying out physical exercise is the fact that he sweats profusely; this is one thing that really turns me on sexually and I take full advantage of his tongue! I've discovered that a woman can gain ultimate sexual pleasure without having to indulge in full sexual intercourse. Whenever I detect that my slave is becoming frustrated at not being able to relieve himself sexually, I usually make him repeat the whole process all over again! As this arrangement has developed, I've become more aware of my feelings towards his denial of pleasure. It sends a mean streak through me and makes me very happy indeed!

Although denial of his sexual pleasure pleases me, I know it can be dangerous to leave it too long. My solution to this is simply to allow him a controlled and supervised period of relief. I will designate either a specific amount of time for masturbation, or a number of 'pulls' on his cock. For every second or pull below my figure, he receives one stroke of the cane. For each second or pull over, he'll get two strokes and so on. This is, of course, in addition to my compulsory punishment for allowing him such a privilege in the first place. One has to maintain strict discipline at all times.

Any humiliation of my husband makes me laugh no end. Most of the time, I'll make him dress as a baby and treat him with the same kind of love and affection that any 'mother' would. And he hates every minute of it! I'll make him carry his teddy-bear everywhere and he must crawl at all times. He's never allowed to speak, and always has a 'pacifier' in his mouth. Obedience re-training involves exercises of self control and discipline. An example of this would be to simply have him put into a 'stress' position for an hour or two, such as sitting cross-legged, back straight and arms outstretched horizontal to the ground. To make this particular exercise harder, I'll place a book in each of his upturned palms. Every fifteen minutes he'll be given a litre of strong orange juice. The aims of this exercise is to train his posture by ensuring his back is kept straight, strengthen his arms so he will be able to carry out heavy labouring, and to train his bladder to hold a lot of fluid. The final aim is especially important, because I only allow him three toilet breaks each day!

Although I have come round to the idea that dominating males makes me very happy, content and important, I've never found the idea of personal abuse very appealing. A slave is an asset, a tool that a woman can use to make life easier. If you don't look after the tool then it will break and become ineffective. To this end, I will never do anything that would jeopardise his health or personal safety. It may be very well for a lot of other women to make their slaves eat and drink body wastes, but I don't agree with that at all! The body ejects this waste for one reason only, and that's to rid itself of toxins and unhealthy material. I actually cringe at the thought of anybody readily accepting these by-products from another person!

I don't condone the practice of burning the flesh, either. This seems well over the top to me. I punish my slave hard and will create superficial markings, but they soon disappear and, unlike burning, leave no permanent scarring. Candle wax is acceptable, however, because it merely leaves marks that will disappear quickly and without trace. I've recently discussed with my husband the subject of 'branding'– the ultimate symbol of ownership! He suggested a tattoo and, once he had designed my symbol, I became very excited at the prospect that my obedient husband actually *wanted* a mark of ownership on his body. Needless to say, he will be getting it etched very soon!

Though my compassionate side sometimes comes out, I'm still introducing Richard to even tougher regimes! One way in which I constantly remind him of his place is during mealtimes. He must prepare a meal for two, as normal, but then prepares his own a stage further. First of all, he blends his entire plateful together. Then the resulting pulp is transferred into his dogbowl and placed on a plastic mat at my feet. This is how all of his meals are taken at home now, and I get enormous satisfaction watching him struggling to eat them. Again, I can't explain why I like to see him eating in this way, I just find it so amusing, that's all. Another reminder for him of his place in my life is the wearing of his collar and personal restraint. This also serves to increase my own awareness of the power I hold over him!

The regime I now run is based entirely upon my own ideas (some of which I've read about and adapted) of exactly how I wish my slave to conduct himself. For example, his own fantasies had never touched upon the complexities of domestic subservience which I've now successfully groomed him to. Basically, his ideas all involved dressing up, getting beaten and finishing a few hours later. He wasn't too keen on losing his dominant-male status for too long, but I soon made him realise exactly who the dominant status really belonged to! One thing that has made this all too clear to him is the control of his finances. He gets nothing unless he works for it and has to pay for his mistakes. Losing control of his financial affairs is something he hates because he likes to spend money. Now that he has to *earn* his 'pocket-money', he's become much more aware of the value of cash. I won't hesitate in 'fining' him for misdemeanours either, as well as chastising him. This has become a double incentive for him to behave and work harder, because he knows I will charge him for every stroke I have to give! The way I explained this to him was that I had to ensure that he remained obedient in order to retain his privileges. If I had reason to punish him, then he must feel the true cost of his disobedience. A chastisement soon wears off and is forgotten about, but actual loss of earnings creates a long term period of guilt that ensures he thinks twice in the future! It's human nature to prefer a loss of face rather than a loss of cash, and even more so with the inferior male species!.

That initial week-long session has now lasted over twelve months and is showing no signs of change. I've become so used to my new role as a Dominant Female that I really can't see me ever reverting back to the way I was. My slave-husband is now trained to an acceptable standard to serve me for the rest of my life. I need only refresh his memory occasionally! Of course, being an inferior male he isn't perfect and does make mistakes, but I find great pleasure in rectifying his lapses in concentration! So enjoyable have been my experiences, in fact, that I feel I now want more. My aim in the future is to provide a service that will train bachelors to become 'instinctively' domesticated. I'd also like to train couples in their responsibilities; that is, for females to adopt a strict regime of dominance, and for males to accept that their place in society is to obey, work hard for, keep contented and to protect the females who are far more superior than they are!

My husband now has a weekly routine that must be strictly adhered to. He has compulsory chores which are carried out every day. In addition to these, he gets tasked with a list of jobs and chores whenever 'Madam' thinks of anything else to keep him busy! It must be stressed that his list of chores is *realistically* set for a normal household where the male is in full-time employment. Inspections are absolutely dreaded by him these days. I carry them out every day and will search every square inch of the house for dirt! One mistake means severe disciplinary action, a repeat of the chore and possible loss of any hard-earned privileges as well. A daily report is made in order to access performance. It all leads to viable excuses for punishment. Richard is never punished unless there is a genuine reason, by the way. His life is now *totally* regulated by the desires and wishes of his

Governess. The situation is such that I now decide everything that happens, when it happens and for how long it happens!. My husband is now, in effect, 'on duty' for the rest of his life. Marriage is the ultimate in ownership!

Unfortunately, his shift work can play havoc with my requirements of him, so he's encouraged to always try harder. In addition to physical chastisement, I will at any time remove or restrict any hard earned privileges he has been granted, such as pocket money and credit cards. As you can imagine, this is highly embarrassing at work when his mates find out that a husband's allowance has been stopped by his wife!

A stringent set of rules has now been devised and must be constantly added to. For example, meals must be prepared to high standards of nutritional and caloric values, presentation and without use of pre-determined menus or recipes. Clothing is to be cleaned, ironed and neatly put in its correct place. The house must be kept at a comfortable temperature and extreme care taken to avoid draughts. It's also the slave's responsibility to keep fit and healthy at all times, as this will ensure a positive and efficient approach to hard work.

Due respect will be given to *any* woman, no matter what her looks, age or attitude. Admission of misdemeanours are to be given every day – better a slave admits rather than his Governess finds out! The word 'sorry' will not be used at all. After all, a punishable motive or excuse can easily be hidden by an insolent or insincere apology! Compulsory chastisement will be given every day, at no fixed time, in the form of a caning. Additional tasks will be given as and when required. A collar will be worn at all times unless told otherwise. Only I may command the removal of subservience devices. All meals for the slave will be served in, and eaten out of, a dog bowl. Only in exceptional circumstances will a plate and utensils be permitted. I will be attended to at all times. Upon summoning, the slave is to be at my feet in less than five seconds. Sluggishness constitutes gross disobedience and will be severely punished.

My level of commitment to the Fem-Dom lifestyle is growing with each day. So far, I've enjoyed the powers I've developed immensely. Although my activities still remain strictly private, I have, as I said earlier, got the urge to command other submissive males into my presence in order to test my skills by training a complete stranger. Although I hate to admit it, my slave-husband is now showing a certain degree of efficiency in some areas of work! Mind you, when he feels I can't find fault he does have a tendency to get a bit cocky. The perfect excuse for some concentrated lessons on his behaviour and conduct!

All in all, my husband now finds himself serving a self-made dominatrix who demands a great deal. I believe it is in every woman's interest to commit herself to a deserved life of luxury. For it is women who do the real work and deserve the best things in life. Ideally, and it is slowly becoming fact, females should dominate every position of power and supervision in all areas of life. Men have ruined this planet and need so desperately to be supervised and disciplined by the Superiority of the Dominant Female Powers. May Female Dominance prevail!

MISTRESS HADES

Well known and much respected on the British fetish scene as the power behind the London Fetish Fair (the capitals monthly 'scene' market), 28 year old Mistress Hades is also an accomplished dominatrix in her own right. Though American-born, she was educated in Britain and now lives and works in North London. Interviewed July 2000.

I would call myself a life-style mistress because I could never see myself *not* being kinky or into kinky sex or *not* being into games of dominance and servitude and all that. Running The Fetish Fair, for example, I'll sometimes see a mistress who wants to give up her dungeon and she'll come and take a stand and sell all her stuff. I couldn't do that! I'm too emotionally attached to my equipment. I'd be remembering what good times I'd had with that flesh-grabber! Happy days! I couldn't get rid of that. I've had too much fun with it.

You also get a certain amount of psychological freedom from doing this work. I mean, I've done a lot of jobs before I decided to become a mistress where I'd have to wear a skirt and a blouse or some crap like that and I hated it! And they hated the way I thought and the way I wanted to dress. It's like if you were an extra in a film and they wanted a bunch of punks, they'd hire some real punks because they'd look comfortable in those clothes. Whereas I just wasn't comfortable not being dressed up in some gothic fetish clothes – and it showed when I wasn't dressed that way.

I became aware of a fetish side to my character at about thirteen when I started collecting whips. I had no intention of doing anything kinky with them, and that's the God's honest truth! I had seven or eight bullwhips, and on Sundays I would practice hitting things. I just wanted them and it interested me. But I didn't know that was kinky and I didn't think that I'd like to hit someone with them. I just knew I wanted to use them. Maybe things come out slowly that way. I've got a picture of me at nineteen at sixth-form college dressed up on Vicars and Tarts Day and I'm holding a whip and dressed up in rubber! So there must have been some inkling there of the shape of things to come! I started buying rubber and latex and stuff at about seventeen and I went into the scene at twenty three. So, if you take that into account, I was a fetishist for a good ten years before I actually got into the scene.

So these things tend to develop. It's not like I had some awful experience and became a mistress to get back at all the men in the world! Some mistresses do have that attitude, they definitely do. And I'm not anti-mistresses, I'm very pro-mistresses. I think they all have their beauty and their own talents and abilities. It's great when they have the presence of mind to empower themselves and be interested in sex and get everything they can out of it. But then, sometimes you get this little undertone that they hate men and they want to make them pay for all the ills in the world. At the end of the day one man is totally different to another. You can't make one pay for the mistakes another one's made. It's just stupid. They want to beat them to make themselves feel better, and that just perpetuates and feeds a sort of monster or hatred thing that has no place in fetishism or SM.

I don't want to be negative, but their motivations are dubious. There's everything from: "I want to prove that I'm the hardest Dom in the world, therefore I'm going to slice you up" – which I've seen and which made me really sick. Somebody came to see me and he'd left his mistress because she'd carved a swastika into his backside with a razor blade. I was absolutely livid. I couldn't believe how irresponsible and stupid that was. And, on top of that, I couldn't see him again because I couldn't look at that. I said: "You've just got to go away and heal yourself up and we'll talk again, but I can't look at this". I don't use razor blades or needles. I've got no axe to grind. I haven't got to prove that I'm the hardest Dom in the business. Who cares?

I spend a lot of time 'mistressing' because I like men. I like being around them in a fantasy capacity. The only ones I have put a little aggression into my swing over have been ones that needed to be taken back down to earth because of their shitty attitudes towards others. I'm not angry at men. I love them, really. I like the idea that I live in the fantasy side of their world and that's it. Beyond their fantasies and that part of their mind, I really don't know them at all. And that suits me fine, actually, because that's the part that interest me. Ironically, if I were to know too much about them, they wouldn't be able to tell me every filthy, sordid, slutty fantasy and then I'd be upset! We're just in a microcosm of sexual fantasy and nothing else, and that's what I'm there for. That's my profession. It's never boring,

I'll tell you that much!

If you're a mistress, it can go either way. You can see so much of men that you want to be with women just to have a change in your sexual experiences or a degree of intimacy – and some mistresses *are* gay and do go home to their girlfriends. Or, if you have so many sexual experiences with men on a professional SM nature, you get *more* hetero-sexual! Basically, you just turn into a dirty old man in the body of a woman!

There are so many different attitudes of people who go into the scene, as well. Some people are like: "Right, I'm leaving behind my old life and I'm taking on my life as a 'perv' for ever more now, and my whole life will be changed". And yet it *doesn't* change. You're still you. You can never get away from who you are and what you are. It's like they think they're joining a nunnery – only it's a 'rubber nunnery'! And that does happen. There's different motivations, but it's nice when people are just relaxed and they're enjoying it and there's no guilt and it's just a facet of their lives.

It's like, if you get a live-in maid, what happens when the 'maid' wants to go and see Arsenal verses Highbury at football? No, you can't go because you've got to stay here and clean the bloody dishes or whatever. It can't work on a twenty four/seven basis. Though people will probably read this and say: "Yes, it does work. It works for me!" But as much as you've got a dominant nature or as much as you've got a submissive nature, you've also got a lot of other sides (or should have), to feed and grow and all that 'hippified' stuff!

I do know one mistress who's got a live-in slave who does everything. She's got this guy at her feet all the time; doing the washing up and the laundry and he just lives in her house. But what about when she wants to do things that are non-SM related? It's one thing if you dive into the SM scene for three hours a week, it's quite another when you live it day in and day out. You've got to have a certain amount of time to actually come back down to earth. If you don't, then before you know it you'll be trying to tie up the guy at the local shop because he's given you the wrong change or something! I mean, you've got to get a perspective if you don't want to turn into a loony. And I've met some *real* loony people on the scene! They started out okay and then slowly lost their marbles over the years. They ended up needing a check-up from the neck up! And I'm not keen to do that.

I've always been into foot worship scenarios; high heels, thigh high boots and all that. I always think of my toes as being five little cocks that need a blow-job! I've one friend who is a slave (though he's not my slave, he's just a mate),and he told me his mistress said to him that thigh high boots only exist in male fantasies, they're not something that women like. Which is bollocks! We *do* like our thigh high boots. We like all the clothes. I like all the dressing up side very much. Above all, I like playing games with intelligent, open minded people. Bondage scenarios, ownership scenarios, humiliation scenes. Public exhibitionism to an extent, but not where there are any children around or people who are going to be really offended by it. I respect other people's life-styles as much as maybe they should respect mine, so I don't impose my life style out in public to that extent. It's better to do something discrete and *maybe* let someone in on the game if you think they might be cool enough to appreciate it. But, other than that, I don't want anyone to know because they might be really upset by it. And I won't allow it on any of our own doorsteps, either.

Having said that, I've had quite a lot of fun with public exhibitionism. I love going to restaurants with long table cloths so you can kick the slave from underneath. I'll make them tip double to the waitress, if they've been stuck up or rude. Or I'll make them tell the waitress embarrassing home truths. I'm more likely to do a public scene with someone who needs mental correction. I'll order horrible things for them that *nobody* would want to eat! I'll put too much salt and pepper on their food and then just sit there and watch them try to muddle through this horrible meal. In that vein, I'll concoct little 'witchey-poo' type drinks for them. I've gone to their cupboard and I've picked out everything I can and mixed it all up in a big blender, then sat there and watched them drink it just for fun.

As for humiliation, that's just whatever makes me laugh at them, I'm up for really. Whatever is degrading or whatever is amusing. I understand the mind well enough to know when you're overstepping the boundary, and when you're starting to 'physically' hurt the mind. Like it or not, there are boundaries to what the mind can take before it starts to get damaged and hurt. You have to be careful to build people up to it. They will be able to do more as they go along. However, a lot of them just want to go straight into some heavy scenario that they mentally can't handle. As a mistress, you're either serious about it or you're not.

As I say, I like games where they're going to be degraded or demoralised, and have to do things that make me openly want to laugh at them. The last one that I really liked was getting someone to openly give oral sex to a rubber teddy bear with a big rubber strap-on dildo on it. That was incredibly humiliating for him because it looked so ridiculous. So there's those kinds of levels of humiliation you can do. You know you've done something mad and something humiliating, but there's no repercussions afterwards.

Another kind of humiliation that interests me is where the person has had a really negative sexual experience in their life. It's possible for a mistress to 'graft' new memories onto it, by reliving that and putting it into an S&M scenario. Say, if something awful has happened to you in your life, and you want to play that out again (only do it in an ultra kinky, sexual way!), then you can actually 'graft' new memories onto it and new associations. It really does work and can be quite healing for a lot of people.

For example, you could re-live the day your girlfriend dumped you. Except I could play the role of that girlfriend and can make you feel degraded, but turned on at the same time. Does that make sense? And then, every time you think about that, the mind flips forward to thinking about when the mistress did the same thing, but used you and abused you in a sexual way. Therefore, the motivations and the reasons are more, well, slutty! And a bit more fun, as well! It can be very therapeutic for you to work through that. You can't help thinking about one *without* thinking about the other. I don't know how many people are thinking about it in that way, but they should be! That's what humiliation is all about for me.

I didn't understand humiliation before I went into the scene, but I understand it now. Before I used to think I wouldn't like that, that it wouldn't be me and I wouldn't want to do that. But now I realise that people into humiliation do have a certain amount of mental freedom, actually, because it doesn't matter what they do, because they're free from their own personal insecurities. They're actually quite strong people. They interest me very much and I'm always happy to see them!

I also love role-play a lot. Things like 'ownership' scenes, where this person is my property and is going to do *whatever* I ask of them!

I like slaves to be thinking about me, as opposed to just thinking about themselves. And they really do *feel* as though I own them. Sometimes I've had slaves phone me up years later and tell me that they never felt like anyone *owned* them more than I did! I remember being young and thinking that I really did want to own people. And that was *outside* of SM! I just felt *that* possessive of people at times that I wanted them as my property. I guess that's why I like that kind of role-play so much.

However, you can only really achieve this level of play with on-going slaves over periods of time. With a one-off visit there's just no point. All you can really do for one-off visits is a 'smorgasbord' of different types of SM that they can try. Because ultimately, if they're a novice (or they *say* they're a novice, which is what they usually do) I try to do two or three things that are completely different from each other, so that the slave can find out what it is that he likes. Because they don't know themselves half of the time. If they've come straight from the world of 'vanilla' sex to rubber, leather and barbed wire, then it's: "Do something kinky, but I don't know what!" The concept of licking somebody's high heels or being trussed up like a calf at a rodeo, or being made to bark and drink from a dog bowl are all very different things, and you wouldn't understand at first why it would be fun to be naked and have this kind of stuff done to you. But then it opens up a part of your mind that you didn't even know you had. In fact, they're usually quite high after a session and have to sit down for ten minutes just get back down to earth. They're not just high on endorphins from being spanked or whatever, it's the fact that it's popped open a part of their mind they didn't even know was there!

That's the good thing about really intimate one-on-one sessions. I know it's probably more lucrative to have six guys in different rooms, and you go from room to room giving them a whack and telling them they're naughty or whatever, but that doesn't really appeal to me. I like the more intense psychological one-on-one sessions. I've been a professional dominatrix for five years, and I don't think I would have lasted this long if I didn't have that sort of rewarding intensity that keeps me interested. And five years is a long time in this business when you consider that a lot of mistresses last about two years nowadays. They go in, they set up, they're on the scene, they're in the clubs, they're in the dungeons, and then they're gone! Usually, they're renting a dungeon from somebody which can be astronomical. I don't know why they rent dungeons, because it would be cheaper to just rent a place and put dungeon equipment in it. Whatever the scenario, I like them to be 'non' run-of-the-mill. No two are ever the same, just as every slave or submissive is different. I like slaves that are genuinely pleased to serve me as my property. I love it when they have the presence of mind to bring me a bunch of flowers. Then you *know* that they really do want to please you. Also, I'll always leave plenty of time between sessions to sterilise all the equipment. I don't care how long it takes. If it were me, I'd want that kind of security. Maybe I don't make as much because I have that high standard, but that's the only way it's going to happen.

It's very difficult, at first, to get used to being a mistress. It's very nerve-wracking. I think I must have broken about three pictures or something by accident during my first few sessions. I was dropping glasses all over the place, because I was such an absolute nervous wreck. I really didn't know what was going to happen. All I knew was that I had to be in control at the end of the day. Now I'm very relaxed and easy with it because I do it my own way. If I did it any other way, I wouldn't be doing it at all. It's sad, actually, that it becomes so nerve wracking and so stressful for some mistresses, mainly because they *don't* think they can do whatever the hell they want. They think they have to please the client. And, to an extent, pleasing yourself *is* pleasing the client. At the end of the day a good submissive should be out to serve you, after all. But maybe mistresses have done things that they didn't enjoy and that would put anyone off immediately. They may feel pressurised into doing watersports or body worship or something else they don't like. Of course, it rubs up against your personality and who you are! And then mistresses will disappear off the scene, which is a shame because a lot of them are *real* stars and are very talented.

Suppose some slave is phoning up *demanding* toilet training, then she should very simply say that she's not going to do that because she doesn't enjoy it, and that's it. But she might feel: "Well, I'm a mistress now so I *have* to do all of these things". Consequently, she does do it and she's totally upset for days afterwards. Who's benefited from that? Nobody. Especially her. So it's very important to maintain a level of individualism that makes her happy to be a mistress. And every mistress is different. I doubt if you'll ever find two mistresses alike, in the same way that no two submissives are alike. Maybe the scenario is similar, but the 'take' on it is different every single time.

This is a crazy world where you'll never walk down the street again thinking that all these people are straight and I'm the *only* one who's kinky! You'll walk down the street knowing that a good percentage of them have, at some point in their lives, tried *something* out of the ordinary. I was at a 'normal' party with a girlfriend recently, and this guy kind of sidled up in front of us both. Okay, we were dressed in black, but we weren't dressed up as mistresses – yet he was visibly shaking! He was actually hanging onto the table as he got closer to us! Now he *must* have got some 'vibe' from us. But, then again, a mistress sits differently, she speaks differently and she walks differently. There's infinitely more confidence there. The more skilled you become at S&M, the less vulnerable you are. You don't have a problem with walking down the street in the middle of the night because you know you've the skills to not be messed with now. That doesn't mean I'm totally invulnerable. But it does mean that, because I'm constantly breaking the barriers with people I don't know at all and just going straight at them, I don't have that same level of personal space that other people have that they feel can be invaded. Does that make sense? It's a psychological vibe I give off that says: "Don't fuck with me".

It's difficult, though. Mistresses are not *completely* invulnerable just because we've got a house full of torture equipment and the skills to asphyxiate someone in fifteen seconds if we need to. We've got the skills, but if someone was determined that they were going to do something, then there's nothing you could do. Having said that, I've never felt threatened myself while working. That's because my clients have all been strongly 'vetted'. I would rather take the time to talk to them on the phone and find out what they want and where they're coming from and give myself the opportunity to say no. But I rarely have to. Most people who have the guts to phone up a mistress are going through their own problems as it is. Anyway, you'd have to be off your nut, really, to go and see a mistress with the intention of harming her, when mistresses spend all their days calculating how to turn almost any item into a weapon! Everything from the bloody spaghetti fork to a plastic bag is a weapon to a mistress! A good mistress doesn't really need any equipment at all to do what she does. An old slipper and a teddy bear could keep a slave amused for hours, if she wanted it that way!

I keep phone calls very concise and to the point because, for one reason, people are notorious for booking a session and then never showing up. That's usually because they've just gone away and totally jacked off on the idea that they've been speaking to a mistress! One guy even put on a woman's voice and called me three times. He must have thought I wasn't going to remember his voice. If they're really impolite, I'll phone them back during the daytime and say: "Why were you so rude to me at midnight last night when you were pissed out of your mind? I don't believe that's right". Generally, I don't have to do that. That happens about once a year. They are usually very polite, very genuine and I have very few problems. Because my website is very well laid out, people know just what to expect. I don't hide any details about what to expect when they come to see me. Sometimes I will even book an appointment over the Internet, depending on how well written the application is.

Every mistress is taking a risk at the end of the day, but if you're intelligent enough you won't be taking that much of a risk. Most of them have got it 'sussed' out enough that they know when someone is just a total 'wacko'. It usually has a lot to do with where you advertise, as well. There are so many contributing factors. Some mistresses are taking a much bigger risk than me. They've got card boys out putting adverts in phone booths and taking anyone off the street. And It could be *anybody*. Any idiot could pick up a card in a phone box. They might be pissed out of their mind and think: "Oh, I think I'll go and see this mistress and maybe I can fuck her". The only way people can come and see me is through my mobile at fifty pence a minute or whatever it is, so unless someone is really serious they're not going to phone me at all. They'll phone one of the local numbers and jerk off there. But, to be honest with you, most of them are really good. They're a nice bunch and I'm friends with a lot of them and I like them. I've also got a good group of clients I've had for five years who I see regularly, maybe once a month. Once a month is enough. It gives them a chance to go away and heal. Over five years, that's a long time and many sessions indeed!

During that time, you become very good friends and the sessions themselves can really go off into 'outer space', because you've built up such a rapport and understanding. If they let you get into their mind, that is. Some people have got a deliberate wall and they want you to break through it, as if to prove that you're intelligent enough to do it in the first place! It's a lot easier if they just put in a bit of trust and give themselves over and let it all happen. The mistress can then get on with what she wants to do. It becomes difficult when they want to play psychological games to the extent that they want you to break through their will. Which doesn't take me long anyway!

Usually, we'll sit down for five minutes, have a cup of coffee and discuss what fantasies have been running through their mind. Things play on your mind, you know. Sexual fantasies can play themselves over and over until you get them out of your system. So I find out what they are. They know they can tell me absolutely *anything* they want, and I'm not going to bat an eyelid. Then, once the session begins, they are my property and that's it. They don't say do this or do that. They don't need to. I've never used 'safe words' once in any of my sessions, either. I never felt I had to. I think they're ridiculous. To me, 'safe words' mean that the mistress isn't *safe* in the first place! Sure, I'd have bloody 'safe words' if I had somebody with needles and hot knives and razor blades at the ready! My 'safe word' would be: "Can I leave now, please?" I've heard some real horror stories, like the swastika on the buttocks, poppers up the nose, scary stuff. It's one thing to give yourself to a mistress utterly, but it's also nice to find out just who you're giving yourself to!

Having said that, I've got a lot of respect for many of the mistresses in the scene. But a mistress isn't the same thing as an escort. They fulfil a different need. I saw something in a Chinese film about escorts working in a bordello where there was this line about a prostitute being 'a wife to many men'. I thought that was pretty much 'on the money', because they do a lot of things for men. And, to an extent, a mistress is doing a similar type of thing. She's fulfiling a lot of their sexual fantasies. I kind of like the idea of that. So I have a lot of respect for the mistresses who know what the hell they're doing and are devoted and dedicated enough to get to the bottom of things.

However, I find it difficult when slaves are willing to give themselves to just *anybody*, and then have a horrible experience and ask why? It doesn't have to be that complicated. It just needs to be thought out carefully to begin with. In a way, the slave must be as selective about his mistress as the mistress should be about her slaves. He doesn't want to end up with his face all cut up or something awful like that, does he? I don't think it happens that much, but they're taking a risk as much we mistresses are. It's a 'hitchhiker syndrome', in that the driver might think the hitchhiker could be dangerous and he might get mugged. But that driver is picking up that one hitch hiker and is in danger once, while the hitch hiker is getting ten or eleven lifts. He could be in danger from all those drivers, so who's really taking the risk?

Many of the scenes I've done have been unforgettable and sometimes very funny, but I won't be able to go into detail for privacy reasons. A favourite was a scene with a man in his late forties. He wanted to be treated like a cheap little whore. I dressed him up in some slutty lingerie and stockings and high heels and sat him (or I should say, her!) on my sofa with her legs crossed high, pretending to be a bordello girl waiting to pick up her next client. I came in, dressed in a suit and corset, asked how much and what she would do for that. We negotiated as if she were a very cheap whore indeed. Then I took her into my dungeon area and made her do as many degrading sexual poses and acts for me as I wanted. I still get turned on thinking about that one!

The furthest I've travelled for a session has been to New York from London. I had a slave there who had such a wonderful vision of romantic idealism about SM. He wanted us to have the best of everything for our private dungeon, with an *army* of fetish costumes and a life of total kinky sex! It was to be an exclusive relationship. I was going to be free to wear fetish gear all day while I got on with things I was interested in, like running my Fetish Fair business. It was all going to be leather corsets studded with semi-precious stones, heavily themed rooms for gothic scenes that go on late into the night, shiny thigh boots and spurs and totally over-the-top trips to the opera, wearing boned latex dresses. We were going to go for the whole lifestyle thing. To hear a man have such commitment to the quality of his sex life was quite exhilarating. But things didn't work out. One day he just started feeling guilty about the way he was and nothing solid ever came to pass.

As a lifestyle mistress, I have accepted slaves in the past who were not that financially well off, but I wouldn't do it again. I had issues with respecting what they were doing with their lives. Also that they just wanted to live with (and usually off!) a mistress. Those types are such losers and I can't be bothered with them. I prefer work hard, play hard types. I only once had a sex slave who lived with me, but I am very selective about things like that. It wouldn't be likely to happen again. A lot of those types of slaves drain you like a vampire. So needy and self concerned.

I haven't had that many really weird scenarios. The people who want to be buried alive and stuff have been carefully told to go and jump in the lake or to go bury *themselves* alive! I had the phone slammed down on me once because I refused flatly to pull someone's teeth out. I thought that was hilarious, but he was deadly serious. I think those types have left their fantasies for so long that they're just getting *too* extreme. I will do extreme fantasy, but I refuse to damage.

Another guy wanted me to put him into bondage, along with his false leg – which I did. Then there was this other guy who wanted to rush off at the end of the session. So I said okay and got him out of his bonds and said: "Oh, have you got a meeting to go to or something?" And he said: "No, I've got to go to my brother's funeral". Okay, fine. Obviously, he must have been so stressed that the only way to get away from it for a while was to come and see a mistress. It wasn't really funny, but it was thought invoking about people's motivations. Sex and death do go together. They go hand in hand. Death is sexy! You can't really say it the other way around, it would just sound too wacky!

Nothing's ever been too 'off the wall', because I've been careful. But it's been very interesting sometimes! My own personal fetishes are always more wacky than the stuff I do in the scenes, anyway! Like zebra-girl and pony-carting. Next week, for instance, I'll be going to a pony-carting picnic and there'll be predominantly girls there. There'll probably be the odd *Benny Hill-esque* running off into the woods for a spanking type of thing going on, I'm sure. With these club meets, rather than anything serious, there tends to be a lot more laughs than anything else. I've been someone's birthday cake, all covered in fruit and chocolate, stuff like that. Then a food fight ensued. How could that be serious? That was just hilarious. Followed by domination sessions on Hampstead Heath in the middle of the night! This kind of stuff is *supposed* to be fun, after all, and you should feel a bit exhilarated afterward.

Sometimes there is a place for that kind of hardcore dominance and serious 'mistressing', and all that. I think it is important. But, if the mistress doesn't have a sense of humour, she'll always be open to ridicule for taking herself so seriously. You know, I've talked in depth to lots of submissives to try and get some background on this, and they say they've sometimes come away from a session giggling their heads off over that kind of mistress!

I think a lot of men really fantasise about being seen as a sex object and as a slut and everything. I don't think they get enough of that. They spend so much of their time being a husband and a provider, they just don't get the time to be the little cheap tramps that they are at heart! And I think they are little hussy's at heart till the day they die! This is the great thing about working in the sex industry; that you can pretty much define to a fine point the difference between a slut, a tart, a slapper and a hussy. They've got distinct meanings between them. I think the sluts pride themselves on being the lowest in the chain of command. They know they're at the low end of the rung and they like it that way. You know you can always go to them for anything and they'll do it, because they're just sluts, after all!

The scene is fun. I think it's difficult for people on the outside to appreciate that. I'm still the same ravingly kinky person I was at the beginning – it just gets worse every year! I think it's a little like rock musicians. You get the ones who produce one good album and then all the rest are crap, because they *only* had that one good album in them. Or you get the others, like Bowie or the Stones, who just get better. So you can choose one path or the other. You can either do your thing and get better at it or just get out.

The beauty of being a mistress is that you don't even have to be young and cute. I like that. I like the fact that you can see someone in their fifties out at scene parties, dressed elegantly in a leather corset or a neck collar or something., and they look excellent and they look elegant at the same time. I look at them and think that's where I want to be at that age! They still have the elements of sexuality that count and you can still relate to them on a sexual level. I guess it depends how important sex is to you in your life – to me it's practically everything!

It's the same for men, they can look elegant too. In my eyes, as long as they stick to leather and velvet, they can't go far wrong. But the rubber T-shirt brigade had better watch out, really. It just doesn't work. It's not about their shape, it's about the way they carry themselves. If you want to be a real body fascist, join the gay scene. Once you're no longer thirty and don't have a perfect physique, they don't want to know. But it's not really like that in this scene. A lot of the guys just buy clothes that will get them past the guy on the door at the fetish club, and they don't think beyond that. Anyway, I think the rubber and the PVC is more of a 'girl-thing', really. It's a shame, too, because back in the seventeenth century the men were the dressed-up peacocks and much more flamboyant. Outside of the fetish world, it's absolutely appaling nowadays!

I like to wear lots of kinky clothes to be sexual. *More* is definitely better and, the more fetish clothes you put on, the kinkier you become. Mistresses who go around with their breasts uncovered are not really being mistresses in my eyes. She's baring something personal in front of someone who is *supposed* to be her servant and who isn't really worthy. I know that sounds awful, but it's true. If a mistress is naked, then exactly what is she doing that makes her a mistress? She's making herself vulnerable to someone who is beneath her. We've got sluts to do all that 'vulnerability' stuff.

Also, I don't honestly think that men like sex as much as they say, or think, they do. I've seen this time and time again with beautiful, gorgeous, young, eligible kinky girls I know. When they meet a man and they offer all forms of degrading pervery to them, the men go completely off their heads. They just can't cope with the concept of getting what they want. They feel threatened. And they just lose it, they can't perform. So be careful what you wish for, because you might just get it!

It's easier, especially in England, to be the kind of girl who wears white knickers and feels guilty about every naughty little thing she does. Then the male can be the one who is perverting the course of justice for her. He can then feel guilty because he's made her do degrading things, and he can get off that way. That's actually a lot easier. This is what separates the fetishists and pervs and the kinky people from the mainstream. Here they're on equal ground where the women are as openly kinky as the men. That can be quite difficult for some people to get their heads round. The guilt aspect gets moved around quite a bit and becomes just another tool for fun.

What I do like about the fetish scene (apart from the lack of ageism, or sexism and racism) is the fact that games begin, are played and they end. The psychological games don't stem *outside* of the sexual relationship. They're *always* sexual games, and then that's it. You don't play emotional blackmail games outside of your sexual relationships because there's no need for it. You get a degree of honesty that I've never seen anywhere else. Most people who have been in the scene a while are very honest in this respect; they don't have to hold back what they're thinking or dress it up.

At the end of the day, my submissives are not 'committing adultery' when they come and see me for domination. Maybe their wives don't like SM, and don't want to know. But they still have homes and families that they don't particularly want to break up just because they like being tied up or subjugated every now and again. Once you look at it there becomes degrees of tolerance. To think I have submissives who are 'maids' with me and are only ever 'females' with me or slaves and things like that, then they go home and they're the husband and the father and all these other things once more. Yet they haven't broken up their home over something like being a 'maid' for a certain amount of time every month or so. People don't find themselves in their sexual mode till their thirties – although it's getting younger every year, thank God. But by then they might have been married ten years, so what the hell are they supposed to do?

I've known people who've shown a hard-core SM video to their wives and said: "This is what I'm into", and the wife has promptly divorced them and given them no access or rights to their children; which is horrendous for them and their kids! So, which is the lesser of the two evils? Those people have screwed up their own lives over something that is important, but not *that* important that it's worth ruining your home life for. It's different for me, because I'm kinky in my spare time as well. It's a lifestyle thing, which means I never have relationships with people who aren't kinky. There are things, like water sports, that I'll do with my partners, but I don't do with my slaves or professionally, so it's all kept balanced and it works. But then, I don't have to answer to any lawyers or anything.

I still have a lot of old friends who are non-scene and who know

I'm a mistress and accept me. We don't go into details because I wouldn't want to do anything that made them feel uncomfortable. Anyway, it doesn't need to be in their face. Most people in the fetish scene have got other facets and other interests. It's very rare that I talk about SM with anyone outside of the SM scene, because they're simply not interested. I'm not going to bore them with SM techniques and politics, anymore than I would want them to tell me about the finer points of stamp collecting or airplane spotting or something. I'd be asleep in seconds!

The scene is a good community, but it's still very misunderstood. Which is a shame because people are missing out on so much. Those people in the main stream of society are turning a blind eye to their own sexual fantasies. Or even finding out what those fantasies are! Or just doing things and thinking about them afterwards. If you can't think of anything, just do some stuff and think about it later. I didn't have that many fantasies when I started as a mistress. I just used to *do* things. Eventually I got an idea of what I wanted. It's like any muscle, you have to build it up! Fantasy is a part of your brain that has to be built up. It's easier to develop it by doing it first and thinking about it afterward, and then you will be able to fantasise. Most people who are into SM don't actually fantasise at all because they don't know where to begin, and there's nothing wrong with that. It's a very under used part of the brain.

Frequently, it's the case where one partner in a marriage, usually the male, is into 'pervery' and the other isn't. Only once, at an SM Pride event, did I meet a woman who told me she was really into all this but her husband wasn't, so she was there on her own. And I really felt for her because I had been in that same situation myself. I 'came out' at the age of twenty three to my straight twenty one year old boyfriend on his birthday, and he near enough had a nervous breakdown! He freaked out completely. In fact, he promptly burst into tears, stating that he didn't want to lose anymore innocence than he already had! I said: "What the hell are you on about?" We broke up eventually, of course. But not without me saying to him: "I want you to remember when you're an old man in an old age home that you had this opportunity of a twenty three year old girl dressed head to toe in latex and high heels and you didn't take it!" So I really felt for that woman. She didn't want to beat her husband up and throw him into a ditch or something. She probably just wanted to dress up and play with her dark side a bit. Where's the harm in that? I was trying to spank or beat up boyfriends from the moment I met them. And it wasn't because I was mad at them. I just wanted to do it. It's an inherent part of people who are kinky. It just runs in their blood. It's not that they had a bad experience when they were a child and it messed them up and now they're into all this unhealthy sex stuff. It's nothing like that at all. And it's not like they got too many gamma-rays, like in a 1950's sci-fi movie, and it turned them into raving latex pervs, either!

My attitude is that I'm here! I won't be here forever, and I *am* one of the most skilled mistresses in London! I have spent many a day with other Doms, be it on the fetish scene, the gay scene or whatever; and I've learned how to do each type of kink that interests me to an expert standard. So, although I am eccentric, I would want someone to treat a session with me as if it were going to change their lives and act accordingly. Once I get going, it's hell's teeth!

MISTRESS AMBER

Originally based in Harrow, North London, Mistress Amber was at one time the resident mistress at our magazine's own Club Domina. She has now relocated to Newport in Wales where, as well as maintaining her own loyal following of personal slaves, she is also resident mistress at the Bristol based fetish club Invasion. Interviewed December 2000.

I first got into being a professional mistress when I was twenty one. I'm now twenty seven. I went up and trained with a mistress in Cardiff, though I was already playing around at it before. I had been going regularly to different clubs and parties for some time, but I wanted to learn how to do it properly, so I didn't cause anyone any damage. She trained me very well. She got subs in for me to practice on and, if I didn't do it right, she'd make me do it over and over again until I had it 100% accurate. She always said that there's nothing worse than a tacky mistress who goes into a club or a session and doesn't know what they're doing and doesn't know how or where to hit someone correctly. It doesn't look good and it doesn't look professional *and* it can cause injury! You've got to *care* about the people you're playing with. If you don't, then you're not a good mistress.

You've got to be very conscious of the safety aspect. If you hit too high, you'll damage their kidneys and, if you hit too low, you can damage their balls. I mean, just one crack of the cane in the wrong place and you'll damage a man's balls for life! I have one lifestyle slave whose testicles are the size of a horses and rock hard like pebbles! This was caused by damage from his previous mistress. I've other slaves whose nipples have been totally torn off their body and there's just a piece of skin which covers where the nipples used to be. This happened because they were into such heavy nipple torture they ended up doing it to themselves and didn't go to a professional who knew what she was doing. Others have come to me who've been sticking things up themselves – up their penises, that is. When I've examined them, I found blood coming out of them simply because they didn't know how to do it properly, which is quite worrying. Now, I can extract the sperm right out of a man *without* him even ejaculating *and* do it safely! I know how to do these things properly. I use a syringe and take it straight from his testicles. There's maybe one in fifty who've done some sort of permanent damage to themselves because they wanted that sexual thrill but didn't know how to achieve it.

I had one slave who was into hanging very heavy weights from his balls. I didn't have anything heavy enough to satisfy him, so I got a male friend to come in and hang off the rope with his full body force– and it *still* wasn't enough for him! In the end, I refused to see him anymore because he was becoming a danger to himself. In the heat of the moment some slaves will want more and more. A good mistress will know when enough is enough and put a stop to it. And slaves will respect you for it. They'll tell me that I was right and that they were going too far. I don't mind doing more extreme stuff, but not to the point where it's no longer careful and safe. In this job you see everything from burst veins on their balls right through to such bad scaring on their genital areas that you wonder whether they should be at counselling rather than a mistress!

I had another slave come in who'd actually had my name tattooed on himself. It was a bit of a shock, I can tell you! When I'd realised what he'd done, I refused to see him anymore because it was becoming obsessive. 'Amber' is a fantasy name, it's not my *real* name. These people become so obsessed with the character, it starts getting dangerous. I've had slaves who've put my initial in a tattoo, but then you find out that their girlfriend's name is Amanda or something, so it's not so bad.

In fact, I see myself almost in the role of counsellor sometimes. Different people come to me for different reasons. Some people come because they're bored with their married lives and want some kicks, while others come because they just fancy a change. They want something different, but they don't want to be unfaithful and they don't want to have sex. Anyway, there's no sexual contact with me *ever*. Incidentally, I think that only the mistress who can't think what to do with a slave will ever offer sex. A good mistress will have them eating out of her hand in five minutes! Some men come to see me because they're at their wits end. They're going through a divorce and they're thinking that they're forty-something and they've never *done* anything, so they decide they want to do everything now! And that's the wrong time to go and see a mistress, because they're insecure in themselves. A lot of people going through mid-life crisis come and see you.

Having said that, there's no average age group I see. You can get people in from nineteen to ninety. I've got one old fellow who's eighty-odd. He has six spanks on his bottom and off he goes, but he'll have a couple of cups of coffee and a chat as well. I still see a few from London, though now it's too far for most of them to visit. They'll still phone for a chat though, which is nice because I worry, especially about the older ones. If you're used to seeing them every two weeks or whatever and they suddenly stop coming, you wonder what's happened to them. Is there something wrong? Is he ill? You do build a relationship with your regular slaves. It's not the same kind of relationship that you'd build with a partner. It's not a sex relationship, but it is a *sexual* relationship.

There are all different types that visit you, but I'll tell you the *worst* type for any mistress to deal with. There's nothing worse than a slave who does nothing and says nothing and gives you nothing back. What I would say to any slave who is considering going to a mistress is that if they don't make the right noises and give some feed back the mistress won't know what to do. Although she's good with body language, she is *not* a mind reader! It's like, if you're a man and you're having sex and the woman you're fucking is just lying there looking at the ceiling, are you going to have the energy and enthusiasm to carry on fucking her? You're not, are you? Which is a shame.

Whenever I have potential slaves phone me up and ask me what I would prefer to do to them in the session, I always tell them that I love *any* session as long as there's something between me and you. There has to be some sort of communication or some sort of spark. If you get on with the person, it doesn't matter what you do, you'll still enjoy the session more. On the other hand, you might enjoy what you're doing, but might not like the slave you're playing with. Those sessions won't work out as well, so there's got to be some rapport between the mistress and the slave. Any slave who rings up a mistress should always chat to her first to see how they get on. We're not talking hours on the phone, but just enough to see if they like the sound of a mistress because of her personality.

Then there the funny ones and the odd ones and the weird ones. One of the funniest ones I remember was from my London days. I had my slave girl with me at the time, and she'd let this guy in and taken him up to the dungeon. I hadn't seen him myself at this point.

Anyway, she walked in and she was laughing so much she couldn't speak. I went up to the dungeon wondering what I've let myself in for here? I walk in and there's this guy tied up to the cross, dressed from head to foot in rubber, with a huge pump-up hood on his head and little 'alien' tentacles sticking out of it! He looked just like *E.T.* I thanked my lucky stars that he had his hood on because I giggled all the way through the session. I was biting my lip so hard, I couldn't eat my dinner that night it was so sore! At the end of the session, he did complain that I could have done more to him. But he had really expensive rubber on all over his body, so there really wasn't much I could do that wouldn't have damaged his outfit!

On the subject of rubberists, I'll illustrate just how deep someone's fetishism can go. I had one slave come to me who was heavily into rubber. He was down on his hands and knees and I noticed he was coming a bit close to my crotch. So, knowing what the answer would be in advance, I told him that if he would take off all his rubber then I would *consider* letting him go down on me. That was the condition. He, of course, said he would rather keep the rubber on and forgo the pleasure. Now, I've told a lot of my straight friends that story and they've all said that they couldn't believe a guy would react like that. If you understood the way a rubberist's mind works, you'd understand it. But the straight guys just can't get their heads around it.

I've got a TV slave who can literally put *anything* up his bottom! Two fists together, dildoes the size of someone's leg, you name it! It's quite a freak show when you take him to club and do it! He's actually very skinny, so you do wonder where it all goes? But he loves it, bless him. He called me the other day and told me he'd bought this new butt plug, but hadn't been able to use it yet. I went round to his house and he showed me this butt plug that, honest to God, was the biggest thing I'd ever seen! He told me that he hadn't quite stretched himself enough yet to take it all, but he was working on it! You do worry about them sometimes, to be honest. I mean, this can't be too healthy for them, can it?

Another time, I was doing an interrogation scenario and I said to the guy: "You've been fucking a dirty old slut, haven't you? I've got the pictures. What's her name?" I did some cock and ball torture to get the name of this imaginary slut out of him letter by letter. As the letters came out one by one, I could barely stop laughing. By an absolute freak coincidence he'd chosen my real name! He didn't realise it, of course, but he *still* got in big trouble for saying my real name, as you can imagine. That was quite a funny one. I do much better at the fantasy scenarios, anyway, as I really enjoy them. I'm very good at the verbal side of things, so fantasy and humiliation comes very naturally to me.

There are some *very* peculiar ones, too. For instance, the guy who always shows up with a bunch of stinging nettles that he wants me to use on his genitals. Then there's the one who was *really* into torture, but he couldn't have marks anywhere on his body because his wife used to check him over when he got home. That meant that the *only* place left where I could torture him discretely was on his asshole! I used to cane it and wax it and even put cigarettes out up it! Then I'd finish off by sealing it up with candle wax and telling him he was a dirty little slut and that he couldn't use it anymore. All this just so his wife wouldn't suspect what he was up to!. That was quite weird. Well, different anyway. The play was so focused on such a small area!

Then there's our 'circumcision man'. Apparently, he was once invited to a Jewish circumcision party (that was his words) and ever since he's had these fantasies about being circumcised himself. What I'll do is torture his foreskin a bit with needles. I had another who was a 'mouth slave'. He used to come in with cornflakes and chocolate and all kinds of things. I used to piss on the cornflakes and then feed them to him. I'd also stick a bar of chocolate up his bottom and pull it out and make him eat it. That was a bit different, too. Then you've got your obvious ones, like the piercing and needle fetishists. They can be a bit funny sometimes. Not strange, just humourous. I think a lot of my slaves would be classed as odd in the ordinary world but, to me, it's all normal because I'm so used to it.

I had another guy who turned out to be the size of a house. I mean, he was massive! I walked in and just smiled at him, as usual. It really doesn't matter to me how big or small they are. I really don't mind at all. But then he had the cheek to say to me: "Oh Mistress, you are a bit fat". I told him that if he didn't want to stay he was free to go. He replied that, as he'd travelled all this way, he was going to stay. My maid was furious that he'd had the nerve to call her mistress fat. She reckoned I should just give him a very basic session so that he won't want to come back. But I said: "No, I'm going to give him the *best* session he's ever had in his life and, when he phones up begging for another one, I'll tell him no because I'm apparently too fat!" And that's exactly what happened. A bit of politeness at the beginning of a session makes all the difference. Some of them can be very rude when they come in. With some it might be nerves or some sort of power game they're playing, but it doesn't win them any favours. I'm not one of these mistresses who expects gifts every time they come, and I don't want them grovelling on their hands and knees as soon as they walk in the door. I don't expect anything other than a little politeness and respect. I've never had a slave turn nasty, though. I've refused to see some for various reasons, but not because they were nasty or violent.

Actually, being a big girl on the scene is quite good. There are so many small, petite girls out there who don't mind taking their clothes off because they feel good about themselves. There tends not to be so many bigger girls doing this, because they're generally not as confident. It's so nice to see the new generation of mistresses coming up where you do have some bigger built girls.

My attitude is that the guys have come here for a bit of a laugh and a giggle, and that's what we're going to have. Some mistresses forget that domination is about fun. I can see how that can happen, because slaves drain so much from you all the time. They *want* all the time. They want everything you can do. It's perhaps easier for me, because I'm not really putting on a role. I'm pretty bossy anyway. This is just a bigger, more exaggerated version of what I am in normal life. I know what I want and I know what I expect when I go in there. Because I've got that attitude though, doesn't mean I'm rude to them or that I won't make them a cup of tea after the session. It doesn't mean that, just because you're dominant, you have to be horrible. To be a good dominatrix, you have to be caring because you're playing with people's minds, as well as playing with their bodies. You don't want to mess these people up. You want them to go away happy, so you play with them to the best of your ability, and that's it.

I always categorise people, which I know you shouldn't, but you do get your basic 'types'. First, you've got your slaves who want to please and serve. They don't necessarily like punishment, but they will take it for not doing their 'serving' properly. A submissive, however, is a sexual thing. He likes it for the sexual buzz, which includes your mild cock and ball torture, spankings and things like that. Then you've got your masochists, who are just into pain and into themselves. They're not into any fantasies or scenarios and they don't want to be slaves. A true slave is thinking about his mistress *all* the time. A submissive is somewhere in the middle, and wants half for himself and half for you. If you roughly categorise them, then you can work it out quite well. The average person I see would probably come under the heading of submissive.

There are all different types of people, and they all do it for different reasons. There are some that you love to see and you can't wait to see again, because they're fun and you enjoy them. Then there are others where you cringe at the thought! Not because you don't enjoy what you're doing, but because you don't enjoy it with them. There can be a lot of complications behind why they're doing it. A lot of these people have got their own problems, which they bring along with them. But the point is that I would rather they come to someone like me and sort out these fantasies and play them out in this situation. If there weren't women like us, then there would be a lot more weirdos around. The vast majority of my slaves are not weird at all, but you do get one or two who are. I really hate seeing them, and I have to take a deep breath and go in and do it. Afterwards, I know that that's satisfied them for the next six months and, for the next six months, people out there are going to be that bit safer. I'd rather not go into details about the kind of scenarios I'm talking about. All I want to say is that society does *need* women like us who are willing to put up with these people, who really aren't that nice. And I do believe, truthfully, that this is an important part of what we do. We don't really want to see these people, but we do.

This is where the counselling side comes in that I spoke about earlier. I've had people here where I've sat them done and spoken to them for about two hours after a session. Then it comes out about their life stories, and what's happened to them in the past that made want to do what they just did in the session. They'll tell you how straight their wives are, and how they haven't had sex for so many years. They *still* haven't had sex when they come to me, so they don't feel they've been unfaithful with me because there's no direct sexual contact. How can I put it? A working girl will fuck them and have it over and done with and make them come, whereas a mistress will give them their 'wanking material' for the next six months! That's how I see it anyway. I believe I've given them something other than the norm to think about. I try and level out all of their fantasies and get them into some kind of perspective. At the same time, you can't let some of the weirder fantasies get to you. Remember, there are still so many fun ones out there! And those good ones override the occasional bad ones and keep you going.

Nowadays, a mistress is inundated with e-mails. This is an example of a text message that I've just received on my phone. It says: "Amber, not everyone cheats. My words come from my heart and my imagination and my brain. Is not that how it should be? By the way, you are *not* on my mind". So, there you go! Last time I checked, I had one hundred and thirty three e-mails in a week! Some of it's junk mail, of course, but a lot of it is people sending me dirty letters saying they want to spank me, whip me and fuck me till I scream for mercy. They don't even realise that I've got their contact e-mail address on there! They're obviously writing it drunk in the middle of the night. I just ignore them.

There are certain things I just won't deal with. I won't see animal fetishists or anything to do with children or shit. The 'school' scenario is different, that's just about a fantasy. The one thing I do find quite sad is when I get fifty or sixty year old men who were buggered or sexually molested when they were children, and they want me to *replay* that scenario! I do find that quite disturbing. I'll do it because it's obviously something they need to get out of their system and work through. It's something they've had to keep secret all their lives, but it's become such a fantasy inside their heads over the years that they've *got* to fulfil it! It's a shame, really. You do it, and you do it to the best of your ability but, after they go, you do give a sigh of relief. It's more of a pity thing than a fun thing. They don't come out of the woodwork that often though. But it's nice to have my maid with me just the same, because it's not easy to go home and tell your partner what goes on in the course of a day in the dungeon. With my maid I can talk things through with someone who's there, who's seen it and who understands. You don't really want to go home and put all this onto your partner's shoulders, do you?

Going right back to my childhood, I don't think I was *ever* normal! I was certainly never the same as my friends. For instance, I was practicing kinky fantasies from a very early age. I also realised, from a very young age, that I could get my way with men. Not sexually, as such, but things like fluttering my eyelashes and learning how to manipulate them to do whatever I wanted. This was long before sexuality or even puberty hit in. I remember, before I went to college, I was a dental nurse for three weeks before I got fired. I went into the interview with a low cut dress and fluttered my eyelashes at the dentist and got the job, just as I expected! At first, the dentist was fine but then, after a couple of weeks, he started taking off his everyday clothes and throwing them at me as he changed into his dentist's whites. I was only sixteen, but I thought: "How dare you!" So one day I threw them back at him and told him to hang them up himself! How many sixteen year old girls are assertive enough to do that to a fifty year old man? I was terrible in any job I ever had, unless I was the boss or unless I was left to do what I wanted to do.

I suppose my first experience of the sex industry was selling advertising space to working girls in a newsletter that was handed out free at Heathrow Airport. I did it as a summer job. It was put together at the back of a dirty little shop that sold furniture. I did quite well and they wanted to keep me on, but I wanted to go back to college. I was never close minded about sex anyway. I was one of these girls who used to encourage boyfriends to go and see strippers. I wouldn't think anything of going into a pub where a girl was doing a striptease and sit down and watch. I used to find it fascinating and I never thought badly of anyone who worked in the sex industry. I just considered that they were doing a job and, if they had a great figure while they were doing it, so much the better. I never really went through the steps that other girls did. I never had any of the prudery that is put into you as a child, because my parents are very broad minded. In fact, my father came to see me at *Club Domina* when I was your resident mistress! He's also made some whips for me in the past. My mother's fine with it, too. Her attitude is that, as long as I'm safe, it's okay. They were both wild children when they were young, so I suppose it was inevitable that they should produce a daughter who is such a wild animal!

I think most mistresses have followed a similar pattern to me. If you're *genuinely* into the scene you find the 'vanilla' side of things, although it's fun, isn't as exciting. Now I'm not saying I'm one of those mistresses that doesn't have ordinary sex, because I do. But I found my imagination was too much for it, and I looked for other things to satisfy me. And, besides, I like watching people squirm. I really do enjoy that! And there aren't that many women out there who genuinely enjoy it. I like to watch that certain 'thing' in their eyes; it's where they're somewhere between pleasure and pain and ecstasy and hell and they don't know how to get out of it! And you've got to 'lead' them out of it. That's what I like most of all!

This lifestyle certainly does extend into my own sex life with my husband, as well. I think, if you're going to be doing stuff like this, it will inevitably overlap. Though don't get me wrong, just because it extends into my personal life, doesn't mean I don't have a normal life as well. I know slaves like to think that their mistress wanders around in rubber all day long, but life doesn't work like that. I don't go into a shop and demand to be served straight away. I know a few mistresses, especially the younger and newer ones on the scene, who do behave like that. Maybe they've been to a couple of fetish parties and think this is all absolutely wonderful, and straight away they reckon they can do it too! That attitude doesn't last for long. They soon discover that no one will even talk to them in a fetish club! Now, when I go to a club everyone knows me, because I'll go around and talk to everyone. Although I'm a mistress, I don't just sit there thinking I'm better than anyone else, because I'm not. You have to keep your feet firmly on the ground in this business, and you have to get away from it occasionally, too. My hobby is horse riding. But, thinking about it, I suppose that's domination as well really, because I'm controlling the animal.

Basically, I do this because I love it! I know I'll never be rich being a dominatrix. If you're doing this just for financial gain, it's simply not worth it. Mistresses don't earn as near as much as working girls or strippers, simply because they've got so much equipment to buy and all the rest of it. Actually, mistresses are *never* rich. Once you've paid your tax and your rent and your rates, it just doesn't work out as a profitable vocation. Maybe it did once, when there weren't so many mistresses around. Nowadays, there's a ridiculous amount of girls out there doing it. They've got themselves a dildo, a couple of whips and a rubber skirt and *think* they're a dominatrix. It doesn't work like that. And you've got to be naturally like this, too. You've got to actually be dominant in yourself because, if you're not, you're going to get messed up in the head. It's very hard for someone who's not naturally dominant to do this. They have to think about their sessions and work them out in every detail. Me, I can just walk into the dungeon without having thought about it at all, and I can *still* do a brilliant session! I can go from one scenario to the next very easily. I can go from cock and ball torture to a school scenario to a nurse scene without thinking about it, because it comes so naturally to me. I just go in and do it straight away.

Having said that, mistresses don't have good days all of the time. We have our bad days, too. We have problems in our personal lives like everyone else. Yet, every session still has to be the best session you've ever done! Slaves will judge you on the first time they see you. Consequently, you're not *allowed* to have an off-day. If you do, there's the possibility that you'll never see that slave again. And each subsequent session has to be better than the one before, too! It's a constant learning curve. I'm learning something new with each slave I see.

The first thing I was ever taught was to go in gentle. You can always go harder with a slave. But if you go into the session like a bull in a china shop, no one likes you for it. If you build them up slowly and don't reach their pain levels, they'll always come back to you for more. If you go over that pain level on the first or even the second time, that trust is broken and they'll no longer want you. Always play under, because you can always top it up. I was lucky enough to be taught all this at a very young age. Not everyone is as lucky as me. I was fortunate enough to fall in with the right person at the beginning who taught me everything I know today. I owe her a lot for that. Some mistresses don't even allow their slaves to talk or smile. That's great for slaves, but it's no good for subs! Submissives *need* to be able to smile and let things go. I like subs for that reason. I like someone who will occasionally start giggling for no reason. Besides, it gives you something to punish them for, doesn't it?

Different mistresses have different favourite scenarios. I always say, my favourite scenario is anything that's a bit different and a bit fun! I love fantasy role play, and I also like interrogations and kidnaps. Escapologists are fun, too. The kind of scenarios where you tie them up in every position and the little buggers *still* get out every time! Adult babies are simply funny! They amuse me a lot. I don't like the ones who want to be little boys though, like two or three years old. I do worry about them a bit. I like transvestites, but they're all into pretty much the same thing. And you can only fuck so many people up the ass with a strap-on before you get bored with it, can't you? I don't mind if they want to clean the kitchen floor with their tongues or want to be 'force-feminised'. That's fun. I love giving them scenarios where I make them my little prostitutes. I tell them I'm going to sell their bodies on the street. I'll make them walk up and down and bend over to show me their little bottoms, then let me see exactly how they're going to pick up punters in hotel lobbies! Then I'll make them demonstrate how they're going to slip out their little willies and show the punters that they're actually a man and not a woman! I'll do all sorts of terrible things to them! I'll turn them into strippers, and even get my friends round and make them do a full striptease to entertain us. It's amazing just how many guys are into the tarty TV scenario!

My favourite 'kidnap' session was back in London with a slave I knew quite well. He was very much into humiliation and that's what he wanted most of all, so I kidnapped him and took him to a hotel. He'd already booked the room, so he knew roughly what was going to happen. Anyway, I tied him up, handcuffed him and dressed him up as a woman, with red lipstick and everything. I then left him and went home! Of course, the maid found him in the morning. They couldn't find the keys to the handcuffs, because I'd taken them home with me, so they had to get people in to cut them off. He told them it was his stag night. Anyway, it was something he'd always to do, and now he's done it!

I like my little 'human doggies', as well. I usually get a couple of people round to watch them play fetch or something. Ponies are amusing, too. Honestly, there are so many different fetishes. If I went through every single one of them, we'd be here all day! And everybody has a unique one to themselves. But it's all amusing, it's all different, it's all fun and I wouldn't stop doing it for the world!

Really, it's the same in the dungeon as it is in real life. You've got good slaves and bad slaves, but the majority are good. They're fun and enjoyable and I don't know where my life would be without them. When I eventually slow down, I'll still have a few choice slaves that I'll see because I *want* to see them. I'll never retire completely. I mean, you've still got to have a housework slave, haven't you? I couldn't be without one. Good God, I'd have to do my own washing!

MISS SPITEFUL

As her name suggests, Miss Spiteful's interests definitely lean toward the hard-core end of the SM spectrum, including the nailing of foreskins to tables and the burning of swastika's into flesh with cigarettes. She is also a leading practitioner of the intricate art of Japanese rope bondage Despite her predilections for the more extreme forms of game-playing, she strictly adheres to the limits of safety and consensuality. Born in Newport, Wales, Miss Spiteful now lives and practices her dungeon crafts in South London. Interviewed October 2000.

I suppose, like a lot of people, my interests in SM developed over time. I remember, when I was a child, I saw a drawing in a Christmas annual of a man tied up and found that very exciting, but probably didn't understand why I was so attracted to it. I first began to understand SM when I read the *Story of O* back in the 1970's. When I met my partner in 1981, he was already heavily involved in the TV scene and a number of people on that scene were also involved in the SM scene. There was always this undercurrent image of SM in the clubs and places we used to visit, although there was never any action as such. We used to get *Skin Two* magazine and the images in that were unbelievable. During this period, a major turning point happened in my personal life and I began to get more heavily involved in the SM scene. A couple of friends, who were on the scene, and I had a number of sessions together and I got a real taste for it. One friend, in particular, introduced me to the club scene about 1992. To be honest, my first experience of a club was very disappointing, but I'm glad I kept going because I do think they're great fun. Compared to an SM club, ordinary clubs are too tame.

I've always been interested in the images of SM. I love the cold, dark gothic image of the dungeon and the image of the heartless and cruel dominant woman. I also enjoy the empowerment of the SM scene. When I go to the SM clubs and I know people are watching me dominate a sub, it really excites me! I like the shock factor, too. I like the look on people's faces, because some of the things I do are very, very hardcore. Things like burning a sub's penis with a cigarette or piercing their nipples with needles. I've even burned a swastika on someone's back with cigarettes and nailed men's foreskins down with a hammer. It's really *very* severe stuff! I'm not talking about just flicking at someone with a whip. I love knowing that people watching me are really horrified by what I'm doing!

Before I became a professional mistress in 1995, I worked as a secretary for some very high powered companies, including working as a treasurer's secretary in the City. In fact, slaves often comment on how well written my e-mails and letters are. Incidentally, I'm often horrified at the number of illiterate letters I get from men (especially young men) who can't even construct a sentence! Perhaps people should look at their standard of education.

Anyway, in those days, I was doing this just for fun in clubs and occasionally had people back for scenes in my own dungeon. I then realised I was very good at it and enjoyed it so, in effect, I turned my hobby into a profession. I think the fact that I really enjoy it myself comes across in my sessions. That's why people keep coming back. Personally, I don't regard *anything* I do as unusual or weird. I literally *adore* dominating people and hurting them. Having said that, there are certain things I won't do. For instance, I won't do 'hard sports', and I certainly won't have sex with clients. I'm not a great lover of water sports, enemas or anal penetration either. I'll do it, but I don't particularly enjoy it.

What I enjoy more than anything is people who will interact with me. I like people who are slightly impotent. I can feed off that and use it back at them. I like verbal humiliation, too. And I *don't* mean just shouting at people while they're standing there like a lump saying: "Yes, Mistress. No, Mistress". I like them to think and work at it. Then I can use what they say and throw it back at them. I can sound *very* authoritative without having to rant and rave all the time. I don't feel the need for it. In fact, you can get much more out of people that way. I like them looking at me while I'm hurting them, too. If you're just going to shout at someone for an hour or get them to lick your boots, then there really isn't much enjoyment you can get out of that. And I do like to get some pleasure out of a session, too. I don't do this just for the sake of earning money.

I think if you're a professional dominatrix, then you *have* to be intelligent. You also have to keep your wits about you! For instance, if you're going to act the part of a schoolmistress, it's no good asking questions you don't know the answers to yourself! You have to get inside someone's mind and use everything they say against them. As I said, domination isn't about shouting and screaming at someone for an hour, there are much more subtle ways of dominating a person. Most of the dominatrixes I know are well educated and intelligent. I know two who have university degrees. Although I had a normal 1960's education, I'm educated to A-level standard.

Depending on what we do, I'll offer someone a session lasting from one to two hours. The reason I do that is because I don't think it's fair on the person, or on me either, to tie them up in a very intricate fashion and then, after about five minutes, tell them their time is up and start untying them again. Sometimes they'll come down from a session and they won't have a clue where they are, so you have to bring them down gradually. It's very unusual if I don't offer someone a cup of tea after the session and a chance to come back down to earth. If I don't, it's because I'm glad to see the back of them! One case was a chap I had recently who walked in as if he owned the place, took a look around my dungeon and then told me he was really looking for someone younger. He was just about to leave when I said: "Before you go, I'd like you to take your trousers down". I thought he might be a newspaper reporter, you see. If it is a reporter, I thought I might have a problem. And I know they will *never* take their trousers down, they won't expose themselves. Anyway, he dropped his trousers and I said: "Well, actually, it's just as well because I wanted someone bigger!" I've had a few like that who come round thinking they're Jack The Lad and find, when they get in the dungeon, they just can't handle it. You can see them visibly shaking.

As a matter of fact, a lot of my sessions aren't even about thrashing people all the time. They might just like to be tied up and teased with whips or simply touched. There's a lot of sensuality and eroticism in what I do through the feeling of helplessness. Just being touched can be as torturous as being whipped, sometimes more so.

I enjoy the 'adult' schoolboy and schoolgirl scenes very much, too. There are so many subtleties involved and phobias you can touch on. And such a depth of humiliation, as well. Teachers back in the 1950's and 1960's did things to children that were absolutely unbelievable. I mean, *totally* sadistic. They traumatised people for the rest of their lives. It's that generation that end up coming to me for those kind of scenarios. Consequently, there's a whole area you can concentrate on with a wealth of sub plots that go on. I have one favourite who loves to act the part of a 'schoolgirl'. We've been through endless scenarios exploring this theme. He's run away from home and become a prostitute. Other times, I've sent him to Catholic school. I've sent him to the police. It always ends up the same way though, with him over the desk being thrashed!

As I said earlier, I really enjoy nailing foreskins down. I've done it in the clubs, as well as here in my dungeon. To be honest, it looks much worse than it actually is. It doesn't hurt that much, it's more the shock value. I've even done it to someone *without* a foreskin! I've never nailed scrotums, though. How it came about was that I had a friend who was a carpenter and was very heavily into bondage. He was also very excited by the idea of nailing. He was tied up on the whipping horse one day, and we just did it! We experimented with different ways of doing it, using varying numbers of nails and it went on from there. It frightens people at first, as I said, but it's more the shock than anything else. I've had a lot more blood from pushing a needle through someone. That's because a nail goes in faster. And we always use masonry nails made from hardened steel, because they don't rust.

I got interested in bondage in the early 1990's, but I've always found it erotic to watch and partake in. I was always fascinated by the sheer *helplessness* of it! I think rope bondage brings a special sensuality to the session, because it's so erotic being tied up in this manner. My partner used to be in the Merchant Navy, so he was able to show me a few simple knots to start me off. It's the same with Japanese bondage. They're very simple knots, but because of the way you tie it, it becomes almost unbreakable. It's also very decorative. In Japan, it's considered a great art. They have what they call 'Rope Salons' there.

I became so fascinated by Japanese rope bondage, in particular, that I set out to find someone to teach me. I was at *Club Whiplash* one night about four years ago, and was lucky enough to meet an English rope-master, who lived in East London. He fuelled my interest even more and was kind enough to teach me some techniques. I started going over to his studio on a regular basis. Although we have tied each other up, he's in a league of his own. He is far superior to anything I could do. Now I'm *totally* fascinated by it. I can get so much pleasure in tying some one up and just *looking* at it. That might be difficult for some people to understand, but it's such an empowering feeling. And for the person tied up it's very comforting and, at the same time, they feel quite helpless and vulnerable. It's very intense and very erotic, but some people are afraid of it. You obviously have to be very careful what you do and watch to see that the person isn't getting into trouble. For instance, you have to watch their fingers to make sure they're not going numb or very bright red.

I know there's a myth that women who work as professional dominatrixes are men-haters and just do it to get revenge, but this certainly isn't true of me. I think I'm more attracted to men than to women. I can have a great deal of fun with men, as I see them as the weaker sex. I know they like to appear the stronger, but they're not. I like their company, but I also like the company of women, too. I think, at the end of the day, it depends on the man. I see men in all shapes and sizes, and some men you're more attracted to than others. Some men have nice bodies and nice personalities, and some don't.

The SM scene has *always* had a bad press, because newspapers are only interested in selling newspapers, not public morals. If they think a story will sell a newspaper, then they'll print it! They're very fond of taking a righteous moral stance. They'll call anyone who dresses in leather 'perverts', and cause the people involved a lot of embarrassment and sometimes real harm! Reporters will try and infiltrate someone's dungeon because it's an easy story. Next week, they'll expose something else. Of course, you'll always have nosy busybodies who'll want you to live to their standards; but they're going to be very disappointed with me, I'm afraid, because I live my life to suit myself!

There does appear to be a movement to make the scene more open and more acceptable to the general public, with things like the *SM Pride March*. Personally, I don't think this is a good thing. The SM scene has got a certain appeal *because* it is so underground. If it becomes too accessible and too open, then it'll lose that appeal. I don't want to walk into a club in rubber clothes and have people *not* take any notice! I *want* ordinary people to look, because it's not something they come across every day. I enjoy the shock value of the scene. If rubber clothing became fashionable, it would take away that shock value. I understand that *SM Pride* even has a committee. To me, that's ridiculous! Unfortunately, I think I'm in a minority of one on this!

The SM club scene has definitely become more popular over recent years, but whether that has anything to do with the fear of HIV, I don't know. I understand swingers clubs are still as popular as ever. Probably some people will explore areas like SM because of the fear of HIV, but I think there has always been a lot of men, in particular, attracted to the SM scene anyway. I'm sure there are a lot of men who like the feeling of having the power taken away from them and being humiliated in some way by a woman. And there will always be people who think this scene looks interesting and want to experiment with it by going to a couple of clubs. But I also believe those who get involved on a long term basis do so out of simple enjoyment, as well as a deep seated fascination for it. Personally, I don't see the point of publicising SM clubs so widely that they become packed out with tourists. Nowadays, it's quite common at clubs to see young women with riding crops, and you just *know* they don't have a clue what they're supposed to do with it! I'm sure in this day and age anyone who *really* wants to get on the scene will be able to find the information they need on the Internet or through fetish magazines.

As I said earlier, I know some women only look on domination as a way of earning money, but I thoroughly enjoy what I do and I would hope this comes across in the sessions. I get a lot of people who come back on a regular basis and I'm kept pretty busy, so I guess I'm doing something right! If you only do this for the money, people will recognise it and look elsewhere. I've heard of some so-called dominatrixes whose only 'equipment' is a chair and a whip – that sounds more like a lion-tamer to me! One chap told me he'd had a session that only lasted ten minutes! I asked him what can you do in that time? He said there were two women who put him over a chair and beat him as hard as they could, then masturbated him and kicked him out! As I already said, most of my sessions will last anywhere between an hour and two hours. If I don't think the person is responding or is responding too fast, and they're almost at a peak, I'll let them ejaculate and let them get over it. Sometimes I'll end the session myself and we'll have a cup of tea. Other times, I'll carry it on as long as I want, if the other person feels like it and doesn't have to get back to work or anything. I'm probably not coming across as some kind of Lady Macbeth saying all this, but I do feel that just because I'm spiteful and sadistic in the dungeon doesn't mean I want to rip people off.

In fact, I have four or five 'almost' full-time slaves. My most faithful is Quilp, who's in my dungeon at the moment. I call him Quilp after the character in that lovely Charles Dickens story *The Old Curiosity Shop*, who got drowned in the Thames. I met him about five or six years ago at a party. At the time, he was the plaything of a number of mistresses up the West End. He's quite well known on the scene, in fact. We got friendly and he ended up belonging to me. Not that I particularly want him, but he is nice to torture! He's also quite good as a domestic slave. And, of course, I also use him as a kind of 'living model' to practice my new rope techniques on.

One of my favourite incidents was with this chap who actually wanted a session on Christmas Eve, and ended up staying over for the whole holiday! I'd just got to my front door with all my Christmas shopping when he called. I thought *surely* he's not going to show up at this time – but he did! Anyway, during the session he told me he liked to eat shit. I told him I don't do scat or hard-sports, but he said that was okay because he'd brought his own in his carrier bag! I said he wasn't going to borrow one of my spoons to eat it with. But that was alright too, he said, as he'd brought his own spoon as well! He then produced this pot which contained what *looked* like shit, but could have been chocolate sauce for all I knew. I certainly wasn't going to taste it to find out! I must admit, it really turned my stomach to watch him munching his way through whatever it was he was eating!

Anyway, we came downstairs and he happened to mention he was going to be spending the Christmas period on his own. I told him he was welcome to come over for some lunch, if he wanted to. On the Christmas Day evening, as it happened, we had a mistress friend and a couple of gay guys come over who were heavily into CP. Well, it ended up with the five of us queuing up to beat him, and there was blood all over the walls and ceilings and everywhere!. It was an unusual way to spend Christmas, to say the least!

I see couples, occasionally. I had one couple who came to me regularly who were *both* into the spanking scene. Unfortunately, they've split up now. They were both subs and liked me to be their strict aunt and give them a spanking or paddling together. Another guy came up from the south coast who brought his girlfriend with him, but she didn't get involved. She just sat in the corner and watched. I find it a bit disconcerting when there's someone in the room with no interaction. Another couple phoned up a couple of days ago. They both wanted to be tied up, and then I was supposed to sexually assault her while he was watching.

I had a *really* strange one recently when this woman phoned up. She said she used to be a slave when she was in her teens. She said she was in her forties now, and wanted to know if I dominated women. I told her that I didn't mind. Then she asked me if I knew what the legal age was for dominating a woman? This was quite a strange thing to come out with, I thought. She then confessed that it was a young girl that she actually wanted me to dominate. It turned out the girl was under sixteen, so I really wasn't interested. Nothing came of it and, whether it was a wind-up or not, I don't know. But it was definitely a woman on the phone, and she sounded quite genuine. But you don't know what the sub-plot is in situations like that, do you?

I have had 'vanilla' relationships in the past that didn't involve the scene, but found they were just not fulfiling for me. With domination, there's always that little bit extra. Since I met my partner, I've always been involved in alternative, underground scenes. I suppose our relationship could still be termed 'normal', as he's not on the SM scene. But I don't want to be part of a 'normal' lifestyle! I couldn't bear staying at home, watching television and doing what passes as 'normality'. It just doesn't appeal to me, I'm afraid. It's as though something is missing. I *want* to live a bizarre lifestyle!

JANUS

Born into a female body, Janus feels 80% male and 20% female and prefers the non gender specific Dom to the feminine Dominatrix, or even Female Master. As a female-to-male transvestite, as well as a trained therapist, Janus offers a unique and intelligent perspective on the whole minefield of sex stereo-typing and gender role-play. Janus is based in London. Interviewed May 2000.

Many years ago I read a book called *Coming to Power* by the Samois Collective. It had a very profound effect on me. It was as if it really switched something on. It was a collection of writings about women who did S&M, mostly with other females, and was very powerful stuff that challenged both conventional and unconventional sexuality. Some of it was plain erotica and some of it was more political. The book was extremely unpopular with the more radical feminist element, which back in the 1980's was much more vocal than it is today. Apart from the fact that it switched something on in me that I could relate to personally, it also rubbed up the 'politically correct' brigade the wrong way – which really appealed to me, as well!

There was a lot of 'political correctness' around at the time (even more than now), and a lot of rules and regulations about how people ought to behave. Many people were really affected by that. These were small groups that had all these rules and if people didn't toe the line they were regarded as outcasts and ostracised. And, for many people, that was very dramatic and painful to deal with. They lived in fear of that.

The whole thing was tribal, looking back on it. What was coming up as well, around then, were gay groups that were also into S&M. I knew people in these groups and, at that time, I was also involved with a gay magazine called *Square Peg* which, apart from covering a lot of Art and Media stuff was, I believe, the only gay magazine that really felt positive about publishing politically incorrect material. It was, of course, absolutely hated by the radical feminist lot and their 'associates'. We'd publish stuff about gay skinheads and other people who were outside of the gay mainstream. Consequently, it pissed a lot of these people off, and for obvious reasons. Looking back, there was a real element of transactional analysis 'projections' going on there. In those terms, we were the wayward adolescents and the other lot were the authoritarian 'parents'. And, of course, we played our role to the hilt!

At the same time, the Gay and Lesbian Centre opened in London for the first time. That was the scene of a lot of battles because, initially, the people who ran it wanted to keep out bi-sexuals, sado-masochists, transvestites and transsexuals. Huge groups of people, in fact. Yet they really thought it was alright to ban all these people from the Centre. Well, of course, it wasn't alright. There then ensued this huge uproar with meetings and demonstrations and all that stuff, which was great fun!

So really, for me, that was the beginning of it. At the same time, in the mid-80's, there was a fetish club called *Matraisse* around in London, which was a particularly good place to go. There was a good crowd there; a good mix of people. There was such a buzz. Everyone was dressed up in rubber and leather and wearing fantastic outfits, and there used to be quite a lot of action in there. Mistresses would take slaves along, and there would be little scenes taking place on the dance floor and in little alcoves. It was the beginning of the fetish scene. I think it was a little more underground than it is now.

I got to know people in the scene there. I got involved with a group of women who did domination together. That was really interesting and exciting to explore that. The group was called *SM Dykes*. It's long gone now, but at the time it was new and it was about women exploring their sexuality through domination. As well as that, it was a highly visible statement because people were wearing black leather jackets and peaked caps. The whole paraphernalia became a scene, and you could say the clothes became a uniform, which put me off. The people who didn't want these groups in the Gay Centre decreed this to be fascist. They thought that anybody with a chain or a dog collar was wearing 'fascist gear'. Obviously, this had come out of punk rock. I remember people would wear fascist symbols during the punk days. It was just meant to shock, not because they were into it. It was all about being 'in your face' and shocking. But because there was this group of people playing out this authoritative and parental role, it made them do it even more! They'd wear more dog collars and chains just to rebel.

At that time, I also met one professional mistress with a well equipped dungeon who lived quite near to me. I'd go there either as a voyeur or to help out sometimes. It was a very exciting period, because that was the first time I'd seen equipment like that. Her clients tended to be hard-core SM people who knew exactly what they wanted. There were very definite scenes involving caning and being suspended, and sometimes I'd be in there for hours, hanging around, looking through two-way mirrors and things like. It was quite a rapid introduction. It was over the next year or two that I was involved with her and this group of women. It was a gradual process before I set up on my own, so to speak. But I did start seeing individuals myself away from there. I soon found I had a different style to her. She had a fully equipped dungeon and great equipment. It was a very 'active' sort of place. I never went in for that 'dungeon' sort of thing myself, so mine started off in a more subtle way, really; working on a more mental level with people, which is a theme I've continued with ever since.

Because I'd been working with massage, I began to introduce it into my work. I started working with people to explore their fantasies, and not just domination. Over the years, it's evolved around all kinds of areas. It's become softer, too. I don't do the hard domination scene very often. I encourage people to come along with their fantasies which they may or may not want to act out. Some people just want to talk about it. I feel I'm beginning to work more with energy (other people's as well as my own), because I think you can't split up erotic and physical energy. It's life energy; it's all part of the same thing. People can have highly charged fantasies and, if they're repressed, they're also repressing their life energy. Consequently, if it's expressed somewhere, you're releasing a lot of that energy and I'm very aware that that's happening when I'm with people. It's an intensely liberating experience for somebody to share their fantasy, whether or not it's been a secret. I tell people I'm a therapist. I deal with fantasies, eroticism, also massage (because touch is very important) and I emphasise exploration. When I meet people, I help them to relax and to let them know it's safe and that nothing will happen to them that they don't want. It's not like the average mistress who will say: "You'll do this because I say so". That's fine, but this is a totally different experience.

I have been trained in Reiki, which is a way of channelling universal energy, hypnotherapy, spirituality and guided fantasy. Looking back, it's been a good experience, because I apply it to all my work and people have responded very well to that. I teach them relaxation, then they're encouraged to create a whole scenario in their mind. The physical activity of it can actually be quite minimal, but it's all very real. I've studied modern metaphysics, too, and believe we can recreate our own reality via thought. So, to help someone create a reality around an erotic scenario, there's no reason at all why you can't use the same techniques to create that. It's very powerful because after relaxation and guided fantasy the experience is an intense one and people have been responding very well to that. In America, there's something called Hypno-Dom, which is to do with that. You get the odd person who worries about deep relaxation and will say: "What if I don't come round?" or "What if you make me do something I don't want to do it?" Well, the answer to that is that it can't happen. Most people wouldn't go into that deep a trance, so it's all perfectly safe.

In the early days I used to do a lot more Fem-Dom. You know, all that classic stomping around in a basque and very high heels and all that. It was great fun but, as the years went by and I've discovered more about myself and what I'm comfortable with, I've really changed that; which will become apparent as we go on. I think it's great because people going into this think that they might have to conform to a certain image and certain routines, and I don't think you have to. You can have your own way of working with people. I always believed that there's someone for everybody. No matter what your style, or what you look like, or what you've got, there'll be someone who wants that. So, in a sense, I don't feel there's any competition, either. Everybody's an individual. I think the energy you put across is more important than the image you create. And what I specialise in doing is helping people put across the *right* energy. I don't have all that paraphernalia. I have some if I have to use it, but it's about setting the right atmosphere for the psychological dynamic which is more important.

I love role-play. I love it when people come in and say: "I'd like to be your nephew or a younger visitor to your home, and I'd like you to play out the role of someone who's caught me doing something I shouldn't in your house". You know, that kind of thing. And people come in with all sorts of variations. Although there are some themes that are quite common. For instance, they'll say: "I want you to be a headmaster or a senior prefect and I'll be one of your younger pupils". Now that's very popular, for obvious reasons, because a lot of people have been to those kinds of schools.

The most common fantasy is someone wanting to give up control completely, and to feel submissive so they don't have to accept any responsibility in this situation; they can then give themselves up to me to achieve a profound sense of release. It's that 'letting go' of control, which is understandable, particularly in the city where most of us are trying to 'take' control of things that are happening, and that's very stressful. It's about becoming young and child-like, and to be in a baby-state where you don't have responsibility and you don't have to put all that effort in. You can just relax and let it go. Most people wouldn't actually say that, but that's the most common fantasy they want to act out. Also being blindfolded or gagged and bound so they have no control. It's very exciting and I'm always in the scenario with that person 100%, facilitating it; which is why it works out. My most unusual fantasy was with a client who wanted his genitals removed surgically! He didn't really want me to do it, but that was the turn-on, to create the illusion. I can create all kinds of illusions, but this was unusual. Saying that, for a male-to-female transsexual that would be a reality, but for this person it was an erotic idea.

I'll carry out physical play like spanking if it's relevant and appropriate. If I'm comfortable with that situation and with them, then I'll do it. I tend to emphasise the massage side of it though, and people don't tend to expect that. I think most people who are into domination and fantasy don't always feel massage applies, but I think it's good to get people to relax and feel good. They can chat whilst they're having a massage and establish some kind of trust during that process as well, which is absolutely essential in order to talk about intimate fantasies.

But people will come in with quite a variety of scenarios and it's very challenging because it gives me (and them) the opportunity to be very creative on the spot. It's rather like a drama improvisation– only this is domination! It's good when things can flow. I find there's a timelessness within that. I lose all sense of time. I'm not thinking about anything else except the scenario I'm involved in. All my everyday world that I deal with is just not there! It's outside the room. And, of course, it's the same for the person I'm working with as well, which I think is something people really like. You know, they can leave that other stuff outside when they come in and do something they really enjoy. They're able to explore different parts of themselves that, maybe in the rest of their lives, they quite possibly keep the door closed on.

Some people will come along, not so much with 'scripts' as such, but with prepared outlines that you're allowed to improvise within, which is good. Actually, I love it when people come along with things like that because there's more of their creativity coming into it. The whole process is like a living thing; it's an interaction. And it's two-way, both sides interacting together. The more both people are putting that in (and it doesn't have to be verbal, it can just be energetically) then the more it grows and develops a life of it's own – and the more fun it is!

A lot of people home in on the fact that I'm a transvestite, so I attract of lot of TV's. Although I should explain I'm a female-to-male transvestite. Some people ring up and ask: "What's that?" Okay, so they haven't seen that advertised before. I'll have to explain to them that I'm physically female, but I dress as a male and I take the male role. Fortunately, a lot of people do know what it means and don't have to ask.

Many people come in wanting feminisation. Perhaps half the men I see are TV's, and that's a whole area that I absolutely love. They can relate to me as both a male and a female. It's safer for them. In fact, there are a few things I want to say about that whole thing. First of all, they're all *different*. Everyone who comes in is not *just* a transvestite. They range from people who want to indulge in a little bit of cross-dressing and who are clearly and absolutely male in their normal life, and for whom it's very much a small window that they want to go in and express the feminine side a little bit. Then there are the people who, by degree, want to do that more and more. In fact, I actually see some people who are seriously considering making the change. Some of them have begun some hormone treatment. For them it's not just a little episode, it's part of an ongoing process and it's giving them a space to really indulge in it. Most of them are submissive in it. Now, I'm not saying that all TV's or potential transsexuals are submissive by any means but, obviously, the people who come to see me are leaning in that direction in varying degrees. With one of my TV's, we actually went for lunch last year. She came down on the train dressed and we went out to a nice restaurant. She passed off very well. No one in the restaurant batted an eye lid. And that was great! It broadened out the whole scene.

Some people will bring their own clothes, jewellry, shoes and wigs and things, and some won't. So I provide something for them. I really love it because I, myself, don't fit into conventional, stereo-type gender role at all. And so I really enjoy helping other people *not* do that as well; help them explore other aspects of gender. You know, most people think there are two genders and people either fall into one or the other. Yet, the more I've explored the whole area of gender, the more I've found out there's more. For instance, some people are born somewhere in the middle physically. Indeed, some people think there are many more than three genders; that gender is like a spectrum that people can move around on. And at different times in their life, they might move around on that spectrum as well, which makes a lot of sense to me.

Incidentally, I had one client who had not only a blurring of the gender roles, but a blurring of species! He wanted my co-workers and I to be beings from another planet in this particular scenario and actually enact the landing of a spaceship! We were completely involved in it. It was great making whirling noises and getting him to land on the massage table or whatever. And when he landed, I was supposed to be the 'Mistress from the Planet Yog' or wherever. One week we bought some flashing red devil's horns, and didn't tell him we were doing this. When he finally 'landed' on the planet and we ordered him to take off his blindfold, he could just see blackness with nothing but these devil's horns flashing. His eyes nearly popped out of his head!

In the old days, people would think someone who is transsexual would be at one end of the spectrum or the other. In fact, when they went to clinics, they had to present that. You used to really have to exaggerate to receive treatment. For instance, loads of female trans-sexuals who went to a gender clinic would have to wear a dress. If they went in jeans, they would be told that they weren't 'serious', which was pretty ridiculous! Nowadays this doesn't happen, fortunately. So I made the decision sometime ago that that's where I was heading and made the decision to present myself as male in work. Actually, I think a lot of dominatrixes have probably been working as male persona for years, even though the *image* might be very female. You know, basques, high heels and that kind of thing.

There have been people around for ages catering for male-to-female transformation. People advertise facilities for them and there's even shops for them to go, but there's been virtually nothing for female-to-male, and I'm not quite sure why that is. Obviously, if you're a female cross-dresser, you're not going to draw any attention because women can wear masculine clothes and no one bats an eyelid. But, on the flip side of the coin, you can make it very clear as a male if you're not in your gender role. It's quite easy to do. Look at Eddie Izzard, for instance. He just puts on some 'lippy', sports a goatee and he's not in the male gender role anymore! Whereas I can walk down the street, dressed in complete male clothing and some will *still* think I look like a woman. They might think I'm 'dykey', but I don't feel that's what I'm being; which is a bit of a disappointment, really.

In some ways, gender has been the bane of my life. It's been very difficult for me to cope with being in a female body, and that's something I might have to change. And I think there's a lot of other people out there who have the same, or similar, experiences. There's also a lot of people who accept their gender role up to a point, but it's not *all* of them. Those are the people who may like to come along and spend a little time exploring the 'other' gender in themselves. Maybe this space here is enough for them, and they don't need to take it 'out there'. This ranges right through to people who are spending more and more time dressed in the 'other' gender. Of course, it's usually male-to-female I'm talking about. For them, they're making radical changes in their lives.

What I've come to realise in recent years is that gender and sexuality are separate areas, yet people often think they're part of the same thing. They're linked, but they *are* different. So let me talk about this whole female-to-male TV role because I didn't always present myself in the male persona; not just to clients but to people generally. If I go back to my teens I used to pass as a boy a lot, and that's what I wanted to do. Then, in my twenties and thirties, I was presenting in a feminine role and, when I worked with people, I was doing that, too. In the past few years, however, and increasingly in the job, I was working with people coming from a male role. I was working with clients who were very often interested in taking on either a more feminine role, and that could be literally that they wanted to cross-dress and bring their own things along, or I'd have things for them to make-up and take on a completely female role. I increasingly found that in my own life presenting as a female didn't feel right anymore. It kind of served a purpose for me over a number of years, I think, but it's not really about who I am. So fairly recently, I've been telling people. There's a label for this. It's called gender dysphoria, apparently. I don't really like that because it implies there's a syndrome and that there's something wrong. I don't think that's necessarily the case, but certainly I am in a female body and I'm not female. I feel 80% male and 20% female at the end of the spectrum. I'm living the male gender role on a daily basis more and more now, looking at my options, and taking testosterone to masculinise more fully. Whatever I decide to do, I will become more of who I am as a human being by allowing and pursuing this exploration. I've stepped through a doorway and there's no going back now.

I've been talking to a lot of people who have been living their gender differently to how they were born, and I've been reading a lot on the subject as well. I knew when I was younger, when I got into my teens, I was presenting as a boy and I could do it quite easily then. It's not so easy now, although it depends on the context. Then, however, it was relatively easy. I used to ride a motorcycle and I had a boy's lifestyle. In my twenties and thirties I repressed it, and established something that worked for me in my life This meant presenting a female persona which worked in so much as I could function in a society that made assumptions about me, but it wasn't really the truth. Then I realised I was thinking along the same lines as a transsexual in that I got really annoyed if anyone assumed I was a woman and I always have done, even when I looked more like a woman than I do now. It was interesting and I thought that there's something going on here, because it was evident that other women I knew didn't feel like that. I never spoke to anyone about it, so I never checked it out to see if other women were annoyed, too. I did know that something clicked in that respect. I've been talking to people involved in the gender world, and found it's much easier now to get treatment, such as hormones and surgery, than it used to be. There's also a wider tolerance of the kind of person who might turn up now. As I said earlier, men no longer have to turn up in skirts to qualify! They're even beginning to accept that transsexual and transgender people have different sexuality's now. Apparently, quite a large percentage of transsexuals in both directions are gay or bi-sexual, and that would have disqualified them from having treatment before. By gay or bi-sexual, I mean in their 'new' role. When I discovered this, I was amazed and very pleased because I see myself as a gay or bi-sexual transgendered person now. In fact, I've been in this role for years when working with people!

I don't really get female clients. I do get some women ringing up and then not making any appointments. In ten years I've probably seen about four, which is nothing really. Obviously they exist, but they don't come forward in great numbers, and I don't really know why! I don't think *anybody* knows why. I had a young woman come to see me once. She was about twenty or twenty one, and told me she'd talked about it with her friends beforehand. She'd decided that she really wanted to try out something different, and go and see someone professionally to look at stuff she hadn't done before.

I don't work with couples. What I always say to people is that I will consider it if I know them. But I won't see a couple initially if I don't know one of them, and that's just for safety reasons, really. The result of that is that I don't very often see couples. Most of the people I see as individuals are quite happy to keep it like that. Sometimes men ring up and say: "My wife's interested". But you wonder if it's just a fantasy or if it's really true. I always ask to speak to the wife, but she never comes on the phone.

As far as the scenarios themselves are concerned, my limits are what's safe. I won't do anything with people that isn't safe. For instance, drawing blood or creating that kind of damage, and for obvious reasons. I don't do water-sports, it just doesn't interest me. I've tried it, but it's not my thing. I do a lot of typical bondage and discipline scenes. A lot of people are interested in various anal games. Really, my limits are what I feel comfortable with at the time. And that can change according to who I'm with and what kind of scene we're playing out. Some people really stimulate me. It's a question of chemistry. If somebody comes in and they really stimulate my imagination, the scene's going to work a lot better. It can become quite extreme! Perhaps in emotion as much as anything else. Say, if you're chastising someone and you can do it soft or hard or medium, it's the *emotion* that goes with it that informs how successful it's going to be, in terms of what everyone gets out of it. And that's very much down to the chemistry between me and the other person – if we 'click'. I'm pleased to say that I do click with a lot of the people who come to see me. I encourage people to provide me with material as well. I know some dominatrixes say: "You've got to come in and do everything I say"; which, of course, is part of it. But I want to know what's going on with that other person. I want to know what makes them tick and what they're interested in.

One thing I'd like to talk about is people who come in professing to be submissive and are actually no such thing! I don't know if anyone else has actually spoken about this, but it's the sort of person who is *supposedly* submissive, but is actually highly manipulative. The whole session can become a virtual battleground for who's got the power. It's something that doesn't happen very often, but when it does happen, by God, you know about it! It might start off by somebody making hints like: "Oh, wouldn't you like to do this to me or that to me". I can find that really irritating because we've already had a preliminary discussion, so I do know what's okay for them and what isn't! We've decided on boundaries and limits and 'safe words' and all of that, so I don't need them to start dropping me hints that are outside of the discussion we've just had. In fact, I had someone like that just recently, and I realised quite quickly that this person was *not* a submissive! They were playing a game with me where they were trying to get control. It was quite interesting because at the end of the session, he said: "That was really good. You were really in control. There was a moment there when I wasn't sure, but you were". The whole scene for him was all about *who* was in control. Now that was not a real submissive. It's just a power struggle. The other person, in that instance, is usually a dominant who, for whatever reason, is presenting themselves as a submissive. Or is pretending to be one, or wants to be one, but isn't really. Who knows? But that is something I come across, where they have a need to test out their own power with somebody to see who can win. It's very tiring mentally, anyway.

In fact, people can drain your energy in lots of different ways, but approaching it from a professional point of view helps not to drain me. You just move the focus to something more positive. If someone wants to walk in and tell you about a negative thing happening in their relationship that can be draining, you just turn it into: "Okay, what positive thing can we do today?" It's hard to generalise. Anyway, if everyone turned up wanting the same routine, I would find that very boring, but they tend to differ.

I'm very particular about who I see, because I only want to see people I'm going to click with. I'm quite selective on the phone. You can tell almost immediately if someone is serious or a time waster. There's one category of people, which is unfortunate, and that's those who are severely nervous on the phone, which can come across as a possible time waster. But, then again, I think that if they're that nervous on the phone then they probably won't turn up anyway. I weed out people on the phone I'm not comfortable with or who are not coming from my angle. Then, when people come in, we have a chat at the beginning to discuss their interests and it would be clear then. If I don't think someone is on the same level as me, then I won't take them on because the erotic scenario wouldn't work anyway.

I generally see people who are intelligent, usually reasonably well educated to very well educated. Normally over thirty five, but not always, and usually under sixty five. It's quite unusual for people over retirement age to come, although I do see one or two. It makes you wonder what happens after retirement age. Do people have to give up their enjoyment? It would be very sad if they did! I have had a few ring up and ask if I give discounts to pensioners. And I don't, really. I'm charging a quite reasonable rate for what I do and it's a very good service. You wouldn't go into a shop and say that you want to pay less, would you?

It's also very unusual to get a really young person, although occasionally it happens. The youngest person I've seen must have been around nineteen. The oldest must have been in his mid-eighties, and I've had every decade in between. I think, with S&M, it's something people become aware of a bit older for some reason. Although when they look back they'll see the seeds of it there when they were younger, but it doesn't usually dawn on them till they're more towards thirty. That's when they decide they want to look at their fantasies or act them out. People in their teens and twenties are still going out with friends and experimenting a lot. If I see someone who's younger, I think that's very courageous of them.

I certainly don't see lots of people either. Maybe one or two a day. And then I'll take whole days off. I'm essentially part-time. I wouldn't want to have lots of people coming through because, the way I work, I'm 100% with them the whole time they're here. I put a lot into it and need to recuperate. You couldn't be doing that five, six, seven times a day, and still have your batteries charged up and still be enjoying it! And, because I'm working with everyone as an individual, I'm not just churning out the same stuff to everyone who comes in. I like to keep to quality rather than quantity, basically. I have reasonably long sessions, too. I don't hurry people up, so there's probably only time for a couple of people in an afternoon. And, for some reason, it usually is the afternoon, as well. People go home from work in the evenings. Actually, it's amazing how many people can just take a few hours off in the afternoon when they're supposed to be working!

I work from a special room that's very comfortable and tasteful. It's got lots of hidden little points where people can be bound or restrained or whatever, which is quite handy. So you wouldn't walk in and think that this room was used for bondage; but it can be, you know what I mean? It's quite subtle. All my equipment's portable, so I can visit somebody if necessary. I don't need to be in the space here. I would like to get some suspension equipment, though. Which could just be a couple of little hooks in the ceiling. It doesn't have to be an elaborate system of hoists and pulleys. I very much like to use the basic tools of the trade and then rely on the imagination and the creation. Another side of that, which I like (and , I think, the people who come to see me like) is that it's quite exciting to be in more 'normal' surroundings, because then you have the feeling that this is something that could happen to you in 'real' life! As opposed to being somewhere that's a bit more 'artificial', shall we say. Some people find that quite frightening. I remember the dominatrix I used to go round to could be really terrifying sometimes! But then, some people *want* to be terrified!

One of my favourite groups of people, or men I should say, are those that have bi-sexual or gay leanings. They may come and see me because they find it too threatening to visit someone who is completely biologically male. It's a bit of a half-way house for them, in a way. And that's absolutely fine with me. For example, I've had this one client for a number of years and, when he comes to see me, we *are* two gay men! We absolutely are. Recently, he suggested we should pop down to a local gay pub one evening. I said that would be great! I never for a moment thought that we were anything *other* than two gay men! Then he suddenly laughed and said: "But people might think we're a 'straight' man and a woman!" And when he said it, I thought: "Why should anyone think that?" You know what I mean? I don't know if I'm explaining this very well, but it was a really great moment because I realised that we'd just passed completely across the boundaries of gender and sexuality! In theory, that person is a 'straight' man and, physically, I'm a woman (though, inwardly, I feel that I'm a man and I live as a man), yet the idea that we could go into a gay bar and be thought of as anything other than two gay men never even crossed my mind! And I think that's all in the range of human experience. Does that make sense? We haven't done it yet, but I'll let you know how we get on! You know, sometimes I think I get as much out of this as my clients!

As I say, I'm particularly interested in this group of people. It's a different kind of dynamic to someone who comes in and thinks of me as a female, and is *mentally* relating to me as a female. Even though I present myself as male, some people still think like that from time to time. Other people relate to me as completely androgynous, and some relate to me as a man. It's very much based on where *they're* coming from. But, as I say, the people I'm most interested in is this gay and bi-sexual group. Playing with those people has an edge to it that I find more *alive*. It's more risqué! Though it's hard to put it into words quite what it is! I think it's a very personal thing, because it's very much about where I'm coming from, too. Perhaps it brings out the best in me, that's why I love it so much! I think my biggest turn-on is the satisfaction of being able to help someone, and seeing them feel a lot better leaving than when they came in.

MISTRESS BRIGETTE

While promoting my magazine at an Erotic Fair in Valkenburg, Holland,
I had the greatest pleasure in meeting the colleagues of the Dutch SM-
Studio Phoenix. I say 'colleagues', though this is hardly the right word,
for they in fact form a very happy extended S&M 'family' comprising of
a married Mistress and Master together with their male and female slaves
who live, work and play together – and even do the baby-sitting and the
school-run! I was immediately drawn to these people, seeing in them
something special I had never encountered before on the fetish scene. Here
was a professional 'scene' couple who didn't simply put their whips away
at the end of a session and say 'see you next week', these people actually
had the courage and commitment to live out their chosen lifestyle to the
full. Interviewed May 1995.

To most people our story will seem quite unreal, as it's the perfect
S&M story of a dominant couple living together with their slaves.
How did this happen? Well, I think someone who really wants to live
like this can pick up the right signals and find matching partners.
Although there is the danger that if you crave it too much, it'll stay
out of reach.

Let me start by introducing myself and my partner. Gerald is a
tall, well-built, blonde dominant. I am Brigitte. I'm also tall, slim and
gray-blonde. We've been living happily together for over ten years
now. During that time we've tried everything, especially things that
had to do with S&M. After eight years of marriage and lots of experimenting privately, we started the SM studio *'Le Bateau'* in Breda.
The studio was, in fact, a dungeon on a great boat; a 100 square metre
space filled with every possible torture and pleasure equipment. We
worked together. I received the slaves in my floating dungeon, while
Gerald took care of the rest of the business. It was during my time on
the boat that I really grew into a professional mistress. I achieved a
lot with my slaves and was even able to treat the real *'enfant terribles'*
in the Dutch SM community!

Unfortunately, this wasn't to last for long. In January 1994, a big
fire destroyed our floating home completely. A disaster for our team
and for our guests, who didn't know where to turn. Immediately, we

started looking for another location, which we eventually found in Roosendaal; a town between Rotterdam and Antwerp and about one hour drive from Brussels and Amsterdam. Hence, the name of *Phoenix* – as in 'rising from the ashes'!

It was while we were still on the boat that I got pregnant with our first child, but things didn't really change for me at that time. I was perfectly happy, having the opportunity to play a large variety of scenes with my guest slaves. My altering physical state didn't bother me at all. Most of my slaves didn't even notice that I was bearing a child. On the contrary, I felt more and more secure of my capacities as a dominatrix as my experience increased with every scene. Unfortunately, my beloved Gerald didn't have as many opportunities to act out his S&M feelings, and certainly not his fantasies. We decided to put an ad in the newspaper for a submissive girl for him to play with, and to assist me on the boat. A couple of days later I received a telephone call from Pauline. We made an appointment to meet that coming Friday on our boat.

At one o'clock prompt, I opened the door to find a little girl about five feet tall with dark hair and impudent eyes standing there. I invited her in and we talked for a few minutes. The rest of that afternoon I was so busy with my slaves that I hardly got another chance to speak to her. In the meantime, however, Gerald did a good job with her! I was pleasantly surprised to find that she was still there in the evening, so I finally got a chance to meet under less strenuous circumstances.

A few months later and my little baby girl arrived. And, with that, there was suddenly so much to do around the house and studio that Pauline ended up staying at our place more than her own home. A year later and she had moved in with us on a permanent basis. And then the strangest thing happened! Pauline, who had initially been Gerald's slave, had become more and more my personal slave-girl. So much so, in fact, that Gerald began thinking of acquiring another slave-girl. Several young ladies volunteered, but he didn't find the one he was looking for. Then one day, when he was visiting a friend who was renovating a store, he met the owner and her boyfriend. Her name was Anita. Whether this was fate or coincidence, we'll never know. What we do know is that three weeks later she moved in with us. Complete with her little daughter, but minus the boyfriend!

There's one more story to tell: my male slave, Badboy. The first time I saw him was at an Erotic Fair. I was buying some toys for my dungeon and this slave was assisting me. His manner was very sophisticated and elegant. Normally, I don't pay much attention to male slaves, but it occurred to me that this one was different. Anyway, a few months later we met again at a 'couples night', where he had come with his mistress. At least, that's what I presumed. So I didn't pay any attention to him, but that didn't keep me from observing him throughout the evening. A few weeks later I told him that, as far as I was concerned, he could be my slave. So, that's how I adopted Badboy!

One of my favorite things is bondage, especially the Japanese style, because it looks very good on a slave and has a great effect. When I have a submissive tied up the way I like it, it is impossible for him to move, as he'll be totally immobilised. I enjoy teasing my slaves when they are in such a helpless state. Wet games, or 'golden showers', is another of my specialties. It's not just that you piss on somebody, it's more the way you do it that gives the thrill. It can be a very exciting act, even to me, but I can also do it in a very humiliating manner. I seldom visit the bathroom in the studio these days! In fact, my capacity has become famous in Holland, because I've never disappointed anyone who wanted a wet game. One slave even compared me to Niagara Falls, though that was going a bit over the top! I have to admit that I love my slaves to 'swim' in my juices. Actually, it's one of my favorite recipes in an SM scene, because it's dominant, erotic and intimate all at the same time.

As we manufacture most of our equipment ourselves, I possess a large variety of whips. Each has it's own character and individual purpose. There are whips that caress, whips that punish, whips that threaten and whips that tickle. For me, discipline is one of the major principles of SM. It belongs to the basics that one has to learn when becoming my submissive. Rules have no meaning if there's no sanction on disobedience. A slave that doesn't behave according to my rules will be punished! I always make myself very clear to my slaves. I talk slowly and articulate very well, so there can be no misunderstanding between the two of us. If a slave doesn't listen to the things I tell him, he will inevitably be punished, either by physical pain or by humiliation. I can be very severe if I'm disobeyed. I think listening well is what marks a good slave. One's reaction makes my action. For example, when I tell a slave not to move and then I hear him move behind my back, he will be confronted by my power and has to take the consequences of his behavior. Therefore discipline is, in my opinion, one of the basics of real dominance.

So what do I mean by 'basics' in SM? Well, when a slave first comes into my studio, I will have an honest conversation with him. I'll try to find out what kind of mood he's in. Not every slave is the same, they all have their specific passions and limits. It is important for me to know what he really dislikes, because that leaves the rest up to me. I need room for my fantasy, too. I don't like to be dictated to in a scenario. My games are spontaneous, impulsive and full of surprises! As a professional dominatrix, though, I realise that my guests pay a lot of money to spend time with me, so I will always respect their feelings, keep in touch with their emotions and never push them beyond their limits. In return for my total dedication, I want them to put their faith in me, trust me and let me be responsible for my actions as a woman of art.

It seems to me that nowadays a lot of slaves dictate their favourite treatment to a mistress, who then fulfils their desires like a puppet. I'm nobody's 'puppet'! I always act upon my own observations. The kind of game where the dominant follows blindly the wishes of the sub has got nothing to do with SM as an erotic play of power and submission. If you want to be my submissive, take your chance and let me guide you through the labyrinth of fantasy. That's what I have to offer as a dominatrix, and so far my slaves seem to like my way of treating them. At least, they keep coming back for more!

I can be a very severe mistress if necessary. I can be very tough to deal with, especially in the psychological way. Bargaining is not possible with me. Often new slaves are surprised to discover my attitude. Though I'm only severe when it's needed, I'm always strict. When someone is under my supervision, he has to listen very carefully. If not, he will be punished for not paying attention. Sometimes the 'threat' can be worse than the actual punishment. For slaves who can take it, the treatment can be physically very hard, and in ways they don't always expect! Remember, discipline is one of my favourite games and it has many faces.

People ask me for my definition of a 'good slave'. It's a difficult question because there are so many different kinds of submissives. So many men, so many ways of expressing themselves. I think the most important quality is respect, and by that I mean 'mutual' respect. I love the very obedient, dedicated kind, but I also very much enjoy playing with the naughty ones who will grab every opportunity to disobey – even when they know the sanctions I have laid down! They may even try to manipulate me and, as long as I consider it fair play, I will eagerly pick up the gauntlet. However, let me give a warning to future playmates of mine who may be reading this: never challenge me in my role as dominatrix when you can't take the consequences!

So what does *Studio Phoenix* have to offer? In the apartment we have created three playrooms, each with a style of its own. The moment you walk through the door you enter a totally different world filled with a large variety of professional equipment which can be used. There is no bar, no video show and no stage acts. What we offer is pure SM for those dedicated to this thrilling kind of eroticism. Don't expect standard games or forms to fill in. We prefer a personal approach in dealing with guests visiting our studio for a private session or for our special monthly evenings.

I believe *Phoenix* is for anyone who likes, participates in or is simply just curious about SM. Men, women, couples, whether hetero-sexual, homo-sexual, bi-sexual, active or passive, single or in a group, we will make your fantasies come true! And not just SM fantasies. All sorts of secret wishes or erotic adventures are a challenge to our team! Above all, however, SM is our greatest passion. We want to share our passion with as many people as possible. For example, have you and your partner ever taken an interest in, or have already been experimenting with SM and are looking for new challenges and possibilities? Then you could try our unique, free-play couples nights. You can play as much as you like, experiment in all kinds of ways or enjoy watching others play. This all happens in a relaxing atmosphere. We are always willing to explain our special, often self-developed, equipment. If you feel like it, you can invite one of us to join your play for assistance or to create an extra dimension. And don't think it's too expensive. We only charge 125 gilders. For this you can play, eat and drink as much as you like at no extra cost. The high standards we set for SM, incidentally, also apply to our catering service, so we recommend not to dine before joining the party. Our couples nights are meant for all kinds of couples, no matter what their composition, as everything's possible. You can even bring your personal house-slave with you as a couple, if you wish.

If the idea of playing in public is too big a step for you, we can offer the opportunity of renting one of our rooms in which to experiment in private with your partner. Nobody will be watching you, and you'll find lots of new toys to use, and *without* restrictions! Of course, you can also have your first experiences as a couple in a private room under the guidance of a master or mistress. Or even live out your dominant fantasies with one of our well-trained slave-girls, who will most certainly enjoy a 'triangular' game! On the other hand, if you are a submissive male with exhibitionist tendencies. In other words, if you like being watched, where would you go? Here you can get in touch with others who share your submissive feelings. Every second Tuesday of the month we have an open play-night. This special 'slave education' night has been organised with the intention of giving every slave present proper treatment. On your first visit you may choose to just watch the mistress play with other visitors. Though, I should add, the general rule is that on this night you are 'victim' as well as 'spectator'. The success of our formula has proved itself over the years. Witness the still-growing attendance and enthusiasm of those who regularly attend. These evenings provide an excellent introduction to SM, as well as to our studio.

Where do you go when you love SM, but have no one to share your fantasies? During opening hours you can visit the studio to experience all kinds of SM: from soft-erotic to extreme hard or bizarre-perverted. The first informative conversation is very important; that is the key to your fantasy world. As long as it stays within the borders of discretion and hygiene, we can fulfill *all* your wishes— the choice is yours! We offer every variation with mistress or slave-girl. Both together, with a master, together with a slave or with two slaves or two dominatrixes. If you want to know about SM, this is the place! So, that's my story. So far, that is! You don't have to believe it, but just remember it could happen to you!

LADY GREEN

Based in California, Lady Green is both a professional and lifestyle dominatrix. In addition to her own dungeon practice, she regularly runs workshops for aspiring dominant women, as well as lecturing and writing extensively on the subject of sado-masochism. Interviewed July 1996.

First, some background. I'm 37 years old now, which means I grew up in an era when whether or not you left the hair on your legs meant something. I've had an abortion, been married and divorced, and raised two tough minded children! I've worked for men who know less than I do and been fired by them. I've been called all the names that women who demand what they want get called. By almost anybody's definition I'm a feminist. I'm also a practicing sadomasochist.

Does that mean what you think it does? Well, if you're picturing leather, whips, blood and chains, you're right. If you're picturing tenderness, sensuality, moments of primal emotion, interludes of astonishing intimacy, then you're right again. I've gotten into scenes with my lover that wouldn't raise an eyebrow (well, not too much, anyway!) in the most strait laced household. I've also attended parties where the air was literally sizzling with sweat and screams, and where every person in the room was busy torturing or being tortured. I love what I do. I think it's one of the highest achievements of the human mind, body and spirit. And I'm going to tell you why, and then I'll tell you why I'm so profoundly offended by my feminist sisters and brothers who'd love to label me, and those like me, 'tools of the patriarchy'.

Ever watched Rover and Fluffy making it? Then you've seen for yourself that dominance and submission are essential components of animal sexuality. Rover's been programmed deep in his doggy genes to overpower his mate, grab the scruff of her neck and hang on tight. If you tried to make him caress her tenderly and respectfully, neither one of them would function sexually. However, I'm not implying here that only male domination over females is 'natural'? If Spot comes along and overpowers Rover, he in turn will respond with sexual submission. My point is that most forms of mammalian sexuality is inextricably intertwined with primal, ritualised behaviours of dominance and submission.

Rover and I are alike in a lot of ways. One way is that we're genetically programmed to respond sexually in certain situations that make us feel dominant or submissive. We differ, though, in that he has no choice in the matter and I do. My instincts aren't in charge of my behaviours, at least not in this area. Instead, I choose my sexual behaviour. The instincts that are so irresistible to my pooch are, to me, material for safe, negotiated, and very exciting voluntary sexual behaviour.

It's no coincidence that SM folk call what we do 'play'. Just as children's play incorporates the human drives towards aggression, nurturing, creativity, bringing them down to a manageable, not-too-frightening level appropriate for children, so my SM play gives me a safe way to explore inborn drives toward sexual dominance and submission without being manipulated or overwhelmed by them. Anti-SM feminists (and their sisters and brothers, the anti-porn feminists) are swimming against a strong genetic current. Domination is hot. Submission is hot. Pretend they don't exist and you get tepid sex. I believe that doing SM, either as a dominant or as a submissive, is a profoundly feminist act. And, I'll give you a few reasons why.

Within the context of SM, I've learned that power and powerlessness, control and helplessness are a temporary, negotiated, consensual dance. Tomorrow, you and your boss will 'do a scene' in which you'll follow his orders within certain pre-negotiated limits, and in exchange he'll give you a pre-negotiated sum of money. The next day, you may negotiate a different set of rules, and your boss won't necessarily be the 'top'. Bosses, understandably, are not wild about SM people!

Virtually every recent mental health movement, from EST through 12-step and beyond, struggles to teach its adherents that they are responsible for their own choices. Sadomasochists understand this concept at pure gut level. The knife's edge where resistance meets capitulation is the balancing point of many a hot SM scene. Short of reducing your mental functioning to a subhuman level, nobody can 'make' you do something, they can only increase the incentive to do it. Even in the 'real' world, with its sordid history of non-consensuality and abuse, the torturer and the blackmailer can only up the ante – they can't eliminate your choices.

When I first began practicing SM, one of the most difficult challenges I faced was figuring out what I wanted well enough to instruct my partner how to give it to me. Most people never have to figure out exactly what they want, much less describe it accurately enough to negotiate a scene. The people I've met in the SM community have learned this lesson well and are therefore, almost without exception, breathtakingly honest with themselves as well as others. You rarely encounter sneakiness, manipulation or hidden agendas. Our communication skills are all that stands between a mutually rewarding scene and a physically dangerous or emotionally devastating disaster, so you bet we're good communicators!

Aristotle stated that the purpose of art was 'to evoke pity and terror'. Within the context of the SM scene, the submissive expects to approach the extremes of emotions like terror, pain, humiliation, arousal and awe, while the dominant experiences pity, power, tenderness, arousal and empathy. Most people have to go to a theatre or museum to see emotions like these! I've turned my sexuality into an art where I can experience these emotions and a whole lot more every time I play!

SM is about choice, too. You'll have to excuse me if I seem a little hostile here, but how dare someone espouse my right to choose how I love people? I understand that whipping someone may not *look* like love to you, but missionary position intercourse under the blankets with the lights off and without speaking doesn't look much like love to me either! Even if you believe that SM is 'acting out patriarchal values' or 'reliving old child abuse traumas', or whatever your politically correct catch phrase may be, can you tell me a safer, more rewarding, more intimate way to work on these issues? I choose to explore my interior landscape in a dungeon rather than on a couch, and with a partner who cares for me rather than an impersonal professional. I choose that my partner and I will both receive profoundly intimate contact and tremendous sexual arousal from the interaction. I feel extraordinarily fortunate to have the opportunity to make those choices, so you'll have to pardon me for getting a little testy when someone who ought to know better denigrates my choices as 'patriarchal', 'exploitative' or even 'sick'.

Perhaps you're thinking that the behaviour of perverts like me has nothing to do with you or your sex life? But, ask yourself, have you and your lover ever experimented with sex in which one of you remains entirely passive, while the other takes full responsibility for providing stimulation? Have you ever held your lover's hands down, or had your own hands held down, rendering you temporarily and consensually helpless? Have you ever taken pleasure in sexually stimulating your lover to the point where she or he loses control, while you remain in control? Then you've played with SM energy, and those that contend that sex should be egalitarian and respectful would love to deprive you of a source of tremendous pleasure and stimulation. You owe it to yourself to fight the forces of censorship, behaviour control and invasion of privacy. Remember, these so-called 'feminists' believe that your desire to play with dominant or submissive energy cannot be a valid, meaningful choice! And if that's not patriarchal, what is?

In my experience as a sexually dominant woman, I've found that many more men than women admit to an interest in erotic power play. Yet women discover that they can deeply enjoy dominating their man *if* they're introduced to sexual domination in an understanding, appreciative and non-pushy way. If you're a man with submissive fantasies or experiences, and your lady is inexperienced but open-minded enough to consider exploring alternative sexual styles, now could be the perfect time to introduce her to the delights of sexual domination. But, *please*, don't 'surprise' her! Although some men find this hard to understand, sexual domination is difficult and scary for many women. Your lady has spent her entire life being conditioned to be pleasant, accommodating and giving. She may be a little afraid of what your reaction will 'really' be to her change in personality during the scene. Talk to her about your ideas at least a week in advance; give her plenty of time to think about it, and plenty of reassurance as she does. If she doesn't feel comfortable with this style of play at this time, accept her decision gracefully and lovingly. She may eventually come around to an interest in sexual domination, but she certainly won't if you nag her about it.

You've also got to be very clear about who is exactly giving what to whom! For instance, you may feel an impulse to 'give' her your submission as a present. Look, I've played both the dominant and submissive roles many times, and I know you have to be completely clear about this – her domination is her gift to you! Taking power, control and responsibility for the duration of a scene requires a tremendous outpouring of energy. If you want her to go on giving you the gift of sexual domination, be appreciative. You could start by making sure she is as fresh, stress-free and as well-rested as possible.

A domination scene, especially a first domination scene, requires a lot of energy. How about giving her a 'day off' to prepare beforehand? Send the kids to your mother's, or take them out to lunch and the movies. Or, if you can afford it, give her a day of total pampering with massage, manicure and pedicure, hairstyling and so on. She'll be far more able to give you her best energy if she has some energy to spare!

Next, you'll have to negotiate fully and honestly about what you want. Experienced dominants will never play with a man who is less than honest about his needs and preferences. One of the 'great lies' of SM is: "Anything you want, Mistress". Set aside at least an hour of uninterrupted time well before your session in which to discuss what activities might work well for both of you. A good structure to use is a three-part division: one category is for activities that both of you find erotically exciting; another is for activities that one of you isn't excited by, but can accept if one of you wants to try them; and the third is for activities that are a total turnoff to either of you. If you've fantasised a lot about a particular activity, but not actually experienced it, be honest about that too. For example, being hit with a riding crop can feel quite different in reality than it does in fantasy, and she needs to know that you may not like it as much as you thought you would.

And use a 'safe word' too. This is a code word that either of you can use to mean: "this really isn't working for me; let's talk". It's an important reassurance for both the submissive and the dominant. If you've agreed on a safe word, you know that you can beg, cry or whatever turns you on, and she knows that whatever she's doing is still basically okay with you. Also, arrange for her to 'check in' with you every so often during the scene. She can quietly ask you: "How are you doing?" or "Still with me?" A soft "I'm OK, Mistress", or even a 'thumbs up' signal, lets her know that the scene is still working for you.

And, please, please don't expect this first session to be the hottest, wildest scene you've ever experienced. Be realistic in your expectations. After all, you don't drive the Indianapolis 500 the day after you get your driving license, do you? If your scene ends up with both of you having had a nice time, and feeling loving and intimate with one another, that's a good beginning. A day or so after your scene, sit down to discuss how it went. Remember, she's given you a great gift.

Give her plenty of positive strokes. If something happened that didn't work for you, be honest about it. But for heaven's sake don't be harsh or critical, she was doing her best! Tell her about the things that did work for you, and how excited they made you feel. And make sure she knows how grateful you are for the energy she gave and the emotional risk she took for you. I know you've been fantasising for months, if not years, and it's tough to be gentle and supportive when you're aching to submit your body and soul to her. But I feel sure that, if more submissive men follow guidelines like these when they introduce their partners to erotic power play, there will soon be a lot more dominant women in the world. And won't that be a great thing for all of us?

We sadomasochists demand that the 'vanilla' world respect our choice to engage in activities that may seem dangerous, unhealthy or disgusting. We insist that we be treated as fully functional adults, able to educate ourselves about our preferred modes of sexual self expression, and to balance pleasure in a responsible manner. Why then do so many of us seem so reluctant to respect the choices our own people make about their SM play? For a bunch of supposedly independent-minded, iconoclastic perverts, this community levies a tremendous amount of pressure to conform with various 'sadomasochistically correct' standards, and I'm sick of being told who to play with *and* what to wear while I play with them! Even those of us who pay lip service to freedom of choice often derive our A-lists, party invitation lists, program speakers and so on from a set of prejudices that would shock Rush Limburgh!

For the record, this isn't sour grapes. I'm a female dominant who switches and who plays with both men and women; which, apparently, makes me extremely 'sadomasochistically incorrect'. But unlike many SM opinion leader, I genuinely believe in respecting people's ability to make intelligent choices about play styles, and that means I genuinely believe that people who choose to top or bottom exclusively are not doing so because they're 'repressing' the other side of their nature. Believe me, they've examined the possibility of switching and found that either, it doesn't turn them on, it's too threatening for them, or there's some other important and pressing reason to stick to one role. Pressuring them into switching probably won't open them up to a new realm of possibilities. In fact, it may well infuriate them, alienate them or just plain bore them. They're certainly better judges of this than you are, so respect the choices they've made.

I also strongly feel that bisexual play is not 'better' than gay play, which is in itself not 'better' than heterosexual play. Anti-het prejudice (particularly anti-het-male prejudice) is one of the ugliest secrets of the SM community. Someone who ought to know better recently told me that "so-and-so is probably bisexual, as he's a very open minded person!" I heard also that gay and lesbian players are often mocked or ostracised when they express an interest in playing with the opposite gender. In this day and age, people's sexual and SM orientations are almost certainly not a function of repressing their attraction to one gender or another. Let's respect one another's ability to discern which people we're attracted to, and which we're not. In the same vein, I feel that female-top play isn't 'better' than male-top play. To equate any form of consensual SM with real-world patriarchy or abuse is to join forces with repressive right-wingers and anti-SM feminists. Enough said!

Non-monogamy isn't 'better' than monogamy. Yes, monogamous relationships are the cultural norm, but that doesn't mean that those who are monogamous make that choice *solely* for the sake of conformity. Let's respect our people's ability to choose the relationship structure that enhances their relationships. And while we're at it, your play-style is not 'better' than my play-style. One male-top party group requires that all women attending with a date be collared. While another female-top party group specifies that 'all male slaves' (by which they mean all males in attendance) may not enter their dungeon unaccompanied, and must be either naked or in 'slave clothes'. Unfortunately, many people are so eager to attend parties that they'll put up with whatever is necessary. But for players who play in roles other than master or mistress and slave, or who play as sadists and masochists with no role involvement at all, rules like these are insulting and offensive. We'd never dream of requiring that everybody attending a party accept, say, twenty whip strokes, would we? Let's respect people's ability to negotiate play activities that work for them. And can we *please* leave dress codes to the 'vanillas' with their black-tie affairs? If the way someone's dressed doesn't look kinky or sexy to you, then don't play with them! It's as simple as that.

Also, your safer-sex practices are not 'better' than my safer-sex practices. In fact, there's only type of SM activity that most party directors are eager to outlaw as 'too dangerous' for their parties. Is it knife play? Breath control? Suspension bondage? No, it's unprotected sexual interaction, regardless of whatever the players themselves have negotiated as an acceptable risk! Sadomasochists who insist on legal recognition for their ability to educate themselves and to play safely with SM should be ashamed of their willingness to dictate other people's decisions for them in this one area. One party invitation I received actually *demanded* that monogamous couples practice safer sex because otherwise their excitement might overwhelm non-monogamous couples playing near by! This showed a disrespect for its own members intelligence and negotiating skills that I found utterly appaling and, I'm afraid, all too common.

Remember, too, that if you're fortunate enough to be in a position to be 'out' about your SM, lucky you. Those who stay closeted are probably not making that choice because they're chicken, they're making it because 'coming out' could cost them their marriages, children and/or livelihoods. Instead of scorning them for secretiveness, how about respecting the life they've built; a life that's so important and precious that they're willing to live in the closet to protect it.

We all choose a level of play that suits us at the time. The housewife who spanks her husband may find the experience every bit as thrilling, risky and fulfiling as the 'piercing-and-branding-and-suspension' scene you did last weekend. She may evolve into a bullwhip brandishing dominant, or she may just go on spanking her husband twice a month. But as long as her play meets her needs and her partner's, she's every bit the SM player you are. Anybody who has played with SM has overcome doubts and fears to get where they are. Instead of scorning them for the kinds of play they don't do, how about respecting them for choosing a play level that's appropriate to their needs and skills?

The list could go on and on: women aren't 'better' than men, couples aren't 'better' than singles, tops aren't 'better' than bottoms, and so on ad infinitum. But my real point is this: until we start respecting the choices our own people make, how can we expect the vanilla world to respect our choices? Let's keep in mind that we are an oppressed minority and are likely to remain so for some time. Instead of drawing lines that separate us, let's try to stick together as an adhesive whole fighting for our legal and ethical rights. Save your disrespect for the people who try to pressure you into partners, playstyles or intensities that don't work for you; who don't believe in your ability to negotiate safe, exciting play without outside interference; who base friendships and invitation lists on externals such as gender, relationship status and sexual preference. Let such people know that you believe they're not working for the overall good of the SM community. And while you're at it, search your own heart for prejudices that may be blinding you to some interesting friendships and relationships. Remember, the closer we all grow together, the more powerful we all become!

MISTRESS R

Before becoming a full time professional, Mistress R ran a transvestite shop and dressing service in Manchester. She has been working as a professional mistress since the age of twenty two, during which time she has become a prominent spokeswoman and well-respected figure on the fetish scene. Interviewed July 2000.

I started training to be a mistress twenty four years ago. I was working in recruitment at the time, having originally trained as a make-up artist, followed by a spell in the merchant navy. I had a friend of mine who was a 'working girl', and it was through her I got to know this lady (who was actually the wife of a police officer!) who had a dungeon. I was fascinated by it but, like most people, I thought it was funny at first. There was an element of 'if I giggle it will make it all right', do you know what I mean by that? I went along and I loved her. I thought she was a fabulous person who had enormous humour, depth and loved what she did. Like myself over the years, she would turn her hand to other things, but she always had her dungeon. And, eventually, she trained me. I started, initially, going in and watching. And then she would say: "This is how you hold this" and so on.

In a way, I think it's quite sad that people set themselves up in dungeons as dominatrixes, and then you hear the most horrendous stories of clients being battered and marked. One of the first things she taught me was that nobody is *ever* marked unless they ask to be. When someone comes here the rule is they do not walk out with anything more than, possibly, a red bottom or cuff marks or whatever. So that, certainly within the hour, there's nothing left at all. She also made me do exercises with certain whips, showing me how to handle them and the way I should use them. For instance, she taught me that when you're using a whip or a crop, you're not taking the force from your shoulder, but from your elbow. Even with someone who wants a severe battering, you start off lightly. These were all invaluable lessons. So what I did was to go on doing my own job and work with her in the evenings and at weekends. Then this lady, unfortunately, became very ill with cancer and had to have a series of operations, so she asked me to run her dungeon for her while she was in hospital. I can honestly remember the first day working in there on my own and thinking: "Fuck! I've got to do this!"

One thing I learned very quickly was that it's very important for a dominatrix to have, not exactly telepathy or psychic powers, but very good intuition about human beings. And not just with their clients, they have to have it as a person in their life. Because, let's be honest, when someone comes to this front door, I've got to judge within a second whether they're any threat to me. After that, I have to be able to take somebody's money and give them what they want *without* asking them. As a dominatrix, I'm never prepared to ask them what *they'd* like! The way it works here is that they come in the door and they're told to take their clothes off and have a bath. When they're clean and dry, they'll knock on this door and I'll take them through to the dungeon. What I then do, while they're in the bath, is to go to the bathroom door and wait with a collar and lead. They have to go on their knees to me there and then. I don't care if they're into it or not, that's what they have to do. That's a respect thing.

I'll then take them into the dungeon and the first question is whether they have any health problems I should know about like epilepsy, asthma, or bad heart, knees, backs. It can make a huge difference. I once had somebody on a whipping stool with a noose round his neck who decided to have an epileptic fit and hadn't told me he was epileptic! And it's very frightening, as I could have killed him. All he had to do was tell me, and we wouldn't have had the noose!

Then what I'll do is ask them if they've ever visited a mistress before. If they say yes, I'll ask what did she train you in? Now the ones who know the scene and know the score will say corporal punishment, bondage and so on. They'll list all the things they like, so that gives me a clue. If they're a complete novice, I do have a policy that I don't let them book for longer than half an hour the first time on the basis that transferring things from your fantasies into reality is a world apart. In their heads they can be trussed up by a beautiful woman in thigh length boots who batters the living daylights out of them, then crucify them and they come. In reality, she puts a hand on them and they say it hurts, because it's only been in their head before.

So what I do with a novice is give them a little bit of everything! A little bit of foot worship, body worship, spanking, bondage, perhaps one of the implements, but nothing very heavy. After the session, I'll say that I hope this has given them an idea where their inclinations run. Let's be honest, if you're into very heavy bondage, it's unlikely, in my twenty years experience, that you're also going to be into very heavy corporal punishment. It tends to be one or the other. They will cross over, because they understand they are with a dominatrix and she has the power. They will take a spanking or a cropping, if that's what I decide to give them. The difference is that you know not to do it for very long because their thing is bondage. In a way, they've already told you that by you asking the right questions. But you still have to watch their body language, you have to be in tune with them. I've always said it's like a smell. It's not tangible. It's not something I can say to you how I get it, I just do. To be good at this line of work you need that intuition. I don't know if all doms have it, because I've met some pretty awful ones. I have met some very good ones as well, I must say.

But that's how the sessions starts. No one is *ever* asked what they'd like! With people who are into the school scene, because it is a very different scene, I will say to them: "Perhaps you'd like to write down for me what you have thought about". When they arrive for their appointment they can hand me the envelope with the piece of paper in. That will give me an idea because, for instance, with the school scene very often I don't change. I'm not wearing domination clothing, because that's not how it works for them. They actually prefer the long, black, severe look that I tend to wear everyday. So, on that level, you need a bit of information from people. But I think it's very important that people still understand that you are going to do what you want to do, within the limitations of what they like. I've actually 'fucked' people off on the phone who've called and said: "I want this, this and this" and I say: "Would you? Well, in case you hadn't noticed, I'm the dominatrix and I decide what you'll have and what you won't have". If they humbly apologise, they'll still get the appointment. If they don't, they won't.

Having said that, you'd be utterly stupid to think that in this business you could do exactly what you want to do and still make a living! You can't, not if you're going to make money at it. But, on the other hand, the very nature of what and who you are means that you have to define the rules. You have to be the one who says I am *going* to do this, whether you like it or not! Once I take them into the dungeon, I ask them a few questions and then, normally, put them in light bondage. Then I come away and change, because those few moments of being left on their own, naked and blind-folded, helps them focus and be more compliant. There's this sudden thrill of fear when you realise you've just been tied, and you're left to think about what's going to happen to you. For a lot of people this is part of the kick! It's a good way to prepare them for what's going to happen next.

Some people will have very definite fantasies they want to enact. I'll tell them to write it down and send it to me by post and, if I can accommodate it, I will. However, you still have to understand that I decide how it goes. For instance, I had this chap and what he wanted to do was come in and 'burgle' the place. That's quite a common one, actually. Over the years I've had lots of burglars! The idea is that he turns up, pays me, then we all go outside. Then he has to go through this elaborate ritual of 'breaking in', and I catch them at it! Instead of calling the police, I have to call them a bastard, tie them and give them a good battering! The only one I have a slight problem with is coprophillia; the ones who want to eat their own 'poo', or eat mine! I've never understood how anyone, even a dominatrix, can shit to order! I can't, and I don't want to either! It's not something I wish to practice, thank you very much!

I was married for a long, long time to a bio-medical scientist, and this was extremely useful in my work, because he taught me what was safe and what wasn't. He taught me about anatomy and about bondage. How bondage affects the body and so on. And one of the things he did give an insight into was that shit-eating, or shit being dropped around your dungeon or whatever, is extremely unhealthy! On the other hand, urine comes out more or less clean. In fact, I have a bondage chair that's specifically designed for urinating on people; though, to be truly honest, I prefer the bath, for obvious reasons. But some people don't like that. It breaks the scenario for them if they're taken from one room to another. Hygiene is very important, so that's why I never have the 'pooey people'. There's never any sex in my dungeon, either, and there's no element of prostitution. I'm not saying people don't get 'relief' sexually, but they have to do it themselves. That's not our job.

There have been so many memorable incidents over the years. I once had one little man in my dungeon who had piles like you wouldn't believe! When he bent over for a spanking I could see they were like a bunch of grapes! It so happened I had a clothes peg in my hand at the time and, naturally, I just couldn't resist attaching it! Well, he shot across the room, hit his head against the wall and knocked himself out. I ran upstairs to my husband screaming: "I think I've killed him! I think I've killed him!" He came round eventually and was alright, thank goodness. As he left he did ask me if he owed me anymore money, which I thought was quite sweet.

Years ago I had a garage that had held eight limousines, so it was an enormous space. It was actually a former undertakers. One section I had boarded off and turned it into a school room with desks and a blackboard where we used to do proper 'school days' once a month. People paid fifty pounds and their 'dinner money' on top. They had to be there for eight o'clock in the morning for assembly, and then they had to have 'lessons' through to lunch time. My transvestite maid would do the school dinners, making sure there was something like fish fingers or baked beans and all slightly cold! This was followed by semolina and jam for pudding, and if they didn't eat it they got battered! Then I used to make them go out and do P.E. in our enclosed yard. Where we were situated there was a large office block that overlooked us so, every now and then, you'd have all these little schoolboys and schoolgirls (who, of course, weren't so little) all doing their exercises and these people at the windows watching us, and probably wondering whether they were real children or not! That used to really tickle me.

Another time, I worked with a girl called Carmel, who had an elderly gentleman she used to visit. She was still learning the business and this was a private arrangement. They'd met at a club, where he'd waylaid her, and he said he hadn't had enough and would like to pay her to come back to his apartment in London. Now, I know everyone thinks dominatrixes are dealing with lords and earls and judges all the time, instead of the man who works in the supermarket, but on this particular occasion this person was rather well known and rather well-heeled. Anyway, there was myself, a friend of mine who was really into wearing fetish clothes, but wasn't really a dominatrix. There was this other woman, who was a dominatrix, but very much at the training stage, and there was my transvestite maid. Oh, and I took my dog, as well!

Basically, it was her 'call', so I'm not getting paid for this. Anyway, we're all sitting around this rather luxurious apartment, drinking champagne and chatting away, while she starts playing with him. Well, she'd only been playing for about half an hour when I started to see the panic in her eyes that said: "I don't know what I'm doing! I don't know where to go from here". So, I thought I'd better help her out. I got her to bend him over, while I went around the place to see what I could find to play with. I went to his freezer and found a tray of ice cubes, and I got some butter from the refrigerator. Well, on go the rubber gloves and up goes the butter! And then I start feeding ice cubes up his backside. Load and loads of them! The gentleman was extremely uncomfortable, but enjoying himself, nevertheless. However, Carmel made the mistake of telling him to go down on his knees. As he did so, the most awful 'wet' fart sound occurred, and an ice cube literally shot out of his backside and hit her! Then another and another, till she ends up dodging out of the way, trying to avoid these ice cubes flying out of his bottom like one of those Ping-Pong machines. I thought it was fabulous! Absolutely wonderful! Actually, I think the art of having a dungeon is to able to laugh in it. If something funny happens, then laugh about it! As long as you're not laughing at the client, but with them. If it's funny, they'll usually see the funny side of it as well. Most of the really funny things that have happened, I wouldn't be able to repeat, I'm afraid!

I remember, another time, I was walking my three dogs and I witnessed an armed robbery of an off-license! Because I'd made a mental note of about half the registration number and had got a good look at the men, the police told me to get in the car. We raced round the streets till they got a message saying the crooks had been caught. The police then offered to drive me home and take a statement. At that time I lived here, as well as worked here. So we came in and, of course, the policeman saw everything! But his response was: "I'm fascinated by this! I must get my mate in the car". So he brought the other policeman in. It took two minutes to take my statement and four hours to show them all my equipment! Incidentally, I have a good relationship with the police. I was very impressed when they came round once, when I first started. They said outright that they knew what I was doing because they'd phoned up pretending to be clients, but all they wanted was to assure me that if I had any problems they were there to protect me as much as anyone else.

I have the greatest respect for my clients. I love what I do. And I am, I suppose, a lifestyle dominatrix, even though there's a part of me that asks what that word means exactly? Do I sleep in thigh length boots? No. Do I cry when my dog dies? Yes. And there is this kind of thing whereby, if you say you are a lifestyle dominatrix, people think you wear leather all the time and you're never a human being. And that's nonsense! A real dominatrix has her femininity and her soft side. That's what makes her as powerful as she is! I am lifestyle in as much as I have a partner who I play with all the time. Having just said I don't sleep in thigh length boots, I must admit I do keep my boots and my gloves and my nipple clamps all lined up beside my bed – just in case! While I'm reaching out for a cigarette to smoke in bed, I could equally grab my nipple clamps! So, yes, it is very much a part of my life! I'm also a very forceful person, anyway. I don't take a lot of shit off people, but that doesn't mean I'm not *real*. I think it's more of a male thing, than a female thing. Women are more prepared to understand the different facets of a personality.

For instance, I lost a client once, under utterly ridiculous circumstances. He'd been with me for fifteen years, and on that level you'd have thought he would have known me better. He'd been to social events with me and stuff like that. Anyway, of all things, someone had brought me a baby squirrel that had fallen out of tree. This meant I had to be up every two hours feeding it and so on. Surprisingly, it survived. I called him Barney and he was a lovely little squirrel. Eventually, he caught pneumonia and died. Now, this man was there when the squirrel died and saw me crying, naturally enough. Two days later, I got a letter saying he was very sorry, but the fact that he'd seen me crying had shattered his whole illusion! All I thought was: "You shallow bastard!"

Lifestyle dominatrixes are people who *have* to have it in their lives. I suppose, that's what I mean. Even if I weren't working at it, I'd still want to play. I go out to fetish clubs when I can, though I think the fetish club scene has changed in recent years. In the old days, people were grateful to have somewhere to go and express themselves. They could get to meet and talk about their interests and fetishes. Nowadays, there are so many clubs around who operate on a regular basis that there isn't that need anymore to branch out and talk to other people. They tend to stick in their own little groups with people they know. It's all a bit self indulgent now.

I have my own views on transvestites. A lot of them are submissive and are into domination. However, as a dominatrix, I do not want a man to go on his knees to me wearing a frock! If he can't go on his knees to me as a man, I don't want it. Basically, I think, that by dressing as a woman in order to become submissive is slightly insulting to women. I doubt if many people see it that way, but I do. I feel quite strongly about this, too. I will not have men as 'pretend' woman being submissive in my dungeon. I want them to be submissive as men!

Having said that, I will do enforced underwear dressing, because that's part of humiliation. It's not part of being a woman. It's about being made to look silly. Transvestite maids are okay, too. That's doing something useful! I don't mind someone paying to do my laundry and my housework. I think that's a bloody good idea! TV maids are, actually, very few and far between. You get the ones who want to 'fluff' around in a skirt, admiring themselves. But I want someone who wants to do my cleaning. I don't want to have to go around behind them, telling them off all the time. I might as well do it myself.

I used to make it a rule that I would tell any transvestite who came here for all day 'maiding': "Do not deliberately do things wrong, just to get a beating. Because you won't be! You won't get any attention at all. You'll just be thrown out, and you won't get your money back!" I had someone recently turn up for his first ever appointment as a maid, and he was excellent as a maid. But he did make the mistake of asking me if I liked what he was wearing. I said: "No. It's the most impractical thing I've ever seen in my life. To wear a skirt with fifteen thousand petticoats when you have to get behind the chairs and dust properly is indulging yourself. You're not taking your duties seriously". I like maids to wear black and white and be smart. I had a most wonderful maid called Annabelle back in Manchester. I had him for years and I miss him dreadfully. He was a transvestite and he had his own uniform, but we got to that really comfortable stage where he didn't necessarily dress. He'd come in his normal clothes every day and do my housework, my shopping and walk my dogs. My first husband was dying at the end and, thankfully, Annabelle was a qualified charge nurse who no longer worked. He helped me enormously and became a friend as well. A good servant *is* a friend in a way. We were very friendly, but at the same time he knew his place. And that's the sort of relationship I would look for again in a TV maid.

I am very understanding with maids. If one said: "I'm sorry, Mistress, but I can't get down to do the dusting today because I've got a bad knee. I'd say: "Fine, do it tomorrow. As long as it gets done this week, I don't mind". In the same way, I've always had a slight problem with humiliation in the dungeon. I find it extremely difficult to insult and be rude to someone I don't know. I actually think you should always treat your customers, your maids and yours servants with, if you like, a distant politeness. The aristocrats I met as a child were never, ever rude to servants. They were unbelievably polite to everyone, and I have that same feeling towards my own servants and maids. They must respect you as a dominatrix, because of your position. But you must also respect them for what they are doing for you, and for what they are allowing you to do to them. You must have respect for someone who can take that much pain or intensity. If a dominatrix doesn't have respect for her slaves, she shouldn't be doing this job. I've always said that, to do my line of work, you have to love men, not hate them! People think you have to dislike men. I've even heard them say that the best dominatrixes are lesbians. I don't see that at all.

When I go into my dungeon with a slave, he should make me feel powerful, beautiful, all feminine and totally in control. He gives me that status by putting me on a pedestal. Therefore, I must also respect the level he's at, because he's already given me something. Now I have to give something back. It's complete nonsense that in the SM world a dominatrix can just do what she likes – she can't. Trust has to be given and received. If you're not fulfiling what a submissive or a slave is looking for, then he's not going to come back to you – or anybody else for that matter!

I had a client in recently who was extremely nervous. He actually had a bit of a panic attack when I put him into bondage. Now you have to stay very, very calm when a six foot four Royal Marine decides to have a panic attack! The way you handle a situation like that is so important. You've got to keep the person calm whilst getting enough bondage off them till they've lost the fear, but keeping enough on that if they do go berserk, they ain't going anywhere! Now, on that level, you've got to be totally in tune with the people who are visiting you. To have a panic attack means you are very, very frightened – and you're the one who's just frightened them! So you've got to have that sort of empathy.

I'm not submissive myself in any way, shape or form. If someone hit me, I'd chin 'em. This is why I tend to steer clear of the spanking club scene. People involved in spanking tend to swing both ways and like to be spanked, as well as spanking others. I got fed up with people approaching me to spank me. I felt I should have been wearing a label that said: "I don't get spanked".

As a matter of fact, I've always had a slight problem with masters in general, because a lot of them don't know how hard to go or when to stop. I even got barred from one club over this! I went there one night and there was a master there with a submissive woman, and he'd put her in suspension upside down. It was the middle of summer in a club full of people and I could see straight away she was in trouble. She'd gone a deathly white and sweat was running off her, so I went over to him and said: "Look, I hope you don't mind me interfering, but your lady is in trouble". He said he'd hung her up for hours, and what did I know about it anyway? I said: "I'm a dominatrix and I do know about it! You don't hang someone up like that in twenty three degrees in a room like this". He ignored me completely, so myself and another dominatrix got her down ourselves. As we did so she vomited everywhere and fainted. If she'd been left suspended and vomited, she would have choked and died. The lady who ran the club said that SM rules dictate that you don't interfere with people when they're playing. Though this is true enough, I told her she could have had a corpse on her hands and not to be so stupid. But, because he was a regular and was a friends of theirs, they simply told me not to come back. Anyway, I've come across a few masters like that.

I have worked with one master who I loved to bits. He was in Leeds while I was working in Manchester. We really got on well, and we'd get together to do stuff. He was a very gentle man, very gentle. Although he was a huge man, and in fact used to do extra work for bouncer types, he also had a very feminine side to him. He also *adored* women. Actually, I never felt that he enjoyed being a master that much. He enjoyed the clothes and the adoration, but when it came to hurting women, he wasn't that keen. So he had a really good, safe level.

My usual experience of men who are given the power is that they will always push it. Now I'm sure there are hundreds who won't, but I'm just going by my twenty years experience of the men I've worked with or the ones who've brought their submissives to me or whatever. There's always that element where they start to show off. Between them and the female on a personal level, they probably don't do it. But the minute it's on show, they have to go that bit further. I don't think women have that tendency. Personally, I don't feel the need to show off in a scene. I'm confident in what I do, and I'm not really that bothered if someone on the outside thinks I'm good at it or not. I *know* I'm good, because I make a living at it! For instance, I've never used a 'safe word' in my life. You shouldn't need to in my mind. As long as you're watching your person *all* the time; if you're 'smelling' them, and you're sensing them.

Did you know that men's toes can tell you a lot? Watch their feet. Toes do all sorts of things. You just have to watch the person's body. And remember, a lot of the time you can't see facial expressions, not if someone's hooded. In our normal, everyday life, you learn to read a person's facial expressions. But in the dungeon, you can't do that. Our bodies ripple and move, especially if you're tense. After all my years of watching bodies, I can tell if that tension is sexual or painful! And how much pain. I can tell when it stops being a pleasurable pain and starts to go over that edge, so that's why I never use a 'safe word'. I do get clients who insist upon it, because they're afraid. But, at the end of the session, they'll say: "Oh, I never used a single safe word". And I'll say: "No, you didn't, did you". It shouldn't really be necessary. What really irritates me is the ones who tell me they've had loads of experience, and then you slap them with the palm of your hand and they scream for you to stop!

The Internet is giving us all a headache at the moment. Everything is too available! You've got too many amateurs on there giving it out for nothing, but it will roll again. I've watched it gradually kill our business for the last eight years. The last two years, especially, have been hard for anyone in my line of work. It's hitting us all, but there will be a turn around. What will happen is people will get bored, because they can't read it in their beds or take it with them to the toilet. I've recently had a couple of people come to me who've been 'burned' by amateur dominatrixes on the chat-lines. These guys are suddenly realising that they're spending money and getting absolutely nothing back! They're supposed to go out, buy all this stuff for these women, and then go home and beat *themselves* up with a hairbrush! It's not the same thing at all, is it? To me, the Internet is the domain of cowards, and I don't mind if you print that!

Anyone who's a dominatrix is very much in the 'real' world. We are experiencing things that the average person only thinks about. Things have changed dramatically since I first went into this business. For instance, you could never answer the phone the way we do. In those days, there would be all sorts of code words and things like that. Basically, you were terrified the police were listening in and you'd be busted. And if you were busted, you weren't done for prostitution (which was a nice little fine) you were done for Grievous Bodily Harm! And worse, even if the police walked in and you had a client there who said: "Look, I love this. Thank you very much, but I *want* this to be done to me and I haven't paid for anything", it doesn't matter. The law states that he must be protected from himself!

I think one of the biggest changes that occurred was Jean Paul Gaultier putting fetish on the catwalk. Anything that goes on the Paris catwalk gets filtered down into high street fashion and, by becoming fashionable, it becomes more acceptable. The clothes aspect of it didn't break away from the SM, but it became a unit on its own. And the people who like wearing those sorts of clothes very often like doing the sorts of things I like doing, so we had an overlap that has made it much more acceptable.

MISTRESS CHRYSTALLE

Originally from Manchester, Mistress Chrystalle now lives and works in
London. Aged 38, she brings to her style of domination a deep insight into
human behaviour and sexuality gained from her training as a psychiatrist.
She occasionally works in tandem with her bi-sexual dominant partner,
Master Guy. Interviewed July 2000

I've been a professional dominatrix for fifteen years. How long have I
been dominant? All my life! When I was very young (about six or
seven) I was very aggressive because I hadn't acquired the right social
skills. I can't remember this myself, but my mother tells me that,
when I was in infants school, the headmistress pleaded with her not
to upset me in the morning, because if I was upset I would disrupt the
whole school! I would fight all the time. I would never pick on the girls
because they would cry very easily, but I would fight with all the
boys! And I hated wearing 'girlie' clothes! I wanted to wear dungarees
and T-shirts and a baseball cap. And this was in an era when it just
wasn't done at all.

My first recollections of any sub/dom activities is when I was eight
years old. I used to tie up my next door neighbour's son with my skip-
ping rope and flick his penis with my lolly stick. I don't know exactly
why I did it. Certainly, at that age, there was no sexual thrill. I think
it was simply about power, although I didn't fully understand what I
was doing. I know I've *always* intimidated men; though never intentionally, because I really like men. I think men are really nice. It's a
myth that great mistresses are men-haters. I think men are funny and
I've had some good relationships with them. However, I always have
to be in control. I can't have a relationship where I'm the 'defenceless'
female. That's just not my cup of tea. I hate it. I tried it once, I have
to say, because I've always believed that if you don't try it, you don't
know. So I did try it and so I know that it's definitely not for me!

When I look back now, I can analyse it and see how I always
attracted, what I considered to be, 'wimpy' men. But I think, on
reflection, I was just attracting men who enjoyed strong women. I
didn't fully understand it because I wasn't aware of the power I had.
At times I found it frustrating because I thought people didn't like

me, and I would ask: "Why don't you like me, because I'm actually a very nice person?" Now I realise that it's not because people *didn't* like me, they were simply afraid of the power I had. I was twenty four when I started to realise this, and that's when I knew what I wanted to do and where I wanted to go and how I could get there!

As I say, I've always been assertive. When I was a teenager I had problems getting work because I can't be told what to do. I think I was about eighteen when I realised it wasn't really aggression, it was assertion. And what I needed to do was fine tune the skills I had. I'd always been interested in S&M since I first read *The Story of O,* and I used to sneak peeks at copies of adult magazines in my dad's wardrobe. I was always fascinated by the stories where the women were in charge. I used to think *yes*, I'd like to do that!

I was always terrified of having to fit into this role of being the 'little woman'. People used to say to me: "When you grow up you'll find a nice man and get married and have children and have a lovely little house and you'll be able to do the cooking and the gardening and the washing and he'll be able to put the shelves up for you". And I used to think: "Oh, my God!" For a long time I actually felt I was an 'alien' who had been dumped here from another planet, because I didn't belong in this situation that was expected of me. I felt that one day they'd come for me. That was a horrible feeling to grow up with. I didn't want to get married and have two point four children and live in a rose covered cottage. I wanted someone crawling around naked at my feet, kissing my feet and me spanking them! So, I learned to put up my own shelves and fix my own car and do my own wiring and anything else. I enjoy the fact that I don't physically *need* anyone. I don't even need anyone to give me an orgasm. I can do that for myself as well!

I went back to university as a mature student. I didn't go through the normal channels of going at eighteen because I worked. I was and still am fiercely independent. I left home at sixteen and got my own flat and held down two jobs. I did anything and everything, from bar work to office work, to pay the rent. I needed that and I still can't depend on anybody. I am very, very strong.

One of the beauties about Guy, my partner, is that he grew up in very similar circumstances. Only, in his case, he was always afraid that he'd have to meet someone who would expect him to be this 'macho' man. And he *cannot* put up a shelf to save his life! But he can cook and he washes and he irons. And *nobody* makes the bed like him! It's the perfect relationship. But, in every other aspect of his life, he's extremely dominant, so we get on very, very well. In fact, he participates as a master. Although he is dominant, he's very placid and not very good at verbal humiliation. He is extremely strong physically though, and he works on his own now.

Within a loving relationship, you *can* have your S&M games. When I first had relationships, I would tie my partner up as part of the fun and the sexual thrill but, for me, that was just an experimentation aspect. You're very young and, obviously, you care very much about the person you're intimate with. On a professional basis, however, it is so, so different. If anyone is interested in S&M, they should first try to explore it with a partner or go to a massage parlour and ask them to do some bondage, because the women there are quite happy to do that. Explore it in that environment where, if you don't find the sexual thrill you're seeking, you can leave.

For some people, like me, you really are *born* into this. I know there are some ladies out there who do this primarily for the money, and that's fair enough, if that's what they want to do. But, for other people (and you *know* when you talk to them) there really isn't any other job they'd be as good at as this! I mean, where else can you work your own hours, command a really good fee *and* have such a good time? These 'city boys' may get huge pay packets at the end of the day, but at what cost? They're so stressed all the time! And the beauty of it is, I get some of 'em coming round and cleaning my flat for me *and* paying me to do so! It's lovely!

I remember my first fetish party. It was when I was living in the north-east of England. I am going back a long time now, but there were about forty people there and most of the submissives present were female – which rather dispels the myth, doesn't it? I notice today there are more submissive males. Submissive females are much harder to find these days. For me, it was a real eye-opener! I had no idea what to wear, so I dressed more gothic than fetish. It was almost like stepping into a dream for me, I felt so relaxed. I had people serving me drinks and asking me if I'd like my feet massaged. It was so nice to be treated in such a special way, and I thought to myself: "I'm home at last! This is what I really want!"

I originally trained in psychiatry and, when I first came to

London from Manchester, that's what I was doing. Working for myself, of course! I had considered going into the NHS, but only for about three seconds! I practiced privately for a while, which I quite enjoyed to begin with. The problem was there was no escape for me. I felt trapped because I was dealing with people's deepest emotions and desires, and a whole variety of problems they were trying to come to terms with. But I wasn't really happy and, therefore, I felt unable to give them 100%.

And it was so stressful, I absolutely began to hate it! To be honest, I felt that the majority of my clients really just needed to be put over my knee and given a good spanking! It was very difficult to take my 'mistress head' off and put my 'shrink head' on. Unfortunately, you can't simply tell them to get over here and bend over! You have to be very calm and cool, and that's *not* what you want to do. You want to tie them up and beat them, because that's what most of them needed! You're dealing with spoilt brats of all ages! I had these women who'd complain that they only had five thousand pounds a month to spend on themselves and they *still* couldn't handle life! They hadn't a clue what life's about, yet you just can't tell them! They have to come to certain conclusions on their own, and it's *extremely* frustrating. I just wanted to hit them, but I'd have lost my license. In the end, my decision was that I really don't need this!

It became so stressful for me that I began working professionally as a dominatrix part-time. That was the most wonderful stress relief. Looking back, I would have done it and not charged anybody, because it got to the stage where I really *needed* it. In the end, I thought I'd rather just do the domination. You can have a good standard of living without working all hours. You don't have to get up at seven in the morning, and you can have a lot of fun. Not many people can say they really enjoy their work, so I think I'm very lucky. The beauty of it is, too, that the older I get the more in demand I am!

I'd say that 90% of the submissive men who visit a mistress don't want young 'stick insects'. They don't want women who are skinny. They like physically strong women. I'm a good size fourteen and I know I look like a *real* woman. One of my clients recently was a French guy, who was actually very small and slender himself, and at the end of the session he told me that the reason he kept coming back to me was because he thought I was big and strong and powerful. He said: "If you buy a gift for someone, like a book, what kind of book do you buy them? You don't buy them a thin book. You buy them a big book!" I thought that was really sweet. I'm a big book! But I don't think it's *just* the 'matronly' figure they want. I think they want the confidence, and that comes with life events and getting older. For women, I think, their middle thirties is a plateau in their life when they decide where they're going and what they want to do! I found in counselling that, although they say men go through a mid-life crisis in their mid-forties, women go through it in their mid-thirties. They feel they want to reassess life and see what they're doing, and I think a lot of men like that in a woman. They like the confidence of a more mature mistress. They don't necessarily want eighteen year old girls who are more concerned with their lipstick; all that is just for show. I'm not saying girls like that don't know what they're doing but, when I was that age and although I've always been dominant, I look back now and realise that I didn't really have a clue. I wouldn't have considered becoming a professional mistress then, because I didn't have the skills to see the job through. Now, however, I am *extremely* confident and sorted. I know what I want, and a lot of that comes with age. The greatest, most incredible, dominants are in their forties, because they've survived life and all the shit it's thrown at them.

Despite the bad experiences in psychiatry, I do find all that training was very important and is still a great help in this work. For example, I often have people who really get into the scene and, at the end, they may relieve themselves. After they've done that they start crying and then they're very embarrassed, saying: "You must think I'm really dirty". It's good that I have the skills now where I can help them realise there's nothing wrong with it and there's nothing dirty in it. All they're doing is exploring it, and it's only mainstream society who tell us that what we're doing is wrong.

I have a lot of clients who feel guilty about coming to see a professional mistress at all. I certainly don't feel any guilt about seeing married men, because there's no sex involved. If my own partner had a particular fetish I didn't want to participate in, I would rather he saw a professional. There isn't an emotional attachment, as there is in an affair. Some clients won't call me for six months or more and, when they do, we continue as if we're old friends.

There's a psychological idea that women and men have equality, but it's not so. The pressure on men is probably greater now than ever, and I actually feel sorry for men because they get a very raw deal. They don't chat to friends about their emotional problems. They're expected to be macho and go out to work. Men come to a mistress in order to relieve themselves of all that accumulated stress. They find it a relief to be able to concentrate solely on getting a mistresses floor clean, for example. You can see the stress lifting from them when they know that's the *only* thing they have to worry about for that period of time.

The maximum number of clients I've seen is three in one day, but then I'll take two days off. After an hour or two hour session you feel really emotionally drained. You've got to keep that control and, at the same time, make sure they enjoy themselves. There's a lot of preparation work, too, even before they arrive. Afterwards, Master Guy will reward himself with a pint of beer in the pub! But then if I don't see any clients for a few days, I'll actually have withdrawal symptoms! I'll become very agitated, and I'll go out and get very assertive and very aggressive with people on the street. Master Guy will say: "You need to switch the phone on and take a booking". When I've given a really good thrashing to someone, I feel on such a high. I feel exhilarated! It's like taking a drug and, I think, for me it *is* a drug! It's better than sex... well, almost! I have thought about doing something else for a living, but I can't. So, I suppose I'll just have to accept that I'm a 'dom-addict'!

As well as working with Master Guy, I'm training my assistant, Mistress Blue. We've also got a new female submissive called Jennifer. She'll be coming to stay with us every weekend, so we'll then have a live-in slave. It'll be an ideal entourage, as they say! Two mistresses, a master *and* a slave girl! I've also got access to other submissive males who are quite happy to take part in a session as well.

Of all the scenarios I do, I *really* love water sports. I don't just give a little tinkle, I give a real shower! I always tell them that if they want that, let me know in advance so I can drink litres of water. I've also done water sports with Master Guy. Once, I was standing over the bath and he was beside it and he cross fired and ended up urinating all done my leg! I wasn't too pleased. But, yes, I love pissing on them. I could piss for England and get a gold medal! I also love over the knee spanking. I'm really good at it because I'm very heavy handed. Face slapping I love, too. It's really difficult, because I like so many different aspects of it. I like having a domestic slave. I think that's wonderful! Standing over them and making them clean for me

Giving the cane or the tawse or strap, that's lovely as well. I like it when someone has an exceptionally high pain threshold. Some people say they can take a good beating, but you give them a few and find they can't take it. You can't just tie them up and start flogging them, either. It has to be built up nice and slowly, obviously. But, sometimes you're right at the point when you're ready to administer a good caning, and the submissive says: "Oh, I've had enough!" And you were only just getting warmed up! So, it's nice when you get someone with that kind of pain threshold, and you can really just go and take them there! Afterwards, your dripping with sweat because you've flogged them so hard. Maybe little droplets of blood, too! It's lovely. It's what I like! If I give a punishment, I like it to be a *good* punishment. It's almost an insult to my work if I can't do a proper job.

I'm not really into 'adult babies'. I have tried it but, having had a child of my own, I really don't want to go through that again. I don't do 'queening' either. I'll quite happily ride a man like a pony, but I won't sit on their faces because I feel I would be giving them some of my 'power'. Obviously, they'll see me bend over in my panties to tie them up, but I don't mind that because what they see, they can't have!

I get asked to do a lot of role-play: nanny, school teacher and so on. I enjoy it and can get into role-play easily. I wear rubber, leather, PVC and basques, but I don't wear nurses uniform and stuff because that would be too 'girlie' for me. I play a headmistress, too, and I have a suit and a cap that I wear. I also play the role of housekeeper, which I can do quite well. Last week, as 'housekeeper', I 'caught' a client going through my chest of drawers where I keep my underwear. Obviously, I chastised him! But I don't keep vast amounts of props, because I don't think I need them. I have a cage, a whipping bench and stocks. I've seen dungeons where there's lots of elaborate equipment strung across the wall, but it's only for show. I don't believe in having things I will never use.

Master Guy and myself also get asked to do a lot of school scenes together. We do a favourite scenario where they've been 'caught' with a porn magazine or some cigarettes, like you used to do at school. It's fun remembering my own headmaster's habits and drawing on them; like rattling change around in his pocket or hurling pieces of chalk. Last year, we had a big advertising campaign together and we did get quite a lot of work. I think, because Master Guy is bi-sexual, it appeals to a whole variety of people. You'll get men who just like the Master there to sit and watch while I fuck them with a strap-on. They like the fact that I'm doing that and they're looking directly at the Master. For them, that's a really wonderful experience. But, they do like to be 'forced' into it, too.

We did a job on Sunday with this really nice chap who was heavily into massaging feet. Feet were his particular fetish. And, I have to be honest, I do love having my feet caressed, kissed, massaged and washed. I could have someone at my feet all day long and I would never tire of it. He wanted as many people here as possible. We got five people round in the end and he had a wonderful time. When he wasn't needed, he was in the kitchen preparing a light buffet. He served all the guests and then massaged everyone's feet. After that, while we were having a glass of wine in here, he was in the kitchen clearing up. Mistress Blue and I did take him into the bathroom at one point and gave him a good shower as a special treat! In fact, he e-mailed me this morning thanking me for such a wonderful time and he hopes to come back soon. And we enjoyed having him here.

One of my most memorable clients has to be 'Sloppsie The Slut'. He was an Australian chap who rang me and asked for an appointment with me and the Master. I said, that was fine. He then asked if I would allow him to give me oral sex. I said that was out of the question, but he could give oral worship to the Master, so long as everything was done safely. And he was okay with that. Then he told me that he was a cross dresser and asked permission to come dressed. I said yes, no problem. I don't have a problem with the neighbours because it's very discrete here.

Anyway, he turns up in this taxi. He was quite a large built chap and he had a really low-cut dress on with quite a lot of arm, shoulder and chest hairs sticking out, and a *really* cheap wig! No make-up apart from a little bit of lipstick. No tights and these huge, chunky legs! It wasn't convincing at all! I actually started laughing when I saw him, it was so funny. And I thought: "This is going to be fun!" I couldn't wait for Master Guy to take a look at this! After all, he's the one who's got to do the 'business' with him!

In the end, most of the session ended up with him talking. I think we only did about five or ten minutes of actual domination on him. He just wanted to talk more than anything. He told us that the reason he'd got his nickname 'Sloppsie' was that his first wife had a liking for black men. She would go out to the clubs and pick up as many black men as she could, and then bring them back to the house and have them all fuck her. When they'd finished with her, he'd have to lie on the floor while she'd sit on his face and he'd have to clean her out. And that's why they called him 'Sloppsie'! Then he said he could do the same for me if I wanted, and I thought: "No, I don't think so!"

Really, I've done so many scenarios it's hard to remember them all, but I think 'Lulu' was probably one of the nicest. He was a transvestite, and he was lovely. He was quite a high powered businessman and used to treat his wife like a piece of shit. He'd go home, purposefully drop his clothes on the floor, and have her run after him like *R2D2*. But he would come here and spend an hour scrubbing my kitchen! And woe betide him if there was one speck of dust in there! He, or rather *she,* would really get it! He now goes home and, so he tells me, treats his wife much better.

I would say 98% of my clients are really nice. They're clean and polite. You'll always get the odd one that will come through, and I'll have no hesitation in asking them to leave. At least, in my line of work, if I don't like them, I don't have to see them again. It's that simple. Some people have no idea, though. For example, if you want anal exploration, you don't go and have a three course meal. Or you'll get people who will say during the interview that their last mistress let them lick her pussy for hours. I'll just tell 'em to go back to her, because they were getting a really good deal and that they're not going anywhere near mine! That sort of person shouldn't come to a mistress or master, because we find it *extremely* offensive to be asked for sex. I get very angry that some people assume SM is anything to do with having sex. If I was in a loving relationship, however, and my partner enjoyed being submissive, then it would include the sexual aspect. It's a different thing altogether. When my clients get a hard-on, I'll just hit it with my riding crop!

Inevitably, you'll get time wasters. I think some people get off on

125

making an appointment and knowing you're waiting for them to show up. Or they'll just want to talk on the phone. I'll have a chap ring up and say he and his wife want to come along for a session, and then he'll go into great detail about what she'll be wearing, or not wearing, and what she likes to do. And you *know* that this guy wouldn't know what a girlfriend was if he fell over one! The only girlfriend he's going to get is one that he pays for! I'll tell them to get the lady herself to phone and then I'll give more details. Some will call again and again. I find it so offensive that they think I'm that stupid that I don't recognise their voices. If I actually saw them, I'd hit them *so* hard, and it wouldn't be playing!

Then you get the ones who say that they'll come and do all my housework and they *won't* charge me. I'll say: "Is that right?" So, you go through the whole scenario with them. They want to come and stay here for the whole weekend and cook and clean for me and they won't charge me! I inform them that I have people who come here and do all that and pay *me* to do it! If it's already been done, there's nothing for them to do, is there? "No, Mistress", they'll say. So, therefore, I'm going to lose that income, aren't I? "Yes, Mistress". So what do you suggest I do? "Don't know, Mistress". So what do you think now? "I don't think I'm coming round, Mistress". That's correct! Goodbye!

These days, I'm advertising via the Internet more. They can e-mail me and, if they state that they can only receive e-mails at certain dates and times, then I do respect their privacy. I understand that they're married and don't want their partners to find out. I'm not going to bombard them with e-mails saying: "Where the hell are you? My cage is ready for you!" I can be *very* discrete! I think if the client is prepared to make a little bit of effort, then he's worth seeing.

Within this business *trust* is very important. I'm always aware that for a submissive to come and see a mistress for the first time must be absolutely petrifying! They could get tied up and severely hurt or even maimed! It does happen! And it's not like they could even tell anybody: "Oh, I'm just off to see Mistress Whoever, if I'm not back in three hours send a search party!" I'm always very aware of this, and I do try to put them at their ease because I want them to gain something from the session. I don't just want them to come in, take their money and ship them out. 'Conveyor Belt' domination is not for me. What I like to do is see people on a regular basis, so you can build up a relationship. Once you have a relationship established with a client, you'll be surprised what limits you can go to. But you do need to know their limits first. If you've got someone who's married and, even if they sleep in separate bedrooms, you know not to mark them outside their underpants. You don't want the wife to notice. This is where the trust comes into it, and the respect.

I'm very happy with the regular clients I see. They're really nice and I get on well with them. We have a good relationship. I had one chap who was eighty three (he actually died last year), but he was so sweet and I'd been seeing him for a long time. I used to dress him, put him over my knee and spank him. I was very upset when he died, and it *wasn't* just from the financial point of view! I was upset because I'd really got to know him as a friend. Over the years, he'd tell me a little bit more about himself. He was in a very unhappy relationship with his wife, and had been for over fifty years. Apparently, I was the only person in all those years who had put my arms around him and held him. I thought that was very touching and he deserved a hug. I do miss him, actually. And he used to bring me a bottle of vodka as well! He knew just how to get round me!

You do get to know your regular clients, and they make the effort to get to know you as well. But you do get some people who come in here and are very arrogant. Their arrogance is based on the fact that they are paying me for the service that I'm going to provide; which is fair enough, I suppose. But, at the end of the day, manners cost nothing. I'm *never* rude to them. In fact, I'm a very tactile mistress. I like to touch my submissives and to be very close to them, so that they can physically feel me. I think that's very important. And I don't scream and shout at them, either. Unless, of course, they specifically say this is what they're looking for. I don't enjoy screaming and shouting to get what I want. I don't think that gives you power. I'm very calm and soothing when I talk, and I like to instill my authority in a calm voice. But I know, from what my clients have told me, I also instill a great amount of fear in them *because* I'm so cool and calm. I enjoy that! I am more into the psychology, anyway. I like the mind control aspect best.

But, as I say, you get some of them who are incredibly rude. I think they shouldn't really be coming to see a mistress. That's not what they're after. Some of them don't have a full understanding of what this is about. And yet, they'll come in and say: "This is what I want. I've been to see lots of mistresses before". In fact, there was one chap who told me on the phone that his particular fetish was that he wanted to sniff my panties. I put him in bondage and I took my panties off, put them under his nose and he was in absolute heaven. However, after about fifteen minutes, there wasn't really much else to do, and he'd booked for an hour. I sensed that this wasn't really what he wanted. Finally, we ended up talking, and he admitted that he'd come here for sex. I'd told him already on the phone that sex isn't a service I provide. I actually felt sorry for him in the end, and told him he should have gone to a massage parlour. He could have got the things he wanted, and for a lot less money than coming to see me. He then admitted that he had an advert out himself offering oral sex to females. I said: "I bet you've had no replies". He admitted he hadn't.

Perhaps after a long period of time (and this is where the trust comes in again) a dominant *might* consider it. But certainly not in the first session or even the second or third! You need to know that you can trust your submissive and your submissive needs to know that he or she can trust you. That kind of trust can only be built up over a long period of time. For a submissive to put themselves into your hands and for you to secure them, for example, they've got to feel in their heart that their mistress is going to come back! She may take twenty minutes to have a nice cup of coffee and put her feet up, but she'll still come back and she will release them. That trust doesn't happen overnight. You know there's a joke in this business that the worst thing a mistress can say to a slave who's locked in her cage is: "I wonder where I can get a locksmith at this time of night?" That's only a joke, but really it's the pinnacle of what we're talking about. It comes down to that faith.

Then there was another chap who told me his name was 'Ernest'. He was on the phone for about a week. Every day he would call me before he eventually came for the appointment. He said that his fetish was that he had to wear white underpants while being caned. He said he didn't need to be secured, either. He wanted to be made to bend over and hold his ankles while he was punished. Then 'Ernest' informed me: "I have to tell you that I've been to see twenty two mistresses and *none* of them could hurt me! So I doubt if a slip of a girl like you could either". I thought he was just saying that to get me a bit angry when I hit him. I gave him two strokes of the cane, initially, and it didn't have any effect. Then I got one of my old school canes and hit him four times. He stood straight up and said: "I want to go now. That really hurt" I smiled ever so sweetly and said: "But I thought that's what you wanted?"I never saw him again. Surprise, surprise! The point is that for some people it's such a fantasy and, when it comes to the reality... well, they shouldn't do it, really. They should leave it as a fantasy and just do it through premium rate lines or correspondence. I do a lot of correspondence domination and sessions over the phone. I even do e-mail domination now. And, for some people, that's perfect. It all depends on what the submissive is looking for.

I do like doing live one-to-one on the telephone. What happens is they will send me the fee and arrange a time. Usually, they'll call me because it's easier for them. Especially if they don't want their number given out. Or, if they're not too bothered, I'll call them. Then they'll get so many minutes of domination. It really is quite fun. This is a completely different market, because here you're dealing with someone who would dearly love to come and see you, but just hasn't got the courage. Though they're not quite confident yet to *physically* visit a mistress, they still need that thrill. Doing it this way is the safest form of domination you can have. If you slap your thigh, they'll squeal! It's obvious that you're not really hitting them, but they just get so lost in the scene for the length of time you're on the phone with them. I have long term clients who I've been 'phone dominating' for some time. Most of them have seen my picture, so they know what I look like. They'll describe what they look like, though I only have their word for that, of course. They might send me their picture – well, I *think* it's their picture! You can be more sexual on the phone, as well. Which I'm quite happy to do. I can explore areas on the phone which I won't explore in reality. They are aware of that, so it's not a problem.

Sometimes, when I switch my phone on during the day and listen to some of the messages, I'll find I was called at three o'clock in the morning! What sort of person rings you at three in the morning? Someone who's drunk or someone who has absolutely no idea or someone who is definitely *not* a submissive! Half of them imagine you live inside this little cardboard box with your leather dress on and your high heels and, whenever the phone rings, you toddle out and say: "Mistress Chrystalle here. How can I help you?" And it doesn't work like that. I'm a real person. I go shopping in Sainsbury's and I wear jeans and a T-shirt and no make-up. I worry about all the things that everyone else worries about. Do I have enough money to pay the mortgage this month? Oh God, the phone bills just come in and I want this new pair of shoes. In my case, the shoes always win, of course! But the point is that these are just everyday things that everyone goes through, and a mistress or a master is no different. We're still human beings!

When I worked for *Eros* magazine, I had people write in saying how they'd really like to live with me for a week. I can you assure you that they *wouldn't* enjoy living with me! When I'm not working, I'm just so ordinary. The difference is that I'm very assertive. I'm naturally very dominant. So, whereas some people might show signs of submission, I don't. In everyday life, even in the supermarket, I am very assertive. I speak my mind to everybody and anybody. But that's not because I'm a mistress, that's just the way I am. The fact that I'm a mistress only enhances all these qualities I've got naturally. One of the reasons that I can't work for an employer is that I can't take orders. I can give them *very* well, though!

I have always been very open about what I do. No one is ever shocked. I even spoke to people I went to university with and told them what I do, and they said it came as no surprise to them! I have noticed a major Sunday tabloid has given mistresses a really hard time in the past. They've slaughtered female doms, but I have noticed they're not doing it to the men! Yet, men's magazines are so much more outrageous! I wonder if it's still this male hierarchy keeping women under the thumb? For me, personally, if they want to do a double-page spread on me, I'd be quite happy for the publicity! All I'd say to them is: "*Please*, don't do it in a devious manner. Come and interview me! You'll be doing me a favour". There's no embarrassment at all, as far as I'm concerned. My family and my loved ones accept what I do, and that's all I care about. In fact, my seventeen year old son (who is a brilliant photographer) took all the pictures of me!

I would like to explore other areas in the future, and go into different careers. I'd like to do more editing or perhaps run a fetish club. I'd never want to give up being a mistress, though, because I enjoy it too much. I don't see why I should stop doing something I really like and am so good at! If someone could wave a magic wand and give me anything I wanted, I'd say I would like an extremely wealthy male bi-sexual submissive to give me the lifestyle I've become accustomed to. He would be my exclusive submissive and I would be his exclusive mistress. Though he would also have to accept the fact that Master Guy is in the scene. He would provide for all of my needs, and not just on a financial basis. He would escort me to clubs, restaurants, shopping, all those things. He would be my chauffeur and my maid. He would bathe me and dress me. That would be my ideal! If you're out there, please write to me. I'm looking for you!

GODDESS VENUS

Goddess Venus is, in actual fact, a rather striking 27 year old of Italian parentage who provides, in addition to her private one-to one sessions in her London-based dungeon, a fully comprehensive postal training academy for dedicated male submissives who wish to explore the world of Female Domination, but at a safe distance! Interviewed August 2000

I am a life style dominatrix as well as a professional one, as I do have several slaves who are part of my life. Although, I hasten to add, I do have an existence as a human being as well, rather than just as a 'dominant android'. Because that's what it's about, isn't it? It can be very one-dimensional and 'unhuman', which is why it's a fetish and must be kept there really. Maintaining this as a full life-style, especially for the submissive, is quite a difficult role. It's very tiring and there isn't much left for the true slave. I've had slaves in the past who have been so *totally* servile it's unbelievable! Just unquestioning obedience and so *utterly* in awe of me and the whole scene that they're not really in need of much training at all. Obviously, they've got another life as well, in that they've got to earn a living, but other than that they're my property and they have to keep themselves available for me.

I'm actually still looking for that one special slave who can keep my interest totally. I tend to find that over time I become very bored. For me, what would be most interesting would be to try and integrate the dual roles of slave and partner into one, and that's something I've aimed to do in the past. Perhaps there's still hope out there, but I'm not sure. It's something that's very difficult to find. A lot of them want to try it, but I'm looking for someone who is very strong. By that I mean strong within themselves, but not dominant. There is a difference. I think that kind of inner strength and intelligence is what I'm looking for. But it's actually very difficult to find that without getting that sort of aggression from the male, which I really can't stand. That sort of blind lashing out is really abhorrent to me. On the other hand, someone who is too grovelling really makes me want to be sick as well. It makes me want to put the boot in for real! The strong silent type is probably the best for a slave/partner. It isn't anything to do with doing as they're told necessarily, although that helps, of course! It's about a man *honouring* the female. Now that's *my* private fantasy, and we're not just talking about shiny bits of plastic! Perhaps that's why I find a lot of medieval imagery so interesting.

I'm not looking for just a domestic slave, because I expect all my slaves to muck in anyway when it comes to cleaning, cooking, showing clients in and dealing with the videos and music and being 'minder'. That last role is especially important, as I *never* ever work alone. I know some mistresses do because it's much cheaper than if you have to pay a minder, but you do need someone with you, really. I have one submissive who works with me on a regular basis here who's a transvestite, although he's so big and muscular that I prefer to keep him as a slave. Whereas there is another little one, who actually lives in Dorset, who serves me on a personal level and does jobs for me at home, as well as here in my dungeon. He's perfect as a transvestite maid. It really does depend on the guy as to what I want to do with them. If they're not paying me, then I will *totally* dictate what role they play in my life. I'm not going to have *their* stuff pushed on to me!

With my clients, what I do is try to provide a mixture of what they want *and* what I want. I think that's the best way if you're going to form an on going relationship with them, which is what I like to do, obviously. They'll chat to me about their past history, and I'll find that a lot of times they're not *really* sure, when they first come here, what it is that they're into at all! They only know what they've done. So I try and take them on a journey of self discovery, which is what this is all about anyway. As far as my own preferences are concerned, I refuse to get involved in any toilet stuff, because I find that really abhorrent and I'm not going to go there! That's the only thing that *really* turns me off! I don't work with any other mistresses either, because I like to run my own show.

Regarding my work with correspondence slaves, that's something totally different and very involved. The kind of submissives who are attracted to the postal course are very different to those who actually visit. In some cases, they may be even *more* dedicated to me. But I think there's a lot of 'wimpery' there as well, and they don't really want to come. It could be finance, because it's obviously much cheaper to *not* do it for real. And, in a lot of cases, I think they're really very, very deranged people! I mean you have to be, don't you? It's still an interesting idea to develop, all the same. I'm hoping in the future it will be more computer based and I can do it by e-mail. It'll save time for everyone. Although, in some ways, pen and ink actually makes you sit there and consider what you're doing. That aspect might be lost with the computer age, I'm not sure. We'll have to see how it goes.

As I said before, what I'm interested in doing really is attracting to myself someone who would help me forward. At times, I think it might be good to work with another mistress in terms of the scene, but it would have to be someone I felt very bonded to. I would like to find out. I have been thinking of possibly advertising for that, but it's got to be someone (and I know this might sound pretentious) *very* spiritually and emotionally aware that I can really trust. I'm not interested in it just being about business, because really I'm also someone who needs close, bonded relationships. For me, with anything I get involved in, it's never *just* about money or *just* about business. I need someone *very* self aware, certainly. And it would have to be someone thirty five plus. That's what I've got in my head, anyway.

I do have very young boys, around eighteen or nineteen years old, who come to see me, and I like them very much. I know other mistresses never see clients that young, but maybe it's because I'm quite young myself. It's surprising how much they're into this. Maybe they haven't pursued it, but it's definitely there in their heads. That kind of innocence is *very* attractive to me. Over all, my clients range from eighteen to about seventy years old.

More than anything, I enjoy people who are as outlandish as I am, and who can totally get into it! People who are completely absorbed in the scene and are totally uninhibited. It doesn't happen very often, though. I suppose it's nerves for a lot of them. But when you do get one of those, it's a real pleasure. A lot of people (not just in this scene, but generally) are *very* dull, let's face it. So, obviously, that makes for dull scenes in the dungeon, too. The fantasies inside their heads probably aren't dull (certainly not to them, anyway) but it's more to do with how they respond to me with shyness. Although I understand it, I don't particularly enjoy it. I like people who are totally *absorbed* in this!

I would love to meet someone who was theatrical. Probably someone who is quite heavily involved in this industry themselves, because I think they would understand what I'm all about. And money, of course, is important. Not because I want someone to support me, I don't need that. But I certainly don't want to support anyone else. Romance *without* finance is a load of crap! It's a joke! We don't want to sit at home and eat baked beans on toast, do we?

I think that most women who are involved in the scene non-professionally (and this is just my opinion) are perhaps desperately looking for something. And it's not really about sex for them, either. It's much more about wanting be a part of this unique club. A lot of it is about exhibitionism with the gear and the fact that it's something unusual and different. I think that's why fetishism is becoming so fashionable now, because it's glamourous and a bit naughty. It's becoming more and more main stream all the time. The images you see in advertising nowadays have got lots of fetish in them. As it becomes more acceptable, perhaps the people who are *really* involved in it will have to either take it one step further and become even *more* socially unacceptable or go and do something else! I mean, what's it's future and does it even have one?

When I was growing up as a young teenager, I always saw it as street-walker gear. You know, standing on street corners. I think I've come to understand a lot of it now and where it comes from. There are still certain sorts of fetishes and perversions that I find very difficult to understand, though I do try! I actually am very interested in understanding what it is and where it comes from and why. For instance, I was thinking of getting involved in medical stuff but, having gone a little way down that road, I find it's so totally removed from anything erotic or sexual that I've decided not to go there. I'll leave that to the experts or the so-called 'experts'! Honestly, I've seen some absolutely dreadful cases of injury on submissives. They've come to me after having medical scenes done to them, and they've got huge bruises on their bodies where it's been done wrong. There could be infections and all sorts of things! I mean, how can you (unless you're a trained medic, which they're not) possibly know what you're doing?

I come from an artistic background myself, and have been drawn towards kinky clothing for a long time now. I designed rubber wear and got involved in that side of things, but there wasn't really much money in it. Not anywhere near as much as there is in this, anyway! So I decided to do this, instead. But I don't intend doing this work past the point where it's no longer glamourous. As soon as I get past it, that's it! I don't want to end up like one of these old bags, you know what I mean? I'm speaking only about being a professional in terms of seeing clients now. As a life-style, I think it's something that can be carried on forever. But, as a professional mistress, if you're not careful and unless you can raise your profile and actually take pride in what you've created, you can become like some of those women you see in the contact magazines who look as if they've been washed out by the whole thing.

And it is *very* wearing. This is a very difficult job, and I don't think people appreciate that. You're engaging your mind *all* of the time. Plus you get paid half what you would if you were catering for a 'straight' market, so you have to have dedication and you have to have a brain. You've got to create scenarios for people all the time. For instance, I don't have any 'set' scenarios, none at all. Nothing's scripted and nothing's repeated. If I'm not feeling my best and able to give my all, then I won't work that day, it's as simple as that.

I suppose I want to become, I don't know, Queen of the Entire Universe! And I don't think that's too much to ask, do you? I know it's crazy and I realise it's completely demented, but then this is a demented scene, isn't it?. Everyone involved in this world is completely mad! You've got to be to be able to keep a straight face. I think it's interesting the way people in this scene, and especially guys, will say that they'd hate other people to find out about them because it would be seen as very deviant, and all the rest of it. But I think a lot of straight people actually just find this stuff very amusing!

Kidnapping is a huge fantasy for a lot of people. Certainly, things like abductions by witches and goblins and having spells put on them and that kind of stuff. Oh God, yes. I don't really understand that one myself, even though I am very interested in spirituality in the whole of my life anyway. I've been reading tarot cards since I was about fifteen. And I think that kind of spirituality comes over in the domination I practice; which is very traditional, but very, very intense at the same time. It's very much 'mind centred'. I mean, I use hypnosis for instance, which I'm trained to do. For me, it was simply a natural progression, really. If you think about all the 'bits and pieces' involved in this; you know, the leather straps, the ropes and the chains and this, that and the other, then you can see that it's just a way of restraining the body so that the mind is free.

Then you can really get in there, right into the mind, and you can unlock stuff in there. Sometimes I'll do it in combination with bondage, using the two together is good. In fact, some submissives come to me purely for the hypnosis side. That's their *whole* fantasy. This may sound quite evil, but you can actually implant messages with hypnosis. You can also remove stuff over time, like irritating and negative character traits. I don't think it does them any favours to have those traits, so they won't mind if they lose them, will they? I can then replace that stuff with something more positive. It's really all about mind control. I remember back to the first time I was ever hypnotised – I fought it totally! Ultimately, I don't like losing control in any way, shape or form!

My whole upbringing has been based around spirituality. I would like to use it more in my work, and it's great when I get people who are in tune with me. Unfortunately, that doesn't happen very often. And that, in my opinion, has absolutely nothing to do with age whatsoever. I've met people in their forties and fifties, especially men, who are not *aware* in the slightest, even of themselves! They have no self knowledge or awareness at all! And that is the worst thing, when you get someone and you try and try and try to get them to open up and they don't. Eventually I just get bored, whether it be in this way or in general. I will attempt to help them by bringing them out of themselves, but you can only go so far. If it doesn't change, it doesn't change. That's their journey and their problem!

I had a very privileged public school upbringing, but rebelled terribly and got thrown out. I didn't really settle with any one thing. My whole family is very artistic and my own interests are very diverse. Even though I'm a Capricorn, I've got a Gemini moon and so, for someone like me, the grass is *always* greener and something more exciting might be happening over there! Although, I must say that I've become less and less like that as I get older. When I first started out in this business, I wanted to make vast amounts of money from it, but I don't think there are huge amounts of money to be made. It's a good living and that's it. So it really *is* about life-style and vocation for me. What I want to do is get involved much more in the scene, generally; whether it be in magazines, videos or whatever. I'd also love to hostess my own club one day, but it would have to be something that caters for *real* scene people and, obviously, is as glamourous and outrageous as I am!

MISTRESS ANTOINETTE

Born of mixed Spanish and Danish parentage, Mistress Antoinette spent her childhood in both countries before finally settling down in the United Kingdom. She has been a professional dominatrix for five years and divides her time between her dungeon and her nutritional health business. Interviewed September 2000.

One of the first dominatrixes I ever met was this woman in Spain who was actually a high court judge! She was working from a very plush apartment in Madrid, and had given up her career in law in favour of being a dominatrix. She was the only one I knew of in Madrid who *really* understood what she was doing. In Spain, there are a lot of women who 'say' they do domination, but don't really know what it's about. They actually think that men who want this kind of thing are total perverts and hate working with these people. They think it's wrong, but they'll do it anyway for the money. You have to look at the history of Spain, I think. Franco died in 1975, and about 1987 you first started seeing things like pornographic videos and sex shops opening up. I take that as a signal of things relaxing a bit more. But even today, you can still walk into a sex shop in Madrid or any other Spanish city and you'll see very little that caters for domination. It's still in its infancy there.

I got to this level because I'm naturally a very sexual person. As a child in Denmark, I was always reading contact adverts like: 'Well endowed male seeks...', and all this kind of stuff. In Copenhagen, pornography is around everywhere. When I was five or six years old, I got sent to the kiosk to buy normal newspapers and magazines for my mother *and* some pornography for my father! It's quite normal there and seen as quite creative, in fact.

I was involved in the fetish scene while I was still living in Spain, but not on a professional level. By that, I mean an exchange of money being involved. I wanted to get to know more people, but I didn't want to compromise my relationship; so I decided that, if I put money between it, then no one is going to get the wrong idea. They won't think that it is the prelude for a relationship or whatever. I'd gone to Madrid originally just for a long weekend, and a friend of

139

mine put an advert in a magazine advertising for submissives. He interviewed the people for me and sent them a questionnaire to find the kind I would be interested in. I found three or four suitable people from different parts of Spain and, whenever I was in town, I would meet them in a nice luxurious hotel room. It had a wonderful marbled bathroom that was great to play in and old fashioned furniture that was really good for bondage.

When I practiced my profession in Spain, I found people were quite into 'religious' punishments. Here in England, tastes are a little more, how shall I put it, 'traditional'. Overall, I would say there is far more demand for my services in this country. Also, the number of men here who have a 'knicker' fetish continually amazes me. As I am quite a lingerie addict myself, there's plenty of scope for fun and games in that particular area. Interestingly enough, black knickers seem to be the big turn-on with men in England, whereas in Spain it is nearly always virginal white knickers that are the most popular.

Going back further, I really discovered S&M by accident. I was playing with a friend of mine and he told me about some things with domination that he wanted done to himself, and I started thinking: "Well, we can do this and we can do that!" My imagination just got going on it! I thought that this was great and really interesting! When you meet someone you can do this with there is a development between the two of you. It's your skill plus the other person as the recipient as well; how he reacts and discovers new things about himself. It's fun too!

That first time is rather a long story. Let's just say that, during a rather heated exchange of opinions, I got rather aggressive and then saw the astonishing effect it had on him. It must be said that I've always had a dominant nature, even as a child. But I didn't realise, until this particular incident, that it could be used so positively! My experience developed when I got introduced to the subject of spanking. That is, with me being the subject! I was very lucky because it was with a person who was very experienced and very skilled. He was English and had been doing it for years. I was working for a company doing consultancy around 1990 or 91, and we contacted this person through an advert. He showed my partner different techniques and we became good friends. He's since become a millionaire (though not through spanking!) and has moved to the United States. My partner

140

and I just wanted something to add a new dimension to our relationship that didn't involve actual sex with other people.

I wasn't thinking of myself as either dominant or submissive at this point, because spanking in itself isn't like discipline, it's a very erotic exercise. For me, what was interesting was the sensation. Anyway, I don't think a person can be a proper dominatrix unless she knows what's going on from the receiving end. As far as a female can, I've tried out all my equipment on myself, often without anyone's help. I've experimented with everything from nipple clamps to electric's, so I then know how it feels and it helps me develop new ideas on how it can be used. For instance, the medical and sports equipment I use is not erotic in itself, but in the *way* it is used.

I never take anyone on who I don't find interesting. After doing this for some years now, I pretty much know within the first few seconds whether I'm interested in the person or not. It's a personality thing as well, whether you go together or not. A submissive wouldn't find *everybody* dominant to him in a way he or she could accept, so it's important on both sides. If not, it becomes more of a farce than a game! That's not to say that there isn't any laughter. Sometimes there's quite a lot. For example, I was doing something with pegs, and my slave didn't want any more pegs. He put a funny German accent and said: *"Nein, Nein!"* I didn't understand what he meant, so I just said okay and put nine more pegs on him!

I would also refuse anybody who wanted scenarios that I didn't enjoy myself. Lately, a lot of people are ringing up and asking if I do castrations or tooth pulling and things like that. How serious they are, I don't know. I never get that far with them to find out! People also ask for kidnappings or to be chained up in public, but I don't do that either because I don't want the attention it would draw. I don't fancy being 'set up' by some newspaper either! I don't think that would be very beneficial. The people who are interested in the things I want to do are not interested in pushing it in the face of the rest of the public. I'm certainly not, anyway. It's a private thing and I don't think anyone needs to stumble on somebody tied up to a lamp post or whatever. I don't think it's fair on people. If I had a secluded garden or something then that would be fine. It would just add a different dimension.

I'm very professional in what I do, and try to establish a good relationship with my slaves from the outset, that way there is mutual respect. It's also important that people realise I am sensitive to their requirements and will do my best to explore their fantasies with understanding and invention. Sometimes they come along with fairly complete fantasies in mind. However, I'll always try to add something of my own to the proceedings. I am *never* predictable!

It is important that people realise that this has nothing to do with sex or perversion. There is an obvious visual side to it, but many people fail to grasp the mental side. For example, many of the men I see have wives or partners who aren't interested in every aspect of their sexuality. They don't come to me looking for sex (which, I stress, is never on offer anyway), but for someone who understands domination and is willing and capable of taking control of their life for an hour or so. Usually, this control is established through role-play, along with a combination of punishment and subtle teasing.

I get couples and single females sometimes as well, though usually the female is part of a couple and the man will speak to me first. They want to sort out if I will be responsible with her. Then he will drop her off and leave her with me. Sometimes they want to watch, but not often. I will, of course, insist on talking to the female myself to find out if she really wants to do this herself. There's no point for me otherwise. If a person can't relax and trust me, then there's no session. I wouldn't get anything out of it, and neither would they. There's no point in doing a session with someone who is unwilling. When I go into a session I want to be totally *there* and completely 'on the line' with what's happening with that person. When I practiced in Spain, it was not at all uncommon for women to visit me for domination. You must understand that people have become much more liberated there since Franco, and that includes the women! Nowadays, they're not afraid to buy porn videos or to seek alternative forms of sexual satisfaction. I think it's an interesting comment on the social pressures in this country that, despite the occasional call from submissive women, only a handful of them have ever made an appointment!

The couples I see are usually *both* submissive. I'm kind of a catalyst, really; a sort of third element that's safe for them. They're often interested in the use of my dungeon and my experience with things that maybe they haven't thought about doing together before. When you are a couple you often notice that you're too close together, so it's quite nice to watch each other in bondage and see each others reactions. Plus you can play the two against each other, which I think works very well. When you are partners with someone and you've been together a long time, it's quite difficult to keep the fun going in the relationship. That's really how couples get into things like domination, and then maybe they find that they naturally like it, either as a dominant or a submissive.

The kind of clients I see are all very intelligent and very 'on the go'. They are making decisions and are interested in all aspects of life. This is probably contrary to what people have a picture of; that is, someone who just sits there and reads perverted magazines all day long! They are absolutely *not* that kind of people. They're simply looking to expand their view of things on *all* levels, including the sexual side. They're exploring things about themselves and sex in general. It's a very good process on many levels.

I'm sometimes asked if I will teach other women how to be a dominatrix. My answer is always no, because I don't think you can. For me, at least, when I'm together with a slave it's a very special thing. Each session is so totally different, which is what I like. It appeals to my imagination and challenges me. It's not like a cooking recipe! Even with one client, their pain threshold and so on can be completely different from one session to another. My clients tell me that's what they like about coming to see me, that every time is different. And that's not because I sit down and think about it all the time or analyse it too much. It's because when the person is reacting in a certain way, I follow that route and it becomes an exploration for both the mistress and the slave. I dislike sessions where I don't have an imaginative input. I might as well be packing chocolates!

I enjoy role play very much. I have a large wardrobe, so I try to become the authority figure in their dreams. Schoolroom scenarios seem very popular in this country. I can be a strict headmistress, a punishing governess or a bossy head-girl. Then there is, of course, the typical dungeon mistress in PVC or leather. In addition, there are my medical uniforms such as doctor or nurse. Sometimes I will play the part of the hard-nosed businesswoman in a smart suit with 'power-padding' who punishes the office boy for slacking at work. There's no one role that is my favourite, though I must admit I do quite enjoy the policewoman's role. In fact, I've got a Spanish police woman's uniform from a friend back in Spain, and I've done a few interrogation scenes where I've been speaking Spanish. It's fun because you enter completely into the fantasy and shut out the real world. They will try and bribe me as a police officer and, of course, make it worse for themselves! One person in particular wanted to be dealt with as if he were a football hooligan who had been arrested abroad. So I put on my uniform, strung him up and gave him a good thrashing. I also conducted that whole session in Spanish. By the end of it he was so confused, I think he actually believed he was in Spain! It was very funny to see.

I do 'white room' therapy also. This is a tiled room with medical equipment where I do examinations and colonic hydrotherapy and electric's. As I know a lot about the body through studying nutritional medicine, I'll *never* do anything that I'm not confident about or I feel is not safe. The medical room creates the same feeling of fear and anticipation as the dungeon. It brings back all those feelings of going to the hospital or the dentist. Discipline is a very interesting subject, too, because there is the challenge of *not* leaving marks. You have to be quite skilled to do that. The cane has got a very special pain with it. One or two of my clients just want to see how much pain they can endure, which can be quite interesting. I haven't got any particular passion, though. I enjoy a whole range of activities. After all, this is my hobby as well as my job. I'm genuinely interested in it. But it is a very expensive hobby!

I don't really go out of my way to see transvestites, as it's not a subject I'm particularly interested in. I do have some lingerie, but that's used more with humiliation. It's the same with 'adult babies'. I don't have anything against it, I'm just not that interested. Unless, of course, the person is interested in the same things as me and we can incorporate their fantasy with my games. But, if I have to enter completely into *their* game, then I'm not interested. For instance, if a TV wants discipline too, then that's okay. Does that make sense?

My other interest is nutrition and all aspects of bodily health, so I'm always happy to offer that service, too. The dungeon is quite separate, so there is no need for a 'normal' patient to be any the wiser. However, having said that, it's very strange how one thing can lead to another! I had a person come for a 'colonic' once, and he was a few minutes late. When I joked that I would have to punish him, I could tell straight away that he was interested in spanking. Now he comes regularly for domination sessions. So, you could say the clinic works well for me in *all* respects!

I don't go to fetish clubs or scene parties that much, because I don't like all that posing. Maybe I'm just boring! I get to do enough posing in front of a camera anyway, so I don't think I have to prove anything to anyone. But I'm always looking for things I can incorporate into my games. Even somewhere as 'normal' as a garden centre, you'll be thinking "that's an interesting bit of rope" or whatever. For instance, I once used a little paint brush to circle a woman's clitoris until she had an orgasm. I'll also look out for special stones on the beach that I can roll around the tip of the penis. For a man, it feels just like a blow-job! It's not just about pain, but about pure sensation. It's the whole spectrum of things. What is the *most* painful thing is when you have so much pleasure and can't get release.

I really do get a lot of personal pleasure out of my work. I wouldn't be doing this otherwise. And, if the number of my regular slaves is any indication, they're also fairly content. It's always nice when people come back to see me again and, of course, it is much easier to explore the limits of someone I know. Some of the people I see have been very surprised at our lifestyle and the fact that we are just normal, sane people! One American guy from New York who came here told us the last so-called 'mistress' he'd been to had had her boyfriend sitting at the kitchen table cleaning his nails with a flick knife! It's the sublime to the ridiculous in this business!

MISTRESS MIDORI

Born in the ancient Japanese capital of Kyoto and raised in the high-tech city of Tokyo, Midori is the daughter of a Japanese mother and German-American father. Both her parents are university professors. Following a varied and successful career in the United States Army and in commerce, she now works as a professional dominatrix in San Francisco. Incidentally, this is the only interview in the book that was conducted over the Internet, hence the rather stilted and premeditated style of the dialogue. Despite my own dislike for this particular medium, I decided to keep this one in as it seemed to me to be tantamount to a 'master-class' in how a professional American mistress presents herself to the world. Interviewed September 2000.

I had a very unique multi-cultural upbringing that combined Japanese and German-American influences with feminism and a fierce devotion to individuality. It's a background that brings a distinctive edge to my play, I think. I moved to the States as a teenager, where I attended and graduated from the University of California at Berkeley. I studied psychology with an emphasis on neurobiology. Shortly thereafter, I enlisted in the US Army. I eventually received my commission as an intelligence officer attached to Soviet Tactical Intelligence. I'm also airborne trained and an expert marksman. Since then, I've also been successful in the corporate world, but eventually turned my back on it to pursue my true passion of SM.

My current hobbies include working out as well as many outdoor sports. I'm extremely passionate about shoe shopping and enjoy vintage fashion collecting, too. My ultimate fantasy would be to combine world travel with the elegant couture of the 19th century (steamer trunks full of exquisite gowns and with all the sherpas and servants to carry them!) with a grand spirit of adventure; canoeing down the Amazon, trekking the Silk Road in the footsteps of Marco Polo and living among the tribesmen of some exotic rainforest!

I also like very physical sports. I guess I'm a real thrill seeker! The vibrant pleasure of living is reinforced everytime I push myself in a physical or mental challenge. I'm very athletic and routinely enjoy snow-boarding, skiing, kayaking and white-water rafting. I'm even considering eco-adventure racing. I thrive on living life to the fullest, and I'm *very* greedy when it comes to gaining pleasure and experiences. I don't want to waste my time on the vulgar or the mundane.

Fetish for me is a visual, tactile and sensual passion. It's something that triggers my erotic desires and stirs my imagination. It pleasures my animal soul as well as stimulates my intellectual fancy. When anthropologists speak of a 'fetish', they usually mean a religious or spiritual object. Something to focus belief on. My definition is the contemporary usage of the term, as applied to clinical psychology, as well as to popular sexual reference. We're talking about two different things here, because the term has deviated substantially from its original meaning. The word 'fetish' has currently been applied to everything from Zuni amulets to fashion trends, and from sexual novelties to an enthusiast's hobby, and even to sexual dysfunction! My own personal fetishes include shoes and boots, fur, leather and corsets. Those are the things that come to mind immediately, but there are many other things that turn me on in the right situation. The 'second skin' of latex provides a sensual contact, yet denies the animal touch.

I've noticed there's a greater availability of leather in the United States. I've also found in the US that there's a greater influence from cowboys and leather-men in our fetish shops. Here, on the West Coast, we're very influenced by our pan-Pacific heritage, of course. For me, it seems that Europe taps into fashion tradition, and also has a strong history of elegant balls and costumed festivals, which we lack on this side of the Atlantic, unfortunately. Americans, however, have a legacy of organisations, tribes and cultures from which we draw our archetypal imagery. For example, the military, ethnic costuming, motorcycle gangs and even labourer's coveralls. I think that the popular rise in fetish imagery is a by-product of urbanisation, industrialisation and commodifiction of human sexuality. The desire for the 'genital' has been replaced by a desire for manufactured objects.

I think my success in the fetish world is due to the fact that I am a *real* woman, and not just a two dimensional visual icon or an SM caricature. What I bring to all my scenes and performances is intellect, physicality, as well as my own beauty. I bridge the gap between many worlds and communities. My charm appeals to both the SM and fetish worlds, as well as the mainstream community.

NANNY LILLY

Adult Babies are traditionally the most misunderstood, certainly the most marginalised, of our fetish sub-cultures. Even amongst die-hard 'pervs' the idea of a grown man sucking his thumb in a cot whilst dressed up like Shirley Temple's baby brother is viewed as a bit odd, to say the least, and is invariably guaranteed to raise a snigger or two. French-born Nanny Lilly has devoted herself to the nurturing and (when needed) the chastisement of her Big Baby charges. Here she shares her experiences and understanding of this little known area of eroticism, providing along the way a fascinating insight into the world of infantilism. Interviewed June 1994.

One day last summer, as I was going about some errands, I witnessed a scene in the street that was to have a profound effect on me. In front of me, a little boy of around one year old was walking along beside his mummy. Much to my surprise and bewilderment, his mummy suddenly grabbed the child and lifted him high up in the air to sniff his nappy. They must have been very soiled, because she gave a loud cry of disgust. The confused infant, who was still hanging in mid-air, looked over at me with an expression of shock and humiliation on his face at his undignified treatment. It was a common enough maternal scene. But, as I stood there watching, the thought flashed through my mind that perhaps such an experience could shape the future sexual tastes or inclinations of an adult male when confronting his own mixed feelings about why he should secretly crave to wet or soil his nappies and how this should, in turn, provoke a strong sexual arousal.

I'm not a psychologist, nor do I have any interest in becoming one. But as a professional nanny, I have been exposed to the amazing, yet delicately torturous labyrinth of the fetishist male's quest to regress emotionally into his own past through his sexuality. Any person seriously involved in any of the many and varied paths of sub/dom knows that someone can seek a regression through cross-dressing or through humiliation, servitude, helplessness or pain. Why should wanting to be a schoolboy or baby again be regarded as any less marginal?

Infantilism remains a subject that is rarely spoken about. It is neglected and often ridiculed, even amongst so-called 'open minded' fetishists! They remain a section of the fetishist community that is not very well understood at all. Unfortunately, due to their misrepresentation, a large majority remain firmly locked in their own closets. Here, they fantasise guiltily about the security of being a baby once more; the lack of responsibilities, the tenderness of the mother or the warmth of a breast feeding. There is also the intense sexual connotations whenever the mummy or nanny changes the soiled nappy or gives the adult-baby an enema or cleanses his genitals before cuddling him back in the cot in his plastic knickers to protect the bed against any further mess. She will also make him feel precious by dressing him in a pink frilly dress or flannelette baby-boy pyjamas.

All of these details can become powerfully arousing to a lot of adult babies and, needless to say, they have *nothing* whatever to do with 'real' children! These scenarios about bondage in the cot or rubber wear are coming directly from one's own childhood emotions and the profound impact of first sexual memories, whether consciously or subsconciously. These are some of my insights into the world of the adult baby gleaned from my wide experiences of pampering and punishing them, and listening to the most intimate emotions they so trustingly confide in me. Role-playing has the most marvellous benefits in bringing out the best in a person; whether they be an adult-baby, a school boy or 'school-girl', a transvestite tart or as maid or a medical patient or whatever. I have seen some adult-babies nearly crying from the sheer joy that comes from finally being able to express their fantasies! And, believe me, some can be rather on the naughty side! Yet, all my adult-babies know I will always respect their vulnerability and lead them through their regression.

I'm afraid all this is beginning to sound ever so serious! One should not forget that humour can sometimes play an important part in a scenario. For instance, I remember one 'beginner-baby' who literally ran to the cot faster than a fireman! Before I had time to blink an eye he was already stark naked and clutching his teddy bear! When I told this Big-Baby that I had never seen such eagerness before, he simply replied, somewhat mischievously, that he thought he had better jump in the cot quick before he changed his mind!

Throughout the session I often see the adult-baby revealing a freshness in his face; some sort of transformation takes place that makes him lose twenty, thirty, even forty years off the hardened expression of manhood. To me, this is beautiful and makes me feel my job is worthwhile. He finds himself back when he was a little boy juggling with his first images of sexuality through humiliation, pain, helplessness or devotion. I see this man transforming under my control with tears of happiness in his eyes. Cruelty doesn't have any meaning here and is a total stranger to this delicate and intimate moment.

One thing that never fails to make me smile is when I hear one of my transvestites say: "I will never understand how someone can actually *enjoy* a caning!" Or a bondage lover who comments: "I can't get it into my head how anyone would want to be treated like a baby". Then there is the adult-baby who asks: "How can someone want to be your house-duty slave?" Or the corporal punishment fanatic: "What does a man get out of wearing women's clothes?"

At the end of the day, any erotic treatment that is safe and mutually consensual is meant for relaxation, escape and the expression of our prohibitions. Some fetishists out there might well find something to giggle about in image of playing 'mummy', and that I will concede to allow the adult-baby a glimpse of my thighs or, as 'nanny', I will let him smell my knickers after a sound spanking. It would be an invasion of privacy to reveal more, but I assume that there will be quite a few males reading this who can put themselves back in their imagination to such a tender age and are able to recall the vivid sexual feelings they experienced looking at teacher's breasts or nanny's bottom or, dare I say it, mummy's stockings!

LADY CLAUDETTE

For the dedicated fetishist, no trip to the German city of Munich would be complete without a stopover at the studio of Lady Claudette, otherwise rather aptly named 'Bizarradise'. The true connoisseur of outrageous eroticism will find everything on offer and even the more unusual tastes happily accommodated in this liberal, or rather less conservative, oasis of traditionally ultra right-wing Bavaria. Lady Claudette herself is a petite, deceptively soft-spoken brunette who originally started out in the cosmetics industry as a representative for a large company. Like many before her, she originally encountered the SM scene through a relationship. Interviewed August 1995

I had a friend who had masochistic tendencies. I didn't know anything about SM then, until this friend introduced me to it on an intimate level. The relationship broke up, but I knew that with my next boyfriend it would have to be the same. Above all, I was curious to know everything I could about it. Back in the early days, I didn't know any of the private circles. I didn't even know such things existed. And I certainly didn't go into sex shops to buy literature on the subject. However, I did get hold of one of those contact magazines, but it was all full of adverts from professional ladies. So I made a decision then to take some unpaid leave and use the time to look around and simply find out what there was to know. Besides, I thought, at least it would give me the opportunity to meet the kind of men who would suit my interests!

I did a little round trip, first through Stuttgart, but up there I found no demand for a dominatrix. I could have worked as a maid, but that was completely out of the question, naturally! I found out from a friend that there was a vacancy here in Munich. That was here in my present studio. I learnt a lot from this mistress but, looking back, I don't think she had what it takes. Not many clients came and eventually she couldn't pay the rent and had to leave. The proprietor came to me and asked if I would like to take over. I had to make a decision then and there. Because I had already enjoyed myself enormously during the short time I had worked there, I said to myself: "Yes, sure. Before I go back to my old job, why not make my hobby into a profession?" That was back in 1991.

Getting a studio here in Munich is very difficult. Because of the 'No-Go' district, it is restricted to a very small area. The walls in this type of studio have to be quite high, so the cost would increase by about 70%. And then, if you just mention your trade to a potential landlord, he'd rather not let his property at all than rent it to you! Munich is tremendously conservative, as you probably know.

The studio now consists of four main rooms. The first, known as The Leather Room or sometimes, more provocatively as The Cuddle-Up Room, has a bed with four chains where one can tie somebody down really well with arms and legs apart. There's a pulley which can be used to hoist a client up to any height you want above the bed. We've also got a full wardrobe with everything from rubber knickers to catsuits and even rubber suspension suits. Everything is included in the price and all the clothes are in extra large size. I feel that, even though the outfit might be a little loose on a really small person, the main thing is actually the *feel* of rubber against the skin.

Next comes The Marble Room, complete with metal bar for tying up slaves. There are two columns with tying up devices. One of these has a leather harness which tightly fixes a client to the column. Also, there's a rack with metal candle holders. Various play gadgets and some fifteen different masks hang from the wall. The Marble Room gets its feel, as the name suggests, from the flooring made from finest Italian marble, as well as its marble columns.

Besides this, there is The Torture Chamber with a pillory, a punishment horse, cross and a solid wrought iron cage. The whole ambiance is decidedly medieval! Next, we come to The White Room, more commonly known as The Clinic, for doctor/nurse games. This room is divided into two areas. The first, The Treatment Room, has a gynaecological chair, couch and all the medical equipment necessary to offer the patient an unforgettable stay of classic luxury. There's also our Wet Room for lovers of toilet games, with a single toilet and a shower for each guest and lots of space to lay out a client. To ensure absolute hygiene, the floors and walls of both rooms are finished with tiles. Outside there is The Open Space where we have at our disposal a playing field of over 150 square metres surrounded by a three metre high wooden fence to ensure absolute privacy from the prying eyes of the 'normal folk'!

I currently employ four females slaves and three mistresses. The degree to which a client can 'go' with a hired slave depends on the individual girl. Some girls can't take very much, admittedly, and tend to work more as maids. For others, even a good hard lashing that results in whelts would be quite acceptable. Above all, I can assure you, all my slave girls really enjoy it! This is an important factor for me. I make absolutely sure that they have just the right predisposition for the job – which means they love it! Two of my slave girls, in particular, are able to take a considerable degree of harsh treatment. They couldn't do it for money alone. Imagine if you were tied up and required to take fifty lashes on your backside. Maybe you could stand it for half an hour or so. But if it went on for another hour, then either your psyche has had it or you are really into it yourself. There has to be a tendency towards it. I know that's how it was for me.

I'm not suggesting a girl will reach an orgasm with *every* client, because obviously empathy and chemistry play an important part in any scenario. But it can happen that a client, who at first seems unappealing, does the training so well that the sparks really do fly! Sometimes a woman will come out of the room and tell me how fantastic it was!

My slave-girls are all very well experienced in their chosen field and, no matter how excited they may be getting, never let things get out of control. If a client doesn't know how to use the whip properly and goes for the thighs or the spine with too much force, we use a code word to stop the action and the girl will explain to him what she can endure. If they still can't manage to come to some agreement, we'll give the client his money back and suggest he come to a demonstration evening. These evenings are a unique part of the life of the Studio, in which clients new to the scene can learn and understand all its aspects with a particular emphasis on safety. I have noticed that, unfortunately, there are some people who have no idea what SM is all about. They probably think the slave is like a piece of meat they can just hit as hard as they like. I started these demonstrations to show that the whole thing is something more than that!

These Community Education evenings are not for small talk or hesitation. You go for it! All those present are educated according to their disposition, and I will expect them to dress strictly fetish. The classes take place every two weeks, and always with a particular theme. Sometimes there are 'slave only' evenings where slave girls from our house, as well as private guests, are demonstrated on, either by a mistress or by their own masters. Other evenings might be mixed and include both male and female slaves, and are designed to show the various ways a whip can be used. For example, how to gradually increase the force instead of hitting too hard right from the start.

My team and I will also explain how to deal with weights; how many one should use and how to proceed with care. Sometimes there are evenings where they demonstrate The Clinic. Here the 'patient' will get examined by a male or female 'doctor'. Various areas of expertise covered here are catheter or bladder cleaning. I, myself, have gained a proficient level of medical expertise to enable me to carry this out competently and safely. I have acquired all my knowledge from 'real' doctors. My acquaintances taught me everything, particularly when I first began. There was always a doctor at my side, an emergency surgeon who also took part in the demonstration evenings.

Generally, I'll limit the number of people present at any one of these evenings to twenty. The demonstration will take place in the middle of the room and the people stand around the sides. Sometimes the visitors are involved as well. They help with the tying up or are even allowed to caress the slave. But there is strictly no sex-play. The absolute beginner or committed voyeur has also the chance to experience SM live as a spectator during the weekday evenings. Education from soft to hard! The show features mostly female slaves, but male slaves are rigorously handled too! No dress code is required for these display evenings. There are also regular fetish nights here which offer a relaxed atmosphere, whatever your sex or sexual orientation. Naturally, strict fetish clothing is compulsory for these theme parties, which are arranged in co-operation with a local private SM club called *Aktives Munchen*.

There is a strict procedure to follow if one wants to attend a personal session at this studio. First, the prospective client makes a telephone appointment. When he or she arrives (the studio also receives visits from couples and, very occasionally, a visit from a lone woman) we will talk briefly about their wishes, with particular regard to their pain threshold. I consider everything else totally superfluous. We don't need to make a detailed plan of action. I find it important that the girls are able to do their job well and that they have enough fantasy skills and the necessary sensitivity. If someone gives us an exact description of what they want then, of course, we'll do it. We also cater for TV training and have a wide range of clothes, shoes, wigs, make-up and silicon breasts for that purpose.

I'm also very clear with clients concerning where the borderline is involving sexual intimacy. Sex is *not* part of the agenda with any of the mistresses, of course. We keep it strictly separate. A woman takes either the part of a dominatrix or a devotee. There is a limit to how much a mistress will allow herself to be caressed. My absolute borderlines are my thighs. However, we do have mistresses here who will allow a licking to go much further. It depends entirely on their own preferences. Sexual intercourse with a dominatrix is, as I said earlier, an absolute taboo here. But a different rule applies for slaves. After all, that's why they're slaves! Within reason, they have to be game for anything. They must be prepared to kneel down and lick feet or lick anything else the client may desire!

My slaves work two days, then have four days off to recuperate. When a girl comes back she'll be in good form and looking forward to the next session. It would be too much to do this five days a week. She just wouldn't be able to give her best and the whole act would become mechanical.

I'm afraid clients expecting a session with me personally will be likely to be disappointed. I don't do training very often these days, but I do stand in if necessary. My main work is taking care of the organisation and staff. It's important to me that every one of my guests leaves here completely satisfied, and that's only possible if I keep an overall picture of what's going on. It's a pity in some ways, because we used to be smaller and things were easier to manage. But the clients are happy; more women means more variety, after all!

MISTRESS CASSANDRA PAYNE

A one-time leading light on the Canadian fetish scene, Mistress Cassandra was based in Vancouver, British Columbia. Since this interview was conducted, however, and following some bad experiences at the hands of her manipulative Number One Boy, she has now *quit the fetish scene altogether and moved back to Toronto, where she has resumed her former career as a beautician.* Interviewed April 1995

I'm originally from Toronto, and was involved in the fetish scene there for about twelve years. Sadly, the scene there has gone the same way as most serious scenes in recent years; that is, a victim of repressive government policies, opportunistic retailers and a sudden influx of self-styled 'experts' in the fetish world who feel the need to 'educate'. Government policies can be fought (albeit slowly) and money-grabbing hucksters can, and should, be avoided like the plague. Unfortunately, well meaning, but ill-prepared, pendants do more harm than good to a thriving fetish scene and, short of some discipline around the head with a blunt instrument, are almost impossible to stop!

I learned to be a dominatrix by starting out with an assertive nature, asking a lot of questions of dominants whose skills I admired, and taking a thousand baby steps on my own towards achieving the technical expertise I knew I needed. The psychological acumen a dominatrix requires is gained only through experience. I have led a dominant lifestyle for the last fourteen years and have performed almost six and a half thousand sessions, and yet not a day goes by that I don't gain some new insight into the dominant/submissive dynamic. It boggles the mind that there are people out there with, at most, three years experience, actually teaching courses on how to be a 'professional dominatrix'! It's bad enough that 'kink' is being turned into some odd form of 'pop psychology', with discussion seminars and support groups, but to have some poorly trained dominant 'wannabe' committing untold unpleasantries on potentially valuable slaves is at best frustrating and, at worst, downright dangerous! We need more good slaves, not more bad dominatrixes! There are, at most, five people in the world actually qualified to teach 'kink', in my opinion. Sadly, only one of them is doing it. Kudos to the excellent

Cleo DuBois! I will now get down off my soap-box!

I like attention to detail at Payne Manor, but only within the bounds of good taste. I began offering my dungeon as a bed and breakfast several months ago, advertising through word of mouth and in 'select' fetish magazines. The response has been enthusiastic, to say the least! Vancouver is a splendid tourist destination, located as it is between the mountains and the sea, and Payne Manor is a convenient fifteen minutes drive from almost everything. Kinky couples staying here have access to golf, boating, shopping and night life, while residing in relative luxury in a state of the art dungeon. I get to meet the nicest people, too!

I've been thinking a lot about house slaves recently, as I am in the process of interviewing candidates for some vacancies on my staff. However, after two solid weeks of 'auditions', I've sadly concluded that 99.9% of the submissives who covet a semi-permanent position don't have the faintest clue as to what this entails, or even know what's required of a successful candidate. Admittedly, a good house slave is a rare commodity, but from my experiences over the past fortnight, it would seem that this years crop of candidates is the poorest quality ever! I have kept slaves for fourteen years and am *always* on the lookout for quality stock, but I'm totally at a loss for an explanation to the present lack of talent. Perhaps the current glut of 'nouveau dominas' has resulted in a lowering of standards, or maybe the polarisation of sub-dom culture worldwide has diluted the slave pool with dabblers and hangers-on? While not all mistresses will agree with my opinions or standards, I feel that any house slave candidate who adopts what I suggest will be well on his way to achieving his goal. In any case, the situation warrants a comment or two, at the very least. So, indulge me here, while I get this off my chest!

Firstly, when I advertise for house slaves, I am *not* looking for a sexual partner! You should not try and impress me with your genital endowment or tales of oral abilities! I want someone to serve me, not service me! While the scene has a highly charged sexual aura surrounding it, the fact is that sex in itself is actually nothing more than one tool out of many available to a capable dominatrix. I can't stress enough that it is a dirty, largely communicable world out there. Aids, and the various strains of Hepatitis are only the tip of the iceberg. I plan to grow to a ripe old age, and have no intention of risking my health in the pursuit of house slaves!

I follow my usual screening process when examining each days postal applications from would-be slaves. Obviously, if there is no self addressed envelope or token, the letter is immediately consigned to the trash without even being read! If, on the other hand, the letter is sincere, genuine and captures my attention, it gets placed in a document folder for my further consideration come bedtime. I prefer to do my correspondence at night when distractions are minimised. It's interesting to note that fully 80% of the letters I receive are scrapped; a statistic matched by most of my mistress friends. I think there's a lesson here for all aspiring slaves!

I have no interest in listening to a long list of what you would like me to do to you. I have professional clients who pay me lots of money for the privilege of having me consider such requests. Being a house slave is about you doing things that I want done, *not* the other way around! In the context of rewards and punishments associated with your training, I am more than capable of deciding what, where, when and why, without your assistance!

Being a house slave is, to quote my Number One Boy: "Not a gig for the faint of heart". The hours are long and the tasks, shall we say, 'challenging'. I once had a candidate who neglected to inform me of his diabetic condition. While I appreciated his enthusiasm and dedication, his succumbing to insulin shock whilst doing the windows was a terrifying experience for both of us! Luckily, we both survived the experience and remain good friends to this day, but he would be the first to admit that he wasn't up to the task at hand.

If there is any qualification which I would deem most important for a slave, it would have to be 'honesty'. I don't care if you have a wife, but if there is a chance I might encounter her, I'd better be aware of her existence. And I don't care if you've got millions (though it would be nice), just don't make claims or promises that you can't deliver. You'll never be able to make up a story that would impress me more than an honest, heartfelt admission of your devotion and submission.

There's no such thing as a free lunch! Remember that phrase? When you apply to be a house slave, you enter into the 'real world' of domination and submission. It's not like you imagine, not even close. Contrary to popular belief, a dominatrix doesn't roll out of bed in the morning wearing skin-tight leather catsuits, six-inch heels and full theatrical make-up. I won't be standing over you wielding a riding crop while you wash the floor, either. Nor will you receive a fully involved two hour session just for showing up on time!

I have a busy, active life, which is one of the reasons I need slaves. My whole household is busy and active, too. We actually have a lot of fun and, yes, there is a definite 'kink' to the ambiance of each and every day! The successful house slave candidate is an active part of such a household, part of a team of skilled, dedicated slaves whose main reason 'to be' is to serve to the needs of a worthy dominatrix. Yes, there are parties, but there are also dirty dishes and filthy toilets. It is the *real* world, little man. And, if you remember that, you'll not be disappointed.

Your job is do 'things'. So make sure you know *how* to do things! Like carpentry, leatherwork, horticulture and fabric care. Washing windows and knowing which end of the vacuum cleaner sucks is not enough anymore. You must have skills and you *must* be prepared to use them. And don't lie about what you can do, either. I'll be really pissed off and, if that happens, you won't enjoy the experience!

I can't bear stupid slaves – or stupid people in general, for that matter! This isn't the same as being smart. This is a warning not to screw up! Accidentally *or* on purpose. If I give instructions, follow them to the letter. Take notes if you have to, but get the job done. And get it done on time – and to specification! I'm a reasonable person and I won't make outrageous demands. I remember I once sent a slave out to pay some bills. He got on the bus and then got lost. And I mean *really* lost! He didn't even have the sense to ask someone for directions or call me for an update. He stayed lost for five and a half hours and my bills didn't get paid. He didn't know enough ways to apologise for his colossal cock-up. Needless to say, he was fired on the spot. I will tolerate the occasional error, if it's an honest mistake. And, naturally, you will be punished for it. But, if you intentionally err, in an attempt to goad me into disciplining you, I will know it and, as I said earlier, you won't enjoy the experience!

A dominatrix is just like any other girl – she likes to get gifts! Flowers, clothing, automobiles! Don't spend outside your budget, but don't be cheap either. I once had a slave who brought me a used broom and dustpan as a present! This man was a highly placed politician with an investment portfolio worth millions and, I'm *not* joking, a collection of antique automobiles! Don't get the impression that I'm greedy, but I viewed his so-called gift as insulting, pure and simple. That display of disrespect earned him a curt invitation to depart.

As I learn about your abilities, you should learn about my needs. Anticipate them, and act accordingly. There's a definite hierarchy among the slaves of an extended household, with everyone jockeying for Number One Boy status. Friendly competition makes for a vibrant stable, and the most versatile, indispensable slave does enjoy privileges as befits his rank.

My current Number One Boy, Kris, has held that position for three years now, and the lengths he's gone to in order to maintain that exalted state are almost comical! Once, while I was in the process of auditioning equipment 'techies', Kris took it upon himself to build me a St. Andrew's Cross and a vaulting horse (both quite attractive and functional, I have to say), but he then decided to use only his Swiss Army knife and a house brick to complete the task! It took him two days, during which time he also managed to handle 60% of the domestic duties as well! His hands looked like hamburgers when he was done, but he had proved himself to me.

I've had Kris for five years now. Originally, I took him from another mistress and, right from the start of my ownership of him, I had subjected him to the most intense training and conditioning in order to bring his natural submissiveness to full fruition. He's now my most reliable slave, and serves me as my executive assistant, aide de camp, general lackey and convenient whipping boy! He's also the only slave I've ever seen fit to have branded with my personal initials as a life long symbol of his servitude to me. Today, he wears my insignia proudly on his left shoulder. He took the branding very well, staring off into space and muttering his pain mantra under his breath. He never flinched once as the branding iron struck, burning the stylised CP motif into his flesh. A year after coming into my service, he quit his successful rock band to accompany me across the country from Toronto in order to attend to all my needs as I established myself in this wonderful city.

I cherish all my slaves, especially the ones I've trained to my standards. In return, I know my slaves cherish me. The hardest slave to train is the one who has bounced around from one mistress to the next, staying only a few months with each, picking up bits and pieces of training, but never completely committing. I'm usually hesitant to accept such a slave, since he has so many bad habits to break – not to mention questionable loyalty! If you're lucky enough to be accepted by a mistress, commit for at least a one year contract and immerse yourself totally in her world. You'll find your patience rewarded many times over, I can assure you.

The camaraderie between slaves that inevitably develops 'below stairs' can often lead, amazingly enough, to strong friendships. I know of at least one successful rock band whose members met in the stable of a well-known mistress! The role of the house slave is definitely a fulfiling one for the *true* submissive who is aware of the demands of the position, and is prepared to put the time and the energy into serving his mistress with subtlety, precision and humour.

Obviously, these points only touch on the broad issues a house slave candidate should consider. Each mistress will undoubtedly place a different emphasis on these requirements. But, if you take what I've said on board, you're definitely going to be prepared mentally for the job. Believe me, it's well worth the effort because a fully developed mistress/house slave relationship is as rich and as full as any relationship you'll ever experience.

GODDESS DIANNA VESTA

Dianna Vesta is both a life-style and professional dominatrix, as well as highly successful businesswoman. Residing in South Florida, she publishes the monthly fetish magazine 'Attitude', and runs a worldwide organisation called The Fetish Network. Interviewed July 1994.

In 1968, when I was ten years old, it was apparent to everyone around me that there was something very *different* about me! My strong persona extended way beyond what might be called aggressive. 'Stubborn' was my middle name! That's what my mother used to call me, anyway. Although I tended to cause a lot of trouble, my parents seemed to recognise my creative ability to manipulate circumstances to my advantage. At this age, I told my father I would no longer be going to Catholic Mass with them. I felt instinctively that my life had a different destiny. Luckily, he didn't press the issue. He did, however, continue to invite me each and every Sunday.

It was at this young age that I began to realise our world and our God was *all* male! I didn't like the roles women were forced to play. I read the Bible and the books required at school. I also borrowed books from the library. Hour after hour I would day dream about a world I created. I remember crying sometimes because I thought something was wrong with me. I was totally out of 'sync' with the rest of the world and everyone around me.

I played a lot of challenging sports with boys at the time, and particularly enjoyed tackle football. Once I jumped to tackle this boy. I flew at him and knocked him to the ground. He was older than I was, and no one expected a boy to whimper. Holding back his tears, he removed himself from the game. I still remember the sensations I had over that experience. It was sheer power-surge! My heart raced with excitement. I felt a drawing and pulling sensation crawl up the inside of my thighs, and my head became very light. His total defeat excited me beyond anything I could understand at the time!

Through the years I kept most of my religious and personal philosophies to myself. I enjoyed Greek mythology. Unfortunately, at that time, there were very few books that focused on matriarchal attitudes, so I developed my own little world and practiced my own solitary religion. Over the years I cultivated a special energy. I've been asked many times if this energy (that is my 'dominance'), is a reaction to a negative experience in my childhood. Maybe. This goes back to how I viewed our world as being so male, and about the devaluation of women, as I saw it. Women seemed to hold it altogether and, to me anyway, were far more spiritually, emotionally and physically complex. Birth and procreation seemed more god-like, more of a miracle than man's god-like image. I believe *all* women have been exposed to some of the animal instincts of masculine energy. Some survive and some don't. All women have been violated to some degree and it's socially accepted. I knew I wasn't going to accept this as *my* destiny! However, I needed a way to balance this extreme energy. I had to find a truth that I would recognise.

My cultivated powers of persuasion helped me move very fast in the world. I dated some highly intelligent and successful men, and always found it challenging to take their power! I absorbed their knowledge and penetrated internal areas where no one had ever been–certainly no woman! Ultimately, I would break their hearts. I have always felt far superior to any of them. Even to this day these men are in love with me and they hate it. Their words are usually something like: "Why do you exist to torment me?"

I then married a boy ten years younger than myself. I ran my own company by this time, and was very successful. I taught him and showed him how to be the man I wanted. This man moved elegantly in social circles, yet this *boy* crawled to me at home. With this impressionable young boy I explored a sexuality that was considered very forbidden in the circles we frequented. For the most part, he stayed home doing everything a woman is normally expected to do for her husband. This role-reversal was unknown to many in my 'other' business world. I travelled a lot, and in every city I seemed to be able to find some man to do my bidding. Sometimes an eager bell-boy, sometimes an executive at 'happy hour', or sometimes both! Let's just say, I found many ways to entertain myself! My husband and I explored cross-dressing, anal play, bondage, servitude and very intense levels of humiliation. I would have him serve me and a couple of my most trusted girlfriends. After a few years, though, I began to neglect him and he took off.

I dated *both* men and women during this period. Women were submissive to me in a different kind of way. Their submission seemed to me more like an earned prize, whereas I just expected it from men. At this time, the words and the 'theatrics' of domination were not present yet. My female lovers felt uncomfortable with my dominance over men and tried very hard to replace my need for them, but were unsuccessful. I enjoyed dominant sex with men too much, and I liked having them at my service.

In 1988, a friend of mine called me a 'dominatrix'. I didn't know what the hell he was talking about! It was the first time I had ever heard the word. He told me about the clubs he went to in New York and some of the professional dominatrixes he knew there. By this time, I was tired of the double life I was leading and wanted to know more about this world. One day he brought over a bunch of films and magazines. For the next two days, I scrolled through their pages and watched some of the more bizarre forms of sexual expression. To be honest, a lot of it didn't appeal to me. It seemed kind of 'lower end' of the market and didn't seem like anything I was doing myself.

At the time I didn't do anything about it. However, it didn't leave my mind either. I thought a lot about the women in the magazines and analysed their behaviour and the behaviour of the men involved. It didn't catch my attention at first, but later on it occurred to me that these magazines, much like ordinary pornography, were written and published by men! I examined them more carefully and decided to test the waters myself. Having had a lot of experience with advertising and promotions, I began placing a couple of ads in the classifieds and in some of the contact magazines. The ad read: 'Aggressive woman seeks passive man in high heels'.

The letters flocked to my post office box. It was time consuming and tiring to go through them all, and it didn't take a rocket scientist to figure out that a lot of these guys purposefully exploited the game. I made an attempt to become a professional dominatrix and charged high fees to wear leather costumes and use some stupid implements that some of these men brought to me. But I already knew that the most important implement in my arsenal was my mind and that I *already* had that power. At times, I felt more like a common prostitute catering to their bizarre fantasies, while dressed in some kind of *Barbie Doll* fetish attire! I soon realised this was not for me. It wasn't difficult finding the clientele and the money was most definitely overwhelming. Most of the men were white collar businessmen in high stressed jobs or very shy, quiet types. Some of them became friends and I still see them.

Yet, I *still* wanted a way to expose myself to the 'scene' proper. After writing for some of the S&M tabloids, I soon became very well known. I went to New York and rented an apartment there, travelling back and forth to Florida. Eventually, I was able to give up my previous career and could focus on building up a network where people could openly learn about creative play. Having been a victim of misunderstanding myself, I realised that there were a lot of other people out there experiencing the same things I had.

I also realised that there was an awareness that was changing the consciousness of both men and women. Men were forced into roles they couldn't always live up to. They would constantly have to harness their insecurity and their fear of defeat. As women have become more independent over the years, it has only served to intensify their insecurities. The whole sexual arena began to take on a new form. I've studied and analysed these behaviours and read a lot of research from Erikson and Freud to Jung. My Jungian research provided me with more real recognisable truths than the others. My sessions, regardless of their nature, provided many of these men with a therapy they couldn't receive from 'normal' psychology. The simple fact that I actually *cared* enough about human destiny and was willing to extend my knowledge into these esoteric levels of human expression did, in fact, qualify me to help these people explore new aspects of themselves.

I believe that role-play and self exploration are an holistic form of self-discovery. Sometimes a good dose of 'counterbalance' is all a busy executive needs to alleviate high levels of stress. Sometimes we need that other world, because we feel it's a very real part of us. The trick is to 'integrate' it into an already existing lifestyle, and not allow any one part of you to become obsessive. In a world with Aids and a total disregard for sexual intimacy, I feel that role-play and S&M 'alternatives' are a futuristic approach to exploring each other. I envisage psychology eventually becoming obsolete in many areas as human awareness excels. I can also see violent crimes diminishing as forms of role-play and self expression become socially acceptable and taught as an integral part of human interaction.

Imagine the frustration someone might feel when they are confused about an emotional aspect of life and told they are 'sick'. They enter into therapy only to find, after years of sessions, that there isn't really a cure for what they are feeling! Think how that person, who has harboured fantasies that do not fall into so-called 'normal' behaviour, is emotionally *forced* into believing themselves to be strange and unacceptable. It doesn't surprise me that their psyche would rebel. It also wouldn't surprise me if it constantly created interruptions throughout their entire lives, causing limited growth.

I enjoy Female Domination. I enjoy watching a male shake at the sight of me because he realises that I have power over him. He is prepared to relinquish his power to me and surrender his will. He is willing to do *whatever* it takes to please me. I look at this man on his knees and in absolute fear, and yet with the strength of a king, ready to accept any challenge his queen bestows upon him for the sake of her happiness. I look at this man as being superior to other men *because* of his submission to me! I accept his offering as a prize far more valuable than anything else he could offer. These men are my allies. My trusted confidants and assistants in my journey to know myself. This man understands female priorities, and I would consider *only* these men to be my equal!

I suppose I have a passive side, too. Sometimes I feel like a little girl, and my attitude might become very playful or melancholy. However, I think my nature is *definitely* dominant. I can't share intimacy unless I have respect for someone. My dominant expression will often test those who pursue me until they have proven themselves worthy to enter this world I've spent a lifetime to create and nurture. I'm willing to sacrifice whatever it takes and to wait patiently, sometimes for years, just to experience the erotic heights I encounter from the perfect fusion of dominance and submission. Highs that are so high that almost *anything* can take place, providing that person has succeeded in reaching the inner core of my being.

While waiting for these moments, I want to teach other people and set a positive example. I want to teach women not to be afraid of their power, *even* if their power lies in their submissive nature. I think they haven't been given a chance to really know their options, especially when it comes to sexuality. Women don't usually want to entertain themselves with the 'lower ends' of sexual expression. They prefer a much more imaginative approach, which is why you often find that women read much more than men. Often they feel guilty about some of their fantasies and therefore they don't share them. If a woman is given 'free rein' to exercise her own imagination, without influence from a demanding partner, she will eventually pass the erotic heights of her lover. Unfortunately, this is not easy in the world we live in today and, until the priorities of women are really accepted, they will not take this 'free rein'.

MADAME PATRICIA DE GIFFORD

One of the most bizarre and ambitious endeavours I've come across in the Fem-Dom stratosphere is The Other World Kingdom, or OWK for short. Located in the Czech Republic, the OWK has created a veritable country of 'dominant women' and male 'subject-slaves'; complete with palaces, farms, even their own currency and, of course, plenty of prisons! The OWK was the brainchild of one Patricia de Gifford, who now reigns as Supreme Highest Administrator in the Black City, capital of the Kingdom. Incidentally, don't bother looking for a likeness of the Supreme One in any of the OWK's numerous publications. Apart from pictures of her derriere and legs, she doesn't allow photographs of herself to be published. Interviewed November 1998

I had been thinking about the idea of the Kingdom for a couple of years before I did anything about it. I knew I needed somewhere with enough space and in a country which wouldn't afford me problems legally. Then I saw this 16th century castle, which is now the existing Queen's Palace, with it's surrounding lands and buildings here in the Czech Republic. The repairs and reconstruction of the old buildings and purchase of the luxury equipment cost me a lot of money. Nevertheless, I'm glad to say, it's all coming together nicely now!

The OWK comprises various areas and developments, including the Castle of Whips and my countryside residence as Highest Administrator. The most recent addition is a working farm, which we've called 'Happy Farm'. We called it this because I thought: "What can raise the spirit and mood more than the refreshing country air, beautiful nature and a view of naked male slaves working in the noon day heat under the bullwhips of beautiful Lady Warders on their horses?"

Though please don't be misled into thinking this is all just for 'pervy' fun! The farm is responsible for supplying the Queen's Palace. To ensure this is done efficiently, the Warders are only recruited from those members of the Queen's Guard who have received the special 'Cruelty' decoration. The serfs of the Kingdom (i.e. male submissives) are divided into 'servants' and 'slaves'. We can hardly talk about the difference between slaves and servants, because these are unrelated concepts. A slave is a name given to a creature who has lost *all* human rights. A servant is a person who serves a Woman in order to satisfy all Her needs. A servant can be a slave, a subject or a free man. Yet all are subject to taxes and other levied charges. The Kingdom is not the Salvation Army, you know!

The funds raised from taxes are used for state development and the welfare of the Sublime Ladies of the Kingdom. I can't think of a better way for the subjects to spend their money, can you? After all, the Kingdom represents their dream and ultimate fantasy come true; a state controlled by Dominant Women who tolerate males only if they work and serve them in every way. The same applies to the slaves. I consider it only natural and completely logical that, if I obtain a slave for life, I also take over his property. If the enslavement is for a shorter period of time, then only a proportion of the slave's property is transferred, of course. How else should it be? We are not a club where one spends an hour or two. We are reality! And if anyone doesn't like it, then we would have to say good-bye! I believe there is, and will always be, enough genuinely interested male-creatures out there to support my Kingdom. By that I mean those who understand that, in order to live out their dreams in reality, they have to sacrifice something

The duties of the male-creatures depends on whether you mean the servants of the Queen's Palace or my own personal servants. There is a major difference. Regarding the large area of the Queen's Palace and the quantity of work to be done, there has to be a high number of slaves and subjects performing the work of servants. These creatures are mostly specialised in the work of cleaning public areas, the apartments of Lady Guards, the chambers of Ladies at Court and the rooms of Lady Visitors. The *most* privileged are also allowed to launder and iron the Ladies underwear and clothes, cook, serve at tables and polish our boots. Other servants may wait all day long for the honour of offering their faces or backs for a tired Lady to sit on. As a kind of punishment they may also be used as public whipping boys.

My own personal servants have to be more 'universal', though I do have a few that are specialised. My personal servants include one male maid, two universal servants and a hairdresser. Incidentally, I have owned these servants since even before the Kingdom was founded. In addition, I now own ten state slaves, to which I am entitled because of my office. Some of them work on my fields, two of them carry me in a sedan chair and one is being trained as a human pony. Although the basic duties are precisely specified, occasionally the individual jobs are interlinked. Each of my servants has to be able to perform all the other jobs, excluding my hairdresser, of course. He is the only one who has the honour to take care of my hair. And yet, no matter how skillful he is, he still gets slapped!

But let's get back to the point. My personal TV maid, Dana, must never leave my chambers because being locked up all the time allows him to concentrate all the better on the job of looking after me and prevents any external disturbance. Dana must not talk without permission, must not look out of the window and certainly must *never* even look upon anyone but myself. He lives in complete seclusion in my chambers and spends all his time serving me.

Another of my personal servants is called Michael. I have owned him for seven years and, because of his capabilities, is also my personal secretary. He deals with my correspondence, reads me the most interesting letters and dictates my replies. He also accompanies me everywhere and is available at any time. In order to utilise him as much as possible, he also serves as my living stool, personal driver and baggage porter. In my chambers he is responsible for serving drinks to me and my visitors. He also cares for my boots and makes sure they are polished and shining all day long.

The OWK offers the opportunity for interested mistresses and would-be slaves to enter its borders as visitors to view our land of Dominant Women. A male visitor with special status (a white tape is put on the right arm to symbolise neutrality) is allowed, for the most part, immunity from punishments and gives him the temporary right to move through the Kingdom without necessity to obey its laws, decrees and regulations. This status of 'protected visitor' is applied to those males who would like to get a preliminary glimpse of the Kingdom without commitment. Male visitors are, however, expected to follow basic rules of conduct. That is, they must salute all Women, they must not enter into conversation with a Lady without her consent, and must not enter any area forbidden to 'men and other animals'. A Dominant Woman visitor is, naturally, granted all rights of the Kingdom as honourary citizen throughout her stay. The visitor may stay for an hour, a day or a week. The time is unlimited, in fact. If you need anonymity, you can even move around the Kingdom masked.

For visiting Ladies (with or without accompanying male slaves) there is a wide range of luxury accommodation. Ladies who do not wish to share common space with their servants or slaves, may let these creatures stay in the stables where they will be watched over for her by Lady Guards and where a strict regime is enforced i.e. no smoking, talking or walking upright. Alternatively, male visitors can be accommodated in the cells of the underground prison itself. Here the male visitor is required to live alongside prisoners convicted of crimes against the Kingdom and must adhere to the same strict regime of prison life and wear an identical convicts uniform. The only advantage for the imprisoned visitor is that he does not have to eat the wretched prison gruel or suffer punishment at the whim of the Lady Guards, providing he behaves 'modestly'.

We also have a highly specialised souvenir shop, run by Sublime Lady Christine de Lamour, when she's not fulfiling her role as General of the Queen's Guard. The shop is located in the New House and is called simply *Our Style*. It is open twenty four hours a day, seven days a week offering not only a full range of torturing, bondage and 'educational' equipment, but also carriages, fittings for human dogs, cages, pillories, pony carts and so on. Most of these items are manufactured here in the Kingdom's own workshops by slave workers and marked 'Made in the Other World Kingdom'. The visitor will also find books, videos and magazines from all over the world devoted, obviously, to the theme of Female Dominance. And there is one more special service for Superior Female customers. All implements of punishment may be tried out on 'live' test dummies selected from the Kingdom's slaves! As soon as you've fitted yourself in appropriate clothing and changed your money in the exchange office for the Kingdom's own currency of Doms, you're ready to pass on to enjoy the delights of the Queen's Palace area.

The Palace itself was originally a medieval castle rebuilt in the form of an early renaissance building, with a tower that dates back to the year 1580. Today it is the seat of the Supreme Administrator and the seat of the future Queen. The visitor can look through all the rooms, including selected parts of the underground jail, school, laundry room and Throne Hall. You can have lunch or dinner in the

Banquet Hall. For slaves and human-dogs there is a special menu. Ladies may also enjoy a game in the Billiard Hall and, if you are lucky enough, you may also be able to view my own luxurious apartments!

The Queen's Throne represents the absolute power of the first future Queen. At present the only person with the right to sit on the throne is, of course, myself as the Kingdom's founder. The throne itself is hollow to allow the fastening of one or two pieces of throne-slaves (note: slaves are always referred to as 'pieces of furniture') in order that they can take care of my comfort without bothering me with their appearance. (note: the 'comfort' of the Highest Administrator refers to the hole in the upholstered seat where the Lady places Her Sublime Bottom and is just the right size and shape to accommodate an eagerly attentive slave's face to give fun or relief to the aforementioned Divine Ass-Hole).

Apart from this receptacle, there are other strategically placed holes for the arms, legs and heads of shackled slaves to poke through in order to attend to various parts of my Sublime Body as required. In addition, two pieces of 'dog-slaves' are fastened to either side of the throne, and two more slaves hold fans. Taking care of the throne is very demanding. It has to be cleaned with velvet dusters three times a day at eight hourly intervals. The duster may be used just once. The slaves ensure that the throne is kept cleaned and polished and must not under any circumstances touch it with their bare hands otherwise they will be subject to the most severe punishments. The attendant slaves are allowed to move around the throne on their knees while I am not present. Once I, or any other Sublime Lady arrives in the room, however, only crawling is allowed.

Also in the Queen's Palace area, the curious visitor may be able to view the stables for slaves and 'human horses'. There is also a riding hall and sports park (human horse races are held), and even an electric power plant situated in the courtyard (propelled, naturally, by slave power). At 3pm every day erring slaves and convicts are publicly punished at the pillory. I will say more on the subject of convicts later.

Next on the agenda is the Long House. Here, in addition to the covered swimming pool, bar, solarium and massage facilities, one can also enjoy the Library of Honourables. Here one can borrow, for the duration of one's stay, any of the hundreds of books on Female Dominance. Another point of interest is the Gallery of the Other

World Kingdom exhibiting a wide range of artwork on the same topic. A Museum of Dominant Womanhood is also being opened shortly.

Like any other self regulating country, the OWK has it's own laws and prison. Under the provision of the Kingdom's Criminal Code, felons may well find themselves having to serve sentences for crimes against the Female State. To this end, the underground prison in the Queen's Palace is used and operated just like a normal detention centre. This ensures a prisoner's sentence is a *very* real punishment.

The convicted male (the prisoners are, naturally, *always* men) is taken down a staircase and along a short, narrow corridor past a 'dark' cell and a cage to the main corridor with standard size cells and one 'low' cell. The prisoners are, based on the Lady Judge's decision, placed in one of three corrective categories. This is denoted by the type of cell, the permitted quantity of food and the intensity of punishment applied by the Lady Warders. The massive granite walls, thick ceilings and steel reinforced oak doors ensure that no sound penetrates to other parts of the Palace, and further ensures that any thought of escape is dismissed from the inmate's mind.

The special prison meals are prepared by mixing the garbage from the Palace Kitchen with the leftovers from the Banquet Hall. On special occasions the prisoners are given bread slop. The meal, however, is further enriched with necessary vitamins since the cauldron, containing the prisoners food for the following day, is put into the Lady Warders service room the previous evening and is used by them as a toilet. The convicts are given two cold meals a day, but prisoners sentenced to penal servitude are fed only once a day. Needless to say, no male creature repeats the same offense after spending time in our cells!

As will be abundantly clear by now, the OWK is a *real* monarchy and, as such, approves and supports trade in slaves. This is the place where slaves of both sexes who want to experience real enslavement have the unique opportunity to be sold in the Kingdom's regular Slave Market for a day, a week, a year or even for the rest of their lives! Unlike a conventional (if that's the right word!) visit to a dominatrix, the slave lucky enough to be sold at one of OWK's auctions remains a real slave for the whole period of his servitude. This is a condition he accepts of his own free will and can't back down on later. In reality, it means the slave can't choose the Lady who will buy him. Neither has he the right to be treated according to his own wishes.

She can use her new living property for household duties or for sexual/sadistic purposes, as she sees fit. It is completely up to her. The slave, however, is allowed to set the period he wants to remain enslaved before he signs the contract. Minimum time is twenty four hours. Maximum time is unlimited. Every slave is entitled to offer for sale, besides himself, his belongings which will become the property of the Lady who buys him. These belongings may include moveable or non-moveable assets or money. The greater the assets, the greater the interest of the Lady Slavers will be in owning him, naturally!

There are many plans in the pipeline for the future of the OWK, and the majority of them depends on the funds the Kingdom will have available. Most importantly, I want to establish an international network of slaves and subjects who would care for the Sublime Lady's comfort on their travels. I intend establishing OWK embassies in those countries from which the highest number of our Lady Citizens, subjects and slaves come (i.e. Austria, Switzerland, Germany, United Kingdom and the United States). The embassies would grant entry visas, co-ordinate the network of slaves and represent the business interests of the Kingdom by distributing books, magazines and video tapes. And last, but by no means least, the Kingdom will enlarge its territory around the capital of the Black City by buying out land and homes from the original citizens. For myself, I have decided to run for election as the first Queen. If this happens the Kingdom will live under a real tyranny!

Finally, I will answer a few of the questions that potential slaves always wonder about. For example, why is it that I always refuse to show my face in any photos? The answer is that I'm simply not interested. Obviously, all visitors can behold my face when they come here. I'm in no way trying to hide my features, but I'm certainly not interested in some lowly male jerking off over my picture. For them, a view of my ass and legs will have to suffice. To see my face they will have to expend a bit more energy than simply buying a magazine. Women who write to me and send me their photos are an exception. To them, I will send a photo so they will have a better idea with whom they are dealing. Even male-creatures can express an interest in photos that show my face. If their humble whimpering amuses me, and they offer a sensible price for my efforts, I may kindly oblige their request.

People also wonder why I refuse, in all our publications, to be precise about the location of the Kingdom. I could answer that question like the last one. Those who only buy our books don't need to know. It is enough for them to know that we exist at all! Those who successfully apply for an entry visa will be informed, obviously. I will say that it is located on the highway connecting Prague and Brno. About an hour and a half by car from the capital and about the same from Vienna.

And lastly, people always want to know what was the thinking behind the choice of our state colours of red, white and blue? Well, it may sound a bit devaluing, but what really inspired me were the colours of my personal slave Michael's bottom after he has received his regular weekly whipping. I have to admit, however, that if I were to stick to the facts, the flag would have contained much less white!

Reverend Kellie Everts

Kellie Everts is nothing less than a dominatrix for God! Her self declared mission is to help guide society back to the natural and peaceful order of female supremacy that God the Mother intended. Kelly does this, in part, by producing sexually explicit videos that celebrate the worshipping of women by men. Her firm believe is that with every male she converts to female rule, she brings the world closer to the paradise of heaven. Formally known to the world as Commander Kellie of the Fetish Corps, she has recently forsaken the military life and taken religious orders to promote her philosophy of Dominant Femininity and Goddess Worship by means of videos, information packs and a regular newsletter to converts. Kellie operates her church and mail-order crusade from the town of Quaquaga, New York State. Interviewed September, 2000.

You might call what I do brainwashing, but I think it's only 're-balancing'. Since men have been brainwashing women for centuries, I'm just trying to get things back to where they should be. In most of my videos, for instance, you get to have a good look at my vagina, which I've found is a good method of behaviour modification. The point is that men get all wimpy and whiney when it comes to even the slightest glimpse of a woman's vagina, but women are only slightly amused at the sight of a man's penis. Men will do whatever it takes to get their tongues working between a woman's legs.

Every man who's married should be pussy-whipped; the pleasure of the marriage is directly related to how much the husband accepts this fact of nature. Men get the so-called 'seven year itch', which is really just a man searching for a woman to control him. If women take charge of their relationships with men, like they deep down know they should *and* could, there would be no more divorce in this country. There would be better adherence to the word of God, too!

The world began with God the Mother creating the cosmos and all its creatures; each species with a female designed to be the head of the household, and a male designed to be the female's helpmate and bodyguard. They were to work in unison, each with it's important task that only it could perform. Somewhere along the line (the exact date is lost in antiquity) God's scheme was upset by Satan, who is an evil, unanticipated offshoot of creation, a dark side that poisoned paradise by rejecting feminine rule. This intervention by evil forces created the battle of the sexes, which is simply males trying to come to grips with their true selves. Where a man belongs is in his true place in the universe – which is at a woman's feet, ready to serve!

The confusion a man feels about his relationships with women, and the turmoil and grief they can cause us, is an inner battle with Satan, who is afraid of the female and struggles to keep her down. Because of this cosmic battle that started when the world was created, modern man has a difficult time coming to grips with the fact that he was made to serve a woman, and to be ruled by the feminine side. It's this conflict, created by Satan, that is the basis of all the agony in the world.

Woman is equipped for leadership because she is responsible for her children; that is, *all* the children in the world! Man is not responsible and see how his rule has made a mess of things! I don't blame modern man for his shortcomings, though. We know that he can't help himself, after centuries of Satanic indoctrination, from expressing hostility to women and trying to keep the feminine side down. I can only try and encourage males to accept their true nature, and to realise that to serve and protect a woman is the ultimate lifestyle. To do a woman's bidding is all that a man can, and should, aspire to.

The concept of sexual sin comes from the male wanting to control the female. This happens in the guise of conventional religion but, if you look closely, you'll see that most religions are hopelessly anti-woman. Men are afraid of women. They won't even call a vagina by its real name. They will make up names for it, some 'cutesy', most derogatory, that keep them from considering the power of it. And, in turn, the power of the woman who owns that vagina. That's not to say that her vagina is a woman's only strength. It's a symbol of her power, of her rightful place as ruler, as creator of life. I believe men know this instinctually and therefore either bow before the knowledge or fight it. Unfortunately, because Satan long ago poisoned man's brain against woman, most males choose to fight their natural tendency to obey the female.

I also believe that my videos are a small step in the right direction of helping to change this. Men are so horny, they can easily be manipulated that way. And since deep down inside *all* men is the need to worship and obey women, no matter how much they fight it, it becomes possible to convert them back to their true place in the natural order of things. A man is at his happiest when performing a task for a woman, and with only the assurance that she'll pat him on the head for his good work. Of course, he wants *more* than a pat on the head, which makes him so easy to control. If you're honest with yourself as a woman, you know this to be true.

There are men all over the world who are devoted to me and to the resurrection of female rule, and it was my tapes that started the transition for them! To put it simply, every woman knows that she can lead a man around by his penis. What I'm doing is leading them to where they should be. And if I have to humiliate them and subjugate them, maybe even be cruel and play the bitch goddess, then I will! The end is what matters. I'm helping to recreate the paradise on earth that God intended. The female's two X chromosomes are the biological language of God. They say that she is the superior sex and must rule. I suggest you read *The Natural Superiority of Women* by Ashley Montague. In fact, there are lots of books and scholarly papers on the subject of Female Domination as the natural order of nature.

The world is slowly returning to feminine rule. It has to, because the universe *must* find its proper equilibrium. It won't happen in my lifetime, though. But I take heart from the fact that a lot of men are fed up with the violence of their gender and are trying to give up their aggression. These men are becoming more nurturing, more welcoming to life, more loving and Godlike from within. This is their way of cooperating with the planet's salvation, of welcoming God, and the power of womankind back on earth. It's the return of the Goddess, and the world will be better place.

My pornographic images of women reflect the natural superiority of our female sex and, in so doing, depict women as never before. I have an argument with most every institution and publication that depicts images of women. Especially, I don't like mainstream men's magazines which represent women as fuckable sluts and whores, or as playthings for men's amusement and sexual relief. My worst criticism, though, is not for pornographers, but for male domination in society. This shapes the brains of people from the time they are children going to those detention and brainwash centres called schools, where they are trained and programmed to think that men are superior and women are inferior. Even those women who, in rare instances, get ahead, like Margaret Thatcher, are just cocks in frocks!

Even mainstream religion degrades women as being incapable of ministry, and almost every religion on earth is guilty of this sin. Women have nowhere to lay their hat, spiritually speaking, except in some smaller religions. And men who love women have little place to go in the realm of spirituality. That's why I had to create my own religion!

Many men have asked me to find them dominating women. These men are not mainstream macho faggots in disguise, but are men who really love strong women and are in awe of them. These are the kind of men I serve with my videos and photography. But I also have my own feelings and my own concepts of what a woman is, and this is my vision. Perhaps my vision is the highest that one can achieve of what a woman truly is. I see women as the image of God. And I see a woman's sexuality as part of her Goddess nature, a part of her power.

Some people tell me that, as a dominatrix, I'm as guilty as the men who degrade women because I degrade men as part of my profession. But the truth is that a dominatrix does not degrade men who come to her. Women *are* degraded by being shown as whores, pigs, sluts and tramps; devoid of autonomy and spirituality. They are not always pleased with this image, but they do it for the money. Of course, they don't admit that they hate this image, they pretend they love it! Unfortunately, the truth is they sell their brains out as well as their bodies! That's something I have never done, even though I served the mainstream sex trade most of my life. I never said I *enjoyed* being looked on as a pig or as a sex machine!

No, in my business a dominatrix doesn't degrade the men who come to visit her as clients. Even though we are ball-busters and are abusive to men verbally and, to some degree physically, we do this for their sexual pleasure. In fact, men will pay for the privilege of having this sexual abuse. That's one way we make our money. So, we are not degrading men. We are giving them pleasure. We are not taking innocent men who are desperately in need of money and degrading them or turning them into victims. That's what's being done in the male dominated porno trade!

The photographs I take are of women who are *above* everything in the world – they're certainly above men! I make men appear small and weak. They are shown grovelling, kneeling and in awe of the woman in the picture. They are in her shadow, eclipsed by her. The woman is always unavailable and unattainable. She is serene; sometimes haughty, sometimes contemptuous, always in control. She is abstracted from male needs and dominates all. My women have elegance and spirituality. Whether or not the individual model herself is spiritual, I still see spirituality itself in the form of a woman. I portray that woman as if she had spirituality within her. And truly, most women *are* more spiritual than most men. They're certainly more virtuous, more intellectual and more giving from the heart than are men.

Many men have asked me to train their own women to be dominant. Let me just try and tell you how hard that is! Have you ever tried to remodel a hundred year old house? I have. And by the time I got almost done, I realised that it would have been much easier to build from scratch! And that's the problem with 'de-programming' women. By the time they are eighteen, they are so brainwashed that you have to tear down the house, so to speak, in order to produce a new one. That's where the hard part comes in. Women are afraid to assert their dominance, even though *every* woman is a dominatrix within. They have been taught that it is evil, sinful, wicked and taboo to show any strong positive emotions like dominance, aggression, hate, anger and rage with which they can denounce men and get a hold over them!

In my videos, women tell their *real* lives and are encouraged to bring out their *true* emotions and dissatisfaction with male domination. This is extremely rewarding because here you can see videos filled with the natural energies that women cannot vent anywhere else. The women in my videos are the only true stars. They are important, as all women are important. The men are just bit players. And I want the public to become familiar with my stars, and to know who they are and what they are about and the continuity of their lives. Some will inevitably come and go but, whenever possible, I try and give a sense of who they are, what they believe in, what their activities are and where their lives are leading. In so doing, the men watching can have a real sense of knowing these dominant women. In the videos themselves what the women are doing is having fun and, at the same time, giving sexual pleasure to men. Our motto's are: 'We cover a multitude of sins!' and 'We do stuff crazier than porno!'.

In normal male domination pornography, there's a kind of formula that makes women cringe; but many of the videos I make show women who are so powerful, so ball-busting and so in charge that women enjoy watching them, too. For instance, we have videos of women trampling men underfoot, boxing with them and beating them up. They will kick their nuts in, spank them and whip them. I know for a fact that many women would like to see themselves in such powerful roles, although they might not have the guts to star in a video of mine! I will continue trying to serve people to the best of my ability; bringing sexual pleasure to men and, at the same time, lifting the image of women. May God give you happiness, health and lots of money. And may you spend that money on me!

LADY LATEX

A native of Chicago, Lady Latex now lives in Berkeley, California. At present she has virtually dropped her personal client base in favour of conducting the major part of her work on-line via the Internet, as well as through her video and phone sessions. Interviewed September 2000.

People very often make the mistake of thinking of a session as 'punishment', and it's not always that way. Although in a scene, it's normal to *pretend* that it's punishment. It's one of my sayings that *only* good boys get spankings! During a session, a lot of people *feel* they are being disciplined; but for others, like myself, it's simply an erotic sensation. The ass is a very erotic area, after all. People who are into nipple-play, for example, are not 'reliving' any childhood punishment! In fact, the very first person who ever called me a sadist was someone I was doing nipple-play with. I still love to do it, although I don't fantasise about it. It's the same with cock and ball play. I love all the sensation activities which in private are pain activities. In sessions I do a lot of things that are not painful (like foot-worship, for instance) but definitely are involved in sensation.

Golden Showers are the same. If you really have to pee and then you go, the relief feels great. I don't even look at that as humiliation. I feel powerful as I'm doing it, but that doesn't mean that the person I'm peeing on *isn't* powerful. I see it as giving them a gift. And, usually, people swallow my gift! You can do all kinds of activities that heighten sensation without causing pain. For clients who have a Golden Shower fetish (and there's a lot of them) it's a very intense, physical sensation. When I tell someone there's no sex in the session, but I will allow them to worship my foot or be smothered by my butt, they understand that.

There are some scenes where no energy is being exchanged at all. I'll be doing what a client said he was into, but it's dead. It's like putting batteries in the wrong way, there's no connection. Those types of sessions can be a real drain. That's one case, and the worst case scenario is where I'm putting in a lot of energy and the other person is just sucking it away. Even if I figure out on the phone that I like the same scenes as the slave, when it comes down to the actual scene, it's just not there. Sometimes that's simply because it's the first time. Although there was one client who I had two horrible sessions with and I was amazed that he called me a third time. I decided to go through with it and at last there was a connection. He said it was the best session he'd ever had and I've seen him a bunch of times since then. I'm not really attached to any one type of activity. I've enjoyed sessions that I wouldn't go for in private play because that person is so passionate about it. That makes it very exciting. Ideally, I should feel very energetic about a session.

Genital piercing is one of my favourite activities. I love to gaze at the needles in the entire shaft of the penis. It's so beautiful. I also like to pierce around the corona to create a hedge of needles. I get a touch of blood that way. Yummy! As it takes so much energy, I only do it rarely. There are very few clients I do piercing with. That's for clients who are truly into pain and can't have enough of it. I've only branded my initials on to one of my slaves thighs. I didn't even know before I did that if I'd be able to. I was told I would have to be in 'top head space' to do a branding. I wasn't sure if I could get to that space, but I did. My limits would be putting a nail into someone's dick. One client asked for it and I told him to rent the video. I know a mistress who did it and it took her half a day to get her energy together. So why should I do that if I'm not going to enjoy it?

I guess I first became aware of SM, in a way, when my parents told me how they were abused by nuns in Catholic school – but then still made me attend, anyway! They had abolished those practices by the time I went, thank goodness, but that didn't keep those nuns from being control-bitches from hell! Beyond the school-girl uniform, which I'm convinced was invented by perverted minds, I used to have fantasies about forcing cops to have sex with me and rasping them with their own night-sticks, yet it was never anything I imagined would happen in real life!

Sadistic thoughts always lingered in my mind, but I never had an outlet for my fantasies. After high school I went to business college and quickly found myself working as a secretary. My mother thought that would be a good way for me to meet a husband. A flirtatious female co-worker, who always liked the gothic way I dressed, told me about a fetish ball that was coming up. She was helping to organise it, on behalf of a latex clothing company, and wanted me to be one of their runway models. I enjoyed modeling and loved clothes so I said yes. I spent two days before the show just trying on all the different costumes they had! I powdered up my skin chalk-white and bound my body in tight latex. I knew I had to have my own large wardrobe of this dark rubber as soon as possible. Nothing had made me feel so immaculate and beautiful before!

During the show I had a lot of fun doing mock SM scenes with the other models; tying them up and giving out beatings with my riding crop. Afterwards, I trumped around the club in my dominatrix get-up and had a few good laughs ordering men to lick my boots and administering spankings. Then I realised it was more than a laugh, I was getting off on it! I went to the play area and volunteered to whip some eager young men who were hanging around. The master gave me a few tips on whipping techniques, handed me a cat o' nine tails and I was off! The redder their asses got, the more turned on I was! I got into a trance and just started flogging this man, who kept yelling for me to hit him harder! The play-space master eventually had to grab my arm and tell me to stop. I was dripping with sweat, my nice hair-do ruined, strung all over my face – but from that moment on I was hooked! I spent the next few months answering personal ads from submissives and spending all my time at fetish clubs trying to meet sissy-men who would let me beat them up. None of the relationships worked out, but it didn't matter to me, as long as I could dress up and be the 'Mistress of the Night'!

I then answered an ad in one of the weeklies for a small house of domination run by these two lesbians. I became the third girl they had working for them. The first thing they taught me was that I didn't know anything! My apprenticeship began with this guy who had a 'bug fetish'. He would bring in snails, worms, ladybugs, whatever, and he'd then lie on the floor, stomach down, with his face up and the bug right in front of him. Then he'd shout: "I am a worm! I am a worm!" I would then cut the worm in two, then three, then four with my stiletto heels and he would 'come' just watching it, without even touching his dick! The whole scene lasted about ten minutes and I was a hundred bucks richer. I've done some pretty weird shit and I'm totally into bizarre fantasies – but, come on! What was that guy's problem?

I find that a mistress with a true latex fetish is into more sophisticated dominance, generally. Play that's more glamorous, and with richer clients. I have a huge inventory of latex fetish wear now; including corsets, nun and maids outfits, nurse and military uniforms, complete latex skin-tight wear for every occasion. I enjoy sharing my collection and dressing up my slaves. A client doesn't *have* to be rich, but he does have to be fun! And I still go for glamour. I want the illusion. The *ultimate* sex fantasy. Cinderella getting it on in a pumpkin, as opposed to some toilet training scenario. When I do that, I feel like I know what William Burroughs was talking about in *The Naked Lunch* – seeing what's really on the end of your spoon! I enjoy that sometimes, but only in my most debased of moods. I'm attracted to things that are dark, evil and perverted. I enjoy helping people live out fantasies that society would judge as wrong. But there's a limit. I'm not a psychiatrist and I won't act as one if a person needs help.

Most of my clients live normal lives and only want to live out their fantasies for a few hours a week. It's just that at that particular house those women were running, it had a knack of hooking up with particularly weird people! These days I screen out anyone I feel is 'sketchy' on the phone. If I don't want to do something, I won't do it! For the most part, though, I enjoy building relationships with my clients that will grow and that we'll both enjoy.

If I'm doing a caning, I'll order the slave to strip naked before fastening him to an apparatus known as an 'A' frame. I secure his wrists at the top with weighty straps, with his legs spread apart and bound to the frame. If the slave is in for a heavy punishment, I'll shackle his elbows, knees and waist, too. I have a dozen different canes of various sizes and weight, and choose the appropriate one determined by the slave's offense and pain threshold. My favourite cane is a light, but deadly, instrument with delicate, feminine curves. Although steel at its base, I have it coated with heavy red rubber to match my blood-red latex caning outfit. Because of the severity of this punishment, I'll be attired head-to-toe, complete with executioners mask, like a red latex machine of punishment. The only flesh showing is through the open slit exposing my eyes. Each blow is powerful and unyielding. I always draw blood and leave long red scars that retain in my memory for months, even years! Like any flogging, the slave must count out the blows in a loud, clear voice and thank me with sincerity. If he screams in pain instead, then more strokes are added. I concentrate on the buttocks and the top five or so inches of the thighs, sometimes overlapping the strokes. I do this until every inch of his ass is on fire and he is crying unashamedly.

My style of bondage is cruel and foul. I take a man into my reserve brusquely, contorting his arms behind his back and smacking his cheek. I'll taunt and frighten him with my clawed gloves, then tear off his clothes and conduct a police rape with a strap-on. Needless to say, my 'suspects' always confess their crimes! Oh, I almost forgot about the rubber cock I slip into my slave's mouth before I 'face-fuck' him into submission. Then I'll finish off by smothering his face with my latex-clad ass!

I will not work from 'scripts' in my sessions that are based on the slave's fantasies that they've worked out. I'm an unpredictable 'Mistress of Improvisation'! In high school I had wanted to become an actress and went to several summer acting camps where I learned about staging, timing and the pacing of a scene from deep and vehement to restrained and subtle. I collect and spew out a jumble of emotions. My constant train of thought keeps my slaves off-guard in order to build up their tension. I know my feelings are right and I go with them. So much of my scene-play is acting out my alter-egos and those of my slaves.

With me, every execution exhibits nervous tension and is *totally* capricious and without limitations or mitigating conditions! I am also a contemplative role-playing dominant marked by my sober sincerity. Nothing gets me wetter than the spirituality of energy interchange! I feel my worst enemies in the fantasy world are those vampiric leeches, those miserable little worms, who don't return the honour I bestow upon them. Reciprocation of energy is essential. After all, I give you mine with pain, so you give me your's with obedience. As of late I've been partaking in play with what I call 'captive masochists'. These are slaves who might resist my power, while *still* observing the rules of my game. With these slaves I take that extra step beyond typical fetishes and combine it with my metaphysical energy. My sadistic nature must be appeased! My victims leave the dungeon hurting like hell, but are better human beings for it. And I still enjoy the occasional grovelling slave. If a submissive is sincere I will make him or her my little bitch, introducing them to worlds of fantasy they never even dreamed possible!

I now live in San Francisco. I love the Bay Area more than

Chicago, although I know it's a saturated market of dominatrixes out here. I still have a large slave-base in Chicago that I shouldn't leave behind, but I came here to live and be part of the fetish scene, not to work. Most of my work is on-line now, so it doesn't matter where I live. Thank God for the video-phone. It keeps me honest with my old slaves! I now intend becoming Lord Mistress of Cyber-Domination! I just get off thinking men are worshipping the very idea of my existence! It's a realm that can't be explored in-person!

MISTRESS EVA

From her exclusive London apartment, this blonde former dancer and performance artist reigns supreme over her harem of 'little slave boys' in her self created world of dominant delights. Interviewed September 2000.

My first experience of domination for pleasure was when I was in my late teens. Because I'm six foot one tall, I found when I started dating guys that the kind of men I attracted were secretly subservient. I also had a tendency to want to be bossy sexually anyway, so it kind of evolved from there. I just got into it more and more and more. I'm thirty three now, so it's been over a period of about fifteen years.

I went to live in Miami for a while, so I didn't know about the scene in London. I started going to fetish clubs there and, to be honest, the first one I went to was a bit of a shambles, really. It was kind of like a high school dance! There were lots of people with bits of PVC on just standing around and not really doing anything. And I was there ready to kick everybody's head in! I'd even brought my own collar and lead with me ready to drag some slave around the floor! People were looking at me a bit strange, I can tell you!

Then I came back to London. The scene was very underground then. I started going out and meeting people on the scene such as yourself at *Club Domina*. I'd stopped dancing professionally at this point, so I thought what shall I do for a living now? Why not do something I really enjoy and get the most fun out of? So that's how I became a professional dominatrix.

Because I live on the premises, I've redesigned the whole place with a sort of gothic, semi-livable, semi-dungeon feel. That means I don't have to restrict the play to the dungeon itself. I can have a slave as a foot stool in my living room while I'm watching a movie or something and it's still got the right atmosphere. It's not like going from a dungeon to Laura Ashley, which is not my kind of thing, and not the slave's either, I'm sure.

I do a whole spectrum of scenarios from erotic dancing and tie and tease, to quite heavy-handed violent scenes involving fisting, face slapping and flagellation. Because of my size, I can do a good line in beatings! That's top of my list of favourite activities. But I do know just how far to go, so everything I do is safe. My other top favourite is using my strap-on dildo. I find that at least 85% of submissive men like that, they just won't admit it! I have to talk them into it sometimes. I get quite a range of requests for heavy bondage and body bag scenarios but, to be honest, I can't be asked to do anything that I don't enjoy. It's too time consuming and I'd start getting bored. The reason I do this work in the first place is because I enjoy it. It genuinely gives me a thrill to work with slaves. They tell me they can *feel* that I'm actually enjoying it myself, and that I'm not just doing this as a job. Then it would be mundane and I'd do something else to get me out of the house. I really enjoy 'cuffing' someone or having them on their knees staring up at me for hours. I love it! It gives me goose bumps!

You get some mistresses who will just go 'tap-tap-tap' and tell them what a naughty boy they are. You get the impression that they're just doing it for the money and don't really enjoy it at all. I earned enough through dancing for ten years so that I don't have to do this for the money. I do it because I love it. The beauty of having the dungeon in my own apartment is that I don't have to work ten to seven, Monday to Friday. I work seven days a week, but I'll have a day off whenever I feel like it. If I don't want to work for a few days, I won't. I don't work regular hours either. I might see someone at nine o'clock in the morning or one o'clock at night. I think that works better because not everyone can come and see a mistress between ten and seven o'clock. It's also very useful when I get overnight kidnappings and stuff. What I usually do is keep them in the cage and I'll sleep in the bed next to it. They have to stay awake, of course, till I fall asleep. And they have to make sure they're awake *before* I am in order to greet me correctly and prepare my breakfast!

I have some great people I kidnap on a regular basis. I've got one client I always kidnap at Toddington Services on the M1 motorway. It's the first service station you get to leaving London going north. I see him once a month. I won't say his name, but he knows who he is! It's always the same rigmarole. I drive up in the car and buy myself chicken and chips or something. Then, as I'm driving out again to come back to London, there he is waiting at the entrance to the motorway with his thumb out hitch hiking. I love it so much my heart starts beating away with excitement as I stop! I'll get out of the car and ask if he's okay. He'll tell me he doesn't know where he is or where he lives because he's lost his memory. And I'll say: "Oh, I'll take you to the nearest police station, you poor thing". Then I'll blindfold him, open the boot, shove him in and bring him back here and lock him up for two days. He'll be beating on the inside of the boot all the way back and I'll be swinging the car from side to side as I drive along. He's my absolute favourite. Mr Motorway, I call him. It's the most fun, even though it's the same scenario every month, and in exactly the same place. He's probably parked his car there or maybe his house is behind the bushes, I don't know. I've never asked him. I think the monotony has actually become part of the excitement for me! I vary the 'verbals' sometimes, depending on what kind of day I've had. If I've had a good day, I'll be all sympathetic or, if I've had a bad day, I'll give him a good smack as I bundle him in.

Then there's The Milkman. I call him that because he spends half an hour acting like a pussycat. I'll give him the cat bowl and he'll lick me and I'll stroke his head like a pet. I've got The Slapper, too. He likes having his face slapped for hours on end. They're my favourites. Sometimes it can get a bit mundane. When I do a sensory deprivation scenario with blindfolds and earplugs, for instance, I'll be sitting on top of the cage with a cup of coffee and my newspaper or doing some paperwork. It's quite comical really, and the slaves see the funny side of it too.

I'm very much into costumes and role playing. I like the scenarios where I'm wearing a police woman's uniform or Gestapo outfit, and I get to shove a lamp in their faces and that kind of thing. I'm supposed to have caught them and have to interrogate them. I also enjoy 'secretary' ones where the client is my male secretary and they've done something wrong or their sales figures aren't up this month. Basically, I'll rape them and fuck them up the arse! I'll have the strap-on under my skirt. I'll whip it and pound it into them. I enjoy those ones a lot, actually. They're fun to do. Well, I wouldn't be doing it otherwise, would I? And I shall continue to do it for a long time yet!

Scenarios that I won't consider doing are things like 'hard sports'– just the thought of it makes me feel sick! And I won't have any conversation in the session to do animals or children. If they want to dress up as little boys, that's okay. But if they're using connotations of a paedeophile nature, then they're straight out the door! There are things that I don't personally like, but I will do them if the client requests it. Mostly, I mean the kind of things I mentioned earlier that I find a bit tedious, or things that I think are a little extreme. For instance, some harder forms of cock and ball torture is just not good for you and can be very damaging for the future. I've seen someone at clubs actually dangling fire extinguishers from their testicles! That person is going to suffer so much in the future. Even if he's confident in his technique, that technique could fail one night and his balls will be gone! It's up to the individual to do it or receive it, though. I'm not trying to put anyone off it but, personally, I won't go beyond a certain point.

I won't doing piercings, either. That's for professional people to do. Branding is okay. In fact, I branded my ex-husband! He'll have to carry that on his back for the rest of his life! Scarification I won't do, because that's very dangerous, too. Also, the submissive is caught up within the moment so much that, under the spell of the mistress, they really feel they want to be scared. But when the session's over and they go back to their other life, I know they'll regret it. I think that's taking advantage of my position and my power. They're only doing it because they really are under the power of the mistress! I've studied the medical side for each job I do, because there are certain things I need to know. I am also a qualified first-aider, so I know what to do should a situation arise.

Generally, I love all the fun stuff! Tease and please and bring you to your knees kind of stuff! I love water-sports, too. And I absolutely *insist* on body worship, because that always gets the session moving. Remember, a lot of times the clients are very nervous, especially if they're first timers. They're always scared walking into the dungeon for the first time. They think they're going to be thrown down on the floor and beaten unmercifully, but that's really not the way it is. Maybe they've had bad experiences with a mistress who just didn't listen. I'll normally bring them into the lounge if they're first timers, and sit them down and have a chat. I'll give them my 'safe word' and ask them for a list of things that they really don't like. Things that really scare them, that's a good place to start. We'll exchange contributions and then go in and do it. I like the fun of working them into it slowly, and getting them into the dungeon scene that way. I'll put a favourite song on and I'll do a full strip and tease them while they're tied up. I love getting up so close they can *almost* kiss me, then I'll pull back! I love all the teasing and caressing and whispering and taunting them. That's what I like the best because I am a real exhibitionist when I'm doing it. I'm really a quiet little pussy cat inside, but don't tell anybody that!

A lot of domination is theatre, if you think about it. And I'm a born actress! I'll change my hairstyle and clothes to match the scenario; whether it's school mistress or secretary with my hair in a bun and severe glasses, or long flowing red-head vamp. It gives me a great opportunity to dress up in corsets or rubber cat woman outfits and wonder bras. That's what I love about the job the most. I still do some dancing and television work, but out of all the jobs I've had, this is my favourite. I'll carry on for about another ten years professionally, though I know that'll be a big disappointment to all my little boys! I'll still keep a dungeon in my house, but that will be just for pleasure. I love all my naughty boys who come into my life and make Mistress Eva's comical world of dominant delights spin and spin!

It is a wonderful lifestyle, as I keep saying. If I decide to go away for three weeks, I will. I'll just shut down and put on the answering machine and tell them I'll be back on such and such a day. My regular clients, I'll refer to other mistresses who I know I can trust. Rather than let the poor puppies go without, I'll ask them if they can look after a few of my boys for me. I know that the other mistress will take care of their needs, and that they're not going to be mistreated or poached. We don't do things like that. There's enough to go round for everybody.

I've only had to turn away two clients in my life. One because he was so filthy, and I was actually cruel enough to tell him so! And the other because he came in very drunk and was very obnoxious towards me. He wasn't violent, so I wasn't threatened by him, but he was saying things like: "What are you going to do to me then?" and I said: "I'll tell you what I'm going to do to you, love. I'm going to throw you out the fucking door". I grabbed hold of him and threw him into the street! But that was the only two occasions. Generally, I find the submissive male immaculately clean and well behaved. Because they've come to submit to me, they're very compliant and polite. Even if I've almost drawn blood from giving them a beating, they still want to bring me chocolates or flowers, which I think is really sweet.

I don't have to buy flowers ever again. Sometimes the dungeon looks like a funeral parlour!

As I said, I do have a fully equipped dungeon here, complete with leather bed built on a metal cage and all sorts of bit and bobs. But it's not always the equipment that counts, it's what the mistress does with it! You can dominate someone with one hand and with no dungeon at all! If you're that good and that strong, mentally and physically, you can do it. For instance, if any of my slaves tell me they're allergic to my pet cat, I'll put the cat in the cage with them just to torture them a little bit more! If they've misbehaved, I'll rub them a little bit with the cat. It completely freaks them out!

This is a complete lifestyle for me. Even if I go out to a 'vanilla' club, I'll always wear six inch patent heels with rubber trousers, something of a fetish nature anyway. It separates the boys from the toys, as it were! If they see me and they've got submissive tendencies, they'll know what's going on. That's how I attract my personal slaves who I'll bring back to my little harem. That's what I'd like to have really, a harem full of hunky male slaves! They can pamper me all day and serve me and carry me everywhere. I could have them all on leads like little puppies. I can quite see myself as Cruella de Ville!

TANITH AU SET

Tanith originally trained, like so many dominatrixes, as a nurse. She soon became disillusioned with her chosen career, however, and quit to pursue her twin passions for Egyptology and perversion! Now aged thirty six, she has been involved in the fetish scene in one way or another for, as she puts it, half her lifetime! During these years, she also became an eloquent and respected spokeswoman for the fetish scene with many television appearances to her credit. Interviewed July 2000.

I chose the name Tanith simply because I liked it. I first encountered the name in a book by Dennis Wheatley called *The Devil Rides Out*. Unlike other dominatrixes, I don't use the title 'mistress' at all. I like to be different, you see! Au Set is the ancient hieroglyphic pronunciation of the Goddess Isis. I have a passion for Egypt. In fact, I did a college course for five years to get a diploma in Egyptology.

It's a common misconception that the Ancient Egyptians had a morbid obsession with death. That's simply not true. They loved life and just wanted to make sure it continued after the death stage. Their world wasn't dark and morbid at all, but full of light and joy. I think they've have been greatly misinterpreted and misunderstood – a bit like sado-masochists, really!

They were the first people to use fishnet for clothing, incidentally; so there's an interesting little fact for you! They had good surgeons too, so their clinical scenarios were excellent. And they were also pioneers of the enema. Apparently, the Ancient Egyptians got the idea for the enema by watching the Ibis. Now this bird has got an incredibly long beak and what it used to do was suck water up into its beak, then shove it round its tail feathers to clean itself. And that, supposedly, is where the idea for the enema came from. Whether it's true or not, I don't know. But it's nice to think so.

I'm very influenced by Egypt. In fact, when I want to do my fantasy role-play thing, I love wearing flowing robes with a crown with a cobra's head on it and hieroglyphics around the rim. I've got a crook and Egyptian whip as well, just to lend a air of S&M about it. I'll sit on my throne with my most devoted slave of six years kneeling at my feet. I surprised him one day by actually initiating him ancient

Egyptian style as my bonded slave! That was really great for me because it gave me an opportunity to dress up how I wanted and be a goddess and have a lot of fun! That's what's so great about all this. It gives you a wonderful opportunity to dress up. When I was a kid, I had a dressing-up bag full of frocks and things. I used to enjoy dressing my brother up as a girl all the time. Obviously, dressing was a big thing for me. And, even now that I'm a grown up person, I *still* get to do all the dressing up I want!

I've been involved in working on the fetish scene in one way or another for half my life, really. Since I was about eighteen. Not full time, but on and off. I used to be a lifestyle 'perv', though not so much now. I started off working for a chap called John Sutcliffe years ago, who did a magazine called *Atom Age*. That's how I got introduced to it all. He also made couture leather wear. I used to answer the phone, send the magazine out, and welcome the clients who wanted to have leather clothes made for them. He was such a fabulous man and the best person I've ever met on the scene – the old school style! You know, where everyone had a great deal of respect for one another. A lot of people don't have that anymore, and it's such a shame.

The clubs now are full of loud music and geared toward your next 'bonk' and all the rest of it. The last time I went to a fetish club, some guy came up and just gabbed hold of my arse! This is *not* the way it used to be. As a woman, you used to be able to go to these things and have your breasts out or your arse hanging out, and no guy would come up and grab you. They'd come up and ask if they could lick your feet in a most respectful way. Now it's like a meat market, very predatory. That's very intimidating for a woman, and I didn't like it at all. I might go to the occasional private party, but that's about it. I suppose things inevitably evolve and change over the years.

You can't even talk to people in clubs like that. When I was working for John Sutcliffe, he used to have this club once a month in a little wine bar in Victoria where people could dress up and come along. He would even have classical music playing in the back ground! The emphasis, in those days, was on people meeting other like minded people and being able to chat about what they liked to do and make new friendships. Nowadays, if you're a new person going to one of these things it must be quite scary, I would think. You don't get that opportunity to really mingle with people.

It must have been around the early eighties when I first discovered this scene. When you're young, you don't have an inkling that all this exists. When I did realise, I was in there like a duck to water! I thought this is brilliant! I was just out of college and intended becoming a nurse. I had a place ready at a hospital where I was going to train. To fill in the time for nine months, while I waited for the placement to come up, I went to work for *Atom Age* and got my taste for it all. Then I went into nursing, which lasted all of three months! It was so depressing, I just couldn't do it. During this period, living in the nurses home, I used to suffer from 'rubber-sickness', which is a bit like home sickness. At the end of my day on the wards, I couldn't wait to get back to my room and strip naked and put on my rubber mackintosh. I remember one day being 'caught in the act' by two girls when they walked into my room and surprised me. After their initial shock, I did manage to get one of them into rubber stockings, which they ended up absolutely loving! Then I decided to move up to London and worked for different fetish shops for a few years. Next, I went to *Cocoon* and learnt how to make rubberwear. After that, I managed *Skin Two* retail for the first three years of its existence, which was great fun because it was so high profile.

My ambition during this time was to have a shop of my own, which I eventually did. It was called *Libido* and was in Camden. It was run for women, and by women. There were no men involved in the business whatsoever. This was kind of linked up with *Submission* night club because my partner, Tina, was the girlfriend of Rubber Ronnie who did the club. They had the office upstairs and we had the shop downstairs. It was fun, but it was difficult because it was at the tail end of the recession. In the end, because I lived above the shop, it was *all* the time. I was going to clubs to promote the business every week, and in the end I got fetish fatigue for a while and had to leave it. I'd always wanted to go to Egypt and went there for a week. When I came back I decided to go to university and do a part-time course in Egyptology. To put me through college and pay for all the books and everything, I started doing this full time. Unfortunately, a diploma doesn't get you a job in Egyptology! But, because I enjoyed doing this so much, I stayed with it. I've been a full time dominatrix for six or seven years now, and had jolly good fun doing it, too!

This is a very interesting subject for a lot of people. The amount of people who used to phone up when I was at *Skin Two* wanting information because they were doing a thesis on The History of Rubber or this perversion or that perversion. From the outside, when they're looking in, they think this is *so* weird what's going on there. What makes people do that kind of thing? When I first started at the shop, I became kind of the spokesperson for the scene for a while, as I was an intelligent woman who had a good argument as to why doing this *isn't* a bad thing. I was able to say that it isn't just a male thing. Women like doing this as well. I'm not being told I *have* to do this. I'm doing this because I like it. I did quite a few television appearances talking on the subject. The first one was *South of Watford* when Hugh Laurie was presenting it. That was about high heels and heel fetishism. I was also on a few of the *Skin Two* videos. In fact, the first *Skin Two* video I did was about how to look after your rubber wear. They did a review of it in *Time Out* and said I was like a really cheerful *Blue Peter* presenter as I was explaining how to put on your rubber cat suit!

The worst one I did was *The James Whale Show*. Not that James Whale was the problem, he wasn't. It was his female co-presenter. A completely 'bonkers' woman. We were just talking about stuff and she completely lost it. She said we were all mad! That something had to be desperately wrong with us! We had all been abused as children or our parents belonged to strange religious cults and all the rest of it! She was practically spitting! James Whale came up to us afterwards and apologised. I feel I've done my 'fifteen minutes of fame', so I don't go on television shows anymore. I've stood up and done my bit in the eighties. It was great fun; a mad, whirlwind time. But I've settled down a bit now, and I can still get my 'fix' of pervery by doing this.

The nurse training has come in useful, because it has given me the understanding to do the clinical stuff, which has became one of my specialisations. I've always had a fascination with clinical instruments anyway, as you can probably tell by my collection on the walls! They're very difficult to get hold of though. If you phone up a company that makes this kind of thing, they'll give you the third degree! Who do you work for? What's your status? They'll really give you a hard time. Though there are a couple of places you can get stuff from. Anyway, I like everything to do with clinical scenarios. There's something about surgeon's rubber gloves I love; that's one of my particular things. They're so thin and feel so nice against the skin. And I love the smell. And the noise is great, too! Cold steel always looks very nice on a wall or wherever, I think. If you've got somebody blindfolded and tied down and they feel the cold steel of the surgical instrument against their skin, it's a bit scary for them. And that's all part of it. I don't do anything to anybody that they don't want. In fact, I insist on having a chat before we do anything at all. This lets me find out what particular things they're into and whether it's viable or not.

Incidentally, it's interesting when you read *supposedly* true-life accounts about alien abductions, because the 'kidnap victims' are invariably clinically examined! And usually of a sexual nature. They always seem to be having things probed into their nether regions, especially the women, and there's invariably a lot of weird instruments and bright lights and everything. There's always a lot of fetish and S&M imagery in there. I think, in a lot cases, it's a fantasy to do with 'anonymous' sexual stuff. A lot of people couldn't ask their partner to do it to them, but it's okay if an 'alien' does it! And that's the 'excuse' for having these kinds of bizarre fantasies. And they really are quite bizarre!

Again I draw on my nurses training when I talk to people during a session. I remember they told us it was very important to tell the patient exactly what you're doing all the time to reassure them, so they know what's going on because, obviously, it's very scary for them. I find that's a great technique to use in a dungeon situation, too. Only it's more erotic and done for the effect of creating suspense and anticipation. You can describe to them before hand how it's going to feel.

It's like when I'm caning someone. Many years ago, when I was first experimenting with things, I had a partner who was into the schoolgirl-type situation. That is, with me being the 'schoolgirl' and him caning me. So I tried the cane, I know what it's like and know it's not for me. Basically, because it hurts too much and I'm a coward when it comes to pain! I love inflicting it on other people, but not on me! But I've tried it and I know how it feels. And so, if I'm about to cane somebody, I can describe to them *exactly* how it's going to feel. It's a very particular sensation. A slipper or a paddle is a sort of glowing, stinging sensation over a large area, while the cane is very different. Being very thin it's like a crack of fire across their arse cheeks. As I know how it feels, I find it great fun to describe it to them and give them a very clear picture in their minds of what's about to happen. I'll give a few swishes behind their back just to make them *think* it's coming, even when it's not! It's always great fun, especially if they're blindfolded. Then, obviously, their senses are more attuned to sound and touch, so you can rattle chains and pull on rubber gloves. They've got this whole world coming in front of their eyes. They can imagine what's going on and get tensed up ready for whatever is about to happen. It's a bit sadistic, I suppose, but it's good to be able to say you've done it yourself.

I've certainly seen some interesting people over the years, I must admit. I think one of my favourites was a chap I used to see some time ago. He was from Romania or somewhere like that, and what I enjoyed about him most was that he was so happy to be doing what he was doing. He was completely mad and had no guilt whatsoever! He knew exactly what he wanted, told me what he wanted and had it done to him! It was so brilliant! He was completely different from the usual run-of-the-mill slave. He was quite bossy, really. And you do get these 'bossy' submissives from time to time.

I remember he brought a carrier bag with him the first time he came to see me. Inside was a tin opener, a roll of cellotape and a tin of semolina! I thought, this is interesting! What are we going to do with this lot? He asked me if he could put the semolina into two different cups and heat up it up in the microwave. When it was really quite hot, he'd lay some plastic sheeting on the floor and put one cup down. At this point I knew exactly what he was going to do next. He knelt down all fours with his cock dangling just above the cup. The other pot of semolina I had to pour over his arse. The point of the exercise was that every time I poured hot semolina on his backside, his cock went into the hot semolina in the cup below him. He loved it so much. I think he was more of a masochist than a submissive, actually. Sometimes he'd vary it and bring tapioca or rice pudding.

He would also cellotape round his cock, pull it between his legs and tape it up round his arse cheeks. It was my job to pull it off really fast along with all his hairs, so it would be a bit of a shock to his system. When he got it all off, he went over to the wall and started banging his cock against it. He was really chucking himself against the wall! I thought this was brilliant entertainment. I sat there throughout the whole session with a smile on my face. He was enjoying himself so much, he didn't really need me. I said to him afterwards: "Have you ever thought about shutting your cock in the door?" He said he hadn't, and immediately went over to the door and did it! I only said it as a joke!

The next time I saw him he brought a honeydew water melon with him. He'd cut the top off and taken some of the pips out. He informed me that one of his favourite pastimes was fucking melons. He liked to keep some of the pips in though, just to make it a bit rough. I suggested he combine it with the semolina scenario and pour some of the hot semolina pudding into the melon. That way he would have the contrast between hot and cold, as well as the texture of the pips. I only saw him a few times. I think he was one of those who go with one mistress and then another, as he wanted constant change and new stuff all the time. But for the few times I saw him he was so entertaining. No guilt or hang ups about it at all. He knew what he wanted and went at it with great gusto and just did it! He was as mad as a meat axe, of course, but was just great!

Aside from semolina, I've found black treacle to be a wonderful thing for playing with. It's fabulous. I had one guy I used to 'do' black treacle with. Though it feels very nice, it's a bastard to get off. But if you spray shaving foam in with it, it becomes very slick. I was just exploring another branch of what people like to do. I've got tins and tins of it in the cupboard. Salad cream, too. I had one guy once who wanted to do bondage. He was tied up on the bench and, instead of using rope, I used clingfilm. I cut out various parts in the 'genital areas', then broke raw eggs onto his cock and his balls with clingfilm over the top of it. He ends up with all these squelchy eggs and scratchy shells all round his cock and balls. It's not very clinical, but it's certainly different!

I've had quite a few people who've wanted testicle inflation with saline fluid. I've never done it, because it's not something I've been trained to do. You do get people who phone up with real 'on the edge' stuff. They actually want you to circumcise them or make them into a eunuch. They say they don't mind if it hurts, just do what you have to do and cut them off. Do these people realise how many blood vessels there are down there? God, it has to be one of the richest sources of blood in a man's body! If I really did cut their dick off they'd probably bleed to death! Fantasy is great, but sometimes that's where it should stay.

I did have one guy who was really shy, and he told me he had this *really* weird fetish! He said he'd never been to see anyone about it before, but it was something he always thought about when he was masturbating, and he wanted to see if there was any part of it he could get realised. It turned out to be a dental fantasy. The big thing he wanted was for me to put my fingers in his mouth and pull his top lip up in the way a dentist would. That was it! When we'd finished he told me that he really didn't think anyone could do that for him because it was so precise. But if you really *listen* to someone, you can realise most of their fantasies.

You do get these people who've really pinpointed their fantasy in a very precise way. There was another chap I used to see who liked me in a PVC catsuit and thigh boots. He would wear jodhpurs and riding boots, and we used to wrestle. Nothing serious. I was much bigger than him anyway and always used to win; which, of course, is what he wanted! But the whole point of it was the 'pulling off' of the boot afterward. I'd get him on the floor and have to twist the boot in a particular way as I pulled. That was the really important part for him!

It's endlessly fascinating that people can be so diverse in their perversions. What interests me is that they've all got this particular 'thing'; this one point that is the whole focus of the session. I'm quite convinced that there will be at least one person out there who has a fetish for anything you can think of. If you were to get a whole load of people together and ask them what triggers certain things for them sexually, you'll find it's quite often a smell or the sight of something. That's what makes everybody so interesting, because it's never going to be the same thing twice.

Years ago I had another very entertaining chap, a bit like the Semolina Man. I think this chap was the first slave for a lot of mistresses that I know. Like Semolina Man, he knew what he was into and totally went with it. He was into the hypnotic, mental kind of domination. Getting into the mind and being in control. He had what he called 'magic tongues'. He used to have his favourite scenario where he'd have two or three of us girls lined up, while he put on a tape of *Phantom of the Opera*. He'd put this big rubber cape on with nothing underneath, and we girls would have to dance around. Then he'd start wafting around us with his big cape, singing away to the

Phantom of the Opera. Then he'd say: "Right, we're all going up to my special place in the sky now". He'd apparently got this special club up there, you see. So, we all went to this 'special club in the sky' thing, and then he'd tell us that he was going to make us all 'cum' with his magic tongues. He'd pull these imaginary tongues out of his mouth and say he was going to count to five and we'd all 'cum' together. We'd all make suitably 'girlie' orgasm type noises, and he'd be happy as could be! He was another guy who was completely 'out there', but also so at ease with what his thing was. I've spoken to lots of girls and they'd all say: "Oh, I did him! He was my first, too". It seems they were *all* initiated on this guy! God knows if he's still around. It kind of sets the scene for all these other people you're going to have afterwards. You know nothing's going to be *that* mad!

What I like is when people really enjoy themselves here. I know people think we're only doing it for the money, but with the diversity of people you have, you couldn't do it just for the money alone. You have to enjoy it or it would drive you 'bonkers'. Imagine having all these people demanding things from you all the time, you've *got* to enjoy it yourself!

That's one of the nice things about this job. Every one you see, although they might come for the same scenario, will be slightly different from each other, so it's never boring. The worst ones are the ones who come in and don't say anything all the way through the session, not a sound. I'm not getting any feed-back whatsoever. I hate that because I like to know I'm doing good, and that they're enjoying what I'm doing. If you don't get the right vibes back off someone it's very strange and disconcerting. You find yourself poking them every now and again just to see if they're still alive! It's so frustrating when you get people like that. They're about the only ones I don't really enjoy, because I don't know whether they're having a good time or not. And that's not what it's about. I know with a lot of people it's all up here, it's very cerebral. The body's going through these things, but it's the brain that's really enjoying it, and that's why they're very quiet about it. Other people are very shy, of course, and keep it all in. Maybe they don't feel at ease enough to express themselves. Which is a shame, since they've been brave enough to come and see someone like me in the first place, they should really be able to enjoy themselves when they get in there. I wish they'd, at least, make *some* nice noises occasionally!

Although I always put 'ladies welcome' in my adverts, I actually see very few females. I think that's because the manner of this particular scene has always been more male oriented. There's a lot more guys out there who are into this kind of thing than women, although it's not so bad now. Years ago, when I worked at *Atom Age*, I used to get guys phoning up all the time and they'd say how they wished their wives or girlfriends were into this, but they daren't tell them or they'd just freak out. Now it's easier. A lot more women are willing to experiment with sex and fun. And, since the advent of Aids, people have been trying to find different ways to have fun that doesn't necessarily involve penetrative sex. A lot more women are open to ideas about ways to spice up their love life. I think that most women who have an interest in this kind of thing will always be able to find a partner to play with. Women in this scene are much sought after people, so I don't think they really need to use a service like this. They'd always be able to find a man who would be happy to 'help' them, shall we say! I like women myself and have had relationships with women, so it would be nice to see women, but there's just not that many who phone up.

Also, you get a lot of guys who come along and it's not something that they even *want* their wives to know about. It's the Madonna and whore complex. Your wife is at home. She has the babies and cooks for you. You have your 'husbandly' and 'wifely' thing going on there. And you wouldn't ever dream of asking the mother of your children to do something that's slightly 'off the mark', shall we say. That's why they don't even want to ask their partners. They want to go somewhere that's completely separate. Remember, a lot of the guys who would come and see someone like myself wouldn't even go to the fetish clubs either. It's a completely separate thing. They don't want to go to clubs or to be a part of any fetish 'scene', as such. All they want is to come and see someone like me every now and again when they get the urge, and then go off back to their everyday life. And that's fine, too.

I've been lucky enough to travel with this job. I've been to Switzerland a couple of times to see a client. I remember the first time I went there with a friend of mine was to see this rich English guy who lived out there. He just wanted a couple of mistresses to come out to visit him for the weekend. That was great – flying out business class, champagne all the way and a bit of 'pervery' thrown in as well! There have been some lovely opportunities like that along the way. Other satisfying parts of the job are the people who are carers in real life. Maybe they've got partners who are unwell or whatever and, now and again, they'll come out and have a bit of fun for themselves. They say it's like a kind of 'mini-break' for them. They come and do this for an hour and forget about the 'not so good' things happening at home.

I think if I was ever going to visit another mistress for a rest, as a little holiday for myself, I think I'd visit Mistress Xena. I think she's really sexy looking. That's who *this* mistress would visit, anyway! But I don't think she does that! I wouldn't want to be hurt or anything like that. I'd just want to be tied up and pleasured really. I always thought that if I was ever going to pay for a service myself, it would be to have a massage, and have them say: "Any 'extras', Madam?" And for them to know how to make a woman 'cum'. It's reasonably easy to make a guy 'cum', but it's much more difficult with a woman. Sometimes, I think I'm doing all this stuff for other people, when's it going to me my turn! At least, I do get my feet massaged occasionally. I've even trained some of my regulars to do it *properly*. It's just one of the many little perks of the job!

MADAME TACHIBANA

Born in Tokyo, Japan, Madam Tachibana originally came to London as a student of Comparative Religions in 1990. On completing her studies she stayed on, working in the City as a bank secretary before embarking on her career as a dominatrix in 1998. Her chosen professional name means Lime Fruit and was used as an erotic metaphor in ancient Japanese poetry. Interviewed October 2000.

I always tell my clients that I am a *natural-born* dominatrix. Although I never practiced this profession at home, I've always been dominant. Even when I was a kid in Japan I was the school bully. I was dominating everyone! When I found this way of life, then I realised this is it for me. It was a name for what I had always been doing, so this is not much different for me doing this to how I was before. For example, I trained my first boyfriend to take off my shoes and lick my toes. If you choose to see that as domination, then maybe he was my first slave.

I didn't have any concept of what I was doing because there really isn't much of an SM scene in Japan. It is very taboo and what little they have is pretty much hidden. Since I have been doing this in London, I have been back to Tokyo performing my SM stage show. At that time I communicated with several SM people in the town. They were ever so hidden. For example, one mistress told me she is always having difficulty doing anything she wants to do in SM clubs. Over there, SM establishments are pretty much institutionalised. So, to do anything at all, she has to get together with the 'rope bondage' people, who are a pretty serious lot in Japan. That is their way of doing SM in Japan, with a lot of ropes. They are fanatics about it. I do bondage myself, of course, but they have this serious attitude about the look of the ropes as well. Once a month they will have a 'members only' salon where amateur models who want to be tied up come along. Lots of members take photos and videos. That seems to be the main activity with those SM people. Apart from that, it seems to be pretty much of an institutionalised sex industry where the so-called mistress will also be submissive or give you a blow job or anything else you want. I don't even know any

209

genuine mistresses in Japan or how to find them.

What I enjoy most in the scene is hard-core play. I don't really like soft 'tie-and-tease' scenarios. All my boys know that, in the end, I'm hard-core. I like nails and needles. Anything hard-core, really. I like 'fisting', too. I don't do that with everyone though. Everyone has a different bone structure. Some people can't take it all. It's a matter of training, really. Even if someone has done it with me before, that doesn't necessarily mean they can do it the next time. They might be out of practice for a while. I met this young man who had his own toy, which was massive! He often used that for his masturbation, so it was quite smooth and easy with him. It depends on the individual.

I like medical things as well, such as scrotum infusions. This involves sticking saline solution into the scrotum, either with an injection or with a hospital drip. It's not that painful really, but it looks spectacular! I always use my house slave as a human guinea pig to test these things on. His scrotum wasn't that big, but he still got about a litre in there. He told me it took about a week to go down and get absorbed into the system. That's why you can't do this with everyone. You can't even walk very well afterwards. It is about mutilation. You have to take a few days off work, so I don't want to give them that much impact. Even with the cane, they can still go to work the next day and behave normally, but with scrotum infusions it requires a bit more serious commitment. Of course, there are plenty of people who don't go to work and are willing to try all of these things. In the end it's all about commitment, I guess. They want to show their commitment to me. Basically, my boys offer me their bodies to do anything I want. That's the adulation thing. They have their own capacities but, within their own limits, they are always thinking of new ways to entertain me and please me. So, you see, I'm a bit out of touch with those 'tie-and-tease' people!

To achieve that level of commitment involves trust, of course. But more than that, it's a kind of love. For example, my main slave girl won't allow herself to be dominated by anyone but me. Okay, she has that kind of mentality but, if it was just a question of trust, there are plenty of skilled masters who want to borrow her. But she's kind of in love with me, so she feels that she'd be letting me down by going to other people. It's not even that she really likes to do these things, but she knows I like it!

I always have to think about the worst thing that might happen in any situation as regards the danger aspect. For instance, 'fisting' or working on the anal area too much might be a danger because you might split it or take the intestine out. But, even then, if you push it back quickly enough or leave them on the level so they don't bleed too much, then it's alright. And even if the scrotum infusion is so full that it bursts, I can always stitch it back up. It's not that bad. Suffocation is more a more direct danger.

There are some requests that I have considered *too* dangerous. For example, I've had slaves who want me to take their testicles off completely. I tell them that this is not possible because it's an organ. I point out to them the death rate as a result of castration. They might say: "Oh, it was so common in the Roman times, so it shouldn't be any problem now". I tell them that those people were *real* slaves! And slaves weren't considered valuable life. If they died, so what? Do you really want to risk your life for a fantasy?

Sure, I've got the equipment to do it, but we would still have the problem of infection afterwards. And the blood he would loose would be so much that we would probably need the facility of a blood transfusion, which I haven't got. So, sorry, I really think it is rather impractical. But, still, I don't refuse them completely because that's the fantasy that's going on in their heads. I might suggest that we do a mock castration or something like that, instead. I usually see people for a consultation first where we discuss their fantasies. I am able to cater for most fantasies, except where there is an obvious danger to life, as I've explained.

My hard-core boys are very happy that they've found me. They have been round to lots of mistresses who just laughed at them and didn't take their bizarre fantasies seriously, but I take them *very* seriously. Some have such specific ideas, very fixed and visual. It's almost like a video tape in their heads, and that's the only thing they will get excited about. That can be a bit weird sometimes. But, then again, I understand how someone can be stuck to one particular thing. I am very sympathetic. Often, the fantasy will come from something in their childhood. One of my boys, for example, is Italian and whenever he is in the country he comes to see me. He always brings three bars of soap with him. In his case, I have to be his cousin Luciano. He plays out the scenario of a young boy with constipation. I have to tell him that his mother and sister are worried about him, and they think the only way to deal with it is to shove the bars of soap up him. But he always refuses, so I have to spank him. That is a bit weird because it's always the same thing. There's no room for improvisation or variations at all!

It's the same with the school room scenarios. It's always pretty much the same with me being the headmistress. I always use some 'excuse' for some caning or spanking. I will punish them because they've skipped Japanese lessons or something. Then, one day, one of my boys actually studied Japanese and started speaking it to me. I was quite impressed with that.

Everyone has their own particular thing. Basically, if you start trying to put your own objective understanding onto it, you'll realise how bizarre it all is. It's beyond your understanding. But, then, if you don't apply that and just accept that everyone has their own way, then it doesn't matter. There's no way, for example, that I would eat someone's shit, but I know lots of people who do. So how can I understand them? There's no way. But because I don't understand, doesn't mean I can't still feel sympathy for them. So I will let them eat my shit, if that's what they want. I mean, if I don't do it, who will? When people come to me, and I can see they are desperate and serious about what they want to do, then I will do it. I don't do sex, but any other activity that I regard as safe SM is okay. Even if it is something I can't do or don't feel comfortable with, I will try to help. For example, I don't do wrestling as I don't feel it is true domination, but I will still feel sympathetic to them. I will refer them to another mistress who will take care of them. I feel this is my responsibility as a mistress.

Another complication is that a lot of people who come to me are into Oriental women. I'm one of the few in London who does this work, so I can't cover everything. They are *very* particular about what they want. They want a certain dominatrix of the right age and looks, and so on. Also, many of the men who simply want a Japanese girl will find me too much, because I am far more domina than geisha! I'm no good for them at all.

One of my most faithful boys, who has been with me a long time and never been to anyone else, had never even done any SM before! But he was very intrigued by Japanese women, that's why he came to me. But then he developed his SM side very well, too. Now we do all kinds of very serious stuff together. Just the other day, for example, I put a needle down the shaft of his penis. It is like there are so many different forms of love in a relationship. Some become very good slaves of mine, and some don't. It depends on the amount of commitment they are prepared to give me.

The reason I decided to live in this way as a dominatrix is that I wanted to be in touch with *real* people. I'm not interested in money games. One time I had a job in a bank. There I was simply moving figures and dealing with 'unreality'. The people I met there I thought were in an 'unreality' with all those figures, just fighting with shadows. I have enough boys who support my lifestyle, so I can carry on like this as long as I want to carry on. I like the way I do things, and the boys come to help me out in order to carry on going. That's the way I see it, anyway.

In fact, when I finished my degree at university on Comparative Religions, I thought about how I could go about living in this religion *and* make a living. I did look into those religious areas, but so many of those are just institutions. A lot of them have lost the original idea. It's about power and politics, and I'm not just talking about Christianity. Many religions have started out good and then somehow ended up in a mess. Even Buddhism in Japan is in pretty much of an appaling condition.

For a while, I thought about joining a religious order. But I thought that's not quite what I want to do, because it is not religious *enough* for me. They follow their regulations and timetables okay, but they are in a very protected environment all the time, and that's not really being in touch with people and helping them. I have stayed in those monasteries in Japan and went along with the lifestyle, but I just thought it wasn't quite right for me.

I am pretty much a spiritual person and, in the end, I found my own spirituality in SM. I don't mean I tell the slaves to worship me because I am a spiritual being or anything! I see myself as being a bit like a medium or a shaman who is trying to get them to somewhere else. Like in a trance or something like that. To me this is a modern shamanism, if you like. Not even modern, really. SM has *always* been there in human history, so there is nothing modern about it. I found this job is very much close to religion, which is what I am very happy about.

As I say, these practices are nothing new. You can find them with North American Indians and Hindus. It's always been there in religious practice. So, in a way, I am taking this activity out of a religious context and just doing the physical side. Religious dogma doesn't come into it, as we separate the experience. I'm not forcing anyone to get into any religion. The mind has great power. Once they strongly believe in something, a person can do quite amazing things, because they get access to their subconscious. My boys strongly believe that I can take them somewhere else. Without their receptiveness I cannot do it. Because they are willing to take it, I can do this. That's another thing I found with religion, it is very pushy. They like to be missionaries. They want to recruit people who aren't into it. I keep it quiet and, when people come for help, I can sort them out. I do my best for them.

As I said, to me, it is pretty much a religious life. Nothing to do with sex – well, to me, anyway. I am just using that sexual SM energy as a vehicle to get onto some other level. They come here for a safe haven to have these 'out of body' experiences. I am like a conductor who gives more and more experiences to create a harmony. I give them different sensations and see what happens. Sometimes it feels that it's not me that's doing it. It's something else flowing through me. It's a bit like a medium, really. If I do a really good session, I feel very happy. It's not just that I've done something for them. It's more complicated than that. My maid tells me that, when I'm doing a session, I don't hear what she says and my face changes because I am concentrating so much. I enjoy that transcendental state.

Sometimes I will deal with several slaves at the same time. And that's *very* interesting! It's more complicated to conduct the whole thing, though. I might let them swap roles and make one of them a bit more dominant than the other. There's all kinds of combinations. I let them spank each other and do all kinds of things to each other. As I say, it can be very interesting! But, ultimately, I would describe myself as a sadist. I get a serious buzz out of *very* serious pain. I find that, when people are in serious pain, they can't pretend anymore. Maybe they have responsible positions and jobs in the outside world but, when they come to me, they just become a 'thing'. There's not much difference between an animal and a human being in that situation. There is an honesty and truth in their pain. It's about dealing with the reality of the people when everything is striped away.

I am *never* submissive myself. That is another reason that put me off the idea of being a nun. You have to submit yourself all the way through to taking the mercy of the god or something. And I'm no good at that. I'm a bit too much of a 'control freak'. If I ever did submit to anyone it would be to gain a deeper understanding of my subject. I would take no pleasure from it.

I am very proud of my job. All the people in my local pub know what I do. I am proud of this lifestyle and I want other people to enjoy it too. I used to do more interviews with the media, but I found I just got flooded with the same stupid questions. They treat you like some strange animal in a zoo. I didn't feel comfortable with that, so I rarely talk to the press now. I use this as my way of living. And it's good, it's working. To me it's perfect. I don't want to exploit other people. And I don't want to be part of those false things – that fighting with shadows. I just deal with real people who have problems because they have such a peculiar desire. I don't look down on them, I help them.

Although I'm pretty much a lifestyle dominatrix, my boyfriend isn't into SM at all. Which is good for me in a way, because I am flooded by slaves. If I'm not careful they'd be with me seven days a week. So, even though I'm a lifestyle mistress, I need a little bit of time that is non-SM time. In fact, *because* it is a lifestyle, I don't want to get fed up. Once you are in that environment too much I think your imagination blocks. You have to be open to everything all the time and let the imagination flow in.

Mistress Shane

This dark haired and deceptively petite, Antwerp-based, mistress is an intriguing blend of former punkette, Big Apple fashion queen, self styled 'arrogant American bitch' and unrepentant sadist who manages to combine a passion for strap-on dildos and equal opportunity multi-gender fucking with a weakness for romantic fiction and a love of opera and antiques. She was also the first dominatrix who ever brought this intrepid researcher a box of chocolates during our meeting in London and then threatened/promised to beat him up! Just your average girl next door, really! Interviewed August 1996

Well, first I'd like to say straight out that I class myself a life-style dominatrix, first and foremost. I'm originally from New York and first became aware of Fem-Dom when I started going out with a guy from my local neighbourhood who I, very innocently, turned into my slave! How it happened, I couldn't even remember. It just seemed so natural and things kind of snowballed from there. What I can tell you is that, when I was about eighteen, this friend tricked me into dominating him! He said he was doing an improvisational class at acting school, and what they were studying was how to be a prop or a piece of furniture. Supposedly, everyone stuck their hand into a bowl for their assignments, and he pulled out a slip of paper telling him to be a floor!

Of course, I didn't realise that this was just a rather cunning ploy. He just came up to me and said: "Can you help me out with my project? I'm gonna lay down and I just need to know what it feels like to be the floor. So pretend that I'm not here, and when you feel like walking on this side of the floor, just do it". So I did it and found I spent most of my time on that part of the 'floor'! Actually, I found it very enjoyable. Years later, when we talked about it again, he said that I was one of the few people he'd gotten to do that who'd had no hesitation about really stepping hard on his crotch and on his face. Ever since then I've just loved stepping on men's penises. Not because I don't like them, but just because it feels so good underneath my foot.

I really think I first grasped the concept of erotica and power dressing when I was in my baby carriage! My mother always wore stockings and high heels. I used to play with them all the time. She had this huge closet and that was my favourite place to be. She used to have stockings dyed to match her shoes. Red and pink and yellow and green. I used to try them on all the time and get yelled at.

Then later, I went through the whole punk rock thing, which was similar, but not quite the same as fetish. But I was still wearing fishnets at the time. It was around then that I bought my first pair of fetish pumps that I used to wear occasionally. As a matter of fact, I bought them in London, during the height of the punk days. I must have been around nineteen. Right after I put them on I noticed a difference. Men reacted markedly different to my pumps than to the Doc Marten boots. Then I realised that someone with a big mouth could fit my shoe in it. And then when he'd start sucking on it, I realised that this was a good place for it to be! I found I just loved having that kind of control over a person; especially one who wouldn't normally be in that kind of position.

Although I charge for my services and make no excuses for that, as I have a certain lifestyle to maintain, I'm not just into this on a professional basis. Even when I'm not working I surround myself with 'scene' people. I have a full time slave in New York and have Tanya, my full-time transvestite maid, here in Antwerp. So, to say I enjoy all this is a gross understatement, I positively love it!

In the early days I worked in New York; that was for about six years. I started working in someone else's studio before working independently. About eighteen months ago I moved to Belgium, mainly because I love Europe, but also because I wanted to broaden my horizons. I wanted to travel and meet scene people in different countries. Now I divide my time between Antwerp and Manhattan. But I also love to visit San Francisco and London. It's interesting to get to grips with the different tastes in perversion in these different places. For instance, I think the Europeans are definitely more into rubber and breath control than they are in the United States. I've worked in other places, too. Like Holland and in Manchester, England, which was a lot of fun. I particularly like the English slaves. They bring out the best (or the worst) in me! San Francisco's great, too. Perverts everywhere!

I go to a lot of clubs and do public performances, too. I was recently at this amazing private party in London at a gentleman's villa; complete with a dungeon built in an air raid shelter. One of our hosts was a caning maniac; he went through literally fifty people in one night, never once losing his precision or his skill.

I also love *Power Exchange* in San Francisco. I was there a few months ago for their scene auction, which is a very fun and frisky charity event. I had my strap-on attached and auctioned off a good reaming. A handsome young guy bought me to do his girlfriend. He was a real gentleman. He just handed over her leash and disappeared. She was a breathtaking blonde with great breasts. I put her in a sling and fucked her until she came. There must have been about twenty people crowded around us watching, some of them playing with each other.

Right now I've opened a new studio in Antwerp. I've been open for business for about a month now and already it's looking good for the future. I've been involved in a lot of other projects, too. I've made over twenty fetish videos so far. I've also been featured in seven cable television specials dedicated to the SM lifestyle, including HBO's *Real Sex*. I'm also in the middle of writing my own autobiography. So, as you can imagine, I'm pretty busy at the moment.

I think my most favourite kind of pervert is the obnoxious kind! No, but seriously, I do like a challenge. Unfortunately, most of my clients are pretty easy for me to dominate. I believe I have earned the reputation of being a sadistic, but understanding, mistress. I accept novices, but only the most sincere. Real and intense sessions in true S&M are my specialty – as well as my passion! My sessions are designed to bring my subjects to their limits in both physical and psychological torment. My favourite methods of torture include heavy whipping and caning, cock and ball torture and advanced nipple torture. For the true connoisseur, extensive and extreme treatments are available and definitely encouraged! Utter and complete humiliation is another area in which I excel. Piercing and scarification. Toilet stuff. I've even branded people, too.

I'm also into wrestling scenes. Again, I think that stems back to childhood. I was the only girl on the block and a real tomboy. I used to get really angry at my mom because she used to call me back into the house and make me put my skirt on. I didn't see what the big deal was. And I guess there's still the tomboy in there, especially when I don my strap-on penis! In fact, I think it's one of my favourite toys. When I put it on it becomes a part of me. I'd describe myself as an equal opportunity fucker as I enjoy both genders! I think the main difference between screwing a man and screwing a woman is that the guys scream more. At least the first time, they do! Actually, I've had a lot of male virgins, but never any female ones!

I think there's a lot of bi-sexual men and women in general in the scene. They've learned to be more open-minded. I help a lot of guys out of the closet. I remember once in New York, I had a client who wanted to be fucked anonymously by another man. So I tied him up over a horse, blindfolded him and hooded him and, by coincidence, I had another client who wanted to fuck a man for the first time. So, voila! Having the power to create that scene was what turned me on the most.

There is a distinction between my professional clients and my personal slaves in terms of what sort of scenes I'll get involved in with them. Obviously, I'll have a much more intimate relationship with my personal slaves. It's much more emotional and there's a greater intensity between us, no matter what the particular scene might be.

I do a lot of fantasy sessions as well. There are lots of pictures of me as a nun and as a school teacher. Actually, no one has asked me to dress up as a nun yet for a session, but I think I would really enjoy that! I like to be teacher and I like to be boss, naturally! Out of all the stuff I've done, I think the most memorable scenario would have to be the mock crucifixion where I nailed this client to a cross. Not with real nails, I hasten to add, just piercing needles. But all the way through, just the same! I guess deep down it must have had some religious significance for him. I feel a lot of times I'm really helping the client by acting as their therapist. I don't mind. If I can help someone discover themselves through a little kinkiness, I'm happy to do it.

Though I have lots of fun, I do take my work *very* seriously. There's a lot of people in this business who aren't serious and honest or even safe and clean! There's a real lack of communication there. You have to bear in mind that you're dealing with important parts of people's lives; things that happened in their childhood, things they're hiding from the world. Things that they're really afraid of sometimes. You must be aware of their limits. That was a road of self examination I had to go down myself, too. I mean, I can joke about stepping on guy's cocks or crucifying them and all of that stuff, but it took me a long time to realise that there was that part of me that I had to get out in a healthy way.

But getting back to the new studio, I've got a lot of ideas to try out. I want to be able to unfetter my own imagination along with my client's and see where we both might go that neither of us has been before. I have been thinking for some time that there needs to be a place where true submissives can stay for prolonged periods. By that, I mean all day, overnight, weekends and even all week stays. This kind of session is obviously only suitable for someone who is truly into the scene. But, I must admit, the idea of training someone for a full week really excites me!

What appeals to me about working here in Antwerp is that it gives submissives the chance to visit both a beautiful city and a beautiful mistress at the same time! The cost of travelling from places like England or Holland is so cheap so, by offering long stay sessions, I feel this would be an experience not to be missed. And for those submissives who can't make it over here, I also offer full postal and phone training, photo sets, custom videos and a visiting service. People can also feel free to send me respectful e-mails. I'm *always* interested in learning a new kink or two!

As you can see, at this point, being a mistress is pretty much my whole life. But I'm eliminating all elements that might lead to burnout. That's one reason I'm building my own dungeon. When I do have time outside of the scene, my hobbies include collecting antiques, classical music, going to the opera and reading. Believe it or not, I adore romantic novels most of all!

MISTRESS LINDA

In this interview we meet a couple who, instead of merely playing at some very dangerous extra marital games, have actually made it the basis of their marriage. Mistress Linda and her Slave-Husband Gary have been married for seven years. Both are now in their early thirties. After the first two years the cracks began to show and Linda tried to end the relationship. When Gary begged her to reconsider, Linda decided to draw up a unique contract! Interviewed November 1998

Who can say when the balance of power shifts in a relationship? There was a time, though it's hard to believe it now, when Gary and I were just a straight forward, normal married couple. By that, I mean we were quite content with our relationship and the way things were. Quite boring and suburban, really. Gary made all the decisions. Well, he still does, actually, as regards our normal daily life. It's just that, as far as our sex life goes, I am in *total* control. He has to bow to my demands and has absolutely no say in what I do or who I see for sex.

The balance shifted when, quite simply, I started to get bored with our marriage. As the cracks began to appear, I became increasingly distant and cold toward him. He, on the other hand, found himself desperately trying to overcompensate by pouring on the love and affection to the point where he just began to irritate me. Inevitably, he only ended up earning my complete contempt. He became a pathetic wimp in my eyes, as I was always fond of calling him – both in private and in front of my female friends!

It was a classic scenario, I suppose. If he had been more of a man about it, he would have told me where to go and got out of the situation then and there (as many of his friend's urged him to do), knowing the damage it was doing to his self esteem. But, as they say, these things are much easier said than done when obsession takes over. Little by little, his self respect was chipped away, almost without his being aware of it. He bowed to my every whim, no matter how demeaning, in his efforts to win back my affection.

As time went on, and this pattern of behaviour became more entrenched and ingrained, Gary found himself becoming strangely excited by his treatment. We'd never thought of ourselves as 'dominant' or 'submissive' before, and knew nothing about any 'scene', so all these feelings were very alien to both of us and a bit frightening too. In effect, we were finding ourselves turning into different characters. Or maybe it's more correct to say, these were the 'shadow' sides of our personalities.

At first, I was ashamed and guilty about the way I found myself treating Gary during that early period. And angry and frustrated with him, as well. I desperately wanted him to stand up to me and put me in my place, the way I had been brought up to believe a 'real' man should. But, he simply wouldn't. He just became nicer and more 'clingy', bringing me flowers everyday and breakfast in bed, and all the rest of his pathetic attempts at seducing me. Of course, it just served to make me even angrier. To think, that if he had slapped me down then and there, I might well have ended up being *his* slave, instead of the other way around!

Anyway, as time went on, I found myself actually beginning to enjoy my power over him, like some horrid child pulling the wings off an insect. I still felt the occasional pangs of guilt and shame, but the excitement and sheer fascination of finding out just how far one human being can push another closer to the edge was certainly better than what had passed for sex up until this time with my 'ball-less' excuse of a husband!

I kept pushing him further and further, and took a cruel delight in humiliating him at every opportunity – even in front of my girl-friends. I'd have to be careful which ones, of course. Some of them found it all a bit embarrassing, while others took his side out of pity, and thought me an absolute cow! There were a few who, I think, became quite turned on by the idea of bossing a man around, as long as it wasn't their own! If it had been their own husbands or boyfriends, they would have been as frustrated as me at having such a spineless wimp hanging around, I'm sure!

In an effort to goad him into some sort of manly response, I'd even discuss his sexual shortcomings with my girlfriends while he was present. I still hadn't quite cottoned onto the idea that he was actu-ally getting pleasure from this humiliation. This was something beyond my understanding at the time. I just knew that I wielded all the power in this marriage and that if he was so hell-bent on being such a total jerk, and letting me get away with it, then I was just as determined to exploit the situation for all it was worth!

From then on I literally became the 'bitch from hell', and loved every minute of it! I made him do all the housework and the shopping (except for luxury items for me, of course!) just to show him who was in charge! My rules were very simple – I either get what I want or he gets out! And I meant it! Meaning it is the important part, because you can't play act at this. If he had shown the slightest objection, I'd have simply shown him the door. And I still would, if it came down to it! He knows and respects my will and, above all, he fears the consequences – which is losing me! He accepts that he is the weaker half in this marriage and that he needs me far more than I need him, so he has no choice but to obey my every whim.

I believe this is the essential key to a woman's control over her man. The inferior male is so focused on his narrow desires it leaves him wide open to exploitation by us Superior Females. The sad truth is that most males would gladly crawl across broken glass or swim through a sea of pig's vomit if they thought it would get them even the remotest chance of sniffing round a woman's cunt! This is a man's greatest weakness and a woman's true strength. Females have no such obsessions. Their fantasies and desires are never as obsessively focused. It's hard to imagine any woman making a fetish out of a pair of used boxer shorts, even if they did belong to Robert Redford!

I remember clearly the night I broached the idea of my taking a lover. Even at that stage, when I had asserted my dominance in most areas of our relationship, I was still not completely certain he would go along with that idea! I thought that he must have some grain of self respect left, surely? What kind of husband could possibly agree to such an outrageous suggestion? But, agree he did. And, as they say, I've never looked back since!

In fact, I already had my eye on a guy who I knew fancied me at the gym. He didn't know anything about my circumstances as to whether I was married or not (I'd long since relegated my wedding ring to the bottom of my knickers drawer)and saw no reason to tell him. Anyway, by this stage I regarded myself as single in all but name. Gary was no 'husband', as far as I was concerned. In fact, I regarded him as little more than a dogsbody around the house. Now that I had moved him out of the main bedroom and into the tiny box room with all the other 'odds and ends' that cluttered up the place, I felt myself to be a completely free agent and warming very quickly to the idea of enjoying my new found freedom, as well as sharing my bed with a variety of new and exciting lovers for once!

Gary knew that I had completely lost interest in him sexually at this point, though I was (and still am) very content with the rest of our relationship. To be honest, that side of things had never been very strong on my part. It was still difficult for him to accept my decision at first, understandably enough. Now that we've been doing it for so long though, it has become quite natural for him to play second (or even third or fourth!) fiddle to whoever I decide to become involved with. And it can be very much a spur of the moment thing! I'll certainly never ask if he likes, or even approves of, my selection of bed mate. In fact, quite the opposite. As often as not, when I feel like really 'slumming it' after a night on the vodka and cokes, I'll go out of my way to pick up the most loutish yob I can find, just to wind him up even more! I thoroughly enjoy a 'bit of rough' as the perfect antidote to Gary's exasperatingly sweet and genteel ways.

Our, or rather I should say, *my* favourite method of finding one-off sex is for us to go out hunting in pubs or clubs. Though not, I hasten to add in our home town, where there might be the danger of running into anyone we know. The way it works is like this. I will select the young 'meat' for the evening and Gary's job is to break the ice by engaging the object of my desire in some friendly banter at the bar while buying the drinks. It's usually quite easy to arouse the interest of even the most stupid of my targets and induce them to join us once the yobs realise there's an attractive woman with him who's taking an interest in them and, as far as they're concerned, is available for uncomplicated sex.

If I'm really interested in a particular guy, I'll waste no time in making it clear to him that Gary and I are 'just good friends' and the way is open for him to make a move. If I'm feeling especially wicked that evening, I will tell the guys that he's gay and then ask them if they have a problem with that. Naturally, with the promise of some easy sex at stake, they'll say they haven't. But it's usually pretty obvious, bearing in mind the kind of very macho young brute's I tend to be attracted to, that they are rabid homophobes who at best tolerate my husband's presence with barely concealed contempt.

Gary will then be promptly relegated to the role of 'guardian of the handbag' while I flounce off to flirt, dance, grope and whatever else I feel like doing with my new toy-boy conquest. What makes it even worse for poor Gary is that as he's cast in the role of platonic or gay friend, he's expected to endure this sort of torment without showing the least signs of arousal. If he should be silly enough to give out the slightest indication that he may be getting some voracious sexual pleasure from watching other guys getting what he can't from his wife, I will promptly dismiss him with a perfunctory reminder that he has to be up early for work or that his mother or mythical 'boyfriend' will be expecting him home. In this way I make him suffer the sneers of contempt from the louts to add to his humiliation. Though, of course, I must point out that he is a *very* willing victim in this scenario and gets as much of a thrill from these games as I do.

So, I'm a bitch who enjoys tormenting men who desire me. So what? Show me a woman who doesn't enjoy lots of male attention, and the power that comes with it, and I'll show you a liar! Women have something men want, and they're willing to pay almost any price to get it. That's the way it's always been. I get an almost unbearable excitement from torturing and manipulating men sexually. This is where a woman's power lies, and the girl who doesn't learn this is cheating herself of her rightful legacy of superiority. This is something I've learned since becoming Gary's mistress and the centre of his world. I wish someone had explained this particular fact of life to me years ago. I think it's something all mothers should teach their daughters at puberty!

It's an incredible turn-on for me to pick up some young man at a club and get horny with him while Gary is forced to watch. And then taking one home, and all the while knowing I'm putting my husband through such a psychological hell of frustration and jealousy that he'll be jerking himself off in his little single bed, while I'm having some *very* noisy sex next door with a complete stranger that he loathes, but his own pathetic lack of backbone makes him absolutely powerless to do anything about! Now that's what I call a buzz!

I've had so many wonderful encounters since we established and developed the full potential of the Fem-Dom side of our relationship, it's hard to think of the best examples. Certainly one of the most memorable episodes so far wasn't even with a man, but with another female I met through a contact advertisement. Mandy was about the same age as me and, like me, very bi-curious as well as eager to explore her dominance over men with another dominant woman. Needless to say, we wasted no time incorporating Gary, as well as a few other males that took our fancy, into our games. We found we got our biggest kicks out of putting on sex shows for Gary and the other men. Of course, with him the rules we laid down were *most* definitely look but don't touch! I'm afraid with the other men, we usually ended up screwing.

Mandy and I have been seeing each other on a steady basis for about six months now and have had a few *very* dirty weekends away together with lots of sexy adventures. These are usually without Gary, of course. Unless, that is, we decide we need a chauffeur or a butler to carry our luggage around for us. Even a male as pathetic as my husband has his uses! I must say Mandy has really got into the mistress-role and is very good at it. She's certainly more physically sadistic than I am, and can really lay into Gary with a whip or a riding crop a lot harder than I'm capable of doing. I'm much more into the psychological stuff myself, as you've probably noticed. Lots of humiliation, mental torture and endless cock teasing. That sort of thing.

Anyway, Mandy has decided she likes the life-style so much she has recently acquired a slave-boyfriend of her own. They have a pretty similar idea about things as me and Gary, which adds an extra dimension to our playtimes! In actual fact, Mandy and I have some very wicked plans hatched that will incorporate both of these wimps. Apparently, her slave Rick is an even bigger wimp than my Gary though, I must admit, it's hard to imagine such a pathetic specimen! We've already humiliated guys together on a couple of occasions, which we always found very exciting. Our favourite scenario is to make them suck each others cocks in a sixty-nine position for our entertainment. As both men involved have been completely heterosexual, this is a totally emasculating and demeaning experience for them; which, of course, is the whole point of the exercise. The more they're emasculated then, by implication, the more empowering it is for us girls!

Sometimes I will allow Gary to treat me to a holiday abroad. Occasionally, I might *even* let him come with me! On these holidays I can really let rip as a total super-bitch, due to the fact that we are completely anonymous and there isn't any chance of running into anyone we know. I don't even have to pretend that we have any connection with each other at all, if I don't want to – which suits me just fine! We'll book into separate rooms at hotels and take our meals at separate tables. I've even been known to ignore Gary for the whole holiday!

All I require is for him to be within sight and earshot at all times while I'm having my fun and get me out of trouble if it arises. So far this has never happened, as I can usually take care of myself. Actually, I've been known to play some pretty wicked tricks on him when he's simply been trying his best to protect me. Like the time when I was getting up to some pretty steamy action with two young guys on the beach one night and Gary, bless him, was keeping a wary eye on things with his binoculars from behind a sand dune. For a bit of a laugh I told the men he was a pervert who was snooping on us. The two of them went over and gave him a bit of a beating up, I'm afraid. It was a bit naughty of me, I know, but it was such a giggle seeing the look on his face afterwards!

I suppose there are a lot of people who would think our relationship is a bit odd, and probably wonder what he can possibly get out of such a life of abuse. We only know that this way of life works for us and we are happier than ever. Whatever it is, it enables both of us to get incredible satisfaction and a sense of purpose from our game playing. By this time, I think it's safe to say we are *both* hopelessly addicted to the suffering and torment I put him through and the empowerment it gives me in return. Maybe we are both completely mad, I don't know! Gary often jokes that he should be locked up for his own good and have the key thrown away but, then again, he'd probably enjoy that, too!

We've been doing this stuff so long now, I believe we've actually lost touch with what so-called 'normal' relationships are supposed to be like. I honestly think we'd both be totally incapable of having one even if we had the chance, so we're much better off staying as we are, which is what we love anyway! I know Gary certainly wouldn't voluntarily want to swap his life of servitude for the kind of bland lives we see other couples leading. They always seem so bloody boring! With a dominant lady in charge, each day is a new challenge in humiliation for any man with submissive inclinations. I know he can put up with my, admittedly, rather sordid little affairs because he knows they are all very short-lived and mean nothing to me at the end of the day, beyond immediate gratification and thrill-seeking. Whereas our life together as mistress and slave is totally secure and forever.

Nowadays our mistress/slave lifestyle is very well established and I see no reason why it shouldn't continue like this for the rest of our lives. I have the very best of all worlds in that I have a gentle, caring partner to look after me and support me, plus I have the absolute freedom to do anything I feel like doing and to take up with any lover I might fancy. I know some of my girlfriends disapprove of the way I carry on, though I think it's more a case of jealousy on their part, if you ask me. What woman, if she were totally honest, wouldn't envy the kind of lifestyle I have demanded for myself?

I feel no guilt these days about the way I treat my husband, not like I did in the beginning. And why should I? It was his decision to stick around when I wanted to end the marriage, wasn't it?. If he had been a 'real' man he would have left me long ago and found himself a new wife. But he didn't, did he? So, the way I see it, he's brought his servitude on himself. I didn't make him a slave, did I? He enslaved himself through his own male weaknesses and, what's more, I know he wouldn't have it any other way. What I always say is, why settle for a wife when you can worship a goddess!

MISTRESS JACQUELINE

With the publication of her autobiography 'Whips and Kisses', as well as her many TV appearances, mail order company and lecture tours, Jacqueline has established herself as quite a formidable force on the American fetish scene. Formally based in Los Angeles, California, she has now relocated to the San Francisco Bay Area. This interview is a good example of the no-nonsense, business like approach so typical of American mistresses. Interviewed May 1994.

I've been a practicing dominatrix for over eleven years now, and they've been very successful years full of fun and growth. I've met thousands of wonderful people. I'm very active and involved in the SM lifestyle, and I have a full stable of slaves who serve my *every* need. The 'scene' is my life and my life is the 'scene'! In fact, to mark my tenth anniversary in the scene last year, I launched my own magazine which records highlights from my career. I'm very excited about this project as I know that anyone who has followed my career and even your people over there in Europe, who don't know that much about me yet, will get a lot out of it.

I've had SM fantasies ever since I was a young girl. My sexual proclivities always included pain and pleasure. I played SM type games with my boyfriends without even understanding the meaning of my actions. I've always been a naturally commanding type of woman. Boys and men have been doing my bidding ever since I can remember. After I divorced my first husband, I went all out on a sexual exploration. When I finally had the guts to answer an SM ad in a local sex newspaper, I knew that I'd come home. I took to the scene like a duck takes to water. The rest, as they say, is history.

I've been on so many TV 'talk shows' that I really can't list them all, particularly when my book was published. I did a national tour that included *every* radio station in the whole country! Plus, I appeared on major TV shows like *Donahue, Joan Rivers, Sonya Live* and *Montell Williams*. I actually decided to go on shows way before the book came out. I wanted to do these shows because I knew how healing it was for me when I first came out of the closet and admitted my SM side. I hoped I would be able to reach others like me. Judging from the mail response, I feel that I accomplished this. However, studio audiences have traditionally given me a hard time. It seems that the nature of the game is to badger and provoke. Talk shows are, by their nature, very exploitative. I'm still glad that I did them, but I think there are better ways to reach people. Since then I've turned down *Geraldo, Maury Povitch* and *Jane Whitney*. I'm no longer willing to go on shows with slaves in hoods and be treated like a freak or cartoon character. I have better things to do! Did you know I didn't even get paid?

The book is my own personal autobiography. It's mostly about how I got into the scene, and the struggles within myself, and how I've overcome a lot of the crap I've had to deal with, both in my family and in society. Again, I wrote the book because I *truly* felt my story could help others like myself. As a leader and spokesperson in the scene, I've found it very satisfying to have the opportunity to educate the public and let them know of our existence. I'm a firm believer that most people have sexual fantasies that could be considered 'out of the norm'. Because we live in a sexually repressed society, most men and women choose to suppress their feelings, and only admit to what they perceive as 'mainstream' sexuality. Those of us in the SM world should hold our heads high as we have taken the risk of admitting that there is more to sex than tits, ass or a conventional 'roll in the hay'! I have a great deal of respect for all of us who have come out of the closet and made a decision to be who we are. As an educator, I plan to dedicate my public image to help all men and women better understand the interplay of fantasy and human sexuality.

And I would consider myself fairly well qualified for the job, too. As well as being a professional dominatrix, I'm also a licensed psychotherapist. I have a Master's Degree in Clinical Psychology and I have my Marriage, Family and Child Therapist (MFCT) designation, as authorised by the State of California. I disclose this not to impress people, but to give your readers an insight into my own orientation toward the scene. I believe that bondage play and fantasy fulfillment are healthy, creative outlets to explore the feelings we have deep inside ourselves.

Recently, for example, I had the pleasure of running two support groups on a weekly basis for both men and women. One group was for people into dominant/submissive relationships. Everyone involved in these groups learned a great deal about themselves. They found it healing to meet with other like-minded people, and to have a place to talk about the kind of things that they wouldn't even *dare* mention to their friends or colleagues. Lasting friendships were formed and participants left with the feeling that they weren't so very different after all! Because of the success of these groups, I then did a series of one-day seminars across the country.

On a personal level, I'm also currently involved in the best relationship of my life. I've waited a long time for this, so it's very special to me. What makes this so good is that we are true equals and love each other unconditionally. Of course, it's not a 'straight' relationship, you're talking to Jacqueline here! However, even though we do live stage performances together, our personal play is done in the bedroom only, and what we do there is intimate and private. Because my slaves are *never* my lovers, my private relationship does not intrude on my mistress/slave activities.

In my SM play I'm very versatile. Depending, of course, on who I'm playing with, I really enjoy *almost* everything in the SM spectrum. The most important thing is involvement. I love passion and excitement. When there is true commitment to a scene, no matter what it is, I find it personally very exciting. Mood, music, creativity, good costuming and theatrics all lend themselves to the drama I crave.

I'm certainly a great spanking enthusiast, for example. I'm very much a part of the spanking community and will always be. I think spanking is something that is very separate from SM. The people and the 'mindset' behind it are completely different. In addition to the D/S support group I mentioned earlier, I also run a second group in Los Angeles specifically for men and women who are into spanking. I've separated the spanking group from the SM group because the issues are not the same. Incidentally, I've done seminars on spanking in various locations throughout the country, too. These one day workshops are called *'Spanking: The Definitive Seminar'*, and not only provide important information, but also allow spanking enthusiasts to gather and meet others in their area. The workshops cover a variety of topics, including how to place advertisements in the 'personals', how to meet others and how to overcome any shame and guilt associated with being part of an 'alternative' sexual lifestyle. It's another project I'm really excited about. *And* It's lots of fun, too!

Unfortunately, because I'm so busy these days, I hardly ever have time to do private sessions myself anymore. However, I'll still see very 'special' slaves for sessions from time to time. I'm *very* selective, naturally, but I can generally tell how honest and sincere someone is by the way they write to me. I always feel that anything of value and quality is worth the pursuit, and I'm confident that my slaves will all testify to the fact that I'm definitely 'top-notch'!

I'm extremely versatile and fluent in *all* aspects of SM, fetishism, slave training and corporal punishment. Since I love spanking so much personally, I give a particularly good discipline session and absolutely *love* to role play! Though my favoured 'look' is leather/rock, I can easily turn myself into a governess or school teacher and administer sound, firm discipline. My dungeon lends itself to all kinds of scenes. I have great bondage hardware, as well as facilities for cross dressing scenes. My wardrobe is, basically, leather, leather and yet more leather! I love it all! SM fashion will *never* go out of style, as far as I'm concerned!

In addition to my male slaves, I do have female slaves who serve me as well. However, I must add, the females in my stable *always* have priority over the men. That's just my personal way of doing things. You could say I'm a *real* believer in Female Supremacy! Whatever the sex though, I'm always very selective in the type of people I associate with. Only those who prove themselves worthy get to come near me. Honesty, sincerity, loyalty and trustworthiness are attributes that come to mind. My slaves dedicate themselves to me in mind, body and soul. To me, slavery is the highest form of commitment! Consequently, the mistress/slave relationship is *never* one that should be entered into lightly. Before I accept anyone into my stable as a real slave, they must undergo rigorous training. As the saying goes: 'Only the strong survive!'

You'll notice I make a strong distinction between 'slaves' and the type of person I see as a professional dominatrix. However, even as a professional, I don't see just anyone. As my time is very valuable, I see only those who are truly into the SM or fetish scene. And let me just say this: I don't think slavery is for everybody! For the *right* person, I think that it's very healthy to play out fantasies in a safe, sane environment. A session with me in my dungeon is a *very* therapeutic experience. Many of the people I see are very powerful, influential people. Their lives are very stressful. When they come for a session, they lose their status. In my dungeon what I say goes! I help these people balance out. They release tensions and leave feeling *totally* relaxed.

Though, as I said before, I enjoy all aspects of the SM and fetish scene, I must say that my personal favourite is corporal punishment. To that end, I have a wide assortment of paddles, hairbrushes and straps. I get very aroused when I administer a severe whipping. Flogging on the back is one of my favourite activities. Believe me, I can flog a submissive for hours without *ever* getting tired!

I'm also well known for my 'transformations'. Everybody knows that Mistress Jacqueline turns naughty boys into *very* nasty girls! I absolutely love playing with transvestites. I have a great deal of respect for this population. Our society plays up on the 'macho' image so much, I think it takes a lot of guts for a guy to come out of the closet and explore his feminine side. My TV sessions are always lots of fun!

Although my dungeon and business is based in Los Angeles, I do travel whenever I can. I love the scene in New York. I also recently took my first trip abroad. I was most impressed with *Club Doma* in the Netherlands. I attended the Friday night show and it was very well done. I also have a wonderful slave in Australia whom I visit frequently. The SM scene is very strong 'Down Under'. I've had the pleasure of befriending Mistress Amanda of *Salon Kitty*. She and her establishment are truly first-rate.

At least there's *some* kind of scene in L.A! And that's better than most parts of this country! My favourite scene place here, as I said before, has got to be New York. In fact, NYC *is* my favourite place, anyway. Maybe that's because it's my hometown! I like the New York scene because it's wide open and always happening. Whenever I go there I'm always at *The Vault* or at *Paddles*. I love the freedom these clubs exude! The scene in L.A. is reflective of this city, and that's very 'showy'. It's pretty underground and it gets more uptight every year. However, I'm very lucky in that I have my circle of friends to party with and get plenty of activity. The local club, *Threshold*, is very active but, for whatever reasons, they have gotten so rule-oriented and have so many regulations when it comes to parties, that I've become very inactive. I'm a true anarchist and it's important for me to always to be able to do as I please.

But don't get me wrong. In my play I work within strict limits. I totally believe in safe, sane SM play. As long as a fantasy is between two or more consenting adults it's perfectly okay in my book. I wish more people understood that it's not only okay to explore fantasies, but it's also healthy and healing. Like dreams, SM play reveals a great deal about one's inner psyche. It's a great outlet with which to express hidden parts of our personality within a non-judgmental environment.

I'm also busy with a number of very exciting projects at the moment. My magazine *Power X Change* is published bi-monthly. Each issue gives an in-depth profile of several real life domina's as well as interesting scene places to visit, well written fantasy stories, letters to the editor, beautiful photos and lots more. The layout and design is top-notch. I'm very proud of it.

I'm also producing my own line of videos and CD-Roms, but let me tell your British readers that I *never* send videos out of the United States. However, there are plenty of items for foreign customers. In addition to the *Power X Change,* I have three other 'specialty' magazines, including *Mistress Jacqueline Magazine,* which everyone who knows me, or wants to know me, simply *must* have! This magazine is unlike any other scene-type magazine in the United States. I've made it very classy, sophisticated and intelligent in the way it approaches the scene.

Though I've been selling items through the mail for many years, I'm now revamping my entire mail order business. I know that everyone will be very pleased with the results. Most exciting, I have a fantastic line of leather items for sale at incredibly affordable prices. These items are specially made for me by my Slave Anton in Australia. He is a skilled leatherworker and has designed a complete range of bondage equipment especially for me. My catalogue includes hoods made from quality kangaroo leather, plus leather restraints and collars which can be personalised, a one-of-a-kind Koala blindfold made completely of fur, novelty key chains and other unique items. My fetish phone lines are also owned and operated by me and me alone. The mistresses who man the lines for one-on-one conversation were all personally trained by me, too. Maybe your readers should call and find out just how good my training really is!

Ms Christine Deering

Ms Deering is one of several Chapter Leaders of the Femina Society; an organisation that promotes female supremacy in a matriarchal society. The society, based in the United States, is quasi-religious in its leaning toward the feminine archetypes found in such diverse belief-systems as paganism and Hinduism. Interviewed May 1996.

Maybe I should start by outlining the process a trainee slave must go through before being admitted into the Femina Society. During his initial period of rigorous and thorough postal training, the slave will learn one of the basic tenants of the society; that is, that a slave has no *free* time. Free time is for free people. A slave is *not* free. All his time belongs to his owner/instructress and, through her, the Femina Society itself.

Part of his training is in 'sensual servitude'. Besides the 'sensual tapes' he receives, the prospective slave candidate is constantly instructed to do erotic writing assignments that give free rein to his fantasies. Topics include giving his mistress an extremely erotic massage, worshipping her feet, serving her in the bathroom as a toilet and many other topics. He'll be given lessons in humility and taught the Femina Society's twelve positions of respect, so he'll know how to behave when he's finally given the reward of serving a lady in person.

Another aspect of the training is the serious study of Female Supremacy: why it's natural, why it's right and why it's necessary. For example, I've currently set a slave to work on his matriarchal studies summer study project. To complete this project, he must read and report on three books – and I don't mean 'fuck books'! I'm talking about serious studies on the natural superiority of women, the origins of human society as a matriarchy and how the patriarchy has unnaturally reversed the roles of the sexes and oppresses women. Another topic of study in this project is male violence in society, and against women in particular. Also included are lessons in honesty, loyalty and how to be a proper and pleasing servant; which means learning to do useful work and serve only to please the mistress, effacing one's own wants and desires. As you can see, this is serious all-encompassing education!

The would-be slave is also trained in networking to promote the growth of the Femina Society and to spread the Society's goals of female supremacy. In order to describe this training, I'll need to explain the nature and structure of the Femina Society. The Society is a sisterhood dedicated to re-establishing women in their rightful place in the world; that is, as rulers of society! Men are allowed to participate in the Society only as students, servants and workers. Women are catered to, make all the decisions and have *all* the rights. Males have no rights, but simply serve, obey and carry out assigned tasks. The Femina Society is definitely *not* a sex club, and males who only want to have their fantasies fulfiled have no place in it. Submission to feminine authority is a serious business and requires a serious attitude. I have a saying that applies: "If it was fun and easy, they wouldn't call it work." And being a servant for the Femina Society is work and not *always* fun!

Structurally, the Society consists of a Mother Chapter, Sister Chapters and Associate Branches. Located in New England, the Mother Chapter, under the leadership of the foundress Ms. C, organises all facets of Femina Society work. Education is carried out through the School for Servants and the Centre for Matriarchal Studies. Networking is carried out by communication with Sister Chapters, Associate Branches, other non-member Dominas, mailing projects and advertising. The Mother Chapter is the final authority in all matters concerning the Society, especially membership, but works closely with Sister Chapters.

Sister Chapters are established under the auspices of a Chapter leader; that is, a Domina who wishes to promote the teachings and goals of the Femina Society in her geographical area. In the Society hierarchy, a Chapter Leader is second only to Ms. C., but is considered a partner, not a subordinate. The activities of a Sister Chapter mirror those of the Mother Chapter.

This brings us to Associate Branches. A Branch exists where there's a worker or a trainee but, as yet, no Domina has stepped forward to become a Chapter Leader. It is the duty of a Branch worker to conduct networking through mailings and in person to promote the growth of the Society. Branch workers are assigned to the Mother Chapter and receive instruction and supervision from it. The goal of a Branch is to become a Sister Chapter.

Whether a person is a submissive male who wants to surrender to feminine authority in all aspects of his life, or if she is a woman who wants to work toward the rule of women in a matriarchal society (either as a Domina or as a Handmaiden who serves other women; though, it must be made *absolutely* clear, no woman in the Society ever serves a man in *any* way!), I urge you to consider the Femina Society as the place where you may fulfil yourself and advance your goals. The male will find a life of useful servitude (which should be the *only* reward he seeks), while the woman will find a Sisterhood that offers both a shared vision and practical support for her chosen lifestyle.

Here I can use my own case as an example of how this can be fulfiled within the Femina Society. Being both a nurse *and* a dominant woman, I naturally find I can blend these two aspects of myself together as a Domina. They fit together beautifully. For example, when I'm giving a slave my version of a physical examination. To start with the slave will disrobe and either remain naked or don some suitable apparel worthy of his station in life. This depends entirely on my whims and how much I want to embarrass him. Most times I like them to be totally nude. Then comes some suitable bondage. Usually this involves simple handcuffs; sometimes in front, then in back, then behind the head. This last one is a lovely position to have a slave in; standing with legs spread out, hands tucked behind his head. He is so vulnerable. I'll usually have a riding crop handy, just in case he shows any signs of moving about!

First, I'll deal with the 'vital signs'. These are assessed and recorded on an examination sheet made of rubber. Hands fastened out in front for this. Temperature is rectal, of course. Blood pressure, pulse and respiration are next. Should the slave ask what the readings are, he'll be told that they're none of his business and that curiosity can get him into a lot of trouble!

Flashing the eyes with a penlight is especially fun! This is to determine the level of alertness. Woe to the slave who is found not to be alert for his mistress! Next, to the extremities. For this I like to spread-eagle the slave, untying and retying as seems appropriate. There is much pulling, pushing, pinching and a lot of fun – for me, of course! I especially enjoy working on the toes. Then a more extensive taking of pulses at various parts of the body, both lying down and erect. I like to tease the slave mercilessly, at this point, because the pulse invariably quickens quite dramatically! The results of which you can imagine!

Perhaps the most fun is to have the slave erect with hands behind the head and legs spread as noted earlier. In this posture, I have the slave talk while monitoring his breathing and tormenting him in endless little ways. I work with particular attention to the cock and balls. Heaven help the slave who even twitches while I play my little games! It can mean the riding crop where he is most sensitive! In that sensitive area, I'll poke, prod, pinch and apply pressure to his balls. I'll even poke the end of my riding crop up his asshole, making him bend over to make it easier for me!

Then I'll have him kneeling, nose touching the floor, while I question him intensively about his diet and eating habits. Most slaves are overindulgent and have sluggish systems. It seems willpower is also a missing factor to the true submissive psyche. Of course, the remedy is a good cleansing enema. The beginner gets a small enema, but those with more experience will receive at least two quarts. The slave is instructed in breathing during the enema session.

After his enema, I always like to administer my golden fluid. This is done in various ways. Most often in one of three ways: a shower over the slave's body, in a drinking cup or down a funnel straight into the slave's mouth, so he's forced to swallow it as quickly as I produce it! After he's cleaned himself up, I'll assess the slave's skin condition and sensitivities are noted. Disciplinary implements are employed to discover reddening factors and his reactions to various types of instruments. This is essential in setting limits for the discreet slave who must remain unmarked. Next it's time to turn to the question of slave posture. The slave is taught to kneel properly, stand and walk. Also, he'll be instructed in the correct positions for discipline and submission to a mistress. The body is examined at each step for correctness of form.

Finally, the slave's psycho sexual make-up is assessed. This is accomplished through intimate questioning and observing reactions throughout. This helps the slave to better understand *why* he is a slave in the first place! To finish the examinations, the slave is given a herbal drink. These are individualised for each slave, and contain calming herbs, potency herbs, diuretics or cathartics. I find these examinations extremely helpful in finding out the potential of the novice slave. They're also valuable in assessing the changing conditions and attitudes of more experienced slaves. And, most importantly, they're fun for the mistress, too!

MISS PRIM

Based in Herefordshire and Wales, Miss Prim works exclusively within the world of 'adult' schoolboy and schoolgirl fantasy scenarios. In her role as headmistress of the Muir Academy, she assists people in the authentic re-enactment of their own schooldays. Interviewed March 2001

The schoolroom role started from home, really. It was always a fantasy I had dreamed about. I've always been interested in the classroom scenario and, even as a young girl, I wanted to go to boarding school. However, looking around on the edge of the SM scene, I couldn't really find what I was looking for. Then I read an article somewhere about some ladies who were running a school in Ireland, and the ladies were in uniform. That really set my imagination racing! I just couldn't put it down and felt I had to find out more! I couldn't go there, but we had a close circle of friends who suggested we start something ourselves. We used to get together on an informal basis and take turns being the headmistress, headmaster or pupil. That's how I know what my pupils expect from me, because I have been a pupil myself! The headmistress role developed from that. I know how pupils visualise me and how they like me to look. I try to put a good picture to their fantasy.

I am very good at communicating with people. I worked as a courier for fifteen years, so I learned to deal with people. That's, unfortunately, a talent some doms don't have. I'm afraid they simply lack the ability to communicate or deal with unexpected situations. I treat people as a *real* headmistress would, and that is to treat everybody as an individual, but with the same rules applying to all. Everybody's different. Some pupils like to come and sit and listen. They get great pleasure just by sitting in the school atmosphere, or enjoying ridding themselves of adult responsibilities by dressing up in 'school uniform'. The actual discipline aspect might be a very low priority for them. For others, however, discipline is a very high priority, and it's important to discover who's who and what they need.

People with all kinds of fetishes are welcome here, as well as transvestites, transsexuals, bi-sexuals and straight. I don't deal with the heavy SM scene as such. I don't use whips or riding crops to cause pain. I've nothing against it, it's just not what I do here. I'm not comfortable with mixing other forms of SM with the school scene. In our literature, we actually say that nothing will happen at *The Muir Academy* that wouldn't have happened in a real school at some time in the past, and that's very true. I use the birch, the cane, the martinet, and the tawse; plus the slipper, paddle and hairbrush. Some people who come to me are regulars for discipline, and they need a lot! Occasionally, they may get a blood blister, but I don't like that because it really doesn't fit the role and we try to avoid it. This *isn't* SM because, for one thing, there's no bondage involved. The nearest we get to that is for dramatic effect, more than anything else. I may hold a pupil down, but again, that's corporal punishment.

To become an 'active' member of *The Academy*, a person has to have a three hour interview with me and, during that interview, I will go into just why they enjoy what they're doing, and find out what they're looking for exactly. And that's *before* we even get into a classroom! I also want to know about their medical history. This is *very* relevant; things such as whether they wear a pacemaker or if they're diabetic.

This is a full-time job for me, although I only make an average living out of it. If I were working as a professional dominatrix (which I don't consider myself to be, by the way) I would be working on an hourly basis, which I don't. I would be earning a lot more money that way, certainly. But this is very personal to me and it's very important that I enjoy it, otherwise I couldn't do it. If I were seeing two or three people a day, I just couldn't enjoy it. It would become too much like work and I would lose interest.

It is mentally draining, though. And, often, I've got a lot of people in my class. It's physically draining, too. There's a lot of preparation that goes into this. People don't seem to realise that I actually *do* prepare lessons, and I *do* teach. If people come to our day school where there are six or eight of them, they will have a school dinner and lunch, too. So there's all that to prepare, as well as the lessons. We give certificates at the end of the day and there's diplomas at the end of the boarding school. It's hard work!

Sir Guy Masterleigh, my partner, while concentrated mainly on his *Pony Club* activities, is also involved in the school side of things, too; but more on an organisational level. Occasionally, we have crossovers where members of *The Other Pony Club* will also belong to *The Muir Academy*. Sir Guy is very supportive. He helps me in that he produces most of the written literature and the journals that go with memberships. The pupils contribute to the journal themselves. I know some people think we make it up, whereas in fact, all we do is tone it down!

There are *very* strict house rules, of course. I don't like toiletry or watersports. It's just a particular turn-off for me. Pupils have asked, and I've always said no. I have a schoolroom in my house. It's a beautiful study, completely oak-paneled, and has a genuine blackboard and cupboards which came out of a girl's school and wood floors with authentic school pictures and desks. My grown-up sons and daughter know what goes on, but they don't see it. I make sure they are never on the premises when activity takes place. All my family have been 'historical' role players, and we're all theatrical. We're all into role-playing, and we have a lot of costumes and props in the house.

All our uniforms, incidentally, are made by authentic school suppliers. When I first started, I couldn't get anything. It's taken me literally years to build up suppliers. In the early days, I had dressmakers and it was always hit and miss if you got a good thing or bad. I had difficulty in finding even the short trousers, but these days I have good suppliers and all the clothing is good quality.

I do telephone lines, too. When we first started years ago, we were the only discipline lines in operation. Our lines were 100% genuine and still are. When doing recording sessions, the recorded session is *always* live. We make the sketches up, obviously, but the purpose of the sketch is for them to capture the *real* discipline, so you actually hear the real thing. We'll all put our uniforms on, so we get into the feel of it and do it for real! Apart from anything else, we really enjoy it!

As well as our place in Herefordshire, we also have a property in Wales where we do boarding courses. It has a classroom set-up, and there are dormitories, a maid, a cook and a matron. They all come under the one heading of *Academy Incorporated*. This encompasses *The Other Pony Club, The Academy Club*, and the school and maid training as well. I do the maid training in exactly the same way as I take on the school role, which is *very* seriously. My maids are trained to a high standard because I actually am a caterer. Whilst doing dinner parties, they will wear *proper* maid's uniform – not French maid's outfits, but the real thing! Fewer maids want physical discipline, incidentally, but still a lot do! It's not compulsory to have discipline when you're a maid. We can arrange for other kinds of punishment, such as being made to stand in the corner of the room and that sort of thing.

When I'm out in front of a class, I *am* the headmistress! My hair is severely pulled back into a bun and I wear a school mistress cap and gown and suitable black shoes. I also wear glasses. I have a pair of particularly severe ones, which I wear on occasions. You could say I'm 'matronly'. I always dress smartly for business, as a headmistress would. I certainly *don't* wear miniskirts and fishnet stockings and things like that because it's very important to get the ambiance right, and to be as authentic as possible. Most of my pupils are looking for the experience that a more mature woman possesses. Some people, on the more sexual side, would want a young, pretty thing, but that's a very different scene to the one that I play. What I do is *strictly* classroom scenarios, which is a real CP scene.

I don't care what age the pupils are in 'real' life. When they are sitting in that classroom during registration it's what age I *believe* they are that counts, and they act accordingly. It's all down to believing in what you do. The school scene is mostly down to psychology. It's a good 80% in the head, and only 20% physical.

It is made very clear to everybody that there is *absolutely* no sexual involvement. We go through all this during the initial interview. I will not give 'relief' of any sort. If a chap gets to a state where he's uncomfortable because he's aroused, then he can put his hand up and excuse himself out of class. Then he can do something about it in the privacy of his room. I have been asked to 'help them out', but I've always refused. If they do that in front of me, they will be expelled immediately as a member of *The Academy*, and they don't get a second chance! Of course, what a pupil does with their partner when he or she gets home, as a result of their 'higher sense of awareness', is another story – a 'private' one!

Any pupil who has been naughty, or has engineered bad behaviour, has got to bring a letter from their 'parents' or 'guardian' saying they have done something outrageous, and then they know they're in trouble. I *never* pretend where discipline is concerned! They have to wait outside my office with a prefect watching them, for up to half an hour sometimes. They can hear the punishment I'm giving to someone else and they know they're for it. The minimum they'll get is six of the best from the cane. But they have to *deserve* the discipline. People have actually *asked* for some very severe punishments that I have considered too dangerous, and I've turned them down.

I think most of the people who come to us and enjoy corporal punishment, actually haven't a clue why they do it! Mostly, it's a release of tension and it's escapism. They come to me to switch off. Some need an adrenaline boost and physical discipline gives them that. There's also an element of exhibitionism, of course, in both the girls and the boys. Then there are others who can't cope with the group scene of the classroom at all. I have to give them one-to-one private tuition. We also run special courses for couples because I think a lot of couples are worried their partner might get molested or excessively beaten, but that's isn't going to happen, I can assure you! Often, one half of the couple is a dom, while the other is a sub; but it's not unusual to have a couple who are *both* submissive in class together!

A lot of my job, in fact, involves being a counsellor. I have successfully persuaded several gentlemen to confide in their wives about what they do. If there's any hope the wife can be accepting, it does make life easier. It isn't always the case, however, and for some it is actually best kept secret. I had a call from a wife one day, who wanted to meet me. It turned out her husband had died and he had been a member. She was heartbroken he'd never told her about this side of himself, because she had always wanted to be a member as well! That was the saddest thing I had ever heard. They wasted all those years when they could have been playing together. I've helped many people come to terms with this scene after locking it away for years. I'm always being told what a relief it is for them to find others on the scene. They no longer feel isolated or alone.

What we offer, I think, is something quite unique and special. What's been available up to now has usually been of the 'put on a school uniform, go along to a dominatrix, act a bit silly and get caned and spanked' variety. Whilst I do make a living out of this, I'm certainly not milking it! I respect my members and they respect me. Having fun's a serious business, after all!

Lady Claudette: "I have acquired all my
medical knowledge from 'real' doctors. When I
first began, there was always a doctor at my
side; an emergency surgeon who took part in
the evening's demonstrations".

Mistress Cassandra: "When I advertise for a
slave, I am not looking for a sexual partner! I
want someone to serve me, not service me!
While the scene has a highly charged sexual
aura surrounding it, the fact is that sex in itself
is nothing more than one tool out of many
available to a capable dominatrix!"

Miss Spiteful :"I'm not into just flicking at someone with a whip. I love knowing that people watching are really horrified by what I'm doing!"

Mistress Amber: If there weren't women like us, there would be a lot more weirdos around! This is an important part of what we do. Sometimes I wonder whether they should be at counselling rather than a mistress."

Ms Deering: "One aspect of our training is the serious study of Female Supremacy, including lessons on how to be a proper and pleasing servant, and effacing one's own wants and desires. As you will see, this is all-encompassing education!"

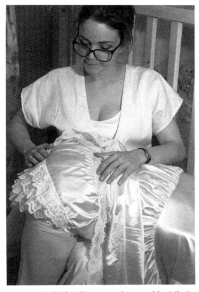

Nanny Lily: "Infantilism remains a subject that is rarely spoken about. It is neglected and often ridiculed, even amongst so-called 'open-minded' fetishists!"

Mistress Dominique: "Everyone who walks into my dungeon is like a jig-saw that you have to put together. They really do have difficulty coming to terms with the fact that they need to visit someone like me, especially if they are genuinely happily married."

Mistress Antoinette: "The kind of clients I
see are all very intelligent. They're looking to
expand their view of things on all levels,
including the sexual side."

Miss Martindale: "Part of what we're doing in
Aristasia is giving girls a place in a hierarchy,
as well as a place in our hearts. This is created
through the bond that's formed with the person
who's disciplining you. It creates a sort of
magical connection."

Mistress Xena: "My mum thinks this is the safest job I've ever done – especially compared to when I was a body guard and was attacked on several occasions!"

Mistress R: "I am a lifestyle dominatrix, even though there's a part of me that asks what that word means exactly? Do I sleep in thigh high boots? No. Do I cry when my dog dies? Yes. A real dominatrix has her femininity and her soft side. That's what makes her so powerful!"

Mistress Andria: "I think the best dominatrixes are in the Royal Family, really. I mean, look at the Queen Mother. She's been worshiped and looked after by servants for a hundred years. If that's not being a top class dominatrix, I don't know what is!"

Tanith Au Set: "It's endlessly fascinating that people can be so diverse in their perversions. I'm quite convinced that there will be at least one person out there who has a fetish for anything you can think of!"

Lady Amber: "This is a real service I provide. It's also an interesting and wonderful way to make your living. I would fully encourage any woman to give it try!"

Goddess Venus: "I think that most women involved
in this scene non-professionally are looking for
something. And it's not about sex, either!"

Mistress Brigette: "I need room for my fantasy, as
well as my submissive's. I don't like to be dictated
to in a scenario. My games are spontaneous,
impulsive and full of surprises! I like them to put
their faith in me as a woman of art!"

Mistress Tachibana: "I found my own spirituality in SM. I see myself as a bit like a medium or a shaman who is trying to get them to somewhere else. To me, this is modern shamanism."

Miss Irene Boss: "In reality, the submissive is often the selfish one, and the dominant is merely satisfying the fantasy of the submissive! Most dominants I know are like teddy-bears in real life!"

Mistress Mai Ling: "When I first started I was very shocked by some of the requests I got, but I never showed it. I pretended I knew what I was talking about, even though I didn't!"

Mistress Hades: "I became aware of a fetish side to my character at around thirteen when I started collecting whips. But I didn't know that was kinky, and I didn't think that I'd like to hit someone with them. I just knew I wanted to use them."

Mistress Jacqueline: "I'm a firm believer that most people have sexual fantasies that could be considered 'out of the norm'. Because we live in a sexually repressed society, most men and women choose to suppress their feelings, and only admit to what they perceive as 'mainstream' sexuality."

Madam Karra: "Dominating the male of the species is the only thing I've experienced that has made me feel content and confident as a woman. My life was very average and routine, but now I feel I have a real vocation!"

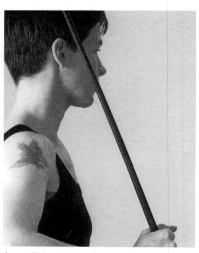

Mistress Eva: "The submissive is so caught up in the moment, so under the spell of the mistress, that they really feel they want to be scared. I think that's taking advantage of my position and my power."

Janus: "I encourage people to come along with their fantasies, which they may or may not want to act out. Some people just want to talk about it. People can have highly charged fantasies and, if they're repressed, they're also repressing their life energy."

Goddess Dianna Vesta: "I believe that this is an holistic form of self-discovery. In a world with Aids and a total disregard for sexual intimacy, I feel that SM 'alternatives' are a futuristic approach to exploring each other."

Mistress Shane: "You're dealing with important parts of people's lives. Things that happened in their childhood, things they're hiding from the world, things that they're really afraid of sometimes. You must be aware of their limits!"

Madame Patricia de Gifford: "What can raise the spirit more than the refreshing country air, and the sight of naked male slaves working in the noon day heat under the bullwhips of beautiful Lady Warders?"

Miss Gen: "We had an incident at one of our SM shows where a middle-aged couple ran into their seventeen year old son! I think it definitely fostered a lot of communication within that family!"

Mistress Chrystalle: "I originally trained in psychiatry, but absolutely began to hate it! The majority of my clients really just needed to be put over my knee and given a good spanking! I just wanted to hit them, but I'd have lost my license!"

Reverend Kellie Everts: "A man is at his happiest
when performing a task for a woman. And, if
you're honest with yourself as a woman, you'll
know this to be true."

MISTRESS DOMINIQUE

Ex-librarian turned lifestyle, then professional mistress who famously suffered at the even crueler hands of Britain's notorious 'gutter' press! Mistress Dominique now lives in quiet, rural seclusion in Sussex on the South Coast of England with her two transvestite personal maids. Interviewed July 2000.

My late husband was fascinated by the SM scene, and we used to visit the clubs in London quite regularly. After he died, I drifted out of the scene for a while. Then, when I remarried, my second husband shared my interest in S&M and we used to go to some *very* heavy parties and private events. In those early days, before Aids, there used to be blood all over the place, but never any sex. Nowadays, I don't really know what goes on.

About five years ago, my husband became very ill. I needed to work from home to be able to look after him and, if you live in a very small village miles from anywhere, there aren't too many types of work you can do at home, so I decided to turn my main hobby into a profession. I wasn't sure at first whether I'd be successful as a professional. All the professional ladies I'd met at clubs and parties seemed to be more into the verbal humiliation and boot licking type of scenarios, whereas I was primarily into bondage and mental control. At first, I just advertised in *Axis*, my favourite contact magazine, but I was lucky because everyone I met I got on with. In fact, the very first slave I ever saw still visits me now, despite the big change of location.

Jayne, for instance, who's now one of my live-in transvestite maids, was originally a guest of mine. I always think of people as 'guests', by the way, never clients. They're guests in my home. Anyway, Jayne's wife had died a few months previously, so she was brand new to the scene. And I really didn't know what I was doing either! It really is a whole different ball-game, being amateur to professional. We decided to do an outdoor session with a cross in the garden. It was my very first session outside and it was the unintentional bits that were the best – like me trying to use a dressage whip while the cat was sitting on the other end!

As I said, I don't deal with verbal domination; all that shouting and screaming that they are pathetic worms who should be grovelling at my boots etcetera. It all seems a bit false and simply doesn't work for me. The idea of pretending to be cross with every single person who comes in leaves me cold. I just like having fun.

I love bondage, especially rubber! And, as you can see, I'm fairly TV friendly! My ultimate favourite is electric's. They're marvellous! I first got interested in electric's when I worked as a librarian in a health library. I adore making people helpless and playing with them. A lot of people, for instance, don't like corporal punishment. It's either the wrong sort of pain, that is, too intense, or there are problems with marks. There are also people I know who'd literally wear my arm out and they'd still not get the endorphin 'high' they need from caning. However, electric's are so accurately targeted (and I only use safe boxes, most of them have got medical applications anyway) it's an incredible, erotic pain/pleasure sensation. Nothing to do with the old idea of banging something into the mains and putting a couple of bulldog clips on. At the top end of the boxes, I can get a 'mercy' out of *anybody*, particularly with the electric catheters which are seriously lethal, nasty, painful little things. But at the bottom end of the scale, you've got pleasure all the way along the line. It's gorgeous! It's like turning a radio down. It starts off low and builds up. I can tease and torment. Everything from a mild tingle to excruciating pain with just a switch of the dial. The reason I've got about ten, twelve boxes and counting, is that I need the different sensations. I'd get bored with just one or two. I get bored very easily. Plus, like every mistress, I'm frightened of one day burning out. There are so many different things you can do with electric's. They're very versatile.

In fact, one of my fondest memories of Julie, my TV housekeeper, is of finding her, one blindingly hot summers day, head to foot in rubber, gas mask on and doing the ironing with a tell-tale little lead from her apron pocket to another part of her anatomy. She had actually wired herself up to the electric's while she was doing the ironing! That's how non-painful they are. You can actually walk around with them in. If I think Julie's falling asleep when she's supposed to be on duty, I'll twitch the dial a little bit. That usually wakes her up!

I remember an hilarious conversation with my accountant about electric's. At first he thought I was re-wiring the house! When I explained, he said: "Let me get this right. You mean people actually pay you to electrocute them? And you even need different ways of doing it!" The conversation sounded like that Bob Newhart sketch *Introducing Tobacco to Civilisation.*

What can I tell you about the transvestite side of things? Well, I don't do 'dress for the day', as I just don't have the time or the facilities. I feel that if you're going to do that you've got to have a massive wardrobe. What we do have is the skills to transform someone into maids uniform or perhaps little tarty stuff, that sort of thing. I find it's a total switch for people. It makes them far more vulnerable. I love TV's for their soft side. I think they get a very raw deal in society anyway. I can't understand why there's so much resentment against them. They're also afraid of being ridiculed themselves. But, to me, it's a chance to wear nice materials and to have a complete change from the outside world. Loads of people are latent TV's, but either don't have the courage or the opportunity to do anything about it.

The important thing is that when people visit us they can see straight away that we are genuine and this *is* our lifestyle. It's not a case of them walking in and finding that the mistress really doesn't like TV's, and all she's got is a few 'glad rags' and that's it. We live this way *all* of the time, and very happily so. Then they'll come out of themselves and admit that they'd quite like to try it themselves. They know we're not going to turn round and think they're a weirdo. For us, it's our normal way of life. I remember one person commented that he was surprised this wasn't sordid, but was really rather cosy. Of course, it's not sordid! This is my home as well as my working environment! One of the reasons for moving down to this area is that it is so TV friendly. In the Midlands, if Julie or Jayne had gone out dressed, they'd have been stoned! We'd already had dead animals thrown into the garden. Down here, even my hairdresser knows what I do for a living!

Not many TV's are into SM, actually. They're mostly into the fetish side and the verbal humiliation and so on. When Jayne first came to see me I was advertising as a headmistress. I got this long letter from her asking if I gave 'correct' lessons and did they include Latin? I thought I must have a nut-case here! She wanted to be 'correctly' dressed for each occasion. I'm sitting there trying to work out what is the 'correct' dress for a dungeon, and what is the 'correct' dress for outdoors, and... oh God, the list went on and on! I think transvestitism is a kind of uniform fetish as much as anything else.

What I'm curious about is what I can show on the Web, and what I can't show. I'm interested in doing things like 'live-cams'. I'm certainly going to do a recorded video clip of the dungeon, so that people can see what I've got to offer. I've heard so many times of people who go to a mistress and she'll say things like: "Oh, that's on order" or "The electric's aren't working today" or "No, I didn't say the room was mirrored" or "You should have told me you were a size twenty". So if I do a video, people can link in on the Internet, have a look around the dungeon, and *see* it's real. Okay, I'm not exactly photogenic but, this is me, it's not a studio shot and I *am* the person who will be seeing them. People will go and see a mistress and she's nothing like the illustration! Maybe they'll find that they haven't even spoken to the person who's there on the day. That seems so unfair. I think the Internet is going to be the way to go, but how much will they let me show? Will they let me show a live session, bearing in mind that, after the Spanner Case, it's still technically illegal here?

When the national newspapers exposed me, it was devastating. I was immediately homeless. I had to move right out of the area and was unable to find work for several months while I relocated – which was financially devastating. A lot of ladies have contacted me and asked me how the newspaper decided on me. Was it a tip off? How can they avoid being exposed? The answer is that, in this profession, there is no way you can avoid exposure indefinitely. It's all down to pure luck, I'm afraid. In my case, they never even entered my dungeon! They just took photos from the outside, including one of me in a summer dress! So even the ladies who wear wigs and masks aren't safe. They will just take a normal 'snap' as well, if they can. It's something you just have to live with. Down here, I doubt very much if anyone would be bothered if I was featured again.

My local newspaper thought it was all marvellous at first! The previous week their front page had been about double parking in the town centre, and now there was this 'sex den' on their doorstep that they didn't know about. They were knocking on our door at all hours for weeks on end. Then they tried to break into the house. They even contacted the local police and said, basically: "Hey, look at this! There's a vice den here. What are you going to do about it?" And the police told them that they had known I was there for years. Their attitude was that I wasn't doing *anything* illegal. I was advertising in a private magazine and there had been no complaints whatsoever. One very unhappy reporter! He was the bane of my life for months, that guy. They were very upset in the end that it had been going on under their noses and they hadn't a clue, and that a national newspaper had taken, what they considered, *their* story.

On the day the paper came out, we had something like fifty-odd people camped outside, trying to take pictures. But, because we knew it was going to happen, I was already house-hunting down here, so I wasn't even there! In a situation like that you certainly get to find out who your friends are, too. All the people who used to come round once a week and borrow books, have a drink or whatever, didn't want to know. One or two people stuck by us. But the amount of people who said: "Oh, I don't really know the lady", and I'd known them three or four years and thought they were friends! It's an abrupt way to find out who your friends are! It was a nightmare. I don't think anyone I've spoken to has had as many problems. But I do know three or four mistresses who've retired because they've realised these people don't *need* a reason. In my case, they printed my address and everything! I think they've got a file on all of us and, if there's nothing else, they'll use it. A mistress friend of mine was done recently, and she wasn't even working at the time! It's a very gray area. What they should do, of course, is legalise it all and run decent safety checks. They should come in to check for things like basic hygiene and safety, particularly. If someone is upside down and you've got 'wonky' suspension, you're in big trouble! It would be better for everybody all round.

We were very green when we started out. We used to lend books and clothes to people. The amount of underwear I lost in the first year! We had so many things that never came back that you harden up in the end! I think every mistress goes through it. I once caught someone walking out, quite openly, with a pair of nipple clamps! He said he thought he'd just take a souvenir! I was so dumb founded I didn't even tear his head off! This is the side of things that people don't see. Like the stalkers, like the newspapers, like the people who ring at two and three in the morning. I've actually been physically attacked half a dozen times in the dungeon! That's why a lot of ladies give up. But they won't change the law and let us work together for self protection. As the law stands that would be considered a brothel and be illegal.

People see what they think is an idyllic lifestyle of the mistress and her bevy of slaves, but don't realise the pressures – especially if the mistress is renting a property. If your landlord knows what you're doing, he'll probably charge you four or five times as much rent for the privilege. If he doesn't know and does a spot inspection, as he's entitled to do, you may well get evicted with very short notice. Then have a battle on your hands afterwards to get the deposit back! And you learn very quickly that you can't have an awful lot of friends in this business, either. If you're too friendly with people, the next thing is: "Can I pop in for a cup of tea?" Well, no, because we do strict one-on-one sessions here, and privacy is a luxury for both me and the guests. People come to me because they don't want to see someone else sitting in a waiting room like in the massage parlours. They know that the only people who might be here will be Julie or Jayne.

When a guest arrives, he is probably met by my TV maid or housekeeper, who'll give them a brief questionnaire to fill in and then bring them down to me in the dungeon. It saves me having to stand there and ask them about fifty different questions. If I've already spoken to them at length on the phone, I'll say: "Look, take a little bit of time out. Write down the things you love and the things you loathe. Put me inside your head". The first session is always about building up trust, more than anything else. Especially with people who've had horrendous experiences. Perhaps they've gone to a 'so-called' mistress and, no matter what they asked for, they've just got straight CP. They're in and out in twenty minutes. What we call the 'whip and wank' brigade! The thing to remember is that there are bad apples in every profession. People just have to keep ringing round, keep asking questions. If a mistress won't talk to you on the phone and there's not a lot of information on hand, then she's not going to take the time to listen to you during the session and try to get it right.

When we first came down here one of the things I needed to know was the quality of the mistresses in the area and what sort of competition I'd got. It's quite amusing that mistresses will actually send their own slaves round for a session to check each other out! It's really just to see what the competition is like. It's happened to us dozens of times and we've done the same thing. Sometimes they will admit at the end of the session: "Well, actually, I've been sent by Mistress Whoever. I'm her live-in slave". Or a mistress will phone up and ask if they can send their slave over to get some information on electric's in exchange for something else. That's okay, it's not a problem.

It's lovely to talk to other mistresses, because then you don't feel so isolated. We have a very good relationship with each other. I regularly go out to dinner and socialise with other local mistress friends. Sometimes we find we share the same clients! A few weeks ago I was chatting with one friend, Mistress Diane, and realised we had had a client who had booked with me at one o'clock, with her at three, and I bet he'd booked with Mistress Antoinette at five! What happens is that someone will be having a meeting and not be sure when it's going to end, so they book three different appointments to make sure they get one session in!

We have a good relationship with our neighbours, too. From their point of view we're quiet, conservative people. We never go out dressed. If this place were let to a group of students, there would probably be parties every night. The only risk now in this business is the gangs of kids who might find out what you're doing though the Internet. And, of course, all the kids are on the Internet these days. But, if a very young voice phoned up asking for details, we wouldn't accept the call anyway.

One of the problems with this job is the adrenaline surge in the morning. I look in the diary and see I've got four people booked– which is fully booked for me. Everybody confirms between nine and eleven o'clock. You think, this is going to be a great day! Right, how much money can I spend? Where are the catalogues? And a little voice in the background is saying 'overdraft'! Then, perhaps, the first one doesn't turn up and we're thinking that maybe he's got lost? Or we're standing here and see him going to the wrong house across the road, despite our very explicit directions! That's heart attack time!

Like any other mistress, I've had my fair share of, shall we say, the more 'unusual' requests. There was the 'Parcel Tape' man, for instance. We actually discouraged him in the end. What he wanted was to be wrapped up from head to foot in Post Office brown parcel tape. It was a fantasy he'd had for years, and he'd even brought his own tape along with him! I took one look at it and pointed out that it would take all his hair off if we did what he wanted, so we switched him to tight rubber-wrap, instead. He hadn't worked out the results of tearing it off, you see. We often say to people: "Yes, it's a very nice fantasy, but you've got to think it through'. From the sketches he showed us I could also see that he hadn't left himself any breathing holes. I know it might have been a trivial thing to him, but I'm the one who would have had to dispose of the body! Then there was the guy who wanted to ironed and then put in the oven and baked! I turned him down, too. I couldn't get my head round that one, to be honest. Another man wanted me to stand on his tongue. Another wanted to be hanged, and I won't do asphyxiation. Another wanted to be beaten senseless and raped. They've got this picture of their fantasy in their minds, but it just won't work or is too dangerous to do in real life.

Some of them are so amusing though. We had one guy, back in the very early days, who said on the telephone that he wanted to be interrogated. Now, I *love* interrogation scenarios. I told him to just think of a story line; with an address or a telephone number that I can drag out of him gradually. He assured me he was quite tough. He even brought me a little note saying that marks weren't a problem. We took him upstairs and he took one look at the room (which, by our standards today, was really quite basic) and his jaw dropped! I went straight into the scenario and bellowed: "Right, you're going to tell me how you got my name and phone number!" And he mumbled: "From a contact magazine, Mistress". No, no, I thought, this really isn't how you play this game. So I tried again: "I don't believe you! I don't advertise anywhere like that. How did you get my address?" Again he blubbers: "I just went to the phone box and you gave me your address and I think I've changed my mind and I want to go home now!" We had to sit the poor chap down, give him a cup of tea and suggest that we started all over again. It was like that *Monty Python* sketch where the chap pays to have an argument!

Another one arrived and handed me two envelopes. What's this all about, I thought? Anyway, I ordered him to undress and put him on the frame and I could see he was petrified. He was standing there in the most beautiful metal chastity belt and shaking like a leaf. One envelope contained my 'gift' and in the other was the key to the belt and a brief note from his mistress telling me that if he performs properly I could release him, if not I was to send him home. What am I going to do here? Oh, I thought, you poor little love! I just gave him a little hug in the end.

I do the same with the female submissives who are occasionally brought to me. They walk in and they're petrified. I tell them to calm down and assure them that I'm not going to hurt them. And, if they're afraid their male partners are going to hurt them, I remind them that women rule supreme in this house and I'd tie him up and beat the living daylights out of him! I'm not bisexual, so I really don't know what to do with the little darlings anyway! It can happen the other way round, too. I've had couples where the male is submissive and he wants me to teach his wife how to dominate him. Well, it's hard because you're either into this or you're not. Sure, I can show them a few basic techniques, but I can't *make* them enjoy it! I'll see couples very rarely. It's not something I encourage.

There's one lovely old gentleman of eighty five who comes to see me most Sunday evenings. He always has to have his little joke, whereby he'll 'hide' my gift in something unusual. Once he handed me a piggy bank sealed with superglue! Another time it was in a coffee jar with a chain and a combination lock! Or it might be a sweet jar with 'bomb' written on it! Oh, and there was the tiny hippo that took me ten minutes with a pair of tweezers to extract my gift from. He must spend hours thinking of all these novel ideas and, not only does it amuse me, I really appreciate the effort he puts into it. He goes to so much trouble, and he's always making me little things for the dungeon.

Then there was another one who'd come along for maid-training, so I set him to work cleaning my kitchen. Now, I'm used to having to go in and telling the maid that they haven't done this or that properly as an excuse for punishment but, in this case, I walked in and the kitchen was spotless and he was looking round for other things to do. Instead of punishing him, I found myself saying: "Oh, you must be exhausted. Sit down and I'll make *you* a cup of tea!" We've also had power cuts in the middle of intricate bondage sessions and all sorts of things. Luckily, there are always plenty of candles lying around in a dungeon!

You have to have a sense of humour in this or you'd just go mad. You also have to laugh when things don't go quite right, or even totally wrong! One of my submissives, Steve, who has been with me from the very early days, and who I treasure greatly, tells me he always knows when the session is going right because I *radiate* peace. He's more concerned that I, as the mistress, enjoy myself rather than just go through some set routine. The last time he came, I'd just seen a picture on the Internet that was quite intricate bondage, and I was playing around with this and it wasn't going right. He assured me not to worry about it. I got there in the end, and he said that he could feel me relax as the scenario was starting to go well. That's the kind of empathy you can build up with a submissive.

I always invite people to write to me after the session and critique it. Yes, I know a mistress is *supposed* to be perfect, and never gets things wrong – you know, the goddess image! But, in actual fact, I like to know how the session went from the other person's viewpoint. The feedback's terrific, and I've learnt a lot like that. I want people to let me know if something didn't work for them. I also keep notes with the questionnaires and the critiques. When they come back in six months I look up my notes. I'll know their likes, dislikes, clothes sizes, everything. People are hurt if they phone up and you don't remember who they are. Steve never fails to write after every single session. These critiques have been invaluable to me over the years in enabling me to see the sessions through the slaves eyes and to learn from that and enhance my skills. He has helped me evolve and I appreciate that. We have what we call our 'Lottery List'; which means, if we won the Lottery, what submissives would we continue to see for free? Steve would be right there at the top. He's kept a pictorial record of every dungeon I've ever had and is the only person, apart Julie and Jayne, to have seen me evolve as a mistress. He has suffered (or enjoyed!) my every passion and enthusiasm, and I always experiment with all my new toys on him.

Another favourite, and the only person I've ever done a 'hotel visit' for, is my 'little corset girl' in the Midlands. She's in her eighties now and adores tight corseting and CP. It was 'her' birthday recently and I went back to the Midlands, stayed overnight and she visited me at the hotel. She's written or telephoned me every week for five years– that's loyalty! As I said, when we left the Midlands so abruptly we found out very quickly who our real friends were. We desperately needed references so we could rent somewhere to live, and we were desperately hurt by the people we thought were close friends and then totally disowned us. My 'little corset girl' did everything she possibly could to help us. I was very grateful and I have a *very* long memory.

Most of all, I like the lovely people who bring me new ideas to try, and the ones who don't care if I wear similar clothes each time (having a 46" bust makes trying to find new clothes in PVC or leather a nightmare), people who appreciate what I do and are enthusiastic and I can have fun with! What I *don't* like are the time wasters and the people who try to play psychological 'games' with the mistress. I'm very explicit about what I do and what I don't. Most people can get a first appointment, but even at that stage I'm still weeding out the time wasters, and people have been known to be asked to leave. One 'gentleman' turned up, refused to fill in the questionnaire, took one look at the equipment and said: "Yeah, fancy decorations. Now what do you charge for sex?" He proceeded to pull out about one thousand pounds in fifty pound notes from his wallet. I promptly informed him I don't 'do' sex under *any* circumstances, and further suggested he put the notes into a particular orifice and I would light them for him! However, after we had sorted out this little difference of opinion, he became a devoted slave, and I still see him occasionally. Apparently, this was a little 'test' of his to see if the mistress is a *real* dominatrix or just a prostitute posing as one. I did ask him once which ladies had passed the test and who had failed – but he's very discrete, and so am I!

There are a lot of people I wouldn't want to see again, yet there are also a lot I would. I wondered at first, when I turned professional, whether it would spoil it for me. But you get more and more involved *and* it's fun! Everyone who walks in here is like a jig-saw puzzle that you have to put together. They're all so different, and looking for such totally different things. That's why I encourage people to send me fantasies and feedback.

Often there is no logical end to a particular fantasy or, as I've said, you make the fantasy real and they find they don't like it. One unexpected problem I've encountered is when someone has brought me a fantasy, and I've done it for them, and they've said: "Yes, but that's my fantasy, and you've done it! What do I do now?" I got an e-mail from someone recently, saying: "Thank you very much, but I don't know where to go from here! I'll be in touch when I've thought of a new fantasy!" What happens often is that they will go to a mistress and they'll get a 'little bit' of their fantasy, perhaps. What we do is enhance that. We do the fantasy *exactly* as they want it the first time, then try and make it more and more realistic.

A good example is one gentleman who's come to see me half a dozen times for a 'prison warder' scenario. It was quite detailed.

When he came to the front door, Jayne was dressed, as near as we could get it, in a trustees uniform with leg irons on. I'd blanked out my old librarian's security badge and written 'prison warden'. We'd got files with his name on and details of his offenses. We enhance the fantasy each time.

Jayne and Julie will get involved in sessions only if they are specifically invited by the guest to join in. It is useful to have an extra pair of hands with the more complicated bondage; particularly the cling-film, as we use very large rolls which are too heavy for me to handle on my own. But they would *never* enter the dungeon without being specifically invited. In a dire emergency they would slip a note under the door, and we do have a subtle alarm system that the guest isn't aware of.

Julie, in particular, loves to join in rubber bondage sessions as she's an ardent rubberist. She's probably responsible for my love of rubber, and she makes all my rubber clothes as I can rarely get anything in my size. Our main problem is finding a strong rubber adhesive, I tend to put rather a strain on the seams as I love rubber skin tight! Julie's always busy and, if she isn't making clothes for me, she's repairing things like hoods, making maids dresses, sorting out my Internet site, doing the accounts – not to mention all the housework!

As I said earlier, I don't consider that corporal punishment is an essential part of every session. Some people simply don't enjoy that type of sensation, and many are worried about marks; though only an inept or careless mistress leaves telltale signs on a guest's body. That's not to say that I can't cane *extremely* accurately! I've had plenty of practice, particularly with Jayne (who is also a wicked schoolgirl called 'Jennifer'). Not only can she be unsuitably flippant at times, she just happens to enjoy being caned in front of people, too! It's very often well deserved and, at the end of each caning, she always kneels, kisses my hand and thanks me for her punishment. She's only forgotten once in five years, but the resulting extra strokes ensured that, oddly enough, she has never forgotten again! And I broke my favourite cane in the process that time!

When we go away, we usually stay at a gay hotel so that the 'girls' can dress if they like. It's very funny sometimes, because people can never quite work out what's going on! We'd come down together and one minute the girls would be dressed and the next they'd be straight.

For a start, there are three of us, which is an odd combination. They'd be thinking: "What is this woman doing with *these* people?" They always assume that anyone TV has *got* to be gay, so it totally confuses the life out of them!

An awful lot of people who come to see me are very stressed out businessmen. If they've done competitive sports, particularly, they're used to an adrenaline surge or an endomorphin high, and the body can't replace that. They really do have difficulty coming to terms with the fact that they *need* to visit someone like me, especially if they are genuinely happily married. But their bodies are going crazy. They need some sort of deep relaxation, and that's what a good SM session should give. They need to be divorced from the outside world. The sessions will usually end on the long bench with the slave bound tight with either latex or rubber; which gives unbearable erotic tension, followed by ejaculation and, finally, relief! Then I'll let people relax and unwind for a few minutes before I slowly remove all the bondage and they gradually come back to the real world from the 'twilight' world. I think it's a much nicer and friendlier way of bringing proceedings to a close. I know some mistresses who will simply bang on the light and they're jerked back to reality. We'll chat for a while and it's amazing the things you talk about. Like their guilt, for instance. I'll explain that really this is *true* stress therapy, in the same way their wives may go out and get a new hair-do or even have aroma therapy! She doesn't feel guilty, does she? I don't break up marriages. They're still faithful to their wives, but they go home happier and more relaxed. Men don't leave their wives for this kind of mistress. Being totally 'out of control' from daily life and its responsibilities is the main thing. Being able to trust somebody enough to hand yourself over to them and empower them, that's my thrill! It's a total power kick for me, having that finger-tip control over somebody. That's the beauty of this job, and I get to wear my favourite clothes, too!

As long as you remind yourself that there is a *real* world out there. On the other side of these walls there are cars going by and people walking about. This is the fantasy world, the twilight world. Step through that door and *bang*, it's reality again. There are mistresses who've come to believe in their own 'immortality', if you like. That's silly. I saw one mistress at the Fetish Market once who had her slave trailing around behind her, bare footed! Now, come on, this is the *real* world! There's

259

broken glass on the floor at events like that. He's going to get stamped on. To me, this isn't about having a slave who'll do whatever I want. This is saying: "I'm an idiot and I've got one with me to prove it!" There was nothing dominant about that. It was a screaming health risk and a total disregard for the well being of the slave. One of the main responsibilities of the mistress is the slave's welfare.

I've always maintained that *anyone* can inflict pain, but not many can make it erotic and fulfiling. Building it up sensually is a very different matter. If it weren't, there would be an awful lot of ladies doing this because it is very lucrative. I certainly couldn't be earning this in the library service, unless they've drastically changed the rates of pay! It's easy to beat someone into submission, but I wouldn't find that fulfiling and it would ultimately bore me. What I do is to combine erotic stimulation with pain until people *want* to submit! And I always make sure I give people 100% in the dungeon. If I'm not feeling my best, or I'm not sure about a particular scenario, I'd rather not do it than give less than my best.

This may surprise some people but, outside of my role as a dominatrix, I'm not a particularly assertive person. I'm even quite shy. I like a peaceful life with a good book to read and I'm not terribly sociable. I think that's probably why I can't get into all the 'shouting' aspect that some other mistresses are very good at. We know one mistress who is absolutely brilliant at it. She'd worked in a care home *and* she'd got two kids! She was used to arguing with people and being assertive all the time in real life, and this came across brilliantly in her maid-training.

I couldn't stop doing this now. It's like a drug. Look at it from my point of view: I've got people who, in normal life, would pass me in the street or in a night club without a second glance and they're coming here, kneeling at my feet, licking my boots and telling me I'm a goddess! And you think I could give that up? No thank you!

MISTRESS ANDRIA

Andria is a 29 year old, full-time transvestite dominatrix who specialises in married men seeking something that extra something special! Originally from Birmingham, she now lives and works in the South Coast resort of Brighton. Interviewed September 2000

I started working as a dominatrix seven years ago and it was really from a theatrical angle. I regard myself as a fantasy figure in that 'Andria' doesn't actually exist, and I think that's where some of the excitement for both me and my clients comes from. I use the persona of Andria to create a situation that excites somebody. It's all theatrical illusion, really. When you're a transvestite dominatrix you create a character that's unique and, to a certain degree, you are guaranteed to be successful because they won't find that character anywhere else. And the better you do it, the happier you'll be and the happier the guys will be.

Before I became 'Andria', I was in sales. I was selling holidays in Tenerife, and also doing exhibition work. I travelled all around the country doing exhibitions. I would be in a different city each week. That was how I first came to visit Brighton, when I did an exhibition in Hove. I used to run along the sea front every morning and I realised what a nice town this is. Even further back I was in engineering, which is a pretty tragic thing to be in, if you want the truth. But there's really not an awful lot to say about my past, there really isn't.

Andria came into being in a very round about way. When I first came to Brighton, I started out on the gay scene. One older gay guy introduced me to simple things like caning and spanking. I used to visit him three or four times a week as a guy. He told me his first experience of being caned was by his local vicar when he was a boy. I was very green then, I didn't know about any of that stuff. Later, I used to advertise in the phone boxes as a headmaster called Mr Cummings!

I started doing domination as The Headmaster, but I didn't have very much equipment, so I used to mix it in my head with fantasy clothing and with girl's clothes. I went out and bought Doc Martens and leather shorts, which was the male gay side. The next item I bought was a pair of thigh high leather boots with six inch heels. But when I started mixing the male and female gear, the gay guys didn't like it at all. They wanted a man, not someone like me who was completely shaven and wearing female clothes. Gay guys don't like transvestites or transsexuals. In fact, some of them are very hostile towards us.

My gay clients started drifting away. That was when Andria was born. Most of my guys are straight, and they certainly wouldn't want to go near another guy if he was hairy or looked like a guy. They wouldn't want to know, so you've got to represent what they want – which is a girl with extra bits! They want a girl with a cock, basically. An ordinary girl they can find on any street corner but, occasionally, they want something different. If you can supply that something different *and* you're very well endowed as I am, then you'll go down a storm in Brighton! But they're definitely not gay. They're straight and nearly all married. They might just be bored with their wives.

I do get approached by couples but we never get round to setting it up because I'm not really interested in girls. What happens is that the guys will try and persuade their wives or girlfriends to come along and see me. When a couple phone, I'll always ask if I can speak to the girl when he's out of the room. Two things I always check is their ages, because I don't see anyone under the age of thirty. And, if it's a female, I'll ask her if he's been pressurising her into doing this. The answer to that is usually yes. I'll ask her to pop him back on the phone and then I'll discretely tell him that I don't think it's going to work because we might clash, and leave it at that really. I'll make some excuse for not seeing them without him thinking that she's put me off. I'll even continue the conversation with the two of them for a bit and cool it down naturally, but one way or another they probably won't be coming to see me. It's just not something that particularly interests me.

Concentrate on the married guys and keep it simple, that's my motto! The simpler you can keep things, the better. As soon as you begin to complicate it, it starts to fall to pieces. That's why I concentrate on the married guys. Hopefully, they're sensible. They're less likely to carry any diseases. They don't want any embarrassing things to crop up. And they're very, very discrete. So there's lots of positive aspects. Besides, I like married guys. They treat you good.

I see guys between the ages of thirty and eighty. Everyone has to have their standards and rules. In this game you've got to create your own rules and then stick to them. That's why I won't see guys younger than thirty. That way it's safe, sensible and secure. There's no need to see anyone younger than that. My oldest guy has got to be in his eighties because he used to drive tanks in the war. He comes for a combination of cock and ball torture, domination and restraint. Maybe a little bit of water sports, too. The majority are in their forties and fifties.

I do everything from domination, humiliation, water sports, bondage, seduction – all those kinds of things. And, of course, all the personal services to go with them. I wish now that I'd specialised solely in domination when I started. But I do like to enjoy myself. I've had a great deal of fun.

You've got to have a good figure for this and a good smile! A good smile will always win through. Plus an understanding of what's required. I used to have different routines. One routine I used when the guys arrived was that I was always wearing a micro mini skirt and I'd make sure one of my switches was turned off, either my television or CD player. I'd sit the guy down, take his coat and fix him a drink. Then say: "Oh gosh, this isn't working". And then, of course, I'd notice the plug and bend down and *every* single guy would grunt and groan when I did that. So you know you're okay then. It sounds a bit simple, but you have to have that assurance that the guy is approachable. The guys are great, but you have to be sure.

A time when that routine was a real asset was when I had a lot of army guys come to see me. It was during that period when the army were talking about homosexuals in the armed forces and I was getting a lot of quite high ranking officers coming along. I think a lot of the guys who had to make decisions on it wanted to experience it for themselves. Whether they were actually ordered to come along and see someone like me, I don't know. But I did quite a few and some of them were very hard. This goes back to what I was saying before about having to be sure. Even though the guy is sitting on my settee, I've got to know I'm okay to approach him. I'll always keep my distance and have a bit of a chat and make him a drink. Then I'll offer him a massage.

I always remember one guy who was really hard. You know, these army guys are *really* tough. I ended up giving him a massage and I think he was determined that nothing was going to work in that department. I think I gave him hand relief or whatever. Afterwards, he admitted that he didn't think that would happen. I just smiled sweetly and said: "But it did, didn't it, Sweetheart?" I think he went away quite changed in his attitudes towards things. To be blunt about it he was stiff as a board!

It's the facts of life. If you're not taught the facts of life when you're a kid, you've got to learn them at some point during your life. For some people that could be quite late. Some of my guys might be in their seventies and they say: "Andria, I've always wanted to do this". In fact, I based one of my adverts on that. I put: 'For gentlemen who've always wanted to, but never have'. It was very successful. They don't feel alone then because there are lots of other guys who want to try.

A lot of the guys who call me are very shy. They're just phoning to see what's going on, but deep down they really want to come and see me, so I never write the phone calls off. It's my life line, after all. Even with the Internet, the phone is still the best way of getting business. The only time I get a lot of hits on the Internet is when my contract is due for renewal and it's the company themselves calling up and pretending to be clients. What will really change the 'hooker scene' is when they have phones with vision, because you will actually see the person you're booking the appointment with. If you're not up to scratch, you'll be out on a limb. There won't be any hiding place. The world is changing and you've got to change with it or you won't be as successful as you should have been. A photograph is worth a thousand words, as they say. A guy will fall in love with a photograph. He won't fall in love with words, unless he's a philosopher and I don't get many of them!

People don't realise the huge amount of preparation you have to do as a transvestite. It's a lot different to any other scene, even the gay scene. A girl's a girl, and a guy's a guy. A transvestite creates an image, which could take you between an hour and an hour and a half every day. You have to have a full body shave, do your hair and your nails. If you're like me, you might have spent an hour in the gym in the morning to keep your figure in trim. And then there's hygiene and cleanliness if you're offering personal services. So, just to become your creation, you've already spent a lot of time and effort. Then, if that creation you've made isn't really accepted by society because, basically, they will always see you as a guy in a skirt, then you really are a prisoner in your own dungeon! You've created your own little world and you have to live in it. You can't even pop down to the shops for a newspaper or go out for a cup of coffee. That's why you need to have a lot of advertising out there to make sure you're busy and don't get bored. It's not easy. When you're a transvestite, it's very restrictive on your life style.

A transvestite mistress has a shot at about one guy in every hundred. If a hundred straight guys are visiting town and you take away the ones who are just looking for girls, you'll end up with five or ten guys who *might* consider visiting you, if you're lucky. So, you've only got about a tenth of the hit rate a girl has got. At the moment, for instance, we've got the Labour Party conference coming up in Brighton. That's my busiest week of the year. The town expects about twenty thousand people coming here that week. Another changing face of this scene is simply that more of those people are going to be women. Equality has done nothing for me! A lot more of the people involved in these conferences now are female and they're not out there looking for sex. Not only are they not out there on the street looking for sex, the males at the conference will spend a lot of their time chasing *them*. So, they're taking the business away from all the working girls and people like me. Sex is more available for them away from home if the conference is split fifty-fifty between men and women.

I think if you're only doing domination it's probably better to isolate yourself away from somewhere like Brighton. I've enjoyed Brighton and I've had a great time here but, looking back on it with my experience, you are better off moving out somewhere to a bigger premises and just do domination. The clients will travel for a good mistress. In Brighton, there are just too many people offering these services, so you've got to be very good. You're only as good as your next appointment with the client you've got at the time. I'm always thinking about the next appointment and making sure the guy wants to come back.

I've been asked to do most everything over the years. I had one guy who wanted to sit in the bath while I did some water sports. Then he'd bring out his shaving brush and shaving foam and he'd want me to fill his eyes full of soap, because he wanted me to be a very wicked mistress with him. Another guy asked if he could bring a banana to eat out of my bottom. When he arrived he had a whole bunch under his arm! Even after he'd left I was still passing bananas every time I went to the toilet! They do want all kinds of weird things.

If you're doing bondage scenes, you've got to be very careful that they're not on 'poppers' or drugs. You've got to have eyes in your bottom. And they all think they can hang upside down for hours on end. All these things are in their heads. You just don't do anything dangerous, you direct the scenario another way. I've had at least eight guys faint on me. It's not a very nice experience having someone pass out on you. It's very frightening. I've been a hairs breadth from phoning an ambulance on two occasions.

Some of the guys want extreme scenes. They've seen things in videos and that's what they want to do. But if you're in control, which you should be, you direct it another way. And, to be blunt about it, I don't get paid the kind of money for me to do the absolute bizarre stuff. If you're specialising in bizarre scenes, then you want the money for doing it. If the guys haven't got the money in their pocket or aren't willing to pay, then I don't do them. It's as simple as that. I won't open my dungeon door unless I get the rate I want.

I don't understand how anyone could be submissive professionally. If you're being subservient all week, your body is going to end up being bashed and battered. You'd have to be on hundreds of pounds for doing it, and you'd only be able to see about one client a week. I used to have an opera singer come down from London to spank me, but I always had to make sure he didn't hit me too hard because I didn't want to be bruised. You experience all these things, but you soon learn that being sub is not a good idea as a profession. You can't control the guys if you're being submissive. Once you show you're submissive, you're in trouble, aren't you? You've got to be in control all the time. You can't hand over the controls to the client. It gets too dangerous.

Everyone in this business should work with somebody like a maid around, especially the girls. Even a dominatrix needs someone there for security. I have thought about working with a female dominatrix, but the problem is that if you get two dominatrix in the same room, they're going to collide. There's inevitably going to be a clash of egos, and unless you've got your own separate premises or a big enough place that you can split down the middle and just come together for certain scenes, it's going to be very awkward to get your personalities to mix.

I knew a guy who had a dungeon who rang me out of desperation because he was looking for a girl who could come and work for him. He'd got his dungeon but couldn't find the girls who could do the business. It's not as simple as you think. A lot of people can't do it. They can't be violent. They can't spank or use a paddle or a whip. It's just not in them. This guy had employed two girls, but they would just stand around and giggle. They were finding it comical. If he'd just had one good dominatrix, it would probably have been fine. But his mistake was having two girls working together in that situation. They just saw it as a comedy.

I wouldn't describe myself as a lifestyle mistress. A lifestyle mistress is a very serious woman and a very serious dominant. Some mistresses just are the way they are. They believe they are that persona. You wouldn't cross them, otherwise they'd automatically expect you to be on your knees to them. They wouldn't doubt you were going to do it, either! If they've got a husband, he probably panders to them as well. If you think about it the best mistresses around are in the Royal Family, aren't they? The Queen Mother has been worshipped and looked after by servants for a hundred years. If that's not a top class dominatrix, I don't know what is!

MISTRESS XENA

Champion body builder, female wrestler and ex-bodyguard, Xena was also one of the first female night club bouncers in Great Britain. And still only twenty seven years old! Interviewed May 2000

My mum thinks this is the safest job I've ever done – especially compared to when I was a bodyguard and was attacked on several occasions! She's quite happy with me doing this. As soon as I become jaded, I'll stop working. I have to enjoy it to do the job well. People will know if you're just putting it on.

I always insist on a detailed consultation to establish the areas a client's interested in; plus a medical check, as well. If they've got any problems like epilepsy or diabetes, for example, I need to know. I had a session just the other day where the gentleman passed out. I got him down into the recovery position and when I got him back he said: "Oh, I always do that". Now why didn't he tell me that before and I'd know how to structure the session and know what positions to avoid? Some mistresses are very conscientious, but unfortunately, some aren't. It's unbelievable the situations some people get themselves into knowing full well that the mistress isn't capable!

There are some *very* good mistresses in London. But, for people who don't know that much, they don't realise the difference. They might go and see some girl who's got absolutely no idea about safety whatsoever. They're just not trained up. I've heard of some horrible experiences from clients. I wouldn't even call some of them 'mistresses', because basically they're prostitutes with whips. I always tell the guys that the best way to find out if the girl is a *real* mistress is to ask her if she does sex. If they say no then they're a professional mistress and they're relying on their skills as a mistress. If they do provide sex then, in my eyes at least, they're not a professional mistress.

Talking about 'horrible experiences', I've known clients who've actually been blackmailed by mistresses! They threaten them with photographs, you see. I may take Polaroid's once in a while, but that's for the client if he wants a souvenir. And it will always be with discretion, it has to be. I've got one client who lives round the corner from my mum!

I know some mistresses who 'switch'; that is, they can be submissive as well as dominant. But for me that's never been a question. I've always been a dominant person in everything I've ever done. I've also known mistresses who've been slave-girls themselves. A lot of people think you can't be a dominant without also being a submissive, but I think you are either one or the other. Your mental capacity is for either being dominant or submissive, not both. Having said that, if it works for you then do it. But, for myself, I'm naturally dominant and that's it! I've always worked and competed on an equal level with men and very successfully, too! I've always been very good at every thing I do, and it's always been along with a more dominant role anyway. I was one of the first women night club bouncers in this country, as well as one of the first female body guards!

I've always been quite physical and I'm very confident in myself, especially with body guarding and door work. It's all about control. You're very aware of what you can do, if you have to. You'd much rather *not*, of course. You'd rather hold back and talk your way out of a situation or deal with it in some other way. I think that's why I enjoy this work so much. It's fun! Or it *should* be fun. Some people take it so seriously, though. I've got a regular who comes to me once or twice a week *just* to do my house work and the gardening and so on. I'll put him into bondage and it's just fun. He's a nice person to have around. And he's got this incredible history of seeing mistresses for over thirty years – that's longer than I've been alive! To me, that's fascinating.

I've got 'domestic-slaves' who come here, too. They'll normally wear a boiler suit while they're working out in my garden, but they'll *always* have ladies lingerie or something on underneath! If anyone sees them, it just looks like I've got a contractor working out there. They'll get a session at the beginning and another at the end *and* they get the opportunity of long-term submission as well. I get a lot of businessmen who are used to being the boss themselves. I'll put them in an apron and a collar and order them around all day and they love it! It's because they don't have to *think* about anything. That way I always have my house clean, and I *hate* house work, anyway! Of course, if they misbehave, they're punished. That way, everyone's happy! If someone has a skill they can offer that I need, I *may* consider them for service. At the moment, I've got plumbers, electricians and everything!

I only do about three sessions a day, and I'll spend about an hour and a half with each client. I prefer quality over quantity. And, besides, I do need some time to be able to sit down and relax between scenes. Because I do a lot of role play and I do wrestling as well, it can be very physically and mentally exhausting, so I need that time to myself. You find that you've just got a particular session working well and you've tuned into someone completely, and then you've got someone who is totally different! You can't keep that level of intensity up throughout.

I get so many clients from my web site these days. I spent such a long time setting it up and now it's just gone mad. I had a guy from Turkey with me yesterday. A lot of Americans, too. They come to see me from Heathrow Airport, which is only fifteen minutes away. They might only be in the country for a few hours, but they'll still come round, have a shower and a session between flights..

Every other person who comes to see me seems to be in computers these days, and they've *all* got access to web sites. I see so many different kinds of people – not *just* the high court judges, as people seem think. Everyone from corporate lawyers to postmen, in fact. That's why this has to be accessible to everyone who wants it. Lots of accountants, too. I remember joking with one of the clients that I should advertise in *Accounting Weekly* (if there is such a publication), because I had one week where I saw about five accountants! I think it's because their jobs are so logical, and they can just go in and do it. Their brains just go off into this vivid imagination. And the same with postmen, because their jobs are quite boring as well, I think.

Remember, for a lot of people this will be the first time they've ever sat down and actually talked about these things! That's why I keep a lot of magazines around, because it's good to introduce people to things they've never thought about before. I've got a young carpenter who comes round and he always says he loves coming round to this house, just for the magazines! It's the fact that he can just sit down and read this stuff that is so great for him. I like to talk to people anyway (if they're nice, that is), so it's a lot of fun for me when they haven't seen something before; just to watch them discover something new is great! That's why I particularly love the sessions I do with beginners because *everything* is new to them! Sometimes it might not be what they're into, but then you move onto something else. There's always going to be something that will trigger them off.

They've got no preconceived ideas about anything. I'm afraid you get some of the old guys, and they'll say: "I want this and I don't want to be tied like that". There's no element of surprise, there's just control right the way through the session. And I'm wondering, just who is the 'Top' here?

Obviously, because there is so much that can be done, I like to talk to them to find out what does interest them and what they do like and if there are any big no-no's. If you do something in a scene like water sports, say, or electric's or something else that they *really* don't like, it can stop a scene stone-dead! So I need to know in a consultation what they're into. And that's why I give them a safe word, too. Fortunately, I'm very good at 'reading' people through working in security for so long. All of them are polite and respectful, though. One of my bugbears is uncleanliness. Long toe nails, too. I think it's disrespectful to the mistress, because a session can get very intense.

There are a lot of things I simply *won't* do. I don't cater for sex, for example – which actually really surprises a lot of people. They think sex is all part of it. But, as I said before, sex isn't something a 'genuine' mistress *ever* offers. I do allow leg and breast worship, but I don't allow oral service. It's just not hygienic. I don't do any cutting of the skin, either. But I will do 'safe' electric's. I enjoy 'enforced feminisation' combined with role play scenarios. Like, for instance, I'll catch a guy going through my clothes and I'll make him dress up in them! Making a man go around in four-inch heels is very funny because the tilt of the pelvis is so different. It looks quite uncomplimentary, too. So that's fun to do.

Then you've got the 'serial' callers. These are the ones who'll phone up and book an appointment with no intention of turning up. It's only through experience you learn these things. I've got a very good memory for voices, and everyone's got set key phrases or something that you remember. This should be treated like an appointment you make anywhere else but, unfortunately, they don't see it that way. Remember, I've put an hour or an hour and a half aside for these people, and I might have turned down two other genuine clients! One of the main pit-falls of being a mistress is that, because you're so involved in people's fantasy worlds, you're inevitably going to get a lot of people who write to you or phone you just to talk about it without any intention of showing up. It's just in their heads. That's why phone-lines are so popular, people can get their 'jollies' without having to do anything about it.

Then you get the 'transit' ones who just go around from one mistress to the next. I've got regulars who will see me once a month or once every six months. I understand that it is a lot of money to some people. But it's more special to them, too. And I appreciate that and show it in the session by giving them my time and attention. For others, it's nothing. They can afford to come to me three or four times a week.

Different clients might like a different kind of girl. Some like skinny girls, some like bigger ones. In some cases, I'm not old enough for some clients. We all have our individual styles. Though I get a lot of regular clients, I might even see someone from another mistress as well. There are a lot of stunning older women working, too. You don't have to be young and 'pretty-pretty'. To be honest, some of the younger girls are just *too* young. They don't have the maturity. And it's maturity that you need in this business, because it's about trust. You don't want some silly, giggly little 'girlie' – it just doesn't work. It's all about suspending disbelief, really.

Because I'm a trained actress, I particularly enjoy the role-play. I've got an American police woman's uniform, that I'll wear for my Captain Hardass character. And I just love 'arresting' people! I've got one old gentleman who comes once a month and I always catch him trying to steal the television set! Actually, he couldn't even pick it up! As I'm a Black Belt and an ex-body building champion as well as a body guard, I try to show people different characters and let them know that there's more things that can be done in role-play apart from just the dungeon side. And when people realise that they think: "Oh, I think I'd like to try that next time".

One of my favourites is the 'kidnap' scenario, where we go out and pick up someone at an agreed point. I've got a couple of body guard friends who are ex-marines that I use as drivers. Sometimes I'll come in with a gun. If it's done somewhere quite public then I'll just come up dressed and take them off somewhere. What I do is I make them come here first and we'll talk it through, plus they need to sign a waiver just in case something goes wrong and the police become involved. We also take Polaroid's to make sure we've got the right person. In fact, I had a friend who was training and they had to do a kidnap off the street and they picked up the *wrong* guy, simply because he had the same hat on and the same jacket and he's pleading: "No, no, you're making a mistake!" They kept the poor man locked up for two hours before they realised! It seems ridiculous, I know, but it does happen unless you set it up properly.

I'm not interested in things like chat shows. The problem with chat shows is that they're only interested in the shock value. They're not interested in the life-style or the safety aspect or how nice the people in it are. There's a lot of humour involved, but *they* only want the sensational aspects. For me, this work brings together all the elements I've been trained for as an actress, as well as body builder and wrestler. I've even done a lot of fencing, which is perfect for crop work. I can use all these things to great effect. I never know what role I'm going to be called on to be next.

In fact, my first introduction to the scene was through being a night club bouncer. I was working for this one security company and they asked me to do this club night, and it turned out to be the *Sex Maniacs Ball*. And it was *really* lovely! The people were great and it was such a mad scene! Visually it was stunning. And I was being paid to walk around and watch it all happening! It was great! I can honestly say that, of all the places I worked in security, I found the fetish crowd were the best. There was none of the drug abuse or the selfishness or macho element you'd find in a normal nightclub. People were just getting off on what they were doing. What impressed me too, was the etiquette and the respect they have for each other. They would approach each other politely and ask: "May I play?" Those people who love to group everybody in as 'just a pervert' would find that amazing! In fact, other friends of mine that I brought in to do door-work with me, because I thought they'd be suitable, just loved it because the people were so nice and there was such a nice atmosphere. After that, I started doing more and more fetish clubs and met different people and went on from there.

Nowadays, I will occasionally take clients along with me to clubs *if* I feel they're suitable and I feel comfortable with them. People just don't realise what's available for them. Also, it's very difficult for people to get into the scene if they don't know where to go. It is coming out a bit now though. And there are the good clubs and the bad clubs. Some clubs are very big and, yes, you've got the play areas, but it is still a bit of a freak show for the 'other' people who are coming in. They may have the clothes, but *not* the attitude – and they know absolutely nothing about the scene! Then you've got the smaller, quality clubs where everyone's playing and everyone understands what's going on, which I much prefer.

At the end of the day, though, you need a life outside of this. I'm lucky in that I've got friends who keep me grounded. I'm still involved in body building and martial arts training, so I've got friends from that. If I say to them: "Go and get me a drink"; they'll say: "I'm not your fucking slave". I'll say: "That's because you can't afford to be!" They purposefully *won't* do something I ask; where as, before I did this job, they wouldn't have thought twice about it! You need to take time out of it just to chill out and relax.

MISS IRENE BOSS

Based in Pittsburgh, USA, Ms. Boss has been a professional as well as lifestyle domina for five years. She has had a varied background in the world of art and drama, the influences of which she draws upon extensively in her creative use of SM play. Interviewed February 2001.

If society were perfect, there wouldn't be any perversions. But we are an imperfect society, and we do find pleasure in our perversions and eroticism in our taboos. However, to compare the modern SM scene with something like a 'Fall of the Roman Empire' kind of thing, as some people do, is like comparing apples and oranges. There is no comparison that I can see. We're now living in the age of technology, not the age of iron! Due to technology, we can now interact with thousands of people anonymously about our desires, and feel we have a kinship; even though most of us have to be very secretive about this side of our lives.

I was at first a fetishist who had sexual feelings towards fabrics, shoes, makeup and scenes involving props, highly charged drama and personal catharsis. These days, I would define myself as a pan-sexual leather person, and I've played and had relationships with *all* sexual orientations. My first orientation was towards women. We would play in groups, doing dress up, spanking and restriction games. All my childhood games before this had included bondage, humiliation and some form of psychological role play. Favourites were 'mean teacher' and 'guard'. I was constantly 'discovering' sexually oriented paraphernalia around the home I grew up in. A few of my father's female relatives passed away during this time and left him large trunks of high heeled shoes and stockings. I would gleefully wear these to school with a lot of makeup and attract all kinds of negative attention, which I thoroughly enjoyed! So you see, from very early on I was an exhibitionist. I also have an excellent insight into the cross-dresser and those who like to be humiliated, especially in public.

The world of the theatre began to interest me around the age of fifteen and, for the next four years, I found an outlet for all my peculiar energies that now could be considered socially acceptable. I began doing scenes with the man I was dating too! Later, I went on to college where I studied art and psychology, graduating from Carnegie Mellon University in Pittsburgh in 1994 with an honours degree. My art was based on abstract and conceptual ideas having to do with male/female and domination/submission in consensual and nonconsensual ways, and used the genre of 'performance art'. My works were extremely controversial and would attract large audiences.

It wasn't unusual for me to play both submissive *and* dominant roles during these performances, which usually included transvestites. I found it very ironic to conceptualise, write, direct and then have to give up the main focus of the show and play the submissive role myself because no one else would do it. A transvestite friend would often be more than happy to play the lead. I learned a lot about the submissive mind-set during these productions, while I was 'topping' from the bottom. Due to my art background, I have an appreciation for the aesthetic beauty of a scene and the mental capacities it takes to enter into that scenario. In fact, when I tell people I used to be an artist, many of my slaves will tell me I still am! It was really quite a natural progression from artist to professional dominatrix, as they are both linked to performance art in a way. What started out as an experiment as 'an artist in the lab' just seemed to carry on. Let's just say I've 'been in the lab' for about six years now! An event that left a deep impression on me was a foreign film I saw. In the film, there was a character dressed from top to toe entirely in black latex. She had on heavy exotic makeup and was smoking a cigarette from a holder. She looked at the camera and, in a deep and sultry voice, simply said: "Hello". I was very attracted and fascinated by her. In fact, I have become her!

I remember the day I told my parents I was doing this. My mother and father just stared at me with their mouths open, and sort of nodding their heads in amazement. All my dad could to think to say was: "I think I saw that on *The Jerry Springer Show*". I just laughed and said: "Well, Dad, I think what I do is a lot more discrete than that!" So they were a little shocked, you could say, because they never thought I would do it. Then they tried to understand it by relating it to things they'd seen on television and in films. I had to explain the difference. They found it pretty fascinating, but also very intimidating.

I've had other kinds of employment before this that affected me a lot more than this job has. I've learned things from each job I've had that I've been able to bring into my current lifestyle. For example, from the archaeology work I did in the early eighties, I learned that I had the 'true grit' it takes to dig holes in the ground in the middle of March at forty-five degrees below zero! Believe me, it's hard work drawing maps and taking pictures when it's *that* cold outside! When I worked my way through college as a waitress, I learned how to 'size people up', so I could make an experience positive. From being an artist, I learned how to be spontaneous and abstract with my clients. And, of course, from being a teacher, I learned patience. What made it hard for me in all those jobs though, was that I'm not a follower or a team player. I'm a *natural* leader, and I'm only really happy working for myself. I'm very lucky to have found this occupation, because it suits me so well!

One thing this job teaches you is how to 'read' someone very quickly. It is actually quite scary! My extra-sensory powers have gotten much stronger, too. I *know* what people are thinking. For example, when I have someone in bondage, I can actually 'talk to them *without* talking'. One way this work has changed me is that now I'm much more protective of my personal time. When I was an artist my work was about my life, and now my domination is really about my submissives. I guess it follows on that the most positive change I've noticed about myself is that I'm a lot less selfish than I used to be. And I'm a stronger person, both physically and emotionally.

I'm proud of what I do, and because of this the people in my life don't feel a need to try and make me stop. If you feel good about what you do, those who care about you may not necessarily support you, but they will be respectful. When I began professional domination I had no perspective and nothing to compare it to, of course. It was an experiment for me, and I approached it with candour. But I had a sense of humour about it, and still do. Even when I'm angry and in 'lecture mode', that sense of humour seeps through, much to the delight of my submissives! In the last six years, I've learned more about human nature than I did during ten years of college.

I've faced and conquered my own 'issues', and I try to help other people with their issues too, but it does depend on where they want to go with it. I am evolving into wanting my subs to experience the same catharsis through the sessions as I have. There are a number of reasons why a person craves submission however, and it can be anything from a desire to escape their normal reality to a need for behaviour modification. I don't think there are any bad reasons to want to be submissive. Sometimes ill-informed reasons need to be reshaped and directed into something more positive though. For instance, if someone is being unreasonable in their expectations of what is possible in a professional domination session.

My childhood experiences and art exploration were obviously key elements in my decision to become a professional top. I also had a live-in submissive male for three years and, during that time, I played the mistress role close to twenty four hours a day. I wouldn't recommend this to everyone though. I strongly feel now that a more well balanced and harmonious existence between the submissive and the dominant can be achieved with a balance of activities, not all of them being oriented towards playtime.

The kind of matriarchal philosophy I believe in and live by is simply not understood in American culture. It's considered a fetish, and the public need to understand that what we do is about relationships and power exchange. People in the scene need to dispel the negative ideas and myths held by the general public. This lifestyle is a conscious choice the individual makes, and it's certainly not something to feel guilty about. I get angry when I see the sensationalism that surrounds the scene in mainstream society, often projected by films and the media. Ignorance breeds more ignorance and anger. People are often hostile towards what they don't understand. This is not just a problem with the fetish scene, but a problem with human nature in general.

Educating the general public about the professional SM community is the only step we can take to insure our future. I believe in humanism; by that I mean human equality of human beings, whether male or female. As a professional domina I don't strike or dominate men out of negative feelings. No bad energy should be transmitted to the submissive. The touch should be cathartic. It's about emotional connection. During my sessions it's essential that my experience level be greater than that of my submissive's, so that he or she can actually learn something from me. I do consider myself to be someone of superior intelligence and strength. I tend to attract submissives who want intense experiences and, if this involves a role-play fantasy where I am a 'female supremacist', then so be it.

You only have to look at our female politicians, law makers, activists and teachers, to see that the standards for female professionals is much higher than it is for males. Also, it's interesting to note that the idea of a woman acting like a man in order to become successful is fast becoming old fashioned and outdated. We do like to poke fun at the old patriarchy, and educated dominant women tend to do this constantly. I feel this is healing when done with humour. Just look at my name, for example. I call myself 'Boss'. Could a man have done this with the same impact? Certainly not. 'Boss' is often looked upon as a male word, but here I've twisted it around for my own use. I have, in a sense, perverted the word and turned it into something else.

There has been a real shift in mainstream perceptions of this subculture in the last decade or so. Due to the new fad of being a modern 'primitive', almost everyone in Generation X has a tattoo or a piercing these days. A whole new wave of club life has also popped up in the last ten years, and it's now considered cool to go out in public or submit to a mistress on a 'fetish night'. These things, unfortunately, take years longer in Pittsburgh to occur with the kind of frequency that they do in places like Cleveland, Columbus, Philadelphia or Washington DC. Personally, I mostly go to Europe to get the kicks I need beyond the ones I get in my studio. The scene here in Pittsburgh is still in its infancy. I think I have had some effect on it, because I tend to attract a lot of couples who, in turn, start hosting their own events. There are several lifestyle groups here who meet weekly. They're called 'Munches'. We also have five or six large scale fetish balls. These events are more commercial than lifestyle, but the turnout of scene people is amazing just the same!

I feel the shift in mainstream perceptions is good in some ways, and bad in others. On the bad side, there's now a new breed of mistresses moving in who are young and beautiful and just want to be worshipped and adored with gifts. They're not concerned with technique, and neither are their clients! It's 'cool' to be a mistress right now. Madonna has been sliding around dressed up like one, and you can find references to domination in many advertisements. The whole 'male bashing' thing gets mixed into the soup as well, unfortunately. People who aren't 'scene savvy' can't possibly understand the difference between immature 'male bashing', professional female domination, or matriarchy and female supremacy, unless they're willing to spend some time on some serious reading.

On the good side, however, all of this stuff is keeping us on our toes! We have to work harder, be more interesting and learn more to inspire our clients to want to continue their sessions with us. Our clients are starting to realise that what we're providing can be found at some bar with a fetish model, or through some lifestyle advertisement on a phone line. There will always be submissives who would rather visit a professional for their own 'separation' from the scene. The convenience of 'no strings attached' is very attractive to them. No matter how big the club scene gets or the lifestyle groups become, there are always going to be the kind of men who want to keep this separate from the rest of their lives.

SM is portrayed nowadays as something titillating, and it certainly sells movie tickets! In so doing, it gets portrayed in nonfactual and negative ways, but these people still want to sell films. They don't care about the 'scene'. People in the fetish community know this, and the more educated ones simply take it in stride. They've also been known to take advantage of it sometimes! For example, they'll get a secret thrill by taking the wife to see *Quills* or something. The problem with SM in film making is that it's too much of a 'hot potato' to do the right thing with or even to attempt to 'send the right message', because someone, somewhere is going to get offended. Film makers who choose to use SM as a subject matter for their projects know this and exploit it. By the way, *Quills* is more of an art film than a commercial money maker, and I highly recommend seeing it with a non-scene person to get their perspective on it.

I operate a private Female Dominant Studio, which we call *The Compound*. We're located in a wealthy gay neighbourhood that has a lot of people moving in and out of apartments, so my activities go unnoticed. The area is a bit like some residential areas in Manhattan; the rents are high and the property values extreme. I did a lot of research and selected a good, upscale area. Also, I am a legal business on paper. I have a business license and I pay taxes. I am a *known* entity and don't hide from anyone. Activities are discrete here and, since we have such a large facility, submissives often come to visit for an overnight or weekend stay. This cuts down on traffic.

The Compound has six fully equipped 'theme' rooms comprising of interrogation chamber, gothic dungeon, school room, sissy parlour, prison cell and clinic. Consequently, there are many role-play possibilities for the submissive here. We have three full-time mistresses working here, including myself. We also have a submissive female, who occasionally joins in to co-submit alongside the males. Sessions can range from half an hour to several days, and the more extended appointments are encouraged. We also enjoy scenes with multiple mistresses and submissives. *The Compound* attracts the more experienced submissive players who want to be pushed yet farther. My ladies and I have the experience and the intellectual capacity to do this. Domination is primarily a psychological experience after all, and being good at mind control and 'mind-fucks' helps the submissive enter into mindset more readily. I don't have any 'apprentices' working here. I'll only work with experienced mistresses, and references are required. Occasionally, I'll take an interest in a lady working at my studio but, if she turns out to be unreliable or not experienced enough, I'll soon lose interest. After all, I have my clients, and their safety, to consider. So you could say that, though I *sometimes* get interested in taking a new mistress under my wing, I find the more experienced ladies are the ones who work out here – much like the experienced submissives!

At the end of the day, this is still 'sex work', because it is a sexual thing to people. However, that doesn't mean that sex has to take place in order for it be *sexual*. I always make it very clear to people that we never supply sex here. Nor do we allow criminal types into the establishment, so a certain 'element of society' is not welcome here! We have standards and our neighbours know that. As a matter of fact, I think they get a kick out of the fact that I'm here. Every studio I have owned in Pittsburgh (this is my fifth, incidentally) has actually caused people to move to be near me, not further away from me! So I guess I must be doing something right! I look at it this way: I am proud of what I do and I have a positive outlook on this lifestyle. When people become aware of this, they can't help but to share my enthusiasm. It's contagious!

I consider myself to be both a lifestyle *and* a professional domina. The word 'dominatrix' has caused much confusion in the professional sub/dom community. It seems that one can be too professional, but *never* lifestyle enough! My definition of the word 'domina' means lifestyle, but a lot of lifestyle dominas also call themselves mistresses.

Our vocabulary to describe such things is vast, and these words mean different things to everyone who uses them. A domina may choose to have her submissive address her as 'mistress', 'priestess', 'goddess', 'my lady' or some other epithet during a scene. There are also women who specialise in providing a fantasy service where 'domination upon request' is provided. This, to me, is a 'dominatrix'.

Then there are women who adopt a lifestyle based on the patterns of their dominant professions and enjoy the scene enough to take things to the next level, or they become a scene professional after amassing personal experience training submissives. These are the 'dominas'; women who train submissives for their own enjoyment, as well as on an hourly basis for tuition or tribute. More tends to be expected of the dominas. These women generally don't accept 'scripts', and don't perform 'domination to order'. It's more difficult to be a domina, but more fulfiling in the long run as a lifestyle choice, because the woman defines her own boundaries and can get very good at doing specific things. She can then feel a sense of accomplishment at developing her own style. A domina is strong, in control and able to inflict punishments. She is also compassionate and truly cares about the physical and emotional condition of her submissives. It is so important to a successful scene that you understand each submissive's interests and limits, and then construct the scene along these borders – perhaps pushing the limits a bit, too. You must be aware of a submissive's emotional and physical state, and use that as a guide in order to know how far to push and when to wind down. Domina's who aren't compassionate can easily give submissives training they don't like, and even actually hurt them. Such people don't get to play very long in the scene. They soon get a bad reputation and won't be able to get any submissive to play with them.

Personally, I have very strong boundaries between my personal and professional life. This keeps me calm and centred. Very rarely do the two cross over, and then *only* with people I know and trust a lot. I'm not even talking about getting directly sexual with someone, I'm talking about inviting people I've met through the scene into other aspects of my dominant lifestyle. It's important to understand that I never throw it in someone's face that I'm a dominant. With some of my friends and family it isn't even discussed, although they know what I do. I'm very comfortable with what I do, so I don't feel the need to defend it all the time by trying to educate or convert people who aren't (or ever will be!) 'scene savvy'.

I find I get mixed responses from non-professional 'lifestylers', too. I am generous with my time when it comes to lifestyle groups, so they in turn are generous with theirs towards me. However, dominant lifestyle men sometimes have trouble with me! They find my girl-friends very attractive, and it seems there's a real shortage of sub-missive girls! Whenever I have a girlfriend on my arm in public, a dominant man will always want to know about her proclivities. I'm naturally dominant and have a strong personality, so I never get asked these questions! Now, I'm not saying I'm any more 'dominant' than some of my friends, but I think my posture gives them the main clue. They often think that I'm the 'man' in the relationship! Lifestyle ladies often befriend me, and I also have a few lifestyle male friends. I've even got a few 'girl toys', as well!

Every day in my studio is different, but that's what I find so exciting about it. Sometimes, I don't want to sleep at night because I would rather be running my studio! I keep an 'ideas book' at the side of my bed so I can write things down if I wake up in the middle of the night. I like the fact that when I wake up in the morning only about 10% of my day is planned. I'll wing it for the rest of the day, and cre-ate it as I go along. If I did it any other way I would get extremely bored. I don't even eat at certain times. I may have only a few appointments booked, but chances are I will get a few more on that day. It's great fun because I get to sit in my office and work on my computer and, if my boys have been naughty, then their own mistress can 'send them to my office' for punishment to see 'Principle Boss'.

I do have personal slaves, as well as clients. I couldn't run my stu-dio without both types of submissive. I'm sure you can appreciate that I can get completely run over with requests from men who are seeking lifestyle positions here. However, I don't try to fool or trick clients into thinking that one day they might be allowed to become my live-in slave boyfriend or husband after a number of visits. I'm honest with all my submissives, and I'm not some kind of 'Fantasy Mistress' who plants silly ideas into people's heads just to make money out of them.

I reinvest as much as 70% of what I make right back into the stu-dio, and the overheads here are extremely high. The studio has five bathrooms, six theme rooms, a guest room, my office plus my huge personal living quarters, which is in the same building. Cleaning some five thousand square feet is a real chore. My lifestyle slaves have to work their butts off for me! Very few submissives ever gain access into my personal quarters, though. At this time my stable is full, and I'm not seeking anymore lifestyle submissives. Male creatures may approach us for professional sessions only at the moment.

I'm not married and I'm not looking for a husband. Personally, I don't believe in the institution of marriage in our society because it has functioned in too many ways to oppress women, or as a kind of 'legal prostitution'. I don't just state my philosophies, I live them! I have been proposed to many times, but I love my freedom too much! Instead, I may allow the man or the woman of my desires to live with me. My word, of course, is law in all my relationships. As a lifestyle mistress I'm extremely unpredictable, and I choose who I want to serve me. When submissives send me applications for live-in positions, I usually just laugh and rip them up because, in a sense, they have already blown it! I keep my personal life separate from the studio. I don't accept appointments on Sunday for this reason.

The world at large is controlled by men. I see good and bad as a result of this. The fact that the Fem-Dom scene is becoming so huge points to the reality that quite a few men are coming to the realisation that they crave role-reversal. This isn't simply a sexual thing I'm talking about here. Men have testosterone running through them and women do not. Men kill and rape other people. Women usually do not. Our prison systems are overrun by men who have committed heinous crimes against society. Some men need more discipline than others. Some men treat women well, and some don't. What we have going on now in society is the backlash of the third wave of feminism. 'Haterearchy' is unhealthy, negative and angry. Yes, for a while it was normal for women as a group to be angry. However, I did not experience the hardships of my mother. I excelled because I'm an aggressive person. I'm a survivor who isn't bitter.

Due to our biological realities and the hormones that are running through our bodies there are going to be differences, and men are naturally going to be more aggressive as a group than women are. Without the reality of this there would be no procreation and continuation of our species. We were written this way biologically. How much of this can we possibly change? Whatever the answer, it's dangerous to use the scene as a soapbox for feminism. The issues of women being in charge as a fetish and women being in charge as a reality need to be kept separate so that people don't become convoluted in their thinking. When too many poisons have ruined the planet, and too many people have died as a result of disease, war and famine, that nurturing female energy is going to save the day. Since I know that this isn't going to happen in my lifetime, I find happiness in the reality of my existence. It's important to enjoy the life that you have, and to make the most of it.

I'm particularly good at the English arts, as well as bondage and sado masochism. I also cater for transformations, and I probably have the best cross-dressing wardrobe in the tri-state area. I also do outings, role-play, spanking, domestic punishment, interrogation and extensive medical scenes. I like to push my bondage people to try new things because usually we find that it brings something back to our regular scene. I have just added a new 'interrogation room' and cell into the studio and have been getting back to my bullwhipping because I now have the necessary room to properly wield the bullwhip and the correct setting to put it to good use! Lately, I've also been administering lots of electrical torture, having recently acquired many new pieces. I've been experimenting on *everyone* from my 'sissy' boys to my bondage enthusiasts and corporal submissives!

What people are looking for when they visit me depends on the individual, as it's different for each person. It's far easier to speculate when one knows what 'type' of submissive they are. There are spanking enthusiasts, bondage 'bottoms', medical patients, masochists, sissy-boys, fetishists and role-players, as well as various kinds of slaves and prisoners. Also, keep in mind that often someone can be three or more of these things. The key is understanding each individual, how their mind works, and why they need a particular thing. Most submissives will classify themselves as such when questioned by me, but will only dig deeper when I get into particulars. While they're speaking to me about themselves, they are also making observations about themselves! This can be a painful and humiliating process, but I believe in making submissives face their facts. I'll always 'read' them with kindness, and I'll tell them what I think. Above all, I'm honest with them. If I don't feel they're ready for a session, or that it might be better to do their session with another mistress, I'll let them know.

Remember, I am a strong, powerful woman! I'm a woman who sets her own rules, and genuinely enjoys being in charge. I have a lot of charisma and sexual energy, that's why submissives like being around me in the first place. I've also got a good sense of humour, and I can 're-present' their scene to them over and over, yet in a different way each time that's more exciting then the last! I'm full of surprises and creativity. That's why these people contact me, they want to make a 'connection' with this energy. There can be other reasons, too. Maybe they want to 'face their facts', in a therapy-style context. Perhaps they want 'not to be in charge' for a change, and to trust someone else to be. It could be for the cathartic experience of discipline, or purely for the eroticism of experiencing their fantasies and 'getting off' on them. Notice that this isn't simply a sexual thing for them, though it is somewhat sexual. Sex is not the 'crux' of it. As I always make clear, I don't 'have sex' with my submissives, I enact mind-boggling scenarios with them! What I do is to shake them up, send lightening bolts up and down their spines, take them on roller coaster rides, make them think, make them laugh and cry and feel previously bottled up emotions! I have fun with them and they trust me. They call to make that connection and, if it feels right, I'll encourage a visit. They keep coming back because trust has been established.

I never ask them what they want me to do to them. Instead, I'll ask them about their interests and, if those interests are compatible with mine, then I'll go into further dialogue with them. I shape what their experiences will be like here, and I'll respect their differences while still encouraging new activities that would be good for them to explore. However, they *have to* give up enough control to allow this 'shaping' to happen. Since I'm a bondage enthusiast myself, I attract a lot of submissives who desire physical and psychological restraint. That's why I keep a lot of equipment that has to do with this. In fact, I've probably got more equipment in my playrooms than they have in most fetish stores! I am a great collector of *devices*! People know I'm a 'gadget freak', and often they'll send me e-mails and letters to talk about equipment. I always encourage this, because that's how I get new ideas!

The kind of men who are attracted to this are extremely bright individuals. They're definitely in the upper brackets and are, invariably, computer 'savvy'. They are the kind of people who make decisions all day, and many of them run large companies. They want to trust and submit to a woman they feel is as bright as they are. And I'm not kidding here! The most important thing to the majority of experienced submissive men is the intellectual capacity of the dominatrix in question. This is often more important to them than what she looks like; though we dominants know that 'looking good' is important as well. Actually, there are men who are so severely into humiliation that they would prefer to be dominated by a stupid mistress, but this very rare. Most of them seek out intelligence, and they want to play with someone they would actually find interesting in 'real' life too. If a dominant lady wants to be successful, she has to be able to mentally spar with, and outwit, these crafty men! An uneducated dominatrix rarely moves out of local circles.

The ideal submissive is one who respects my time before he even places that first phone call. They must be courteous, address me properly and conduct themselves with intelligence. It's very important to be organised, know when you are available for a scene, have a pen and paper ready to write down all the information that is given to you and, above all, be polite! I cannot stress this enough. The basic things are important. He should take good care of himself, practice personal hygiene, be 'scene' educated, experimental and mature.

There are a lot of men who want to 'play' at being submissive; that is, most of them won't even enter the required mindset until the session actually begins. Sessions don't begin for a novice submissive when they arrive here. There's a short consultation that takes place before the session begins. In the case of the men who can only be submissive for short periods of time, and most professional submissive clients have been this way or still are, it's difficult for them to address you properly. They want to dominate the conversation. They'll speak over the top of you and then try to control how they want a scene to take place by actually telling the mistress to do this or do that! They're immediately demanding from the moment you greet them at the door. Sometimes I'll make them walk around the block a few times while I train them with my electric ball shocker that has a one mile remote radius! That always gets their attention pretty fast! Other times, I'll just smile and show them into the waiting room, because I know their tune will change in a very short while. When I tell a submissive to settle down and pay attention and start behaving respectfully or the other ladies and I will evict him, he comes round to my way of thinking quick enough! A true submissive may forget how to address you (usually out of nervousness) but will snap into line as soon as you give him the first command. I'm very perceptive and know exactly when to take control!

I'm in charge of my time and see who I want, when I want. But I like a challenge as well, and will occasionally train a feisty novice, a brat masochist or a bondage struggler who needs to be physically overpowered. The first thing I did when I acquired this studio was to mirror every room, floor to ceiling. People are visual and, although I do a lot of sensory deprivation scenes, I like to make submissives watch. I find their bodies have changed by the time they return for their next session because they have looked at themselves in these mirrors and they genuinely want to make improvements to please me *and* themselves, as well. I give them life changes and, if they're game for this type of instruction, then they must listen to my suggestions and take care of my property – that is, themselves! Don't smoke, don't drink and don't eat junk food. Take pride in being my property! Practice personal hygiene, exercise and know that it is for your own good, as well as to please your mistress.

Physical attributes are only important in the sense that the slave is caring for themselves and, in turn, is showing the mistress that they want to please her by their appearance. A serious submissive craves training. They want to anticipate the scene. They *want* their knees to shake a bit when they first knock at her door! In a sense, I dominate them mentally before they even reach my doorstep! I encourage a great deal of communication before I ever lay a finger on someone and, by the time I do, they are usually electrified by it! Touch is a reward here. Since I'm disciplined mentally as a domina, and I make sure I'm in a peaceful mindset before entering 'Top Space', my submissives are able to experience physical domination as a reward to them, not a punishment. Even if it hurts, it still feels good in the long run because it is, after all, for their own good!

As I've said, the emphasis here is on training submissives, *not* on having sex with them! The submissives who come here to be trained know that sex is definitely not on the menu, and they don't ask! I'm very honest about that right from the start and don't mince words about the fact that body worship to me is proper leg, foot and boot worship, polishing and caring for a lady's leather and latex costumes, and complimenting her verbally with prayers and poems. I never become tempted to have sex with my submissives, because I know it would be a mistake for both of us. Therefore, I never mix sex with training because what I provide *is* sex training! I train men in how to control their base desires, and to become someone a woman wants to be around. It's not uncommon for me to give lifestyle instructions to my submissives on how to improve their appearance and, thereby, become more appealing to the opposite sex. My style of domination is about emotional connection and psychological journeys, as much as they are about punishment and role-play. While all of these activities may *stimulate* sexual feelings, they are not sex.

I'd also like to say here that, believe it or not, sadists are actually nice people! I am a sadist, and I'm a *very* nice person. Your readers have probably met many during their lives and not even known it. It's what we sadists do behind closed doors that is so scary to non-scene people! In this world, the 'victim' is seeking out the 'treatment', and quite aggressively seeking it, too! These so-called 'victims' will often struggle and act like complete brats in order to get more 'attention' from a sadist. In reality, the submissive is often the selfish one, and the dominant is often simply satisfying the fantasy of the submissive!

Most dominants I know are like teddy bears in 'real' life. Really nice people! This is *consensual* 'play' in the world of the professional mistress and her submissive client. It's also consensual play in the world of the lifestyle mistress, only there it's mixed with relationships that are more personal, obviously. Careful negotiations are carried out pre-scene in both worlds, and the submissive ultimately has control over what happens to them. The submissives are partaking because they *want* to partake. This is a crucial and, should be, an obvious element in any SM play. Abuse is something else entirely. People who are dangerous to society are definitely *not* part of this 'scene'. They may try to hide behind its skirts occasionally, but they'll always be blasted out in the end! Remember, there's a big difference between what goes on in D Block in a penitentiary, and what goes on in a dungeon! The energy may be similar, but the morality and the ethics are *very* different.

This 'energy craving' for realism that so many submissives have has popularised such role-play games as prisoner/guard, victim/interrogator, criminal/cop, accused/judge and so forth. Just look at the way the fetish scene has sexualised most types of uniform. Power play is 'hot', and those in the SM scene will often 'play around' with society roles, which may be horrible and forbidding things to actually become! For example, it would be awful to *really* be a prisoner or whatever in 'real' life, wouldn't it? But 'playing around' with it in a sexy way makes it really hot! You need to realise that sadists are often excited by the 'tableau', and that means what we do is literally 'on a stage', even if that 'stage' is only in our minds! It's the *ideas* that excite us, often as much, if not more, than inflicting any kind of real physical or mental pain. It's the power of the spectacle that rules in the mind of the true sadist!

Many professional dominatrixes are genuinely kinky women, who are certainly not repressed sexually in any way! Everyone has sex fantasies at some stage. This is normal human sexual development. There is, for example, a 'lesbian fetish' in the SM community, but then there is in mainstream society as well! I've noticed that women who stay in this business over a period of years are often gay, but they also have male slaves. The sex industry in general is filled with pictures of women who get excited looking at pictures of each other. When we're young, the first pornographic images we see are often of women. It's 'acceptable' for women to look at pictures of other women, and men are turned on by the idea of women being together. A lot of dominant women find the idea of gay male sex really hot, too!

I don't know of very many women in the professional dominant scene who don't like other women sexually. And most of the dominant women I know also have sexual relationships with personal male submissives. From this, I'd conclude that most dominant professional women are actually bi-sexual, with slight leanings towards men or women as a particular preference. I myself may occasionally invite a nervous submissive female caller to come in and make a video at the studio. My videos with submissive women are *all* genuine, incidentally. A danger I've noticed that seems to affect women who have been in the scene too long is to become asexual. This tends to happen if the woman feels 'trapped' by the scene, and didn't develop any other skills to support herself and, as a result, becomes hateful and negative towards men. I am saddened by that, but it does happen.

At the moment I'm studying the Zen Buddhist and Hindu religions. Most importantly though, I strongly feel the world of SM to be my religion. There's ceremony in this, and there are rituals. I feel at times I'm doing powerful things. Conversely, I also do things that make me feel strange. I get off on the strangeness of playing with people I only know in this capacity. It's a real adrenaline rush! The religion I was raised with doesn't work well with my belief system and never did. I found it to be a judgmental and hateful religion that is intolerant of differences and is not embracing and accepting of others, at least that's the way it was presented to me!

Humanism is derived from feminism and is something I see happening as a result of the third wave of feminism. We aren't there yet, but I can see it coming about in the future. Women aren't angry anymore, we just want equal rights for everybody. I'm not a female supremacist, even though I might role play it often! And I'm not a feminist, either. I see myself as a humanist because I'm more interested in equality with respect to equal opportunity; not just between the sexes, but between the races, too. I didn't always feel this way though, it came about because of my own internal struggle and growth that happened long before I decided to become a professional dominant. These are views I've held onto since I was an artist. I never take my role of 'professional dominant' so seriously that I would mistakenly believe that I'm somehow *better* than the people who like to be submissive to me. Never confuse female domination with feminism!

When you do too much of anything, it can become a bad thing. At this point in time I'm regenerating, and doing very few, but very long, quality sessions with people I connect with on many different levels. If a client is rude or disrespectful to me, he has to own up to it and be punished. In this way he doesn't continue the negative behaviour with other women. If I like a submissive's behaviour or attitude, however, I'll reward him instead. The biggest punishment for him is my absence! This is something that has changed me, and how I look at what I do. I have a need to be strong now, and not simply perpetuate SM just to make a 'buck'. I view what I do as an art form. I've studied and learned techniques, and I've attended workshops and travelled world wide to have new experiences. This has become my 'lifestyle', in a very real sense of the word.

I've learned about boundaries in a traditional way. I'm a very fluid person, and I don't think in a linear fashion about sexual things, as in a beginning, middle and end. I'm a different person with different people; although some core things never change, like my rules! I won't allow straight 'vanilla' sex, or dating clients, and I don't partake in scenes that I don't personally enjoy. The fact that I have these boundaries makes the entire experience very professional for my clients, and they can leave here without any unnecessary 'confusion'. As I said, I've grown more patient, yet more choosy at the same time. I want to grow and learn about new things to keep the experience interesting. I know I can't be all things to all people, that's why I have two associate mistresses to interact with those submissives I may not be compatible with. The longer a mistress is in this business, the more important it is for her to do the scenes she actually finds interest in. When I came into the business I imagined I'd do this for five or six years, but now I know that this is something I'll be involved in for the rest of my life. It's as much a part of me now as my right arm!

SARA DALE

Still glamourous at a young 57, Sara Dale is not strictly a dominatrix. Rather, she incorporates elements of domination, submission and SM in her unique approach to tantric sex and counselling. Sara achieved a degree of infamy, some years ago, as the 'Miss Whiplash' character in the scandal surrounding property rented out by a leading British politician. Unusually, she switches in her role playing, that is she enjoys playing both the dominant and submissive roles. Interviewed July 2000.

How I got involved in S&M was an absolute joke! It was in 1984, and I had somebody I was working with as a therapist who was quite dysfunctional. He had no social skills, and his sexuality was totally involved with masturbation and self-play. At the age of twenty seven he had never had a girlfriend and had no ability to receive touch. If I touched his head or his body he would start shaking. Eventually, after about nine months, I got to the point where I said to him that I really thought it was about time I took him out to a wine bar, just to see how people 'get off' with each other. I didn't hear from him for about four months after making that suggestion! Then he phoned me up one day and said: "Mistress, can you help me?" I knew nothing about S&M at this point and, when he started addressing me as 'mistress', I didn't know how to handle the situation. I phoned a colleague called Claire, who I had met when I studied sexual psycho-therapy. She said: "No, I can't take him over, but what I can do is take you to a club and introduce you to somebody who can show you the ropes".

So I went to this club with her, after borrowing some one else's outfit that was much too big, and my first instinct was to stand on a chair so that all the men would have to kiss my hand. I thought, there was no way I'm going to kneel to anyone! At that time, I thought all women were subs and all men were doms. I didn't realise it was the other way around. It was at this club that I met Master Michael, who was primarily sub, but could also be an excellent dominant. He was very creative and that was great for me. He did things that I had never thought of as S&M. For example, we went to a Chinese restaurant and I had a 'batwing' blouse on. He put leather straps on my arms and then collected them across the back with a chain, so that I

295

only had movement from my elbows upwards. I could move my hands up and down, but only partially sideways. He then insisted I eat the meal with chop-sticks! In order to do it properly, I had to move one arm back so I could have movement with the other arm. I was getting pinker and pinker with the effort of it all and, halfway through the meal, he asked if I'd like the chains removed. I said: "Don't you dare spoil my challenge!" So I knew right then that I was *definitely* dominant, despite my sub-role in the restaurant, because he caved in before I did!

Another thing he did on the way to a party, was to have me dressed with just a Victorian corset, stockings and suspenders, a black raincoat and high-heel boots. When we stopped at a garage, he opened my raincoat so that the corset was revealed. He then told me to go inside the garage and get some cigarettes. I had to leave my raincoat open and the corset showing. There was a very shy, young Indian man behind the counter who took one look at me and his mouth just dropped open and he blushed furiously. He dropped the money and everything else! It was quite a turn-on watching his discomfort. Then, as I turned round to go back to the car, I noticed there was a couple in a car with their kids in the back. The wife caught sight of me, put her hands on the heads of the children and pushed them down so they couldn't see me! I thought this was great fun, too! Later, Master Michael made me get out of the car and stand on the centre white line in the middle of the road, and change my stockings with the cars going by. The interesting thing was that the women looked, and then pushed the heads of the men so that they couldn't!

I learnt a lot about the creative side of S&M from those experiences. I still don't particularly care for being caned. I've tried it because I wanted to appreciate what people go through. It takes a special kind of mind-set, I think. I did take a whipping from two girls at a party once. They tied me to a frame and a third girl was standing in front of me. She was whispering in my ear and running her hands down the front of my body, while the other two were whipping with soft suede. I eventually had such an orgasm that I fainted, and they had to untie me and lay me on the bed. All I could do was giggle. I just thought it was the most wonderful experience. What a way to have an orgasm – from being whipped! I would never have thought it possible before that.

To me, the tie-in between sex and S&M is very subtle. I think it's the fact that someone is giving you undiluted attention. The fact that they need a method and a means, like canes or whips or hoods and so on, are all just accessories, they're just variants. Ultimately, it's about a deprivation of attention and then the 'giving back' of attention, and not knowing what's going to happen next. Sometimes, when I blindfold people, I notice they can take the very things they think they *can't* take, and to a far greater degree than when they have sight. This also suggests to me that sight gives us messages about the pain, so we become more tense.

I'm not sure about caning with me, whether I was blindfolded I'd feel any better about it. I think with me it ties up too much with childhood. I was a very bloody minded child, and I used to get whipped with a leather strap quite often. I used to refuse point-blank to cry, as I wasn't going to give my mother the satisfaction. Although I never hated her for it, because I was a very disobedient child and the punishment was deserved, I think the pain of those early experiences would still be associated in my mind.

I've also found with people who can't get erections, or can't get girlfriends, that S&M is a wonderful way of making them proud of themselves. I had one man who used to grind his teeth, which was most unattractive and would put any woman off. I couldn't cure him of it in the normal way, so I said: "Right, I'm going to introduce you to a bit of S&M. On our next appointment we're going to try some bondage". I tied him down and, the next time he started grinding his teeth, I started whipping him, very gently. But, as the grinding continued, I gave him one very hard caning, and the grinding stopped! He enjoyed the S&M because I'd started him off very gently. So, after that, I said: "Okay, what I'll do next time is put you into bondage and, if you don't grind your teeth, I'll caress you and massage you blindfolded. But the minute you grind your teeth, I'll cane you". I can tell you he doesn't grind his teeth anymore, but he's still very hooked on the fetish scene!

He now has girlfriends, too. At the age of forty eight he'd never had a girlfriend. One of his 'homework' projects was that I got him to kneel in front of me and made him promise that, by the following appointment, he would have inserted an advert in at least two newspapers and enrolled with a dating agency. He'd bring the photographs and we'd discuss why I didn't think this one or that one wasn't suitable. He had this thing that he only wanted them thin and attractive. I said he'd got to open his vista and broaden out, because what had he got to offer at that moment in time? He was going to have to take what he can find and develop a reasonable behaviour with them before he could think of anyone finding him desirable. He also had to build up his confidence. The first woman he dated he 'muffed' completely, so I tied him up and spanked him! I told him he had to do better, as I can't have failures! So, it's been a very good medium for me on that score. I see this work, actually, as a teaching of the way people should be in relationships.

I love S&M privately, too. I enjoy going to clubs, though I'm sorry that a lot of the clubs are just fashion places nowadays. If I had enough money I would love to buy a place and completely do it up. I'd be very heavily selective and people could only get in as members. They would have to be people who are known in the fetish scene, or who are recommended. In that way, these 'lone rangers' as I call them, who never have any intention of putting any effort into S&M anyway, would never get in. There'd be a whole variety of fetish theme rooms, not just a dungeon. And a dining room downstairs with long table and slaves underneath creating, shall we say, a bit of fun! There'd be floor shows with transvestites, and maybe have transvestites maids. And certainly butlers and slaves to service the 'needs' of the people! In-house dominatrixes and masters, too.

I'd also like to find a way to attract more single women onto the fetish scene, but as long as there are these guys around who do nothing but bother women, that's not going to happen. There's one Arab guy, for example, who always comes along with his equipment and will throw himself in front of me when I'm trying to do something with somebody else. I usually grab him by the scruff of the neck and throw him out. Unfortunately, he likes that! I wish there was another way of getting rid of him! There's usually about thirty or forty single men wandering around these clubs and very few females, so there needs to be a way to make it more attractive for women.

If I took over such a premises, in addition to fetish and swinging nights, I would also use it as a training centre for the genuine dominatrixes and would-be prostitutes. I'm not against prostitution, but what I'm against is the prostitutes who aren't safe. I have two women who I call on when I need them, because I don't have sex with people who come to see me. It simply wouldn't do. In the massage area, the people I see are wanting a specific thing and, no matter how much they beg for it, they know there's a little 'mental thing' in my head that says no. I explain to them that, were I to allow it to go that far, they would feel betrayed and that would auger badly on how they treat women generally. In the S&M scene, I'm a bit of a purist. I tend to think that fetish *and* penetrative sex is not really appropriate. It has gone into that, unfortunately. Whenever I see it happening in the clubs I leave, as it's not something I want to be associated with. I came into the scene in 1983 or '84 and, in those days, clubs used to be held in some really elegant places. Nowadays, it all seems a bit seedy sometimes. What's happened to all those people?

I like creativity in fetish and I love using ordinary things in fetish. For example, sometimes I'll put the man's own underpants over his head. If he's repulsed, I'll say: "Well, you're happy to put my panties in your mouth, so why not put your own over your head?" It's kind of turning things around. I'll also wear fetish clothes publicly, five inch heels and seamed stockings! I love people staring. Some people come up to me and say they think it's great, and they wish more people had my courage. I even went to my son's wedding in shoes that I'd bought to go to fetish clubs in!

I'll continue doing this until I no longer look like I can get away with it, and then I'll became more sedate. I love doing headmistress scenarios, anyway. I'll pretend this is the study where she sees the parents. I'll sit as if I'm making notes, while they have to write stuff for me. If I don't like their handwriting or their math's is wrong or whatever, they'll be punished. Another scenario I like is where they pretend they've been sent to me by their firm. They've been under-performing, so they've been sent to me for disciplining. They'll come in and present me with their report. I'll read it and say: "You know why you're here". I ask them how they feel about it, and then cane them. It's got a 'cleanness' about it that I love. I'll set them home-work and I'll tell them to report to me in two weeks. If I'm still not satisfied, then the punishment gets harder. You can expand on that one quite a bit.

My favourite scenario (well, it's not a scenario, as such) is when an individual comes in here and the atmosphere is very relaxed for about ten or fifteen minutes, then suddenly I'll snap and the atmosphere will change. Then they'll be told what to do! I also love scenarios that take place out of doors or in public places. You can flirt and do things, and people aren't quite sure. I like pushing it a bit. I like stretching people's boundaries. I have a regular slave who I'll phone at seven or eight in the morning. He'll come round and make me a cup of tea, run me a bubble bath, shower me, shave me and dress me. He'll then prepare me breakfast and disappear. That's quite fun, too. It just feels so outrageous and self indulgent, but it's taken me a long time to get to this stage.

I also love cross-dressing people. Now, my regular slave is the most *unlikeliest* person to cross-dress! It all came about because he bought a red wig one day, and he's just so un-feminine! I asked him how he felt about being cross-dressed, and he admitted he was interested. It so happened that there was an all-day fetish fete and barbecue the following week, so we went 'sort of' fetish. He had on some leather shorts and I had a rubber top, but we had time to get into the 'feel' of things before I took him upstairs and changed him. I'd already decided the way to do it with him was to be very subtle in the make-up.

The scenario was that he had to look for likely people who I might fancy. And the only way he would know if they were the right people for me is that he would have to dance with them as a 'woman'! If they danced well enough, only then could he bring them to see me. He had an absolute ball! People were very impressed. What I did with him was to dress him up similar to me, so they could see we were in some way connected. He had to tell the men that he was trying them out for his mistress. I was sitting nearby so he could point me out. I was being very disdainful, just glancing over occasionally, so the men themselves were quite 'keyed' in, and that was great. I encourage men to dress up as women as much as possible. By dressing up, I feel they will understand what it takes to be a woman. They think women have it easy and they don't realise how much work there is in making up, getting their figure right *and* learning to stand in high heels!

I already told you about that one patient who was very dysfunctional and who first called me 'mistress'? Well, it turned out he'd been raped, and there was nothing to help guys who'd been raped. I also discovered that he was actually a woman trapped in a male body. He had a very feminine body and a beautiful cock which he, understandably, didn't want to let go of. He also had a mustache and very feminine blond hair. It was quite funny cross-dressing him because we had to use scarves and things to disguise his mustache. Subsequently, he's got male partners but, at the time, he didn't know that about himself, and neither did I. It all came about as a direct result of working with him as a dominatrix!

S&M was a way of him realising a fantasy, plus being able to guide him through the difficulties he was experiencing in a 'play form'. When you have a scenario, it's no different from real life, really. If you're genuinely into it, your behaviour should be as you would be in real life. People, therefore, will respond as they would do in real life. I can pinpoint where they are malfunctioning, if you like. I can then steer it around in the way I'm disciplining them. For example, one client had a total neurosis about weight Here was this man of six foot three, weighing out all his food, so that he wouldn't weigh anything more than what he *thought* his body weight should be! As a result he was underweight, so I had to punish him in order to modify his behaviour. I made him bring me the diet sheet I'd prepared for him and, if he under-ate, I caned him. And he hated caning!

This is how I got into the newspapers in 1991 with all that publicity about me as 'Miss Whiplash'. At the time I wasn't even a dominatrix! With this guy it was important to take him out publicly because he had a very low self image. I dressed him so he looked stunning, and people really admired him. I got him into one of the clubs cross-dressed and had a scene with him, right there on the floor in front of everybody, that made every man there wish they were him! It was that night that somebody from one of the fetish magazines asked me if I'd do an interview and have some photographs taken. At first I declined, then I said okay. They wrote all the blurb, half of which wasn't real, but I let it go through as I couldn't be bothered. They called me a 'sex therapist', which is not the description I tended to use. I called myself a 'hands-on healing therapist'. They also had one or two pictures of me in fetish outfit which came out in the *News of The World* story. How they got there, I don't know. And, besides which, I didn't rent just Mr Lamont's flat, I rented the whole house! I only used the flat for work. And I could tell you many stories about that!

However, it did give me the opportunity to go on the television and talk about S&M and the fetish scene. I was saying how wonderful I thought it was and how very misunderstood it was, because they would always portray the worst of it, rather than the best. Fetish 'came out' a little bit after that. I was one of the first to talk about it in the media, as well as talk about the 'swinging' scene. I've always been pro-people exploring sexuality on a non-penetrative basis, because I do feel there's not enough touch. It's not a case of disapproving of penetrative sex at swingers clubs, it's more a questioning. My sadness about the swinging scene is that it's become a 'cock count', or a 'cunt count'. Very few people touch or caress. If there is a union of minds and sensitivities, it *could* go to penetrative sex . Or it could just go as far as it can go, and then make a date another time.

I have had one or two women as slaves, though not professionally, just for fun. Professionally, I've seen women only as part of a couple. And they weren't simply fulfiling their husbands fantasies either, but their own as well. It's just that their husbands are more in the 'know' about who to go to. And, if they're looking for women, they're looking for someone they can trust. My only problem with women who are submissive is this: if they are 'slaves' in their homes as housewives, then what are they doing being slaves in a fantasy scenario?

I'm very good at touch and tease with a female slave. If a woman is too chatty, I speak to them very quietly with a completely blank expression on my face and tell them to be quiet. If they start giggling, I warn them that they will be over my knee for a spanking. It excites me to see the uncertainty, because they're not *quite* sure.

Domination is as much verbal as it is about caning or spanking. It can be all of those things, but it doesn't have to be. I've had couples where the man wants to see his wife dominated, but I like to turn the cards round. For instance, if the woman has been very good, I'll say: "Now slave, I want you to undress your man". I'll get him to touch his knees, and then I'll get her to spank him! My attitude is that no man has the right to fulfil his fantasy without fulfiling the undeclared desire of the woman. It equals the score. I'm a bit naughty, but I do enjoy it. He may not take it from me, but he might take it from her.

I had a girlfriend who wanted me to dominate her in public. She thought it would be a bit of fun, but she very quickly learned different! Because she had let me pay for the tickets to a show and hadn't reimbursed me, I thought I'd better teach her a lesson! She was chatting away to some guys in the foyer and was just about to go through to the theatre, when I said: "And who gave you permission to even consider going through? On your knees, here and now!" The guys just stood there aghast!

Several of my regular male slaves have cock-rings, so one of my favourite games is to padlock them up before we go out. Everytime they want to go to the toilet, they'll have to ask permission, in public, for the key. At the end of the evening, they'll see me put the key into an envelope and post it to their address, so they'll have to hang on till it arrives. I will keep a spare key, of course, just in case it gets lost! I like to create an atmosphere of anticipation; that sense of not knowing what's going to happen next. For example, with someone who I know is very impatient, I may smoke a cigarette or drink a cup of tea while I keep them waiting. I know they're going to be wriggling around! Or I might even walk along the corridor and walk back again, so they're not altogether sure about anything.

If someone writes to me or sends me an e-mail, telling what I've *got* to do, I automatically won't do it! My attitude is I'm the dominatrix, who the hell do they think they are? If it's someone I know or I'm getting a little bit tongue-tied for new ideas, then I might use their scenario as a jump-off. I will work within the boundaries of the scenario they want, but I'll also do things they don't like as the *real* punishments. If they're really into caning, for example, then they'll have to earn it. Punishments are the *other* things. It could be going out to do my shopping for me, if that's what they hate most. The things they like have to be rewards.

To me, the thing that is so wonderful about the fetish scene is that it's like an 'enforced' courtship. A man gets to understand the woman and the woman gets to understand the man. She gets to know his weaknesses and his strengths. And vice versa. We women are portrayed as either weak or bloody minded. If we're intelligent, we're portrayed as being bossy! And they don't see that we can be all those things, but still be quite shy underneath as well. I am quite shy myself sometimes. I need time to feel the presence of that person.

There's more to us women than just the physical, there's also the spiritual element. And what I also like about the fetish scene is that, at it's best, it's got all these different elements. There's a distinct ritual aspect. Sometimes with a slave, for example, I'll leave the door open when they arrive. They know to come in, get undressed and be kneeling with some flowers or a small gift in front of them. If they happen to look up or are not in position when I walk into the room, they're in big trouble! So there's all that pageantry.

We tend also to put our best side first when we meet someone, so they're not really getting to know the *real* person. For some reason people see me as very sexy. I suppose I am, I wouldn't know. I don't know what the word means particularly. But, as a result, there's a side of me they're missing. I'm *more* than just sexy! I'm inquisitive, I'm adventurous, I'm shy, I'm naturist, I'm bloody minded at times. I see my cunt, what I like to call my 'yoni' in tantric terms, as an individual. She definitely has a mind of her own!

LADY AMBER

Originally from Glasgow, 28 year old Amber is an enterprising business woman, as well as professional dominatrix, who now divides her time between the dungeon and her own successful fetish shop in London. Interviewed September 2000

I've been a professional dominatrix for about five years now. I had an incredibly badly paid job in a hospital laboratory at the time. After I initially learned how to do the job, it became boring. This is what I tend to find with jobs. Once I've learned how to do it, I'm bored and I have to move on because I start becoming destructive! Fortunately, I've stumbled across, quite possibly, the perfect occupation for myself where I can be destructive *and* get paid for it! Plus I'm naturally a bossy person anyway. I think, linguistically, my Scottish accent goes quite well with the image, too – Miss Jean Brodie or something!

I've had personal relationships that took in some aspects of S&M, though I wasn't consciously aware that we were playing games. Little bits of bondage games and anal penetration for him, which he used to love. It was basic 'tie me up and hold me down and fuck me like a dirty little slut' sort of scenarios, Obviously, I don't take sex into the dungeon. There's no need for that, and that's not my bag at all. But that's where the awareness came from. When I did my first trial as a dominatrix I found I took to it like a duck to water. None of it shocked me. I started doing it part time, and very quickly came to the realisation that I was allowing myself to spend eight hours a day being bored in the hospital when I could be down in the dungeon having fun *and* earning a living out of it! So I gave it all up and became a dominatrix full-time. I was very happy there for about three years, then decided I wanted to go back to school for whatever convoluted reasons I had at the time! I did a course in English Literature, but then decided that school wasn't going to make me happy either. That's when the opportunity of opening the shop came up.

It's the 'theatre of the mind' that I'm interested in really, so that covers all kinds of role-play scenarios. I like to play kidnapper, boss, auntie, over bearing sister. Anything that I can basically get my teeth into, I thoroughly enjoy. Gang land 'boss lady' is a particular favourite of mine. I also love cock and ball torture, discipline and a bit of rope bondage. I like fairly heavy torture, though not to the point of drawing blood or getting terribly messy. The best bit is getting into somebody else's mind; to be able to know what makes them tick, find out all their secrets, and then use it against them! No, I'm not wicked really, just mean sometimes! How can us women be so beautiful and so mean at the same time? There's many facets to my personality, and domination is only a part of me. I'm also a budding thespian. I suppose what I'm interested in is the idea of altering consciousness through meditation, and I do think there are ways to do it through the S&M scene. There's definitely a bit of a hippie in me, as well as a stern, frosty faced mistress!

Seriously though, you can feel with some people when you're in the flow, and you're understanding each other and the transaction that's going on energy-wise. It makes it all very exciting. You don't often get it though, and certainly not in the first session. An S&M relationship is like any other, and it needs to be built over time. But there some good submissives out there, and I've got some lovely slaves that I've known now for a good few years. It's a thing that can develop all the time; depending on the scenario, of course. If they're simply looking for a constantly overbearing mistress, that's fine. But, generally, you'll find by that stage their ideas are constantly changing and, as long as no one's boundaries are being stretched beyond what they're comfortable with, then it all goes very well. Of course, their idea of being comfortable *is* being stretched beyond the boundaries!

I've always loved plastic and shiny clothes and the texture of rubber ever since I was a little girl, apparently. I do feel it is an empowering thing. When I'm dressed in my PVC, I automatically feel empowered through association, as well as what I'm wearing. In other words, you've got to look the part to feel the part! I've heard it called 'high drama sex', and I can understand what they're getting at there because you've got to entertain more than just your physical senses. There's other bits you can get to as well.

Nowadays, most of the people who come to see me have fairly demanding jobs and, perhaps, demanding families as well. They're in the role of having to tell people what to do constantly. I think everybody's got a little submissive side to them and, if you're constantly having to play that role, on the other side of the coin it's probably going to be good for you to let it out in order to get your balance back. I've probably got a little submissive side in me too, but I've never found anyone who I'd want to submit to. It would have to be somebody who inspired that in me, because I'm so used to being dominant now. It would also have to be something fairly unbelievable! That would be a hell of a scene! Submission is an impressive gift to give anyone, so they're going to have to be a very worthy character indeed! Imagine the power of a mistress submitting! I attract submissive men all the time in my personal life. Maybe it's because when they find out what I do, it becomes a natural progression for them to submit.

There's no solid rules in this world, but certainly on the corporal punishment side, an awful lot of it is linked to experiences at school or parental experiments when they've paddled you with a hair brush or what not. If it happens around about puberty then there's going to be some sort of associated link between sexuality and corporal punishment. I think that's how it a lot of it goes, anyway. With foot fetishism, for example, I would think that is something that goes directly back to a person's babyhood, to a time when you were on the floor and people would rub your tummy with their foot. Their foot is so big that it would reach both your tummy and your genitals. Remember, you were born a sexual being. 'Looking up skirts' is another one that probably goes back to a very young age, when you're crawling around on the floor.

I have been asked to do some quite bizarre scenarios, like nailing foreskins to bits of wood or nailing scrotums out and beating them. That's going too far, I feel. I know someone who does that, but I don't do it myself. I'm also not terribly adept at the 'adult baby scene'. I don't know if that's because I haven't got any myself so I haven't got any 'script' to go from. I've got one man who I call The Rubber Man. He's completely fixated with all things rubber. He's decked his own dungeon out in rubber: rubber pillows, rubber sheets, rubber hoods with pipes out of the nose for restraint of breathing. One thing I found interesting was the 'rubber mackintosh' thing. He wanted the hood pulled over his head and belted, so he was completely wrapped in this thing. Then he wanted me to sit on top of him and sort of rustle around while calling him 'Anne'. That's quite a good one. Here's a man who's totally *fetishised* this mac for some reason.

Generally, as long as I know the person I'm talking to is of a fairly good intelligence, I will make no bones about telling them what I do. All my friends know. In fact, I've roped half of them into helping me from time to time. I came across a negative attitude when I first told them, but within three or four sentences they realised that whatever negative reaction they had was due to their own hang-ups. They realised they were judging people and that *everybody* has a kink, whether they admit it to themselves or not. Most of the people I deal with are very honest in the sense that they've at least looked into their own sexuality and they've come out and said: "Look, this is what I need and I'm going to go and get it!"

Obviously, a lot of them do feel guilt about it, but maybe that's part of the kick as well! The best ones to do scenes with, I find, are the ones who have examined their sexuality, and have come out the other side and are quite comfortable with life. They're the nice ones to deal with. You're not trying to get past this instant barrier of: "I'm here, but I wish I wasn't". Drop that and you're going to start enjoying yourself!

I have many transvestite friends, as well as clients, who are lovely people. I also know one or two who are the most conceited, vain creatures that you'll ever meet in your life! They seem to need to accentuate the worst aspects of what they perceive as 'girly-ness'. Real women just don't behave like that! But, then again, if you spend that much time looking into a mirror, you are inevitably going to become self obsessed. That's what I find annoying about them. To be honest, I don't have the patience for a full-time dressing service. Dressing up in a domination scenario is fine, but I couldn't do a full transformation. I get bored when I have to praise people, especially when they should be praising me!

I used to do a lovely scene with a guy who had a *complete* obsession with ladies underwear! I mean this was taken to the point whereby every single female he met during the course of his day he would get into detailed fantasy about what sort of underwear she might be wearing. The first time he came to see me, I told him he had to guess what underwear I would be wearing and wear the same stuff himself. He would be unerringly accurate right down to the last detail! He was supposed to be coming to see me in a 'doctor capacity'. The idea was that I was supposed to be helping him to stop wearing women's underwear with aversion therapy and various other techniques. For months he'd come round every second week, and we'd have a little session.

I grew fond of him because he was a lovely guy, and he really did want to stop doing this in case his wife ever found out. He was convinced it would end in divorce and he would lose his kids. In the end, he reckoned I'd cured him which, of course, is absolute rubbish. He'll stop doing it for a while, and then start again when he feels his head is going to explode. He'll be back, I've absolutely no doubt! It's always the way. They go through phases where they'll stop for a while, but if it's there they will always return to it at some point in time.

I had another lovely scene once with one of my regular guys where he wanted to be dressed up as a young fashion model who'd been sent to London to do a photo shoot. I was supposed to be his/her protector and chaperone. What I was *really* supposed to do was abuse his trust and talk him into doing pervy photos and generally get him to submit to me! Then there was a fabulous guy who was totally into the whole *Venus in Furs* thing. He had a big fur coat that I'd wear for him and he was into the scenario of grovelling about, being called a worthless worm and pretty much being kicked around. He was so totally believable as this pathetic little specimen that I took great delight in telling him that was what he was. It's great when a submissive gets so heavily into a particular scene like that, it enables the mistress to do the same.

My oldest slave is eighty four and is great fun. He's got a little T-shirt with 'naughty school boy' printed on it, and he wears a little leather thong to save any 'embarrassment'. I've never known anyone who can take a caning like this man can. He puts a tape recorder under the chair to record the whole session, complete with his little 'ooh's and aah's' in various places. He's got a complete ritual that goes with this as well. Basically, I've got to have a stop-watch and time the strokes at fifteen second intervals. He always wants me dressed in everyday clothes and, whatever cane I'm using, he wants red lipstick on it so the stripes are really noticeable!

I can never hit him hard enough. In fact, it's always the older ones who can take the most unbelievable punishment. Maybe they have the nerve endings in their bottoms fried after so many years of taking it, I don't know. He's so little and frail, you'd think he'd break but he takes everything I can dish out. He's also very polite, one of the old school of gentlemen. He just wants to get his arse caned and that's it, really. At the end of the session, he will very politely ask if he can put just one hand on my buttock. If I'm in a good enough mood I will allow him and that makes him a very happy man indeed!

I'd like to find more submissive girls. I do have one girl who's coming round for an interview. She used to be a 'working girl', but she says she's tired of that and wants me to train her up as a mistress. She's basically submissive though and, to be honest, I could make more use of her as a submissive. The pecking order would be: me, the submissive girl and *then* the male slave. I must say she seems thrilled at the prospect of taking orders from me and being generally bossed around!

As far as women in the dungeon are concerned, I've only had a few experiences and the last one put me off the idea hugely. It was a couple where she was submissive and he would sit and watch. She would type out a scenario of what her punishments would be and all that. Part of it would be things like I'd have to blow her nose and stuff. I said: "What? Well, we'll give that one a go and see what happens". But, basically, these instructions were ridiculous, like caning someone on their fanny. I wouldn't even want to do it. She would be in floods of tears and sobbing her heart out just at the thought of it. And this guy's saying that she can take it, it's okay. In the end I told him that I was in charge around here and he could fuck off!

I even asked her once what it was she getting out of this. She said that she hated it when it was happening, but when she got home it was all fine. I picked up from that that she didn't actually enjoy it, but he was making her. Presumably, when they got home she would be venerated for doing as she was told. I really didn't like it, and I eventually told them I wasn't interested in doing this kind of scenario and off they went. Ultimately, I suppose she wouldn't have been doing it unless there was a part of her that enjoyed it, but it's not my bag. I don't want sobbing women in my dungeon. I'm afraid that does absolutely nothing for me at all. I found it all quite distressing, really. Apparently, she's left him now or so I've heard. Great, I thought, he deserved to be binned. She's now shacked up with some guy twenty years her junior and having a ball! She was such a lovely lady and he was such an absolute bastard!

I haven't really come across that many women in my traipse through the S&M world. There was a mad German once, whose husband was a complete voyeur. She was into everything and anything. Then there was a most amazing looking American woman who was fifty, but looked about thirty. She was buying into anything she could get her hands on. She was married to this rich American guy, and he thought he was onto a right winner with the most 'up for it' woman he'd ever met in his life! He must have thought it was his birthday when he first met her, but it turned out she just out ran him in the end. He realised there was no stopping this woman and no controlling her. I think he passed out in the end.

With these kind of women though, I find it's just not balanced. It seems to come from somewhere very dark inside them. My attitude is that if you're already a victim when you come here, I'm certainly not going to facilitate your fantasy into 'victim mode' even more. I'm here for people who are aware of their needs and are quite happy to fulfil this side of themselves. But if you've got an out and out victim mentality, then you're asking for trouble!

What I'm doing in a session is affecting the individual to the extent that they'll come here in one mode, they'll have a transforming experience that will allow them to leave in a completely different and uplifted mode and, ultimately, they are going to affect everyone they touch with their new and improved mode of the day! That's why I like doing this. This and, perhaps, teaching are the few things that I feel are *genuine* jobs. Most of the jobs out there involve just pushing bits of paper around or doing things for people that they're perfectly capable of doing for themselves, but they just can't be bothered. I like to feel I'm doing something that people *can't* do for themselves. This is a real service I provide.

I've never had any *really* bad experiences. I had a guy who went for me in the dungeon once. It was actually his way of trying to provoke me into giving him a genuinely outraged beating! But it's all got to be controlled, as I'm not into just giving someone a good kick-in. This is theatre and there are rituals to be performed. Of course, the whole sub-dom scene is an illusion anyway. The submissive has all the power and the final say. He has power to stop the scene and start it again with something he feels comfortable with, which is fair enough. But, as long as the *illusion* of power stays in my control, I'm happy!

I intend putting on 'couples nights' in my new dungeon for open minded adults who want to play with other people, or just want to be around other people who are playing. I'll have a maid in there looking after the guests. It will be mainly on the fetish side, but these things do tend to take on their own shape, which I won't restrict as strictly as I would if I was just down there by myself. I'm also setting up my own live one-to-one telephone domination. I've found when I'm just amusing myself in the evening by flouncing about on the Internet and generally bossing people around in chat rooms that very quickly you've got men asking for phone numbers. As there's no way I'm going to sit around talking to slaves for nothing, I'll get a special phone line put in to deal with them.

Another thing I love doing is writing about my experiences and putting them up on my web-site, so that slaves can find out more about both me and the whole Fem-Dom scene. I'm getting more and more interested in magic and the whole pagan and wicca thing these days, too. I think we've gone way off track regarding sexuality. Christianity has made sexuality more or less taboo. I believe people can pretty much regulate themselves. They might fuck up a bit now and again, but with controls on them they're just going to overdo it anyway. It just doesn't work. But then, I don't run the world yet! Give us a chance!

My ideal would be to build up the business so I could sell off franchises. Then I could spend one year working as a dominatrix, and one year off working for the peace of the world and helping people worse off than me. Basically, it would be a year of being a filthy pervert alternated with a year of being Mother Theresa!

When this stops being fun, I'll stop working. If I'm not still meeting people that are interesting or strange or weird or whatever it is you want to call it, then I don't want to play anymore. I've got to the stage now where I just don't want to do the average submissive anymore. I like slaves that I can have some sort of connection with, and where our ideas match. I like the ones where I can sit down and work out a role-play scenario with them that we're both comfortable with and bounce ideas around. I like people who are keen and amazed by this whole scene in itself.

This is such an interesting and wonderful way to make your living. I would fully encourage any woman to give it a try! But, then again, not everyone could do this job. And even the ones who think they can, very often can't. I've got a friend who used to try working with me and, as much as she is lovely and bossy, there's something not quite believable about her. Too young, perhaps? Or not enough natural authority? I don't know. Maybe she's not emphatic enough. As much as she wanted to, her personality just doesn't fit the role.

I wouldn't describe myself as a lifestyle dominatrix, there are too many other facets to me. But, having said that, I could quite imagine myself in a stately home somewhere with the maids and the butlers and all the rest of it. I would thoroughly enjoy that. I'm looking forward to that phase in my life when it comes! I will be making a start in that direction by bringing in some slave workers to help me do up my new shop and dungeon. I won't be lifting any paint brushes myself, naturally!

MISTRESS CHRISTINE

Christine and her slave-husband David are well known on the fetish scene as the owners of a travel business in Portugal that catered for SM devotees. Nowadays, aside from their conventional business interests, they still run a variety of Internet sites devoted to SM and Female Domination. They have also written and published a variety of books on the subject, many of which are available to subscribers to their site. Interviewed April 2001

I used to be a computer programmer, back in the days when they filled whole rooms. After I met David, we went into business together in the home-brewing industry, which was a craze back then in the seventies and eighties. The business was successful, but we sold it before the craze died down. This enabled us to set up in the travel business in Portugal.

I first got interested in Fem-Dom when I met David over twenty years ago, back in 1979. I had just finished a bad relationship with a man in which I was supposed to be the dominant partner, but without the style of a fetishistic relationship. Basically, the guy was a shit and, in order to keep him off the booze and other women, I had to try to take control. I failed to control him and, thankfully, we parted.

I met David, who had also been in an unsuccessful relationship, and we fell in love. He explained to me, at the beginning of our relationship, that he had a rather kinky secret which he had no choice but to tell me, as he felt sure his wife would tell me anyway out of spite. He then explained the kind of sex-games he and his wife used to play and, even though they sounded strange to me, I was still interested because I loved him, and wanted to please him. David has written himself about his early experiences and what brought him to Fem-Dom. Basically, it was a combination of unrequited love, sexual frustration and one or two bitchy girlfriends that all fed the fantasy. By the age of seventeen his sexuality became almost completely focused on fantasies of an SM or Fem-Dom nature. He's now forty six, so that makes it about thirty years since he first became aware of this need in himself.

I must admit that, at first, it was difficult for me to understand that the man I loved wanted to be humiliated. In fact, it was incredible to me that he wanted to be punished and hurt. Some of his fantasies, like being urinated on, were quite extreme. Some were quite mild, like what he calls 'prick teasing'. I struggled to understand why it was that these things pleased him. But through working on our relationship together, and communicating our mutual needs and wants, we discovered that there were ways in which I could increase my own pleasure and give him what he wanted. It took about seven years for me to grasp the dynamics of the Fem-Dom relationship, but once I understood it, there was no looking back!

We came to Portugal in 1986 for the sun, and for a more relaxed lifestyle after all the stress of our earlier business. We decided that, because we liked meeting people, we were best suited to running a small guest house or hotel. We developed a complex of small apartments and our livelihood was renting them out to 'straight' tourists. It was never a hotel, and certainly not a 'kinky' hotel. We'd been to one or two clubs already back in London and had enjoyed meeting fetishists. We felt that we would enjoy the company of people like ourselves, and, since there was nothing locally, we felt we could organise a few parties in the winter time.

The idea was to have groups of couples renting out apartments and sharing convivial evenings. We were then trying to help couples 'come out' to each other, and help them come to enjoy the openness that David and I had achieved in our relationship. As we were all kinky, then of course there were some kinky goings on! Unfortunately, newspapers in England and Portugal exaggerated the whole thing and made our lives hell for a few years. We are still suing one newspaper for the fantastic lies they told about us. The court case has dragged on for over five years, and very nearly put us out of business!

We still rent two villas to conventional tourists. Once the press had stopped printing rubbish about us, we were able to resume that business. That provides part of our income. The rest of the time we devote to our Internet interests, and nowadays my primary employment is as a web designer. After the press nearly destroyed our lives, we spent five years writing a computer program. Basically, it teaches a woman how to dominate her husband or lover. It interactively takes her through day to day situations and guides her in choices of activities to indulge in. David learnt programming after me, but he's the 'techie' with modern computers. I helped with that and wrote much of the content. When the Internet arrived in Portugal, we saw the opportunity to promote that software worldwide.

We now have clients worldwide in all kinds of industries, but we also run a free mailing list for loving couples like ourselves, dedicated to improving communication and understanding in relationships. What happened was that the software promotion led us to receive many emails from couples wanting help and advice. So we decided to start the free 'DOMestic' mailing list five years ago. The idea was to cut down the workload by giving the advice to all the people on the list at the same time, rather than individually. The thing snowballed, and now there are over seven thousand people worldwide receiving a daily e-mail digest of messages. People help and advise each other, and we moderate and edit the content. The administration and editing of that daily content is now a full time job in itself!

In my life outside of Fem-Dom, I love reading, mostly fiction. I also write poetry, eat out a lot, draw a little and write some fictional stories. I love to walk on the beach, go shopping for clothes and watch good comedy and films. Within Fem-Dom, I like to dress in sexy clothes, leather, PVC and more conventional fabrics mostly, but some rubber too. I like socialising, especially with fetishistic people, as then I'm free to be myself completely with nothing hidden. Unfortunately, that's not possible nowadays as there aren't any fetish clubs in our area, and we're not going to risk being accused of running one!

By far the nicest and most interesting people we've met have been fetishists. Perhaps it helps to share a common interest, it certainly means we can get to know each other more completely. I think most people have secrets that they're afraid to tell even their best friend, but when fetishists get together openly that level of trust is often there from the start!

The couples who visited us as guests often had fantasies that they wished to play out while they were here. When they communicated them to us, we tried to help them achieve the best results. If they didn't tell us that much, then all we did was socialise and do our own thing, and hope that they would follow suit. We've also had a TV slave in full white wedding dress with a TV bridesmaid go through a wedding ceremony in which he was sworn to complete slavery to his mistress and wife. We've even had a public flogging in the open air with a bullwhip! Some of the other games played here have included transforming slaves into adult babies complete with diapers, dummy, bottle and baby dress. We also do the transformation of a male into a 'dog' in the outside kennel, as well as schoolroom scenarios with school mistress outfits and desks for the pupils.

Role-play is one long 'game' for us, so we live out the roles we both enjoy. I'll start with why I like doing what I do, and then go on to explain what kinds of things I do within the confines of the role I enjoy most. It was the freedom of role-play that David granted me with his fantasies that allowed me to realise that doing what I now do wasn't cruel but, in fact, was giving him what he desperately needed within a loving relationship.

I've always found the passion of petting, necking and love making exciting. As a girl, if a man was breathing heavily and was clearly excited, that excited me too. In marriages and long term relationships the passion tends to fade, and that level of excitement is difficult to maintain. So, essentially, why I do what I do is simply to keep my man hot and lusting after me constantly, because then I feel powerful and in control. That power turns me on. The male body turns me on too, with its erection ever present as a sign that I have him where I want him, and can twist him around my little finger. To have a man so desperate for sexual contact with me that he'll take whatever terms I dictate is the ultimate in flattery! To keep a man so frustrated that he's prepared to literally worship the ground I walk on is the ultimate high!

My favourite 'games' consist of dressing up provocatively while I go about my daily routine. I like to keep David naked and have him do chores for me. I like to lounge in a bikini, or in lingerie, while I have him sweating and toiling away. I love to watch his arousal, while I constantly threaten him with punishment for his lack of control in lusting after me when he should be keeping his mind on his work! When I punish him for unauthorised erections, I also like to get him to admit that I'm being kind to him if I restrain him! I like to point out to him that, if I didn't put him in something that would stop him getting erect, then he would have to be punished every half hour! My favourite is a sharp spiky pad. When he erects it digs in and causes so much pain that the erection is soon lost! That's really amusing! I'll sit there, dressed up so provocatively that he wants to look, yet when he does it brings about automatic punishment of his penis! If I see several erections come and go while he's slaving away, I might start to get turned on myself. Then I can indulge myself in one of my most favourite games, masturbating while I watch his body working!

I get even more aroused when I hear him whimper with the pain of the spikes, as his knowledge of what I'm doing causes his huge tumescence! Knowing that we're in such a viciously sweet circle is a tremendous turn on! The more I get turned on, the more I moan with pleasure. The more I moan, the more he gets turned on and the more he moans with pain and frustration. To bring a man to his knees begging for mercy, simply because I'm masturbating, has to be one of the most powerful and erotic sensations I've ever known! The orgasm is further fuelled by the sensation of cruelty, and the knowledge that this 'cruelty' is taking my husband to his own private heaven! The combination is mind blowing! Of course, we can't spend all day everyday behaving like that. We have to live in the real world too. Most of the time the 'game' simmers beneath the surface, but it's fun when we have time to let it bubble over.

In reality, sex is almost entirely in the mind. The physical sensations are interpreted as pain or pleasure by what the mind cares, or has learnt, to label them. The roles we act, and presumably enjoy, are either the process of social conditioning or our attempt to break those social taboos. If I were to get really intellectual about it then the social conditioning has made the kind things I do to David forbidden but, by their very nature, forbidden fruits taste sweeter! What really turns me on is the combination of several things. There's the knowledge that he is incredibly turned on by it, the knowledge that he finds me so arousing that he will let me do whatever I like to him, and then there's the powerful sensations I feel when I'm inflicting pain and humiliation. It's like the thrust you feel when a plane's taking off!

I like him to beg and plead for mercy, and I like him to whine and plead with me *not* to do things to him! I like him to grovel and plead for sexual release, and I love it when he gets so frustrated and turned on that he'll even break a few rules. Maybe masturbate and come without my permission. I like him to beg for permission to be allowed into my bed, and I like him to look crestfallen and hurt every time I say no!

I'm afraid my husband has a one track mind! Basically, he's sex mad! He likes every minute of the day to have some sexual connotation involved, and the most attractive image for him is the cruel prick-teasing bitch. He enjoys the concept of me doing it for my own pleasure, and being turned on myself at the idea of treating a man cruelly. There are literally hundreds of little ways I dominate my husband on a daily basis that emphasise my sexual power over him, and make him wonder sometimes if I'm really as cruel as I pretend! Things like leaving my knickers on the pillow in the spare room during the evening. When he's sent to bed, there'll be a note there that says something like: 'This is all you are getting and this is what I think of you!' He will invariably get excited by this cruelty, and sniff my knickers. Almost certainly he's going to orgasm without permission, and almost certainly he's going to pay for it severely the next day! Essentially, what turns him on is the knowledge that I know how desperately he wants to make love to me, and the fact that I turn that knowledge against him!

Humiliating him is the easiest, I just tell him what he wants to hear; like he's a sex mad, wanking little shit, who needs to be controlled and punished! Then I'll get him so sexually frustrated he can't avoid proving me right by sneaking away somewhere to toss himself off! If I can, I'll try to catch him in the act – there's nothing more humiliating for a man! Then I'll show him exactly what I think of little wankers like him! Often I'll put him in the bath and piss on his face as well!

I really enjoy saying no to sex in the most cruel ways possible. For instance, I'll allow him to kiss me goodnight and caress me a little bit. I may even return his caresses till I know I've got him hooked, then I'll send him naked to his 'kennel'. This means he has to strip off and get into a small cupboard we use for this game. Anything can happen then. Sometimes I'll come in and simply lock the door on him, trapping him in there for the night. Later, he can listen to me moaning in the dark and draw his own conclusions! Other times, I might open the door and throw a pair of my knickers in for him. Then I'll lock him up again. I might leave the light on so that he can peek through the crack in the door and watch me undress and paint my nails or smoke a cigarette. Actually, that's only a few of the many ways I can and do humiliate him. To tell you them all would take a book, and I've already written two!

MISTRESS ROWENA

A London based, former psychiatric nurse in her mid thirties, Mistress Rowena graduated from being a masseuse and escort to full-time professional dominatrix, specialising in the training of transvestite maids and bi-sexual males. She has since left the profession and gone back to college to study art history. Interviewed March 1999

The first person I ever saw as a dominatrix is still with me. This particular guy rang me one day, completely out of the blue, and asked if he could be my slave. At the time I didn't even know what he was going on about! I was working doing massage and escorts at the time. But he persisted – as they do – and became my first slave, and that's where it all began, really. It certainly opened up a whole new world that I hardly knew existed before. Eventually, he told me that I should be doing this full-time and drop the other stuff. I couldn't believe how busy and popular it was. It was just mad for the first few years. That was about ten years ago and there really wasn't much competition back then. There was only about three or four women doing this in my area, that I was aware of. Compared to what I was doing before, this was great. I could come in and do exactly what I wanted – to a degree, that is. I used to get two or three people a week who'd stay for the whole day, so I could use them as sluts with other clients. They'd love it and be back next month for more!

I don't know why I attract so many TV's and bi-sexual guys, but I do. It seems to have become a bit of a specialisation. Maybe it's my looks, I don't know. But there's definitely a lot of cock sucking goes on around here – and it's not me doing it, I can tell you that! I think they just like being under the control of an understanding mistress while being 'forced' to do something that, actually, they've always wanted to do anyway. None of them would consider themselves gay though.

My first full time transvestite maid was called Natasha. She was also my introduction to the TV and bi-sexual scene. She rang me up and asked if I needed a maid. No, not really. But she persisted, of course, so up came Natasha! To be honest, I was expecting a maid who would keep the place clean and answer the phones and everything, but Natasha was more into seeing lots and lots of clients. She was very oral and a complete little slut – bless her! It was her, in fact, who persuaded me to get a proper dungeon going with lots of equipment and all the rest of it. I was doing it already, but not to the standard I am now.

It makes me laugh when people, especially the feminist lot, automatically assume someone like me is being exploited by men. Honestly, I've had men round here licking my toilet clean with their tongues while I watched day-time television, ate the box of chocolates they brought me *and* got paid for the privilege of letting them do it! Looking at it that way, I don't think I'm a poor exploited female, do you? Having said that, I do honestly think there is a price to be paid as well. Not meaning to sound dramatic or religious or anything, but sometimes I do think I've made a pact with the devil. I've lost a lot of my 'normal' friends from when I worked in nursing. The ones who've since got married and become very respectable tend to distance themselves from you. It's something you also have to keep quiet from your family. My mum and dad still think I'm nursing, so I literally have to live two lives. I drive two cars, for instance. One is a sports car and the other is a clapped out old rust bucket that I use when I go home to visit my parents for the weekend, because that's what they'd expect an overworked and underpaid nurse to be driving. You have to lead this strange double life. It's completely ridiculous, really.

A friend of mine, who's also a dominatrix, told me a lovely story about her little daughter that shows just what I mean. This little girl is about seven or eight now and she's one of these kids who's too clever for their own good, if you know what I mean. Anyway, she's listening to all these 'funny' phone calls her mum is getting from clients and slowly figuring things out and putting two and two together in the way kids do. Then one day she turns round to her mother and suddenly says: "I know what your job is!" My friend is like, oh my God, what's she going to come out with? She says: "Oh yeah? And what's that then?" And the little girl announces: "You beat people up for a living, don't you, Mummy?' Imagine that! I think I'd have fallen through the floor! I mean, what do you say to that?

Then there are the people who wonder why I'm still single at thirty five when I'm *apparently* so attractive and sexy and intelligent and all the rest of it. But the bottom line is, who would I get involved with? The men I meet either want to exploit me (that is, become my pimp) or they want to save me as some sort of 'fallen' woman! Neither of the above is particularly appealing, to tell you the truth. I've known some mistresses whose clients have become their boyfriends. I think that's ridiculous myself, but I can understand how it happens, because that's the only people you end up meeting. You can become very isolated in this business, if you're not careful.

I'm not saying that you can't become friends with clients though. One of my regulars was in his seventies and had been doing this stuff secretly for years, but had only come out with a vengeance after his wife died. He had the most amazing stories to tell, like tying an empty baked bean can to his genitals as a sort of improvised chastity belt, and this was when he was only six years old! Unfortunately, he seems to have 'disappeared' a while back. I've got a horrible feeling his daughters, who couldn't understand what he was about, have had him put away in a home. He used to joke that his family thought he was mad because of his fetish side. Maybe they really have done it and used the 'perviness' as evidence of his madness! It's quite medieval, if you think about it. Like witchhunts or something!

But, then again, some people are very scared of all this. I don't think people in the scene are doing themselves any favours when they call themselves 'pervs'. I know it's only meant jokingly, but it does put a lot of people off who otherwise might get into it. When they hear the word 'pervert' they immediately think of child abuse and wife beating and a whole lot of other dark and sinister stuff that has nothing to do with this lifestyle. Now if they simply replaced that with something like 'kinky', which has got a much more lighthearted and fun kind of vibe to it, they'd find they would get a totally different reaction. People aren't threatened by that word. In fact, most find it quite titillating and naughty – sort of seaside postcards and all that. And that's the way it should be.

The type of clients I get are definitely not just the public school types, that's a great misconception. Although, it's true that they're usually the ones who can afford these little indulgences. But I've also dealt with plumbers, postmen and all kinds of normal, working class and middle class people who'll religiously save up their pennies so they can visit me. Having said that, I would say that many of my clients do come from very repressive backgrounds. Apart from the single-sex boarding school types, I've seen lots of men who come from cultures where women are traditionally regarded as both social inferiors and as sex-objects whose appeal has to be constantly resisted and denied. For these men, the idea of submitting to a woman is the ultimate perversion – it's blasphemous, in fact. Consequently, it's incredibly erotic for them as well, as you can imagine!

What I would add, though, is that most CP addicts are English, or at least, of Caucasian stock. I've dealt with a few Germans, and Frenchmen really appreciate any form of exotic sex, I must say! As for the Latin races, you can forget it. Sado-masochism is simply not part of their macho tradition and the very idea of being punished by a woman is alien to them. Apart from their mothers, I suppose. But that's a different thing. The same is true of Asians and most Afro-Caribbean's, too. As well as the macho aspect, I think the whole thing would be a turn-off for most West Indians. Think about it historically, they've experienced chains and slavery for *real*, and it wasn't exactly sexy, was it? So, I'd say there are very marked cultural differences here with the white northern Europeans dominating – or not as the case may be!

I really enjoy having the transvestites here, but only if they want to 'do' something. Unfortunately, a lot of them just want to sit around and pretend they're at a Women's Institute coffee morning or something! Just the fact of 'being' a woman for a couple of hours is enough, they don't feel the need to actually do anything! Which I can understand is great for them, but it's a bit boring for the mistress who has to sit there with them. I especially like the ones who want to be total tarts! They're lots of fun! Now my favourite was a client called Natalie. She absolutely adored being a little slut. We used to have all the guys who fancied some bi-sexual fun come here one afternoon a week. Natalie would take the afternoon off work and, for that period of time, would be 'the good time that was had by all'! She loved every minute of it, and then would change back into 'masculine mode' and go back to her normal life of husband and father. I think these clients like having a TV join in because they can still kid themselves they're having sex with a woman. Therefore, in their own minds, at least, they've not had a 'gay experience' at all, and they can reassure themselves they're straight. Even though the experience they've just had is not *totally* straight – and neither are they! It's a way of justifying it to themselves, I suppose.

I remember one regular client of mine who was so into transsexuals, as well as domination, that he ended up living with a pre-op mistress as husband and wife. He even helped finance her sex change operation, which was why she was doing this in the first place. Incidentally, you know a lot of the pre-op transsexuals in this business are just doing it to pay for their operation, don't you? I feel very sorry for those ones, because quite often they'll really hate the work. But what else can they do? There's no other job around where they can be themselves or be wanted for what they are, is there? They really are very marginalised in society, much more than the rest of us. Anyway, as I was saying, this guy set up home with her and everything, and eventually she had the operation. Since then, she's turned into a real 'twin set and pearls' suburban housewife who spends her time baking cakes for the church fete and doing flower arranging evening classes! She doesn't want to have anything to do with 'mistressing' either, or straight sex for that matter, so the poor sod's missing out completely! The irony is that he actually helped her to be what she is today. He paid for all this in the hopes that he was creating the mistress of his dreams – and she just doesn't want to know! These days he's having to go back to visiting professionals and paying for it again!

But getting back to what I was saying before, the demand for TV's is so great, especially among the older clients, that I've had a few working for me as maids or submissives. The most memorable was one called Layla who I inherited from a mistress up north who was badly mistreating her. I'd got to know her over the years at scene parties and clubs and so on, and one day she phoned me up in a very agitated state because her mistress was really taking the piss and doing some pretty horrendous stuff to her. I'd rather not go into all the details about what had happened, but it was pretty bad. Let's just say that poor Layla was really exploited something terrible by this bitch. This particular mistress had found out that Layla had left his/her wife because of this lifestyle and had got into a bit of a mess with debts and so on. She was on the run, basically. The mistress was forcing her to do really hard-core stuff, horrible stuff. Anyway, I agreed to take Layla on as my maid and receptionist and told her to jump on a train down here. She showed up with one carrier bag, looking like a bag-lady or a refugee from Bosnia or somewhere. But she was extremely popular with the kind of guys I mentioned – especially as she was hung like a cart horse! I felt quite redundant with all the attention she got!

Even before doing this, I've always been into bizarre sex. I suppose I like things that most women wouldn't even consider. I guess that's another reason I attract the transvestites and bi-sexual men, which would be a turn off for lots of women. But I love them. It's amazing how many men have bisexual leanings. A gay male friend of mine told me a great line that the only difference between a straight guy and a bisexual one is about six pints of beer! I think there's a lot of truth in that. It doesn't take much to bring that side out in most of my clients, I can tell you that!

For instance, another one of my regular clients loves the idea of being forced to have sex with other guys. Usually it's just oral. As I don't do any kind of sex, it's great having this guy as a 'cock slave' to finish the clients off with his mouth. He loves it and the clients, to be honest, are that excited by the end of the session they don't much care if it's a man or a woman doing the sucking. Some guys are blindfolded so they don't even know it's another guy doing it. Another of my guys will *only* suck men off if they're blindfolded. He couldn't bring himself to do it if they were looking at him. I'll be bringing the session to a close and, of course, the client will be all tied up and in a highly excitable condition! Then this guy will tip-toe into the dungeon and go down on him. When they'd finished he'd scamper off back into the other room and I'd take their blindfold off. They all thought I was the one who'd just given them the blow job, rather than this seventy year old filthy bugger! I must admit I find the deception an incredible turn-on!

You hear horror stories in this business all the time. Not all mistresses are as professional as they could be, or even as sane they should be! I know of one mistress who has her black boyfriend working with her who will join in whether you like it or not! He has a real attitude problem where whites are concerned and shows it! As far as his attitude to women is concerned, it's that 'fucking the plantation owners daughter' chip on the shoulder trip. With the sub guys, it's about fucking the plantation owner himself, I suppose. I heard one story from a client, who was also a bi-transvestite, about a session where he was tied up by this mistress, and then this big black guy walks in bare-ass naked and with a big hard-on and says: "So, you want to be a woman? I'll treat you like a woman". The client was bi-sexual, but that still doesn't mean he wants to be raped, does it? The black guy then has his way with him, and what's he going to do about it? He's not going to go to the police, is he? The mistress isn't going to do anything either, because this bastard is her drugs supplier, as well as her boyfriend. I wouldn't mention any names because, apart from the fact that it would be unprofessional, it would be downright dangerous too! There are mistresses out there who are vindictive, nasty bitches. They wouldn't think twice about stitching me up to the police or the tax man.

And some of the things these women get away with, you wouldn't believe! But it shows the way some of these guys get hooked, and the extremes they'll go to in order to please their chosen object of desire. One mistress I know of had this silly old fool come over from the States. He'd worshiped this woman for years and took care of her advertising and bought her clothes. He'd even paid for her boob enlargement for her. And you know what? He'd never even met her! But he still used to sleep with her knickers cellotaped over his nose every night. Then he does come over to Britain to see her. In the whole two weeks he was here, she allowed him to see her just once – and that was only to take her on a shopping trip. Talk about retail bloody therapy! She took his credit card off him and literally drained his bank account. When he got home, he discovered she'd taken him for every cent he had, which was something like twenty thousand dol-lars! And he still worships the ground she walks on! That's the kind of mistress who gives the rest of us mistresses a bad name. In this world, it's not about protecting society from the so-called 'perverts', it's more about protecting some of these idiots from themselves! It's absolutely criminal, but what can you do with someone like that old guy? Not much, really. They really are obsessed some of them. And it's nearly always old men – probably not a lot else going on in their lives, I guess. One old chap phones up regularly, and you really would-n't believe the extent he goes through the contact magazines. He knows all the telephone codes too, so he knows exactly what area of the country a girl's based. It's rather spooky, really.

I don't tend to deal with submissive women, unless they come here as part of a couple. I can tell you that, in my experience, sub-missive women are a damn sight weirder than any of the submissive men I deal with. One professional submissive girl I knew was really into it big time. God, the risks that girl took in pursuit of what she called her 'perfect master' were quite unbelievable. I was telling a mistress friend of mine once that I wouldn't be surprised if she didn't end up floating down the River Thames one day!

Don't get me wrong, it's not the fetish scene I'm having a go at here. The scene in this country is great and the vast majority of people involved in it are fantastic. Even girls on their own are totally safe in a fetish club. I mean, could you imagine a young girl wandering around an ordinary nightclub, stark naked with a dog lead on and a collar that said 'slave' and being left in peace? Of course not. It's just these lone loony ladies like that girl I'm talking about; answering ads and getting picked up by God knows who. She freely admitted to me that straight sex meant nothing to her and that she could only orgasm through being whipped. And we're talking blood on the ceiling here! Quite frankly, I think some of them have got their emotional wires crossed. As far as I'm concerned, these girls don't need a master, they need a therapist! I may be a dominatrix, but I'm not an evil bitch. Call me old fashioned but, at the end of the day, I'd rather give these girls a cuddle instead of a whipping. But they wouldn't thank you for it, would they?

Frankly, I don't like that whole male dominant and female submissive side of the scene, anyway. It's a whole different ball game to what I do in female domination. It's much darker and, quite frankly, gives me the creeps. With Fem-Dom, you can actually have a laugh with your clients and, most of the time, it is fun. It's fantasy, pure and simple. And afterwards I'll sit down with my clients and have a cup of tea before they go. We step out of our respective roles then. And, believe me, the clients I get are not submissive at all in real life. In fact, anything but. A lot are quite high powered businessmen and people who have to give orders and make decisions all day. All those old clichés about kinky high court judges and bank managers are true! I think that's not difficult for even non-pervs to understand, though. If you're in that stressful kind of position then it's like a mini-holiday to come here, swap your pin-stripe suit for a French maids outfit and pretend to be 'Fifi the Maid' or whatever for an hour or two. But it's not like that when it's the other way around. At least, not as far as I can see. Some masters are fine, but many are really horrible guys who just want to beat the shit out of a young girl. They've got a real attitude problem where women are concerned. But, then again, so have the women. After all, there's plenty of willing victims out there.

Like all the other women you've probably spoken to, I've had my fair share of weirdness. I do find other people's sexual fantasies and fetishes endlessly amusing and fascinating, so maybe I unconsciously encourage the extremists, I don't know. Possibly the weirdest I had was this guy who said he'd been a librarian in the French Foreign Legion, for Christ's sake! He also claimed he'd fucked three thousand women including Princess Diana, Jackie Onasis and Bridget Bardot. It was when he got to Cleopatra and Mary Queen of Scots, that I began to suspect I was dealing with someone a little less than the full picnic hamper! And by the time he added Marie Antoinette and Mary Magdelene to his list, I realised he was the full raving article! His main obsession was wanting to drink young girls pee! He even had this idea of advertising in the contact mags offering to pay young single mums to sell him their daughter's urine by the pint!

I can tell you a few stories about vicars, too. That's another cliché that holds true! I've had one as a client, and he was straight round here after evensong to suck off my TV. He'd come straight from the church, still in his dog collar! On another occasion I saw this vicar at a fetish event once. He was leading a slave boy around by a lead. The boy looked like one of those junkies that hang around Kings Cross. I thought, at first, that this clergyman gear was some sort of fetish costume, till I saw him get his cheque book out to buy some bondage gear and realised he actually was 'The Very Reverend'!

One of my favourites is my Dildo Man. He'll show up here with a suitcase full of the things and likes nothing more than putting on a sort of live 'dildo-show' for me and whoever else is here and fancies watching! I have literally witnessed this guy shove at least three bananas up his bottom, and then produce this bloody dildo-thing. It must have been, I swear to God, at least nineteen inches long! When the bananas were nicely mashed up his bottom, he'd shove it all the way up himself. He got it in so far I could see his stomach coming out at the front! It was like John Hurt in that film *Alien*. I expected it to burst open at any moment! He did confess that he was a bit worried his girlfriend was going off him a bit, because he used to shove

bananas up himself at home as well. It's one thing to come to someone like me and do that stuff, but to do it in front of your sweet and
innocent girlfriend is quite another! No wonder she'd gone off him!
All he wanted to do was talk about bottoms and anal stuff!

Which reminds me of another one of mine who was absolutely
obsessed with shit. He'd come for an over-night stay and bring all
these videos for me to watch in the hopes I'd get turned on by them,
I suppose. There were these videos of women rolling around in these
huge tanks filled with cow dung, and he was raving about it! He
thought it was all fantastic. We'd watch these bloody films all night
long and all he wanted to do was talk about shit. Licking it, smelling
it, eating it and smearing it all over himself. He was hoping I'd 'perform' for him in the morning. I did it, but I didn't enjoy it. In fact, I
was a bit disturbed by that one, I have to admit.

Oh, and there was another one who was *really* scary! This guy
wanted to be buried alive. So we took him out to some waste ground
near here and buried under a pile of rubble one night. That was pretty bizarre. We stuck a sort of snorkel made of old hose pipe down for
him to breath through, and then we'd go to the pub for an hour and
leave him there! Another strange thing about him was that he wanted
me to keep all the used condoms I'd accumulated from other clients.
He'd ring up in the morning and tell me he was coming over in the
afternoon and would I keep all these dirty condoms for him. He'd be
dressed up in women's clothes and I'd pin the condoms all over him.
Then I'd have to tell him what a dirty piece of shit he was, and that he
was only fit to drink piss and things like that. He was very controlling
and manipulative too, which you come across from time to time with
submissives. For instance, he'd bring this card with all this stuff written down, which I'd have to read out loud to him, and it was almost
like I was saying I was the one who was a piece of shit! And then I
realised that, with all these condoms pinned to him, it was almost like
a reminder of what I'd done that day! Do you understand? I didn't get
it at the time. I suppose I was still a bit young and naïve back then.
You certainly grow up fast in this business.

But I didn't like him at all, very creepy. In fact, the first time he
came here was to see my TV, and she didn't like him either. She came
into me and asked if I'd stay in the room with her, which she doesn't
ordinarily do. But there was such a weird atmosphere about him. It

was like you felt he was getting a kick out of scaring people. I know for a fact that he goes round all the massage parlours. They call him The Dog, apparently. He used to like to pretend to be a dog on occasion. Woof-woof and all that. He used to like being put into a cage and fed real dog food. But I'm sure that's nothing you haven't heard before.

You do get some real 'spooky' types from time to time. But not too often, thank God. Another one of the weirdest was a young guy who was completely obsessed with all things Nazi. He had a very peculiar thing about concentration camps, which was a bit disconcerting, to say the least. His ultimate sexual fantasy was to be a holocaust victim! He had all the SS uniforms for me to wear and what he wanted, above everything else, was to be tortured to death by some blonde Aryan super-goddess in one of those clinical experiments they used to do! Weird or what? I could well imagine that one going out and murdering someone one day! and everyone would say: "Oh, and he was such a nice, quiet boy! He used to cut the grass!" You know what I mean? Well, they say it's always the quiet ones you have to watch, don't they?

Those types are few and far between, though. Most are just fun loving little perverts that you can have a good laugh with – or at! My most favourite slave has to be someone who I've named Jelly. You can do absolutely anything to him! I've often ordered him to go and get some stinging nettles from the woods round the back of my place – stark naked, of course! I'll then torture him something rotten with them because he's so much fun! I'll have him here all day for no fees, just to entertain other customers. I've made him eat a chilli sandwich and all sorts. And these were raw Chinese chilli's, and they were absolutely awful! They'd been sitting in the cupboard for months and I was just about to throw them out. You couldn't eat them – but Jelly did! It was great fun forcing them down his throat. He was crying his eyes out, poor sod. But he knew that, unless he did it, he wouldn't be allowed any relief. He's eaten a raw onion for me as well, but that was rather mild by comparison.

One of my main 'cock suckers' was this regular client who's now retired. He used to call himself The Sex God. He wasn't really into the pain side or being submissive but, if anyone wanted their cock sucked, all I'd have to do was give him a ring. His famous line was: "I'll be there in twenty minutes". No matter what he was doing, he'd be there. He'd have been brilliant in the Roman times, because his favourite scenario was orgies. Many a cock sucking orgy have we had with him, I can tell you! We used to see him every week. He did have an outstanding libido. But, as I say, he's retired now and gone to live in Spain. He did come back for a holiday recently, and I was the first person he rang from the airport! He was straight round here sucking cocks before he'd even booked into his hotel! He's invited me down to see him in Spain, but family commitments always get in the way.

Some of the mistresses I have a lot of respect for, others I wouldn't give the time of day to. Don't ask me to mention any names, because I don't want any trouble. As I said before, they will stitch you up. They'd do it just out of spite or jealousy or some other reason that was either real or imagined, which is why you can't trust anyone in this business. Unlike a lot of mistresses, I never employ a 'real girl' as my maid for the same sort of reasons that I'm dubious about getting too involved with some of the mistresses. If you can find a good maid, then you're very, very lucky. Most maids work on a commission basis anyway, so they're not worried about who comes through that door. As I said, you do get the nutters, especially the girls who advertise in the phone boxes. One mistress I know quit because she found out that this guy who she'd seen herself on a few occasions had murdered a working girl. She reckoned the only reason it hadn't been her was because she was dominant. Working girls are a lot more vulnerable than us, I think. Still, it shook her up a bit, as you can imagine. She had to quit altogether, in fact, and couldn't face the job for a few years. I think she's back working now, but in a totally different area. So we're not as hard as we make out, are we? You get as scared as anyone else. The most frightening one I heard about was this mistress in Canada who ended up being the slave of her own slave! How it happened was that he was slowly drugging her over a long period of time. In the end, she didn't know what was happening, and he proceeded to rob her blind! He took her for everything she had, and she ended up having a complete mental breakdown!

Because I do the phones myself at the moment, I get to judge who I invite in for the sessions anyway. In my experience, maids will invariably gossip and bitch about you behind your back. They're the ones who get you in trouble. They get paid a wage by the mistress *and* get commission on top, so they're earning almost as much as the girls.

And they don't want to do anything for it, most of them. They're no good on the phone, either. Horrible, fat middle-aged women. If you get the younger ones, they'll have half an eye out to start up on their own. I had one girl working for me who thought nothing of waltzing off for a couple of hours to see her own clients! Yet, she still expected to be paid for her time here on top! And she couldn't see why I was making a fuss! Apart from anything else, I could have been murdered by some nutter during the time she was gone, but she couldn't see that at all. Increasingly, you'll find the girls today don't bother with a maid anymore. They might use a transvestite, as I've done in the past, because at least you'll have some sort of male presence under the make-up to look out for your safety, or they'll just work on their own like me.

I go through very ambivalent attitudes and mood swings about this business. Sometimes, I can't wait to get here in the morning and get whacking and walloping! At other times, I find myself craving some kind of normality in my life. I mean this isn't exactly a normal way of life, is it? By anyone's stretch of the imagination being cooped up in a basement dungeon for eight hours a day, five days a week is a ridiculous way to earn a living! You know, I actually find myself envying the people I pass on the street in the morning. They're off to work in an office or whatever, and I'm coming here to torture people! You can have too much of it. I think it's called 'fetish-fatigue'. I know girls who get out after a couple of years, sell their equipment and everything. But, they come back. They miss the money. Where else can a girl earn the kind of income I make doing this? Having said that, it's not as much as people on the outside imagine. And a lot of the women in this business are bullshitters about what they make anyway. You'll always find some dominatrix who'll tell you about some rich client in California or Hong Kong who paid for them to jet out to their mansions for one evening, and then came home with thousands of pounds stuffed into their handbags! It's rubbish. The trouble is some of them begin to believe their own hype and really imagine that they are sex goddesses!

You know there's a joke in this business that goes: how does a dominatrix commit suicide? Answer: she jumps off her own ego! There's a lot of truth in that, I'm afraid. The trouble is, as I said, they start believing their own hype, and that's dangerous for your mental health! It's a bit like a drug pusher who gets hooked on his own gear, you know what I mean? Some of them are so far up their own bum-holes, that you only see the soles of their boots! I can understand how that can happen, though. When you've got all these silly men telling you how wonderful you are every day of your life, it's bound to affect some of them, isn't it? You see it all the time at the clubs where some silly cow will be standing there *expecting* someone to open the door for her like its her divine right or she's bloody royalty or something, and then treating all and sundry with utter contempt! That's not being a mistress, that's more an 'attitude' problem, if you ask me! If you're a naturally dominant personality, you don't have to keep proving it all the time, and you certainly don't have to shout in order to assert yourself or get respect. You can if you want, but it's not really necessary. Personally I don't feel the need to shout just to make myself feel better. The girls that have to do that have got an inadequacy; it's a character flaw, as far as I'm concerned. In fact, a lot of the girls in this business are actually quite submissive themselves away from it! Did you know that? I can think of at least a couple who ended up being complete slaves to their own clients. Mind you, in both cases the clients were pretty rich, so you sort of understand the motive.

The whole thing is fantasy, really. I know that's a pretty obvious thing to say, because it's *supposed* to be about exploring fantasies. But you do find yourself craving something a bit more real once in a while. You can have too much of everyone pretending to be something they're not. I mean, the dominants aren't really dominant most of the time, and the submissives certainly aren't very submissive away from this. It always makes me laugh the way the guys write their adverts in the contact magazines. Like they're always saying how they worship the superior female and believe in Fem-Dom as a way of life but, when it comes down to it, they're only interested in being a slave to someone who's under twenty five, has got blonde hair and big tits! I wonder how many of them have helped a little old lady home with her shopping? Not many, I shouldn't wonder!

I certainly don't mean to sound like a feminist, because I'm not, but you can't avoid the double standard, or whatever you'd call it, of this business. One the one hand, you have these guys saying: "I want to be your slave. Do with me what you will" and all that old crumble. Yet, on the other hand, they'll say they only like to be submissive in such and such a way, and only in rubber and only with a 'goddess' who's got the big tits and the big hair. It's still about women doing what men want, and pandering to their desires at the end of the day, isn't it? God, I'm beginning to sound very politically correct here, aren't I?!

I also think a lot of the girls in this business get very cynical about men. After all, we see them at their most vulnerable; grovelling around on the floor, licking our boots and our bottoms and all that stuff. If the girl isn't into the scene herself and understands the mind-set behind it they lose all respect for the male of the species. Even after all these years I still find myself having these weird thoughts coming into my head, wondering if my own father isn't seeing a dominatrix himself. You never know, do you? Just imagine if my own dad booked an appointment and showed up for a session! God, that would really put a weird twist on incest, wouldn't it? It hardly bears thinking about. But that wouldn't happen anyway because I work in a totally different area to where he lives. Just as well, really!

I really can't see myself doing anything else. When it comes down to it, I still love the job despite some of the negatives things I've said. It's the same with any job you've done for a long time, you'll have your good days and your bad. And it is just a job for me now. Well, most of the time. I do still have my moments, though! But it's not as much of a life style for me as it was in the early days. It keeps you hooked, though. Like they say in the fetish world – fulfilment lasts only a moment, denial is forever!

MISTRESS ADELLE

Mistress Adelle is a life-style dominatrix married to a master. Now both retired they continue to enjoy a dominant lifestyle with a variety of male and female submissive guests to their home. Interviewed January 2001.

I suppose we are slightly different to most of the people you've spoken to, in that we are both dominants. As neither of us are interested in being submissive, all our games are played with a third party. This can sometimes be together with a transvestite or a female. Usually, however, we play separately, though the other partner is usually around 'in the background' somewhere.

We discovered the 'scene' together soon after we got married. We have both been married before and have grown up children by our previous partners. Neither of us had any experience of sub-dom or SM before that. We initially started out in the swinging scene, but soon discovered that was not really for us. Although they are two very different scenes, some fetish people do cross-over into the swinging scene and vice versa.

I have always had quite an assertive personality. Consequently, I've found that I've always attracted rather weak and subservient male partners. Though I enjoy the dominant role in play, I hate weak people in 'real' life. Does that sound odd? It's two completely different worlds, really. In a relationship or marriage, all women (including dominatrixes!) like to feel protected by an even stronger male. No woman wants a wimp for a husband, that's why I married a master. We are true equals in every sense of the word, and we have no need to try and dominate each other. Why should we? We've got plenty of willing submissives to fulfil that role for us. You do have to keep these things separated. The scene is for fun, it isn't real life! If you start getting the two worlds muddled up in your mind, then you're heading for big trouble! That way madness lies!

We've met people of all age groups and inclinations since we first got involved in the scene ten years ago. Having said that, we rarely meet people under thirty, and usually in their forties or over. As we present ourselves as a dominant couple we tend to meet a lot of other couples, as well as a lot of TV's. One of the most unusual and interesting were a couple in their early thirties who were both submissive. In a way, they were in a similar situation to ourselves, in that they needed outside stimulation in their play. Interestingly, apart from the first time they visited us to chat things over, they don't come here together. I think they both feel a little uneasy about being in a sub role in front of each other.

The wife is very much into 'school girl' fantasies and spanking, but only with a mature 'head master' type male. I played no part in those scenarios, but I think she felt safer knowing there was another female around. She would show up on the doorstep, dressed completely in school mode. She even had a satchel and a pencil case! Luckily, she is very petite and can get clothes straight from normal school outfitters. She had her school girl 'persona' all worked out and very fixed in her mind, as regards her character and 'age' within the scenario.

Her husband, who I took on as my slave, was into extreme verbal humiliation and female-worship. Obviously, on a fantasy level, their two worlds were incompatible. In all other respects, they were very happy and contented together. I'm telling you this as an example of how this scene can work to complement and enhance a relationship, rather than threaten it. Without these little interludes you would have had two miserable people on your hands. In the end, that gulf of sexual needs might well have grown out of all proportion and threatened their marriage. As it is, they can come here, or go to other dominants, and have their fantasy side fulfilled without any risk to their relationship. They then go home happier people and get on with the rest of their lives.

This is only a small part of most people's lives anyway. Sometimes people dip into this for a short period in their lives, it's a stage they're going through if you like. You'll see them at all the clubs and private parties for a few years, and then they'll disappear from the scene altogether. That's fair enough, I've no problem with that. Their curiosity has been satisfied, I suppose. Or maybe they just had certain agendas that they needed to sort out, and that was that. Then you'll find others, mostly the older men, who've been doing this for years. Some will bore you with blow by blow accounts of sessions they've had with mistresses forty-odd years ago! But at least they know how to respect a mistress, and how to behave in her presence, which is more than a lot of the younger ones do! When that older generation of slaves dies out all you're going to be left with are the younger guys who come along and treat this as just another service. I don't deal with paying clients myself, but I know women who do, and this is what I've heard.

For me, and I suspect for many others too, SM and role-play is a wonderful way of exploring different parts of your own personality that maybe you wouldn't otherwise know were even there. It's lots of other things as well but, to me anyway, it's basically a 'gown up' version of Cowboys and Indians or Doctors and Nurses. When I've got a slave kneeling at my feet and submitting to me, it's such an incredible feeling of power. It's a real surge! And I know that it's the same for my submissive – only from the other angle. You have to remember that 'submissive' is not the same as 'passive'. I think this where a lot of people on the outside don't understand what's happening. Passive means 'inert', like a sack of potatoes. In my experience, submissives are rarely like that. In fact, a lot of them are real drama queens and out and out exhibitionists! Basically, it's a sex pantomime – and it *looks* much worse than it actually is! Really, you could say we are both actors in our own play – and our own audience, as well!

Actually, outside of this situation, I am quite good friends with my submissives. We might go to the theatre or whatever. People would think we were just normal people out together for the evening. And the truth is we *are* normal people, because we've left our respective 'roles' behind in the dungeon. We can pick them up anytime we want. That's the beauty of it. As I said earlier, very few people live this way all the time. You couldn't, really. It would drive me mad for a start, having my submissive ask me what he's allowed to eat in a restaurant or when he's allowed to go to the toilet. That kind of slave wouldn't last very long under my charge! You've got to be normal sometimes!

I always take into consideration who I'm playing with: the personality of the submissive and what their limits are and so on. I need to know what buttons I can push, and which I should leave alone. I love being able to walk through the door and have a slave drop his trousers and instantly go down on his knees before me, with just a click of my fingers! I love manipulating a man's obsessions. And I adore being the mean and unreasonable bitch of his dreams – or nightmares! Believe it or not, I'm actually quite a nice person away from the dungeon.

Sometimes, when the session is over, you feel a real bond with the submissive that quite defies description. It's because we have shared something very intimate, very special. At the basis of most dominant/submissive relationships there is actually a strong sense of equality and mutual respect. Although we are playing different roles, we're still equal partners. Does that make sense? A common misconception is that submission is the same as weakness. This completely underestimates the power and the strength of the 'sexual' submissive. In the kind of consensual relationship I'm talking about, the submissive doesn't give up his social or professional power, and he's not very likely to accept authority from anyone else but his dominant partner. You know, many subs have actually told me that when they surrender sexual power to me and fulfil all those taboo fantasies, it's a profoundly empowering experience for them. There's a tremendous sense of freedom in being a slave!

The ideal dominatrix has to control herself before she can think of controlling a slave. In a sense, you have to discipline yourself first. You have to constantly reassess yourself and what you're doing. Well, I do anyway. As far as I'm concerned, anyone who calls themselves a dominant and isn't willing to admit when they've made a mistake isn't worthy of the title – and probably isn't very good at the role anyway! There's a kind of humility in dominance. I found that one of the secrets to being a good dominatrix is knowing, and accepting, that you are not an infallible 'super woman' – even though your submissive is constantly reinforcing that image. That's a very important point to remember when you take up the responsibility of 'owning' someone who is prepared to give themselves to you. Remember, a slave isn't just for Christmas!

In the eyes of the so-called 'normal' world, sado-masochism is a pretty sordid business. They always think the dominant must be some sort of sex fiend who gets a perverted kick out of brutalising some equally freakish victim! The reality is that the exact opposite is true. An SM relationship is the most democratic in the world. Both partners have to work hard to achieve the kind of level trust that you need to share your deepest fantasies.

As long as it's creating pleasure for both parties, we can keep on exploring and expanding. We always set limits at the outset so that we have a frame work in which to play. But, of course, limits can change. By 'limits' I mean when it stops being fun, basically. I'm not doing this just so I can beat someone black and blue. That's not the point at all. The idea is to give and receive pleasure. When it stops being fun, we stop. I always watch my submissive's body, looking for signs and signals. I can always feel the energy flow back and forth between us. If I feel a blockage there, or a sudden change in that energy, I know that's a good place to take a breather and take stock of what we're doing and where we're at. This transfer of energy thing can be very subtle, but it's unmistakable if you're tuned into it.

Contrary to the common held belief that pain is a bad thing, it is a quite natural capacity. Pain is a system that warns of dangerous situations or of physical damage that needs attending to. Basically, it's a biological safety system. If it's given *without* consent, then it is negative and wrong. No dominatrix would argue with that. But, given *with* consent, between willing equals, it becomes a most incredible form of love. In our society, where people conceive of all love as being of the 'gentle and affectionate' variety, that might be hard to take on board. Try and look at it like this. Take fitness freaks who spend a large part of their time in the gym, for example. All that exercise hurts, doesn't it? No one would say there's anything particularly pleasurable about the actual exercises themselves, but what is nice is the end result. They do it because it makes them feel good about themselves when they're finished. People are so conditioned to traditionally 'affectionate' relationships that they can't conceive how anyone could get enjoyment from these activities. We're so conditioned into seeing all pain as being abusive and involuntary that we can't conceive it as a form of love. At the end of the day, SM is about hurting people. But it's about hurting them just right!

This gets back to what I was saying about the dominant being in control of herself and the situation, as well as the submissive. When I'm in control of a scene, I'm in control of the pain being inflicted on my submissive. I control how much pain, when and how it's inflicted. Unintentional pain or too much pain is 'bad' pain, and it means I've lost control and failed in my responsibilities towards my sub. In some ways, it's a lot harder for dominant women than for the submissives. We dominant women are in a weird sort of double-bind situation here. On the one hand, if a would-be dominatrix overcomes all her anxieties that being sexually assertive is unfeminine, then she has to deal with all the feminist stuff about playing up to men's sexual fantasies and all the rest of it. I can assure you I'm not pandering to anyone! As I'm not a professional dominatrix, and I'm not getting paid to do this, why should I? This is a two-way traffic in pleasure!

My favourite scenarios are the ones that are a bit risqué and a bit mad. I especially like open air scenes where there is a danger of being caught. We generally use woods or selected car parks where swingers and guys meet for sexual encounters. That's a whole subterranean world of it's own but, if you know where to go, it is great fun. The most memorable bit of out-door fun I can remember was when I replied to an ad from this American businessman which he'd placed in *The Times* newspaper. It was very unusual for me to reply to any advert, but his was so intriguing. It was very 'cloaked' with only the most subliminal references to what he actually wanted. Apparently, he'd had seventeen or eighteen replies, but I was the only one who'd 'got it' and understood the hidden agenda. He turned out to be a big, burly businessman who'd recently split up from his wife. He took me to a fantastic restaurant, so that was a good start. He had been to a professional dominatrix back in the United States a couple of times, which had really whetted his appetite. Unfortunately, he had made the serious blunder of confessing his desire to be submissive to his wife, who subsequently used it against him during their divorce and accused him of being a 'depraved and degenerate' person because of it.

We have some lovely old, disused windmills in the countryside near our home. I had always thought this would be a great place to play with a slave, so my husband and I took him up there late one night and tied him up to the machinery with his trousers down round his ankles. However, unbeknown to him, we had secretly arranged with a dominatrix friend of ours and her husband to be out walking their dog at this spot at the appointed time. I made some excuse that I had to go back to the car to fetch something and, while I was gone, these friends and their little dog 'just happened by'! She kind of sidled up to him and started talking to him, asking him what he was doing there all tied up with his trousers down and his cock exposed. They then left him and I came back. The poor man was absolutely petrified. I then proceeded to punish him for not having trust in me and thinking I would abandon him. My idea was to teach him to trust me and to put his complete faith in his mistress. Later, we all met up in a pub and he realised it was just an elaborate joke. He explained to me that he had really believed his ex-wife back in the States had set us all up as Mafia 'hit-men' to murder him! That was why he had freaked out so much.

We have been known to take one of our regular male slaves out for a drive in the boot of our car or tied to the roof rack with some tarpaulin over him. We got pulled up by the police once when they spotted his foot sticking out and must have thought they had a dead body on their hands! They were quite befuddled when they found out what we were doing – and a bit embarrassed too, I suspect, as they were quite young officers. In the end they let us go, apparently they haven't got a law against transporting a willing slave around on your roof rack! He was securely tied 'luggage' after all, so there was no danger anyway!

I tend to meet a lot of transvestites. Maybe that's because they like a more mature woman. Some of the guys, especially the younger ones, would be shy of being 'feminised' by a young girl who was closer to their own age. Somehow the 'mother-figure' is safer for them, I suppose. The youngest I've had was around twenty and looked quite stunning made up. If they are particularly convincing as a girl, I won't mind taking them out for a drive or for coffee somewhere. I don't take them into pubs, not even at lunch time, because that's a bit too dangerous and is asking for trouble.

People have suggested to me that I get myself a TV maid as a proper housekeeper, but they don't understand the mind-set of most maids or TV's in general, for that matter. What they're after is the 'trappings' of being female: that is, all the glamourous and 'girlie' bits. The last thing they want is the hum-drum reality! Think about it, you never see many transvestites hanging around *Mothercare*, do you? And that goes for maids, too. They're not at all interested in actually doing any real house work. They just want to flounce about for a while with a feather duster in their hands, most of them. Even if they did do any genuine housework, you'd have to be forever behind them telling them off for not doing things properly. They'd even drop your crockery or ruin your carpet on purpose in order to be punished. So, as well as being time consuming, you wouldn't even get the job done! And you'd probably have your home ruined into the bargain! No, it's best to keep fantasy and reality apart.

The nearest I've come to having that kind of scenario is with my 'butler', who I've dubbed Jeeves. He's not really a servant, as such, and certainly doesn't do any housework. At nearly eighty, he's not really up for doing much physical work. But he loves the role of being my manservant and, I must say, I really can get into that one myself. There's nothing really happens, it's just wonderful to be treated like royalty for a day. He'll act as my chauffeur and run me around on trips up to town whenever I want. He likes all the bowing and saluting and opening doors for me. It's delightfully old fashioned. He's even got himself a proper chauffeur's cap and driving gloves. As he's quite well off and drives a Rolls, we really do look the part. It's an absolutely wonderful game to play, and I do love turning heads when we go out for a drive! As I say, Jeeves doesn't do much work as such, apart from carrying the odd bit of shopping – if it's not too heavy! But at his age, I wouldn't ask him anyway and, besides, the whole scenario is so much fun, it doesn't really matter. Jeeves has been around for years, and was one of the first people we ever met on the scene. Nowadays he's more of a friend than anything else, and he's such a dear old soul.

The strangest slave I ever had was this Spanish bank manager who stayed with us for three days – and couldn't speak a word of English! He'd replied to one of our adverts somehow, and we invited him to stay over for a weekend session. He turned out to be a very 'dapper' little man who was totally obsessed with these Spanish erotic cartoon books he'd brought with him. I must say I thought they were ghastly, with all these pictures of women in medieval times having very brutal and horrendous things done to them. Pregnant women being beaten and thrown into wells, and all sorts of disgusting images done in an almost child-like and fairy tale way. They were extremely strange. Anyway, his ideal was to be one of these abused women! He wanted to be dressed up in medieval sack cloth and ashes and be completely degraded. He refused to sleep in the guest room we'd provided for him. Instead, he insisted on sleeping in a tiny corner of the attic. It was a little hidey-hole no more than a foot high, but that was where he wanted to be! I cottoned on to what he wanted (despite the language barrier) and tore up some dirty old sheets that we used for decorating and made a little nest for him, and he was as happy as could be!

Apart from the sessions themselves, we usually treat our slaves as normal guests in our home, but he would have none of it! He wanted to be treated like the scum of the earth all the time! He loved to eat the scraps off our table out of a dog bowl on the floor with his hands tied behind his back. He also loved to clean the kitchen floor in the same manner, on all fours with a filthy cloth in his mouth. Oh, and he liked to be called 'Begonia' too, for some reason!

We had a party while he was here with all of our 'scene' friends invited. Begonia didn't want to socialise in a normal way, even though there was a Spanish dominatrix present for him to talk to. All he wanted was to be dressed up like a medieval court jester and have everyone push him around and make fun of him! Even the other slaves thought he was stupid! A fact he delighted in, of course! The more everyone (including slaves) treated him like dirt, the better he liked it.

The most amazing thing about it all was that, by the end of the weekend, I noticed that his penis had shrunk completely! What had started out as quite a respectable sized cock was now like a tiny button mushroom! Obviously, our Spanish bank manager was overjoyed at this metamorphosis! The more we laughed at his little prick, the more he loved it! That weekend was about the strangest I've ever experienced. Normally, when we slaves here, I know what they want, but he really baffled us. Maybe we were too nice for him, and not as depraved as he would have liked. He seemed to have enjoyed himself though, and was very grateful for everything we'd done for him – and to him!

Obviously, I do tend to get more people to play with than my husband does. That just seems to be the nature of the game, I'm afraid. It's very one-sided, but there's very little one can do about it. The reality is that male slaves are very easy to come by, whereas the female equivalent is notoriously thin on the ground. As a couple we tend to have a bit better luck than a single master would in attracting the little darlings out of the wood work, but it's still not easy. I know they're out there, but how one gets hold of them in any quantity, I don't know. And neither does anyone else on the scene, as far as I can tell. One can find lots of 'masters in waiting', but never any slaves girls. Apart from the submissive couple, I mentioned before, we've seen no more than half a dozen sub-females.

One couple we knew in north London had a very bad experience with a 'supposedly' submissive female who answered an advert of theirs in a contact magazine. They were advertising for a live-in slave girl, and this young woman answered. Apparently, she was very convincing when she came round for her 'interview' and was very wised up on the scene and everything. They were completely taken in by her. Anyway, ten minutes after she left their house, they got a call from a public phone box down the road. It was this girl saying that she had to inform them that she was from one of the Sunday 'tabloids' and that they would be in the next one! Sure enough, they were. Complete with their names and address and everything! As it happened, they didn't really care that much. He was retired and, being Danish, didn't have any relatives in this country to worry about. She was a little embarrassed when her family and neighbours read about it. Even so, the point is that, if he'd have been a young guy with a family and a career, that could have ruined his life. We know of one teacher who was sacked because he held a private fetish party in his home that was infiltrated by the press! His headmaster was very broadminded and was very good about it, consigning the newspaper in question to the litter bin where it belonged. Unfortunately, the parents weren't so tolerant! They didn't want their precious children taught by this 'monster'! The school had to let him go in the end, and that was the end of his teaching career!

The laws in this country are disgraceful and should be changed to come in line with the sort of invasion of privacy laws they have in France. These newspapers are destroying people's lives just for the sake of a five minute read and a bit of a cheap thrill on a Sunday morning! And for what? What harm have they done? Who cares if someone wants to dress up in PVC and have his bum smacked or whatever! It's not exactly the crime of the century, is it? It's not as if they're a threat to national security or anything like that. We're all adult people, and we're not forcing any of this onto anyone who doesn't want it. We're just enjoying an alternative lifestyle, that's all.

The truth is that fetish people don't pose a threat to western civilisation or have any intention of corrupting your children or abusing your household pets! Neither do they practice wife beating, blood drinking, human sacrifice or whatever the latest wild imaginings of the gutter press may be! In fact, all the ones we've met are a disarmingly well adjusted lot who lead surprisingly normal lives away from the dungeon. Who knows, your readers may even have one living next door!

MISS GEN

The themes of dominance and submission, pleasure and pain has always been a mainstay of heavy metal rock music. Until the nineties, however, these subjects have always been addressed in terms of fantasy and escapism by such luminaries as Ozzy Osborne and Alice Cooper. With the Genitorturers, it's all for real!

Formed in 1986 in Florida, the band incorporated elements of sexual fetishism and body manipulation against an intense tribal-rock sound-track. Steeped in modern-primitive philosophies that transgress traditional taboos, they presented an already notorious stage show that involves the kind of extreme audience participation from which legends are made.

Reports from a New York gig described how a masked woman was chained and suspended from a wooden rack. She is beaten with a paddle and then a man urinates on her. An enema is then administered to a man hanging upside down. Two women had hot wax poured over each other while their breasts were pierced. Mistress of Ceremonies and lead singer Gen simulates sex with an audience member while a masked man jerks himself off. All this while a three-piece band pumps out a ferocious barrage of sound. No doubt about it, these Genitorturers were controversial, provoca-tive and disturbing – in fact, everything rock 'n rock should be!

During a promotional visit to London, I met up with Gen to find out the truth about all those cock piercings, on-stage golden showers and whether she'd be doing panto that year! Incidentally, this interview remains fondly in my memory because it was the very first one I had ever done for my newly launched Domina , and kind of made me feel the magazine had now become 'proper' in some way! Interviewed November 1993.

I was born in Albuquerque, New Mexico; which is a somewhat diverse cultural area, and very much influenced by the Native American and Hispanic cultures. To add another twist in there my best friends were from India, so I was exposed to a lot of cultures when I was growing up. That was something that allowed me at a very early age to accept the fact that there are many different belief systems that have merit. This was a very big influence on me.

Actually, everything has kind of evolved simultaneously, I guess you could say. My interest in piercing, for example, goes way back to since I was thirteen or fourteen. I was doing piercings on myself and different kinds of body play. When I went to college to study medicine, obviously I learned a lot more about the human body. I studied sterile technique, micro biology, surgical techniques and really learned a lot about how the body reacts to stimuli. In our culture, we look at stimuli as either being positive or negative, and many people associate pain as being negative. I've found that pain and pleasure are simply a relative concept of stimuli. Pleasure and pain are the same thing! The same neuro-transmitters are released during a painful experience or a pleasurable one. They're really the two sides of the same coin. A kind of ying and yang.

While I was in college in Florida, I started doing piercing professionally. I trained under an older fellow who had been doing piercings for a number of years. I learned the actual techniques from him and applied them to my medical knowledge. I was already a musician by this time. I played bass guitar and I was in some bands. I always had an interest in music and performance in particular, performing music live. In college the music was really kind of an outlet. Because I was undertaking a very rigorous coarse load in the sciences, music was a way for me to exercise a bit more artistic creativity, which you don't really have when you study a very regimented program such as science. I was working in an organ transplant unit at the time, and was actually performing surgery to retrieve donor organs, so the Genitorturers became for me a real catharsis. Dealing with death so closely on a day to day basis makes you realise your mortality and how precious life is. Then I started to integrate my interests in performance and spirituality, in ritual and in sexuality, into my performance art. It just seemed to make sense to attach that to music, because music has been used in many cultures to enhance ritual.

There's all kinds of rituals in many, many different cultures that incorporate body modification; whether it's tattooing one's tribal insignia on one's body or scarification, piercing and circumcision. All these things are really rites of passage. People ask: "Where does piercing come from?" It comes from everywhere! The Hindu Indians practiced it, as well as the Pacific islanders and Africans. In Victorian England even Prince Albert had a piercing! So it comes from everywhere, it's even talked about in the *Karma Sutra*!

Maybe we're doing a service for people. I hope so. The fact is that bringing some of this 'above board' *is* very scary, but very necessary. When you continually brush things under the carpet it only serves to foster misunderstanding. The truth about the SM subculture is that it's very much based on consent, trust and love. And people have to know that! We've got to get rid of this misconception that what we're doing is violent, and that what we're doing is cruel. People associate SM with something akin to wife beating and this simply isn't true. Everyone in the scene knows that, so let's get rid of the myths that have been created about our reality. No one else can tell us what our reality is. We're going to have to present it in a real fashion for people to understand it. We're not a 'Shock Rock' band, and we don't go out with the intention of shocking; but our reality, and some elements of our personal lives may be shocking to some people. We've been called Rock and Roll's answer to Jim Rose's Circus Sideshow, but our atmosphere is a little different. While they're more the carnival type, we operate in a more ritualistic way.

In our live shows, we do three different versions of our act depending on who the audience is. That's because we do have a strong educational message. We're also breaking down stereotypes with imagery that may at times be shocking to some people, while for others it's a part of their reality. It's not simply the fact that we're trying to talk about sexuality, we're dealing with spirituality too, and opening people's minds to the kind of attachment that Eastern culture makes with spirituality and sexuality. That is that sexuality is *not* a negative thing. In Western culture we've come to view sexuality as being sinful. I find that to be abhorrent and totally wrong. In America there are laws against sexuality as far as presenting nudity. Nudity is very taboo in the United States, so in different shows we're presenting different elements of nudity. In an all-ages show you simply cannot have nudity, so what we do involves navel piercing, male nipple piercing, tongue piercing, Mayan piercing rituals and branding. Things that are coming from a more historical and spiritual perspective. We can even simulate things. The only things that's missing in an all-ages show is the nudity.

When we work a club show for 18's and over, then it's a little more sexually risqué, so we can deal with stronger images of sexuality. Then we go on to our SM club show. Well, that's more of a no-holds barred situation. It's also something that, because of the setting, we're also able to integrate more audience members into the show. We always use audience members in our show to varying degrees. For example, in an all-ages show we might have someone that we put into a dog kennel or we might do different fetish type scenes. Whereas in an SM club we would have people who are into the scene and are in 'training'. We will work them into the show based on the level they're at. For example, we'll have masters and mistresses bring us slaves for piercing or branding.

This is all worked out beforehand, of course, and is all based on consent. It's not based on just doing things half-cocked. Everything's very well thought out, and we always evaluate what that person's limits are. We can usually do that pretty accurately by talking over the different elements of the show and what they want to do. Most people seek me out, obviously, because I'm a professional piercer, and they want to be pierced. Depending on where they're at, we'll incorporate people into enema scenes and the different kinds of castration scenes that we do.

The band is collectively The Genitorturers. We have the musicians and we have the performers. There are four musicians and I'm the vocalist. I'm the go-between, kind of the ring leader for all of this. I work with the musicians and the performers. The show is choreographed with the music, so what you're getting is like a music video; a visual representation of what the song is about. In say, a song like *120 Days of Genitorture,* we have this full medical thing that we're doing. We'll incorporate gynaecological procedures and what have you, depending on the level of the show. The performers consist of a dominatrix and two rackmen, and whatever submissives that we have. And we do have a *vast* number of people we can call on! In America what we've done is to tap into the adult network computer bulletin board, and when we do a tour we post tour dates on this board and put out 'slave-calls' for male and female submissives for enemas, piercings, whatever. Basically, we describe what elements we're going to be presenting. We're *never* at a loss for people!

The interesting thing is that we mostly have professional people who come. When we were in Canada we actually used someone in the act who was pretty high up in the Canadian government! He was masked, but at the same time he was someone who was really into the scene. In Florida, we use a person who is a neuro-surgeon. We attract a very wide ranging audience, such as doctors and lawyers and so on. All professional people. These are higher intellectual folks we're talking about. It's really something that's evolved in the upper echelons of society, historically speaking. It involves a lot of creativity and you have to have a certain intellect to maintain that creativity, especially when you're dealing with sexuality, because it's up here. It's all in the mind, it's not in the genitals. And that's what this is all about. It takes a certain intellect to really get into that and develop it.

We had an incident at one of our shows where a middle aged couple came along and ran into their seventeen year old son! It's interesting, in fact, because where the mother is at in her training as a submissive is that she's really getting into fisting. She really enjoys that. We've done some labial piercings on her and we're going to use her in the show, so we brought her along to watch the all-ages show. It was interesting that her son was there and he saw his parents. And they were, you know, decked out a bit! I mean, they had to explain to their son what Mom and Dad were doing at a Genitorturers show! I think it definitely fostered some communication within that family!

We've had a lot of very interesting things occur over the years. We've had audience members that *really* get into it, and we have the 'Jackin' Men', as we call them, who exhibit themselves on stage in front of the audience. There's a lot of that goes on in our shows. The difference between our normal rock and roll show, as opposed to an SM show, is really the level of interaction with the audience. We have a very strong bond with our audience at these shows. The fact is that here you're dealing with people who are actually coming along to a club to participate in these activities anyway, so it's a much freer atmosphere. The line between the band and the audience gets blurred because we have on-going interaction in the audience as well, as you can imagine. People bring their submissives along to our show and utilise our equipment. We'll invite people up to use their submissives on stage in whatever scene they want to incorporate, and that's another whole element of your psyche. Not only doing the things, but doing them in front of a roomful of people!

It's really back to that tribal ritual thing we talked about earlier. It's a very primal urge. There are many rituals in many different countries in which performing an activity in front of a group of people is part of the initiation or part of the rite of passage. I guess you could say that adds to the experience. The point is that, whenever you put yourself on stage, you're exhibiting yourself. Maybe you see more of me, but Prince Philip has been known to show his ass every once in a while!

There are really varied influences in the music as well. Myself, I grew up listening to a lot of really heavy hard-core music. Our bass player is very much into classical and jazz. The guitar player is really into guitar oriented bands from the seventies. Visual imagery is very important to me, too. I think we are tending towards becoming more of a visual society. With the advent of music videos you can see how focused we are on visual imagery in this society. In fact, film is something I'm very interested in, as I want to explore all elements of performance. I really enjoy integrating different mediums into performance art, whether it's video or a band or the spoken word. To me, it's all performance. And dealing with these things that I feel strongly about, obviously.

In the United States, especially in some of the remoter areas, the kids are really starving for something. And it's fostering something that needs to be addressed, I think. So, I mean that's good. We've only run into trouble in a couple of areas. We haven't played in Cincinnati, for example, because the city is basically fascist to the point of being ridiculous! I mean, they sent us this letter saying they would literally 'find' a reason to arrest us! So we don't go there. As we get bigger and bigger, we're probably going to have to resort to doing fewer shows and limiting them to cosmopolitan areas and then releasing videos of them. It becomes a risk at that point. Like with 2 Live Crew, they wanted to gain publicity when the State of Florida attempted to prosecute the rappers for their 'obscene lyrics'. They wanted to be the people who tore down 2 Live Crew. Well, it so happened that the guy who attacked them is now in jail for child molestation – raping his own daughter, to be exact! And so now that has turned around on them. That was like a big joke. Maybe that's why we haven't been attacked in our own state of Florida, because the people who were screaming the loudest turned out to be the biggest hypocrites!

Florida is a somewhat backward place, but it's changing so rapidly because Orlando is a huge, huge tourist Mecca. People come from all over the world to vacation there. You're seeing beaches becoming topless because you don't want to offend the Europeans and they're the 'tourist dollar'! So, they're kind of having to give in to some of these things. I think it's growing so fast that they can't even legislate against anything.

We're definitely coming over to England to play some shows. We're hoping to do different levels of shows at different places. We're trying to get into places like *The Torture Garden* and doing a different performance there. We've talked to them about that. Obviously , we know that England is somewhat tricky. Anyway, we'll only tour here once, so we'll wait till we get a bunch of dates. What will probably end up happening is that we'll find one or two places in England where we can do our show and people will probably have to come into Amsterdam to see the full show. But that's the way the world is. Anything that is perceived as 'not-normal' is automatically labelled corrupt, because their definition of corrupt is anything that fosters open-mindedness. If that's corruption, then so be it!

MISS MARIANNE MARTINDALE

Miss Martindale takes it further than any other interviewee, in that she has created an entire world of female dominance; her own personal Shangri-La. To me, she represents the 'ultimate' lifestyle mistress and, as such, a fitting point to draw this volume to a close.

Ever dreamed of another, better world where everyone knows their place in the scheme of things, old fashioned values still apply and traditional feminine principles are still rigorously applied; a place in this drab, gray man-made world where the goddess-magic still weaves wondrous spells? Then dream no longer! There is such a place and one doesn't need a magic carpet to get there. The enchanting all-female world of Aristasia lies not at the end of some fairy-tale rainbow. It's location is surprising earthbound, in fact. The suburban fringes of London Transports Central Line, to be exact!

From the outside, there is nothing about the Aristasian Embassy to distinguish it from any other house in a street of quiet, select homes. The more observant passer-by might notice that all the curtains are permanently drawn but, apart from this petty quirk, one has no way of telling that one is standing at the borders of a foreign country, and that the curtains represent the subtle battlements of a well defended empire. There are, in all, five or six Aristasian households scattered around Britain. The embassy is the only one that may be visited by a male outside, and then only by invitation. Miss Martindale, as ambassadress and spokeswoman, is the only Aristasian who will communicate with the outside world.

Ushered into the drawing-room, one finds oneself leaving the present-day behind and being transported back to a world of by-gone charm and elegance. A world that resolutely refuses to acknowledge the march of time or the perceived social decay outside their domain, in what is derisively termed The Pit in Aristasian parlance (yes, they have their own language, too). Artisans ignore all events (even the calendar itself) beyond 1960. There is no television here or any other evidence that the past forty years ever happened. Music is strictly of the 78rpm variety and the required 'current' reading comprises back numbers of Picture Post and Country Life, delivered to themselves through the letter box, according to the day and month which matches the same date in their chosen era. That is, if the present date is Monday May the Sixth, a year will be sought out from the past when that date fell on that particular day. Here the 1950's reign supreme. The 1920's and 30's are in favour, too, although the 1940's are frowned upon as the Second World War simply didn't happen in Aristasia!

Though fervently against so much that has come out of The Pit in the last four decades, Miss Martindale has no problem harnessing the 'magic'(as she puts it) of the modern world, such as the Internet, when she feels like it!. However, even the 'new technology' of the 21st century she embraces in her own iconoclastic fashion. Whilst conducting this series of interviews she sent a fax to my office dated '5.22pm. Monday, July 31st, 1950'! Yet for those with sensitivity enough to see beyond what might easily be dismissed as just another example of quaint English eccentricity, there is something else at work here. Something strange, yet powerful and even magical.

Miss Martindale herself (first names are rarely permitted and an atmosphere of rarefied genteel formality is maintained at all times) dresses and acts completely in the Aristasian character she has created. Her clothes and make-up, right down to the pink Jezebel cigarettes and holder reflect the poise and demeanour of another, more genteel, era. Her voice and manner is authoritative, yet brimming with vitality and enthusiasm for the subject she so obviously adores and is always, unfailingly, the quintessence of the femininity she so passionately promotes. Interviewed May 1995.

I think it's quite interesting how we began, because we started off as writers. We were a group of girls who always had discipline as a part of everyday life, because the conception was related to it. Right from the start we rejected The Pit and the late twentieth century, and looked back to traditional philosophical ideas. This meant we were hierarchical, so there were always mistresses and school mistresses and there were always girls who were servants and schoolgirls. But we didn't begin writing about that. We began writing about other things and then went on to write about what was our everyday reality for commercial reasons. But we wouldn't have anything other than all girls and we would only reflect what was our true reality; which was not about domination, but about having genuine authority and looking after those below you in a genuine hierarchy. In those days, we didn't know what we wrote would sell, because we refused to be deliberately provocative or titillating. In fact, we had no interest whatsoever in addressing the market of dominant ladies and submissive men, even though it was was so much bigger. I must say, we were pleasantly surprised to find there was a market for the quality of our literature, which can't be beaten in any field, I would think.

We were very serious about maintaining our integrity concerning what we're prepared to write about and how we're prepared to write it. That's why we would only write very high quality material. The first book, *The Female Disciplinary Manual*, was actually a collection of papers that circulated around different Aristasian households. They were collected together, edited and typewritten. Miss Snow's novel is a fictionalised version of our reality. The '*Manual*' is absolute fact, and everything in it has happened. For instance, describing what it's like to give a thousand lines. Someone, somewhere down the line has been subjected to the various punishments described.

Aristasia first came into being at Lady Margaret's College at Oxford University in the early 1970's. It was like a little colony. At the time I had no idea about corporal punishment. It was something that had never even crossed my mind. Very soon after I had joined someone saw that I had a 'school mistress' in me, so they just put me in charge of somebody else. I was told a little about it, but essentially I was just told to get on with it. I found that I was naturally strict, and that I liked looking after people in that way. About a year after that I was given the position of being mistress of a household, so I had the dual responsibility of taking care of education where it arises (which isn't everyday, because there are so many other things one has to do) and looking after any household I happened to be in.

The main motivation of everyone involved was disassociation from The Pit. But, as time went on, a small number of us who wanted to live completely privately, having found the maid who was going to be faithful or a companion, took themselves off. It fragmented after the Oxford years, or perhaps dispersed would be a better word. We ourselves went to Ireland with quite a few of the girls and were there for some time. The 'Irish Period' occurred during the 1980's (or the Third Decade of Darkness, according to Aristasian timescale) and found the hardcore Aristasians setting up residence in a mansion in County Donegal. Our numbers ranged from five to fourteen with myself as headmistress. Things went well in our new-found home, which we dubbed St. Brides, for about ten years. Then trouble loomed in the form of a maid who sued me, as headmistress, for actual bodily harm. Although every girl who joined the school accepted the certainty of punishment, and bearing in mind the girl in question had consented to the cane, she won the case and I was still found guilty of assault. In actual fact, I only disciplined her three times in eighteen months, and then only very faintly!

I'm also keen to correct the implication in some press reports that Aristasia is in any way a 'secret' organisation to which there is no admittance. We're always interested in being available to any girl who wants to escape from the dreariness of modern life. This house is the Embassy of Aristasia. If anyone comes here then they're entering another country. It's said at the beginning of another of our books, *The Feminine Regime*: 'Have you ever wanted to go through a wardrobe into Narnia or the looking glass in Alice?' And that's the absolute gospel truth! Because we distill and make so strongly manifest femininity and the feminine principle we really, truly, are not living in the same place as you! And when somebody comes here, her whole experience of herself completely changes.

I can give you an example. A girl came here recently dressed, as many girls in The Pit do, in a very masculine way. I felt, however, that she had a very feminine nature and a very soft side. She was very interested in us and wanted to put her heart into it and join in when she was here. She wanted to be 'good', if you like. She asked me: "Should I wear a skirt when I come?" And I said: "No, don't. You just live your life there. Come through the doorway into Aristasia and be feminine here and have the two completely separate". So she came and I dressed her up as a schoolgirl. She, and I, were both expecting her 'schoolgirl' to come out because, no matter what the physical age, a 'young' side to a girl's character invariably emerges. Incidentally, the girls you read about in the '*Manual*' and our other books may seem like schoolgirls, but they're all adult women feeling like 'schoolgirls' inside.

I took her to a special room that's set aside for this sort of transformation, where I put a uniform on her and a wig. And a character came through that was very fussy, very 'hoity-toity'. You see, what happens is a girl becomes something she could never be in The Pit; something she doesn't realise or perhaps doesn't even have any inclination toward in the outside world. After we gave the girl an Aristasian name (note: in Aristasia 'masculine' names are exchanged for purely feminine ones. Thus, Jameson, or 'Son of James' would be substituted with 'daughter of...') she said to me: "If I had to describe the sort of person I really hated I would have described that character". It wasn't that the character was feminine. It was the fact that here was a side of her personality she was denying. But more than that (and here it becomes very exciting) is that you get a whole sense of the character of the girl. Now I realised this girl was in the fifth year in our 'magical school', even though it was her first real visit. I also sensed, because she came along at about the same time as another girl she knew, that the other girl had a 'prefect' inside her. I could tell by her authority. And I knew the feminine one, the conceited one, wouldn't have anything to do with the girls in her year. She liked to befriend the bigger girls in the sixth form. And I *knew* she had a pony at home and all that sort of thing!

So, you see, they come complete with a whole world! It's not just their appearance, not just the fact that they can look in the mirror and say 'ah!' because their face changes so much, it's that you know their whole history! You can then use that to make it come even stronger. Next time I know this girl is coming I'm going to take some of my own girls (they are passed around anyway) and I'm going to have the girls with a 'younger' personality, though they might all be the same age physically, dressed in gym slips and tunics. I'm going to have the prefects, and the girl who is a bit 'older', in skirts. I'll just let it come to life then! I'll be the schoolmistress, you know, teaching this and that. Then I'll go out of the room and leave the prefects in charge. In the school you turn a bit of a blind eye to what the prefects get up to. If the mistress is away and they want to give someone a smack for something, they do. There is that element of a little bit of bullying or pinching and so on, but it's all part of what is acceptable. Because each girl has a natural 'real life' persona, it doesn't *need* any play acting! They just come to life on their own, and then we just see what happens. You simply enter into it and it unfolds. I don't even know what sort of schoolmistress is going to come, because *different* schoolmistresses come through me. I might go in as a young, glamourous schoolmistress or I might be a very strict schoolmistress who is nearer my physical age. I might go in as someone who is quite tolerant and kind and not terribly strict or I might appear as a terrifying harridan. That's all part of the magic!

It's very much a continual and on-going process of exploration. You create this wonderfully intense, magical thing between the different girls and, when they're out of uniform, then something completely different would happen. For instance, someone who perhaps was a maid in one situation might, in another situation, be something quite different. Though they do tend to be predominantly maids because it's in their nature to serve, even a maid can have an adolescent girl inside her who is on a peer level with other girls in that her personality is of a similar age. She might have a more powerful side which is a bit more grown-up (say, twenty or something like that) who can go to the night club we have created within Aristasia. We obviously don't go into The Pit. She might be allowed to be one of the girls at the club, a waitress or some such.

As well as the nightclub, we create restaurants, rock n'roll cafeterias...what else? Cinemas. In fact, we create a whole world of entertainment. We actually leave the house by one door and come in another, into a room which doesn't look the same as it did when it was just a drawing room or just a dining room. We'll change it around and it creates a very strong atmosphere. Though the schoolroom tends to stay as the schoolroom. The amount of time a girl stays here can vary between one or two evenings a week ,or a couple of days every few months, if they live a long way away. At times we have girls living with us, and at times we have girls 'almost' living with us, depending on peoples circumstances and so on. There's a lot of flexibility there as to what's appropriate for someone's life. Obviously, a lot of girls would have commitments such as earning a living which meant their time here was limited, but you just make sure that someone enters into it fully and is completely in Aristasia and being feminine while she's actually here.

I'm often asked about my possibly admitting transvestites into Aristasia, but I'm afraid that's very much forbidden. This is very much a thing for 'genuine' girls, as it were. That's a different thing altogether. I think the strength of that interest, or whatever it is you'd call it, is because of the femininity in a woman's dress. I feel it's like a reaction to recognising that femininity has almost entirely been pushed out of The Pit, and it creates a sort of longing for femininity which is then transposed into the individual thinking that it's inside him. Sometimes I also feel it's just a reaction to the drab, dreary, masculine world that surrounds everybody in The Pit.

There is a deep spiritual level to Aristasian philosophy. Christianity is a rather masculine religion but, at the same time, I see the Earth Mother as a rather degenerate form of paganism, really. That's a rather late thing. We very much adhere to tradition and, fortunately, traditional principles exist in Plato and people like that where you can learn about ancient things. Incidentally, the 'Arist' in Aristasia comes from Aristotle. But I wouldn't call us pagan, though it is very much connected to matriarchal things such as the hearth and the home, which is the centre of feminine power, if you like. These values that have been denigrated and denied both by men *and* by women in the closing years of the twentieth century. Everything now takes place in a public world, and there's simply no value in the private world; it's not seen as having any value whatsoever.

Part of what we're creating is drawing on the power and the beauty that can spring to life in the sanctuary of the home. The discipline is integral to it in ways that I probably don't even understand myself, such as the exercise of a genuine hierarchy and the instilling of obedience into those below you. I think of myself as serving a heavenly power and serving God, as well as serving everyone I rule. That's the difference when someone has *genuine* authority. This is a whole world, even though I may rule only one household within it. I'm looking after everyone I have power over. I don't have any interest in personal power, and that's why I don't think of myself as a dominatrix. In fact, as will be revealed, Aristasians have no connection or interest in the 'conventional' world of fetishism at all, referring to its practitioners as 'Silly Monkeys'. Take the initials and you'll get the joke!

Here in Aristasia, I train a maid to lay the table almost as if it's a dance, and not just to lay everything in its set place through convention, but to sense the harmony. As a mistress, you try to be the *perfect* mistress; to fulfil an archetype, rather than a stereotype. It's taken me over twenty years to discover what would look from the outside like a dominating personality, because I was so determined that I wasn't going to rule simply from my own whims. I now have a number of personalities that actually enjoy the power and enjoy punishing, but that's after twenty years of being strict with people purely out of duty and not having a sense of power. It's only been given to me, as it were, when I have so completely subjugated myself to the idea of looking after and serving people below me. It's a state of being free, or as far as a human being can be free, of personal willfulness, if you like. And I admit that I like 'enjoying' being strict, and not just doing it out of duty!

In a traditional hierarchy everyone serves other people, not just the servants. The servant serves in a personal bond because they have a character that needs that intimate personal service. Somebody who farms the land or carves chairs serves in a material way, while someone with authority serves by protecting and ruling. In a genuine traditional society , such as Hinduism, you have at the top people who are scholars and priests and priestesses who serve by that function. So, you see, a hierarchy is very, very interesting. And not a bit like the late twentieth century thinks of it!

Somebody looks at a person who has a lot of power and has girls doing things for her and so on, and it looks as if one is leading an easy life. But, as anyone who has responsibility knows, being in charge of people means that you don't have five minutes to yourself, except when you're unconscious asleep! When you're looking after people, you're actually at the beck and call of anyone who needs you, and you've always got responsibilities. You're never an individual when you've got an important function like that. You might have the odd moment when you feel like an individual, but you're on duty twenty four hours a day, really. I feel this is a vocation, and that's true of other girls in Aristasia as well, whether they be maids or commanding maids. I have extra responsibilities because of taking in new girls and helping them to understand things. It's quite clear in one's experience of it and in one's intellectual background, that Aristasia really is a completely separate world and a completely separate country from The Pit. Anyone who visits Aristasia has to leave something behind and step into something else, and you have to understand different things from what you're used to.

There are girls in Aristasia who are above me in the hierarchy, certainly. But they are in closed communities and not under constant supervision in the way anyone under me is. I will get seen and visited from time to time. However, if I've done something wrong, I won't be punished for it as me. I'd be punished as my 'schoolgirl' self. In that way, one isn't denying one's own 'schoolgirl' persona by being a house mistress. For instance, when I see the girls this week, as I was describing to you, and we go out of school, we'll be going to an ice cream soda bar. I'll be going as a sixth former, because I've got that sort of character in me. Obviously, I don't want to miss out on all the fun by going somewhere like that as a schoolmistress or as mistress of the house! That's one of the nice things about it, as I'll still be the eldest 'schoolgirl' and I'll still be in charge of everyone! But, if I've somehow failed in my duty or something like that, and it's seen as necessary to deal with me, then I'll be sat at a school desk myself. I've *never* given a punishment I haven't experienced!

Another part of what we're doing in Aristasia is giving girls a place in a hierarchy and a place in our hearts as well. Those things that are lost in The Pit, such as being able to trust and being able to love without feeling rejected. Anyone who enters deeply into Aristasia finds that they can trust it will be forever. If the girl decides, as has happened at various times, that she wants to go back to The Pit, then she does so and that's that. But if she doesn't, then she knows it will be for always, and that's an important contrast when everything is so impermanent and fragmented in The Pit.

This is partly created through love and affection, and the fact you've given so much time and so on. But it's also created through discipline and the bond that's created through trusting the person who's disciplining you. It creates a sort of magical connection. Nearly all the girls who come to us feel very strongly how drab everything is in The Pit. They discover in Aristasia a whole world that deals with everything from traditional philosophy to how you ought to do your eyes. It covers so much, it's difficult to know what to focus on in an interview. And it's all very fascinating. But, fundamentally, it is a hierarchy; it is about genuine discipline, not 'dominating'. Mainstream journalists do tend to get very interested in the picturesque side of what we're doing, so we do tend to end up as these funny little people doing something odd. And, really, we are doing so much, much more.

Another thing that doesn't often come across in articles about us is that we do encourage females (and females only) to visit. Any girl who feels she would benefit from what Aristasia has to offer is very welcome. A girl who comes along for a chat will find us very approachable. Though, I should say, that not all girls who come here are suitable. Sometimes a girl will be so 'glued' into The Pit, and by that I mean so strongly attached to television values and attitudes and immortality and all the rest of it. In such a case, I would tell her that I didn't think she was quite ready. But if I sense something in her that could be brought to life, I'll invite her to come back. Say somebody came along from the 'Silly Monkey' club and said: "I like what you're doing, but for me discipline definitely has to be sexual". Then I'd tell them there's no point coming because, although our world is sensual, it's subtle, too. It's like the sort of atmosphere you get from our writing. It's intelligent, refined and very powerful, because it's controlled.

I don't think there's any point in pretending that administering and receiving discipline doesn't arouse certain feelings, but it depends what you do with them. One can indulge them and give rein to what I call the 'lower passions' and be 'fleshy' about it, or you can refine it. We are absolutely chaste in Aristasia. It's all girls, as you know, and there is a sort of subtle sensuality, but it is still chaste. Now that might sound boring, but it's actually very fulfiling. It reminds me what Oscar Wilde said about smoking. He said: "Smoking is the perfect type of the perfect pleasure". It's exquisite, but it leaves you unsatisfied. I think that's a very feminine mentality. The masculine mentality demands that you have to go to the end, to attain a certain goal. You have to make it explicit, you have to indulge 'fleshily', as it were. Whereas everything we do is raised to higher things. So you can get very intense atmospheres, but they don't fall into lower behaviour at all. It just makes more magic!

And, yes, I would say that ultimately it is very spiritual, because you have an inward submission to God. There have been times when I've really felt that. When I've prayed to do God's will (who I conceive in a feminine form) and I've prayed to submit to something and wanted Her will to be done, not my own, I've experienced intense ecstatic feelings just by relinquishing my will. And I think that, whether you administer or receive discipline or whether you do both (in a hierarchy you find people who do both, obviously), the true heart of discipline, the key to it, is the submission to a higher authority. It's this submission that gives the delightful feeling, shall we say. It's not the physical aspect of it at all, but the spiritual submission.

Physical discipline purifies, cleanses and encloses. It raises the soul higher. The sensuality you get from giving a punishment is because you're submitting yourself to something that knows better than you what's appropriate. There was once a girl who had been really, very naughty and I gave her six strokes harder than I've ever managed before. Something higher than me had decided it had to be a very severe punishment. I don't know if you're aware of this, but in Ancient Greece flagellation was practiced as a part of a young person's rite of passage.

In Aristasia we have hardly any contact with the outside world. Some of us do live what we call 'up-to-date', which we would deem not later than the 1960's. For instance, I drive a Wolsey 1660 motor car, and one of the girls has an old Austin. They're very good and reliable. We'll go out in the car and we'll play dance band music, jazz and rock n' roll, and you're in your own world the whole time. You take your own world with you. Sometimes we only go out for provisions.

As far as music goes, as with everything else in Aristasia, I don't mean anything past 1960. Rock n' roll for us is the genuine 1950's music. Like 1920's and 1930's music, you can hear the innocence in it, unlike anything that has come after. Raucous, if you know what I mean. I'm very fond of rock n' roll, all the girls are. We have quite a wide musical world here. There are even a few things from that early 1960-61 period we listen to, like the Susan Maugham and Helen Shapiro kind of thing. They're just about acceptable from our point of view, but nothing after that!

The Beatles, as far as we're concerned, are absolutely beyond the pale! They were very, very significant in the corruption of things that brought about the Eclipse (note: The utter collapse and destruction of all order, sanity and feminine values that began in the 1960's, according to Aristasian thinking). They're very, what we'd call, 'sickly'. How can I explain it? Can you hear that rock n' roll is clean and pure as well as exciting? By the time we get to the Beatles, it's become something strange. I suppose you might call it a poisonous element. We view the group as fundamental to the Eclipse, and that's taken as gospel by every Aristasian. They heralded in what came afterward and, even though they seemed appealing, they were pretty well impregnated with something rather poisonous and sickly.

It's the same with jazz. In the actual 1920's, jazz was seen as something terrible. And it's not altogether untrue that, historically speaking, it led on to all those things that came next and got more and more degenerate. But we're approaching it with the philosophy that a road *out* of somewhere is also a road in! Obviously, we might try to deny The Pit as much as possible, but we are historically born into it. That's why one of our books is called *Children of the Void*, because everything we create is created from a void!. So if you back away from a void to a music that's vibrant and exciting, you don't hear what people at the time heard (which was the degeneracy) you hear in it the innocence. Most of the core of Aristasians don't know anything about The Pit after the 1970's and the Second Decade of Darkness. They might know the name of the odd political figure that seeps through or something like that, but the core of us left The Pit completely, and really and truly don't know anything about it. One might hear the odd bit of music walking by a shop or one might know Margaret Thatcher existed, but it's very, very minimal.

We don't have any political allegiances here, obviously. And I wouldn't know much about the details, of course, because we don't read the newspapers or pay any attention to what goes on in The Pit. But one has obviously seen the occasional photograph, though not in the house, of course, maybe a shop or something, so we knew what she looked like. Yes, I thought of her as sort of a governess-type. I thought she made the most of her appearance, which so few women do in the late twentieth century. I liked her having this degree of femininity and superiority, but that's about as far as one would really bother about it. One can't agree with anybody, because we've created a world here whose underpinning is medieval and earlier. Well, not even medieval. It's matriarchal. But we're not trying to bring about a matriarchy, because that's something that happened, or even project anything into the future. It's our internal world, if you like. We're not even saying everything *should* be matriarchal.

We're trying to create a world of beauty and love and firmness; a world that's exciting and stimulating and intellectually sound to live in. And if one has any idea at all, then one thinks (well, I do, personally) that the only form of acceptable political organisation is the kind of small principalities ruled queens and princesses that existed thousands of years ago. I don't know what will happen in the future, because that's in God's hands, not mine. I'm certainly not interested in any form of political organisation today because they are simply too remote from the fundamental principles.

I think that what's happened in recent years is that, through greater public interest in fetishism (which, to me, incidentally, is just another manifestation of The Pit) most people are now aware of a need for discipline. In the past, men have tended to be more interested in it than girls. But through the fashion and publicity of the Silly Monkeys, more girls have begun to think about these things who probably wouldn't have done so before. Generally, I tend to attract girls who haven't had anything to do with Silly Monkeys. The girl will simply feel a need to be disciplined. She might say: "I want a smack, but I don't really understand it and I feel a bit strange". They've never had one before, and never talked to anyone else about it. And many more of these kinds of girls are getting in touch with me in recent years than in times gone by. Also, I was very surprised when I did publicity for the *Female Disciplinary Manual* how seriously I was taken, even by the sort of feminist-type journalists that didn't like me. I was seen for what I was against a backdrop of people behaving in what to us in Aristasia is a very 'suburban' way!

A WORD FROM ABSOLUTE ELSEWHERE

We hope you've enjoyed this first offering from Absolute Elsewhere. As the name suggests, our aim is to bring to the reading public books that are different, challenging and provocative – as well as entertaining, amusing and admittedly, often as not, downright weird! If you would like to receive information about future publications e-mail us or fill in the form below (enclosing a loose stamp or IRC)

Alternatively, find out what's happening and when by checking out our web site: www.absolute-elsewhere.co.uk

At present a full length video documentary is in production to accompany 'You Beat People Up For A Living, Don't You, Mummy?' If you reserve your copy now you qualify for a special discount.

Incidentally, if this book has made you want to find out more about the world of Female Domination and the fetish scene, why not send for a copy of 'Domina' magazine?

The latest issue is available by mail order at a special 20% discount inclusive of postage and packing. That's only £8.00

Please make Cheques/Money Orders (in pounds sterling) payable to 'Absolute Elsewhere'

Name ....

Address ....

....

....

Post Code/Zip Code ....

Signed .... Date...........................

Absolute Elsewhere, P O Box 2, Brighton, East Sussex, BN1 4LQ, United Kingdom.

You can visit our web-site at www.absolute-elsewhere.co.uk